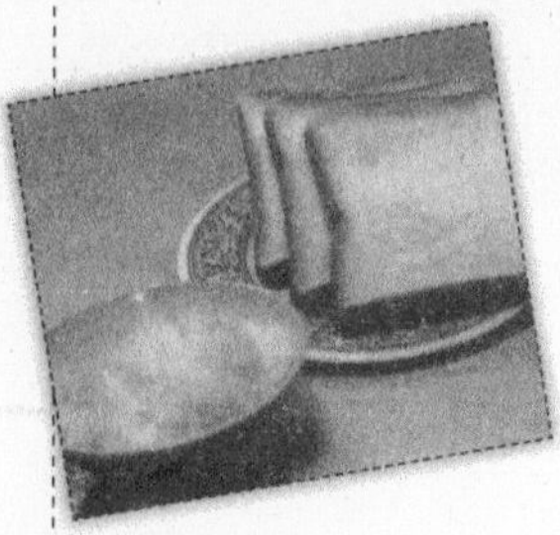

When the series began, there were only three groups at the *Weekly Shonen Jump* editorial department. Now there's a total of five. And Mr. Aida has since become the deputy editor in chief, but I think I'll keep him as a captain for the rest of the series.

—Tsugumi Ohba

Of all the many studios that appear in this manga, I'd say I enjoy the atmosphere of Fukuda's the most.

—Takeshi Obata

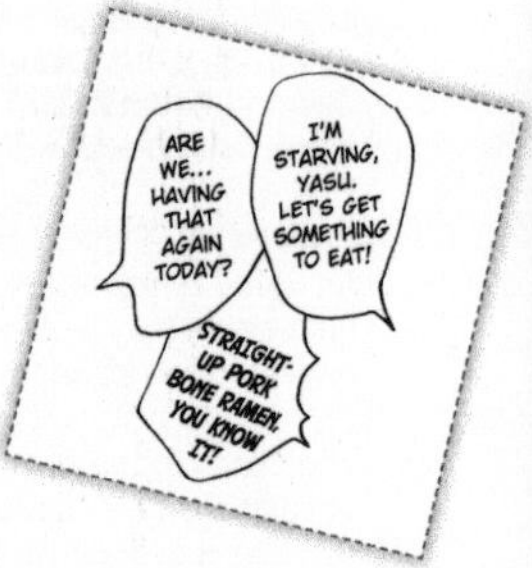
I'M STARVING, YASU. LET'S GET SOMETHING TO EAT!
ARE WE... HAVING THAT AGAIN TODAY?
STRAIGHT-UP PORK BONE RAMEN, YOU KNOW IT!

Tsugumi Ohba

Born in Tokyo, Tsugumi Ohba is the author of the hit series *Death Note*. His current series *Bakuman。* is serialized in *Weekly Shonen Jump*.

Takeshi Obata

Takeshi Obata was born in 1969 in Niigata, Japan, and is the artist of the wildly popular SHONEN JUMP title *Hikaru no Go*, which won the 2003 Tezuka Osamu Cultural Prize: Shinsei "New Hope" award and the 2000 Shogakukan Manga award. Obata is also the artist of *Arabian Majin Bokentan Lamp Lamp*, *Ayatsuri Sakon*, *Cyborg Jichan G.*, and the smash hit manga *Death Note*. His current series *Bakuman。* is serialized in *Weekly Shonen Jump*.

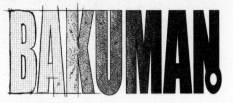

Volume 11

SHONEN JUMP Manga Edition

Story by **TSUGUMI OHBA**
Art by **TAKESHI OBATA**

Translation | **Tetsuichiro Miyaki**
English Adaptation | **Julie Lutz**
Touch-up Art & Lettering | **James Gaubatz**
Design | **Fawn Lau**
Editor | **Alexis Kirsch**

BAKUMAN。© 2008 by Tsugumi Ohba, Takeshi Obata
All rights reserved.
First published in Japan in 2008 by SHUEISHA Inc., Tokyo.
English translation rights arranged by SHUEISHA Inc.

The rights of the author(s) of the work(s) in this publication to be
so identified have been asserted in accordance with the Copyright,
Designs and Patents Act 1988. A CIP catalogue record for this book
is available from the British Library.

The stories, characters and incidents mentioned in this publication are
entirely fictional.

Printed in the U.S.A.

Published by VIZ Media, LLC
P.O. Box 77010
San Francisco, CA 94107

10 9 8 7 6 5 4 3 2 1
First printing, June 2012

www.viz.com

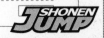
www.shonenjump.com

BAKUMAN。

11

STORY BY **TSUGUMI OHBA**

ART BY **TAKESHI OBATA**

TITLE and CHARACTER DESIGN

SHONEN JUMP MANGA

UMAN。
バクマン。
vol. 11

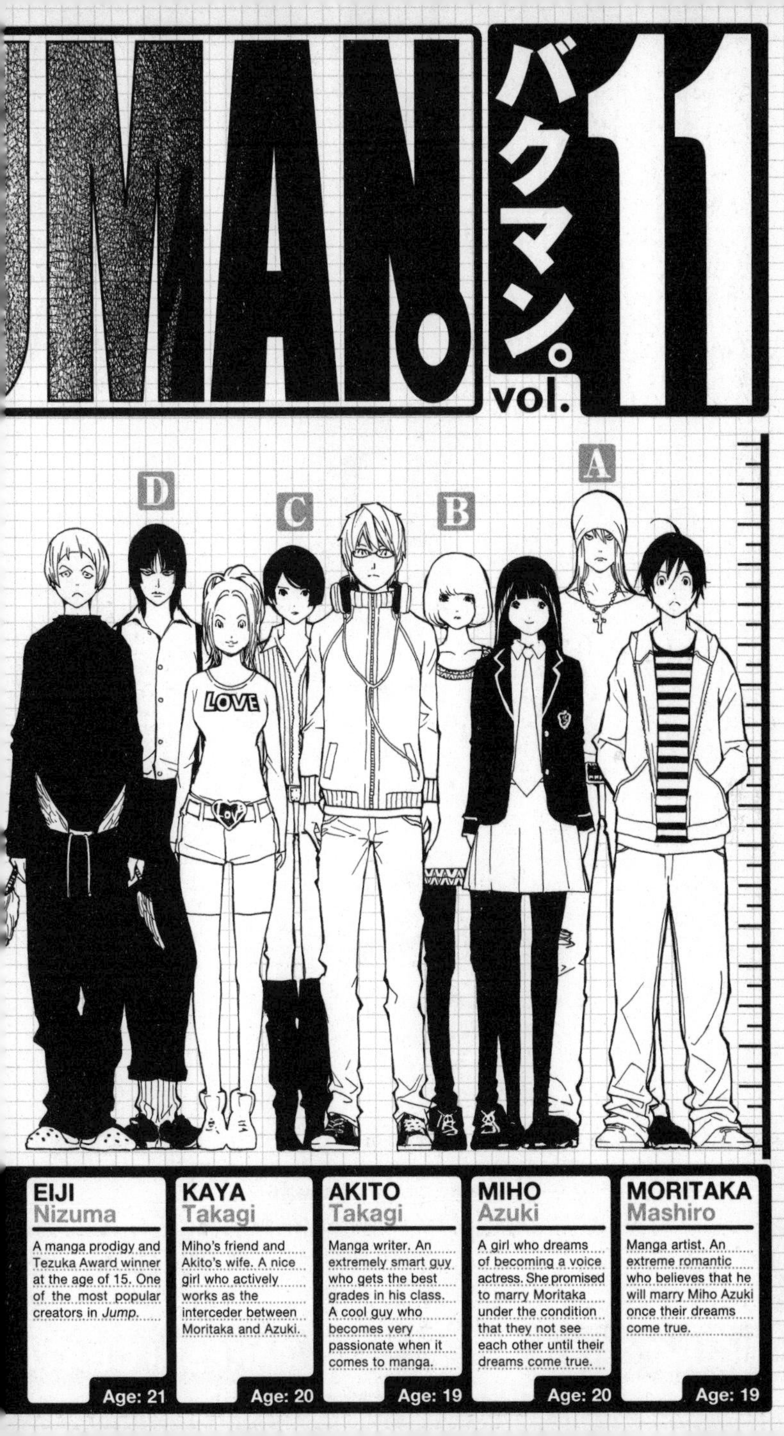

D
C
B
A
LOVE
LOVE

EIJI
Nizuma

A manga prodigy and Tezuka Award winner at the age of 15. One of the most popular creators in *Jump*.

Age: 21

KAYA
Takagi

Miho's friend and Akito's wife. A nice girl who actively works as the interceder between Moritaka and Azuki.

Age: 20

AKITO
Takagi

Manga writer. An extremely smart guy who gets the best grades in his class. A cool guy who becomes very passionate when it comes to manga.

Age: 19

MIHO
Azuki

A girl who dreams of becoming a voice actress. She promised to marry Moritaka under the condition that they not see each other until their dreams come true.

Age: 20

MORITAKA
Mashiro

Manga artist. An extreme romantic who believes that he will marry Miho Azuki once their dreams come true.

Age: 19

*These ages are from December 2013.

STORY In order to attain the glory that only a handful of people can, two young men decide to walk the rough "path of manga" and become professional manga creators. This is the story of a great artist, Moritaka Mashiro, a talented writer, Akito Takagi, and their quest to become manga legends!

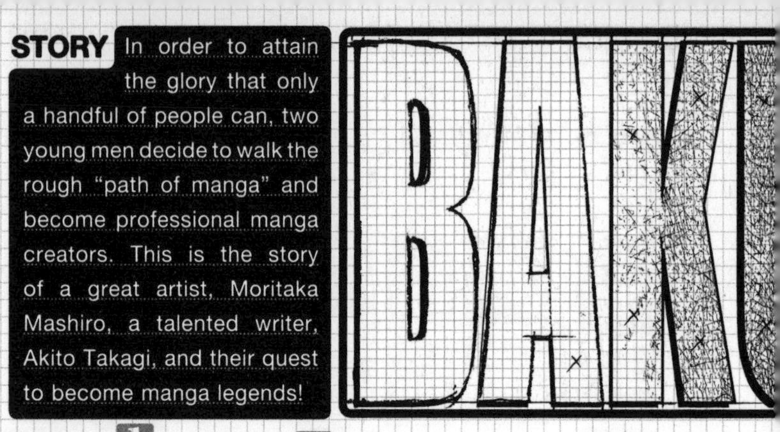

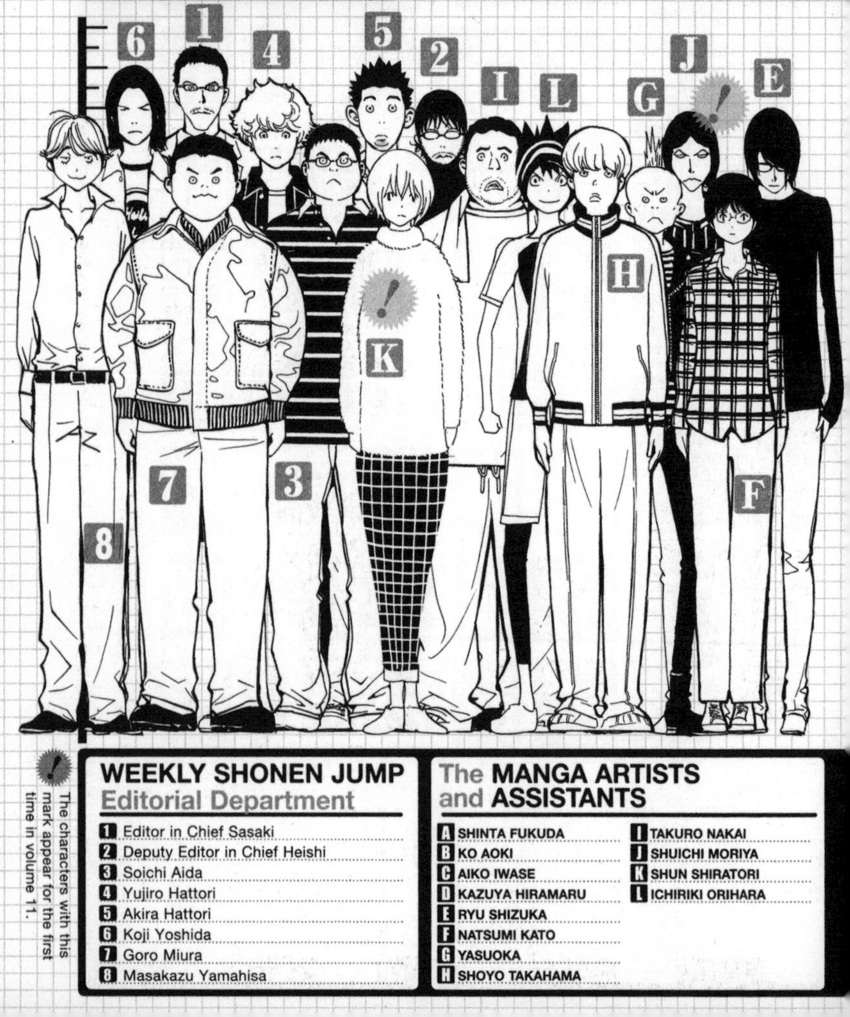

! The characters with this mark appear for the first time in volume 11.

WEEKLY SHONEN JUMP Editorial Department

1. Editor in Chief Sasaki
2. Deputy Editor in Chief Heishi
3. Soichi Aida
4. Yujiro Hattori
5. Akira Hattori
6. Koji Yoshida
7. Goro Miura
8. Masakazu Yamahisa

The MANGA ARTISTS and ASSISTANTS

- A SHINTA FUKUDA
- B KO AOKI
- C AIKO IWASE
- D KAZUYA HIRAMARU
- E RYU SHIZUKA
- F NATSUMI KATO
- G YASUOKA
- H SHOYO TAKAHAMA
- I TAKURO NAKAI
- J SHUICHI MORIYA
- K SHUN SHIRATORI
- L ICHIRIKI ORIHARA

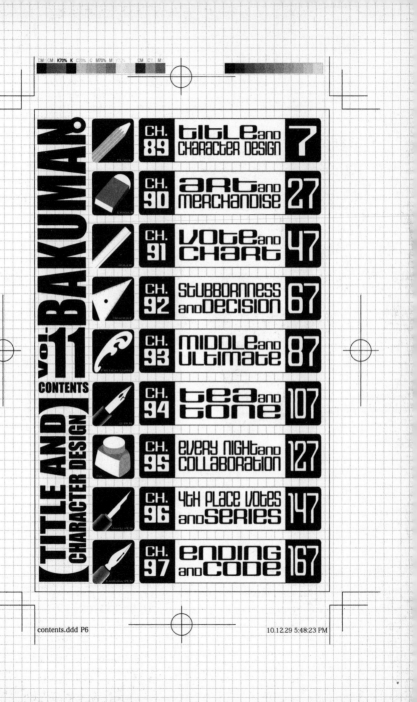

BAKUMAN。
vol. 11

(TITLE AND CHARACTER DESIGN)

CONTENTS

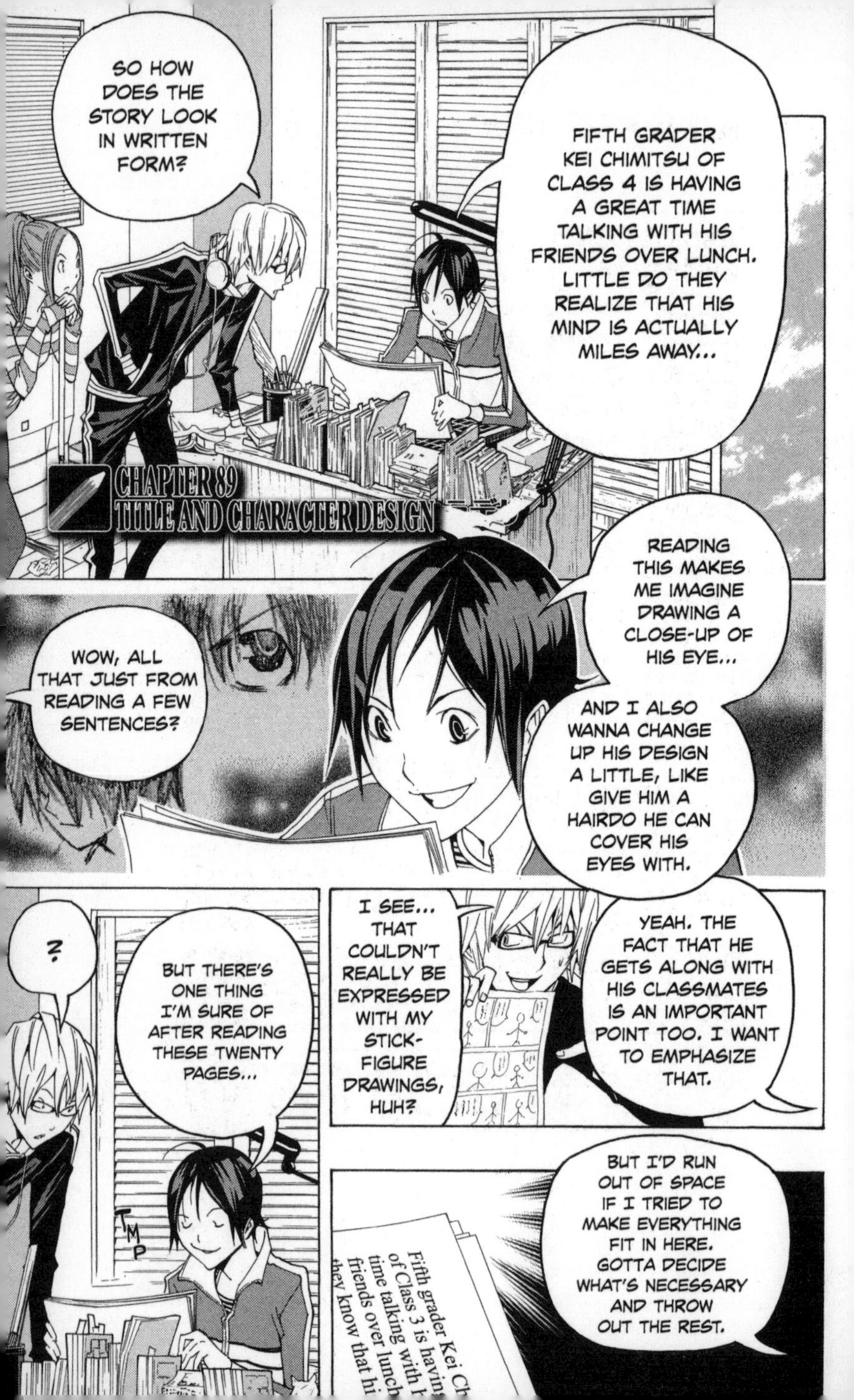
SO HOW DOES THE STORY LOOK IN WRITTEN FORM?
FIFTH GRADER KEI CHIMITSU OF CLASS 4 IS HAVING A GREAT TIME TALKING WITH HIS FRIENDS OVER LUNCH. LITTLE DO THEY REALIZE THAT HIS MIND IS ACTUALLY MILES AWAY...
CHAPTER 89
TITLE AND CHARACTER DESIGN
READING THIS MAKES ME IMAGINE DRAWING A CLOSE-UP OF HIS EYE...
AND I ALSO WANNA CHANGE UP HIS DESIGN A LITTLE, LIKE GIVE HIM A HAIRDO HE CAN COVER HIS EYES WITH.
WOW, ALL THAT JUST FROM READING A FEW SENTENCES?
I SEE... THAT COULDN'T REALLY BE EXPRESSED WITH MY STICK-FIGURE DRAWINGS, HUH?
YEAH. THE FACT THAT HE GETS ALONG WITH HIS CLASSMATES IS AN IMPORTANT POINT TOO. I WANT TO EMPHASIZE THAT.
BUT I'D RUN OUT OF SPACE IF I TRIED TO MAKE EVERYTHING FIT IN HERE. GOTTA DECIDE WHAT'S NECESSARY AND THROW OUT THE REST.
Fifth grader Kei Ch
of Class 3 is havin
time talking with
friends over lunch
they know that hi
?
BUT THERE'S ONE THING I'M SURE OF AFTER READING THESE TWENTY PAGES...
TMP

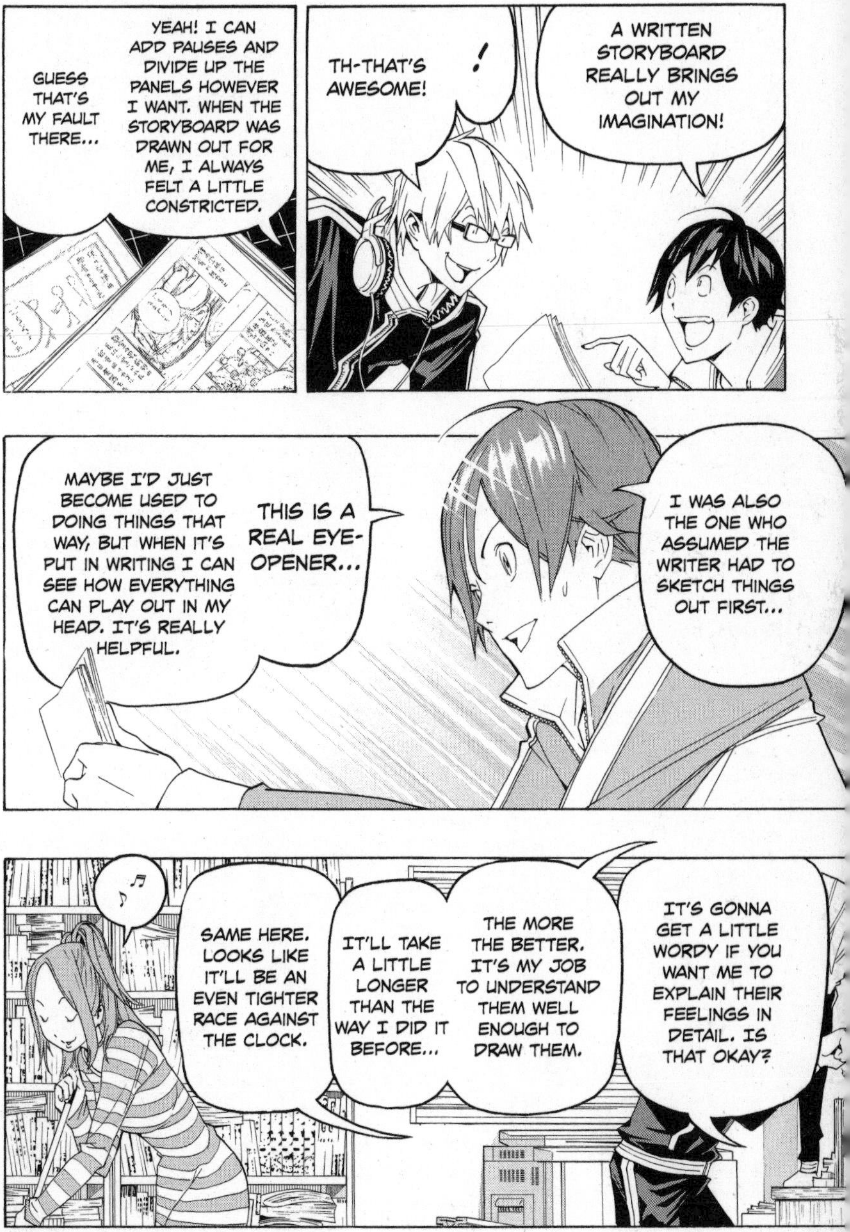
A WRITTEN STORYBOARD REALLY BRINGS OUT MY IMAGINATION!
!
TH-THAT'S AWESOME!
YEAH! I CAN ADD PAUSES AND DIVIDE UP THE PANELS HOWEVER I WANT. WHEN THE STORYBOARD WAS DRAWN OUT FOR ME, I ALWAYS FELT A LITTLE CONSTRICTED.
GUESS THAT'S MY FAULT THERE...
I WAS ALSO THE ONE WHO ASSUMED THE WRITER HAD TO SKETCH THINGS OUT FIRST...
THIS IS A REAL EYE-OPENER...
MAYBE I'D JUST BECOME USED TO DOING THINGS THAT WAY, BUT WHEN IT'S PUT IN WRITING I CAN SEE HOW EVERYTHING CAN PLAY OUT IN MY HEAD. IT'S REALLY HELPFUL.
IT'S GONNA GET A LITTLE WORDY IF YOU WANT ME TO EXPLAIN THEIR FEELINGS IN DETAIL. IS THAT OKAY?
THE MORE THE BETTER. IT'S MY JOB TO UNDERSTAND THEM WELL ENOUGH TO DRAW THEM.
IT'LL TAKE A LITTLE LONGER THAN THE WAY I DID IT BEFORE...
SAME HERE. LOOKS LIKE IT'LL BE AN EVEN TIGHTER RACE AGAINST THE CLOCK.

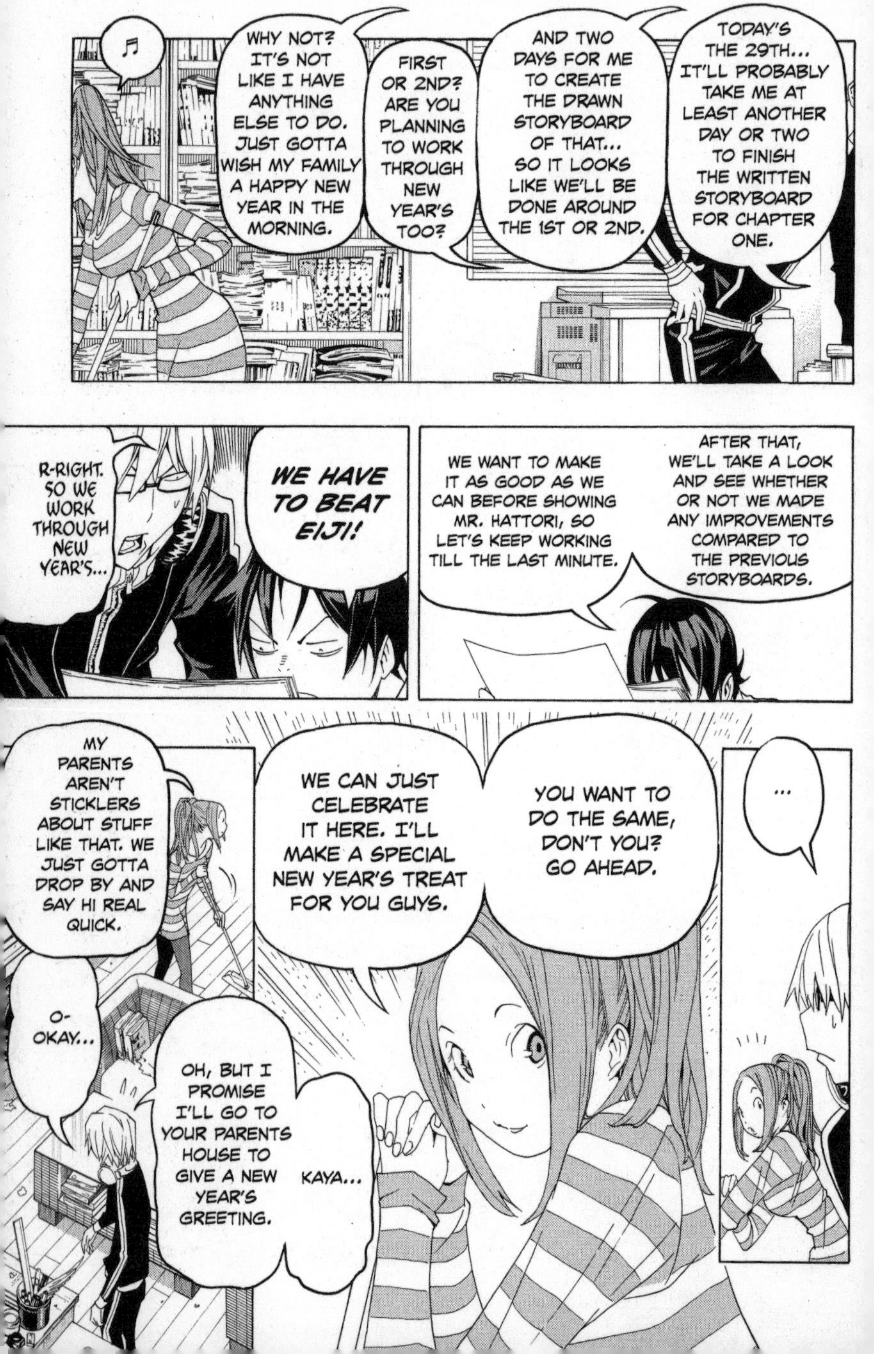
TODAY'S THE 29TH... IT'LL PROBABLY TAKE ME AT LEAST ANOTHER DAY OR TWO TO FINISH THE WRITTEN STORYBOARD FOR CHAPTER ONE.
AND TWO DAYS FOR ME TO CREATE THE DRAWN STORYBOARD OF THAT... SO IT LOOKS LIKE WE'LL BE DONE AROUND THE 1ST OR 2ND.
FIRST OR 2ND? ARE YOU PLANNING TO WORK THROUGH NEW YEAR'S TOO?
WHY NOT? IT'S NOT LIKE I HAVE ANYTHING ELSE TO DO. JUST GOTTA WISH MY FAMILY A HAPPY NEW YEAR IN THE MORNING.
♫
AFTER THAT, WE'LL TAKE A LOOK AND SEE WHETHER OR NOT WE MADE ANY IMPROVEMENTS COMPARED TO THE PREVIOUS STORYBOARDS.
WE WANT TO MAKE IT AS GOOD AS WE CAN BEFORE SHOWING MR. HATTORI, SO LET'S KEEP WORKING TILL THE LAST MINUTE.
WE HAVE TO BEAT EIJI!
R-RIGHT. SO WE WORK THROUGH NEW YEAR'S...
...
YOU WANT TO DO THE SAME, DON'T YOU? GO AHEAD.
WE CAN JUST CELEBRATE IT HERE. I'LL MAKE A SPECIAL NEW YEAR'S TREAT FOR YOU GUYS.
KAYA...
MY PARENTS AREN'T STICKLERS ABOUT STUFF LIKE THAT. WE JUST GOTTA DROP BY AND SAY HI REAL QUICK.
O-OKAY...
OH, BUT I PROMISE I'LL GO TO YOUR PARENTS HOUSE TO GIVE A NEW YEAR'S GREETING.

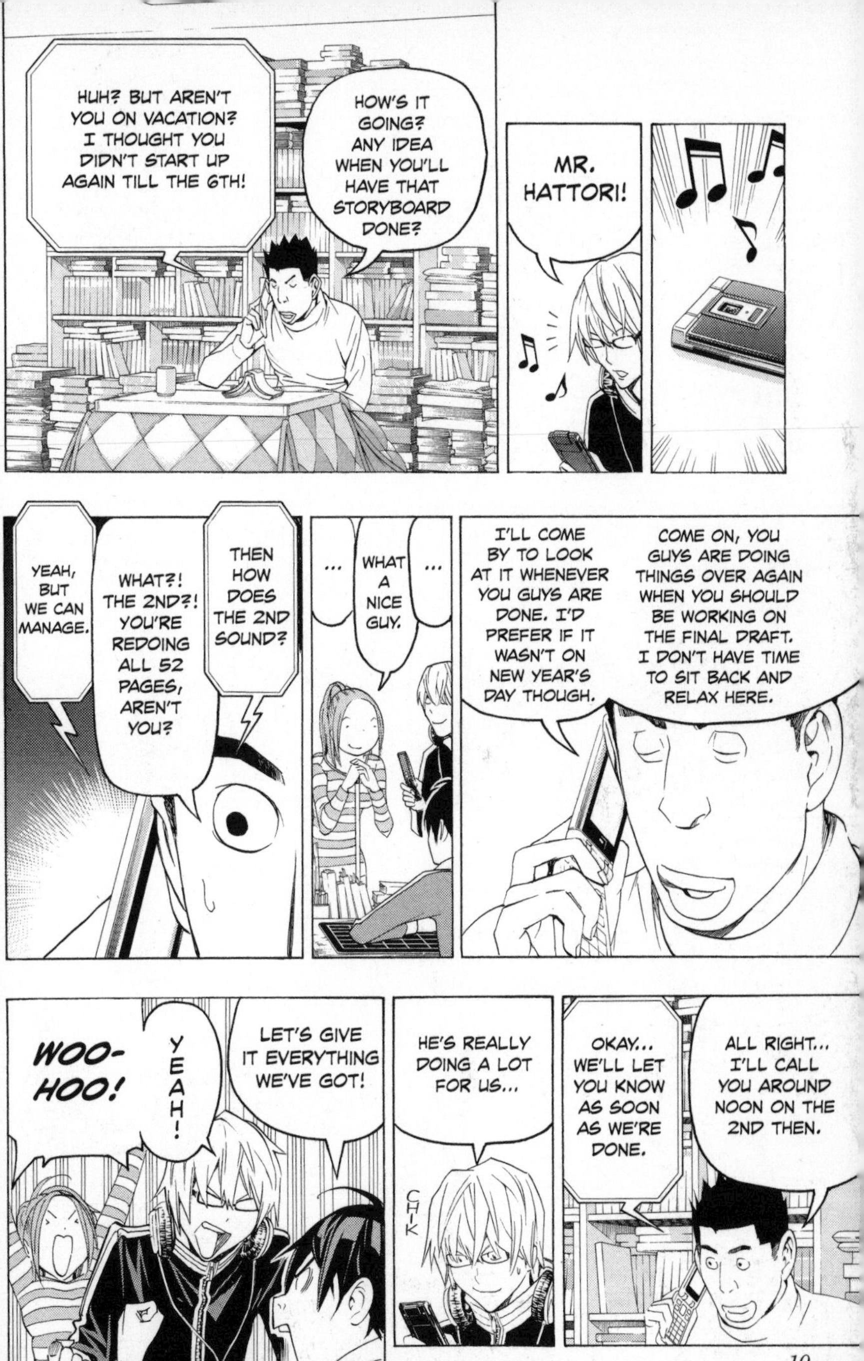
MR. HATTORI!
HOW'S IT GOING? ANY IDEA WHEN YOU'LL HAVE THAT STORYBOARD DONE?
HUH? BUT AREN'T YOU ON VACATION? I THOUGHT YOU DIDN'T START UP AGAIN TILL THE 6TH!
COME ON, YOU GUYS ARE DOING THINGS OVER AGAIN WHEN YOU SHOULD BE WORKING ON THE FINAL DRAFT. I DON'T HAVE TIME TO SIT BACK AND RELAX HERE.
I'LL COME BY TO LOOK AT IT WHENEVER YOU GUYS ARE DONE. I'D PREFER IF IT WASN'T ON NEW YEAR'S DAY THOUGH.
...
WHAT A NICE GUY.
...
THEN HOW DOES THE 2ND SOUND?
WHAT?! THE 2ND?! YOU'RE REDOING ALL 52 PAGES, AREN'T YOU?
YEAH, BUT WE CAN MANAGE.
ALL RIGHT... I'LL CALL YOU AROUND NOON ON THE 2ND THEN.
OKAY... WE'LL LET YOU KNOW AS SOON AS WE'RE DONE.
HE'S REALLY DOING A LOT FOR US...
CHIK
LET'S GIVE IT EVERYTHING WE'VE GOT!
YEAH!
WOO-HOO!

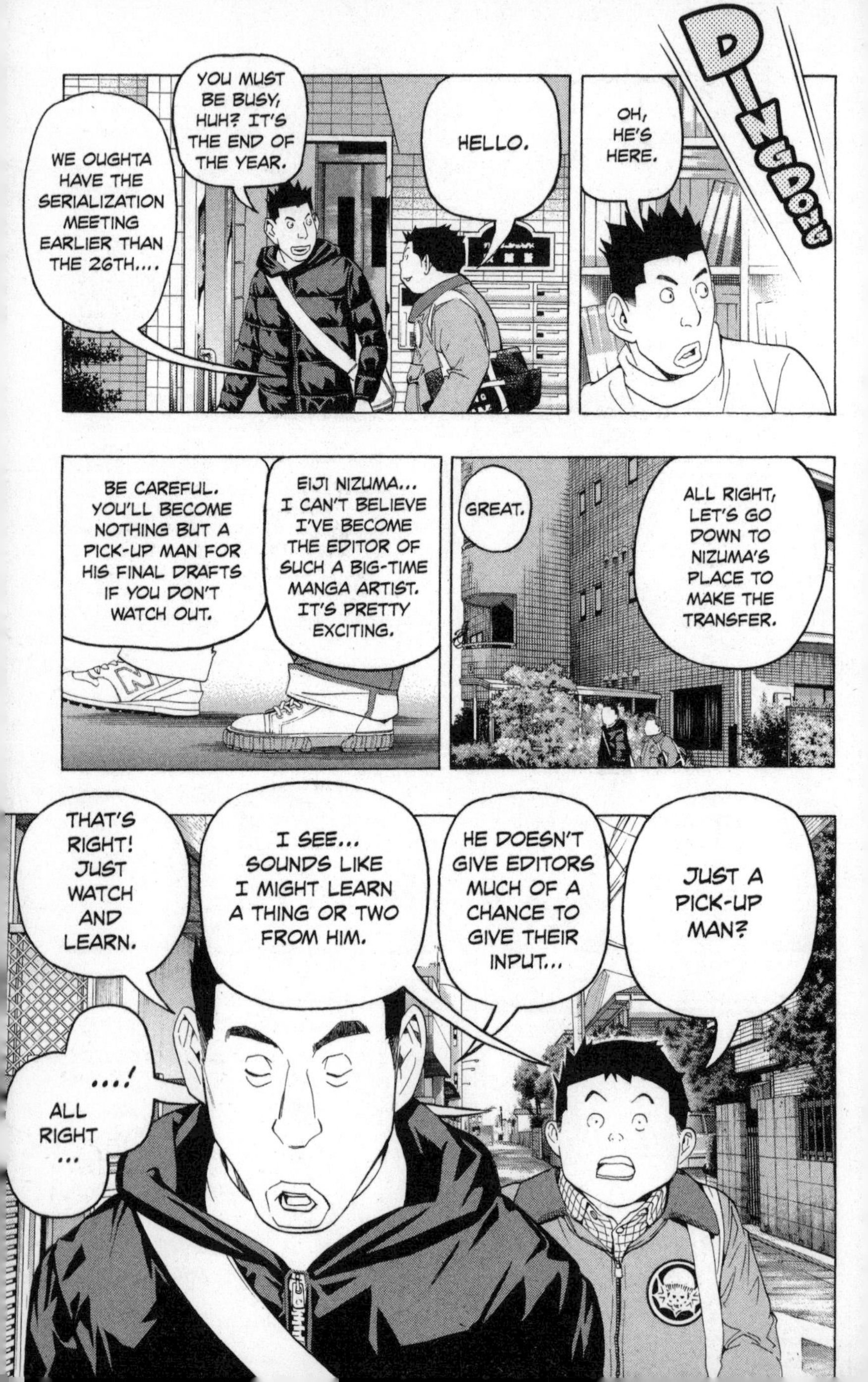
DINGDONG
OH, HE'S HERE.
HELLO.
YOU MUST BE BUSY, HUH? IT'S THE END OF THE YEAR.
WE OUGHTA HAVE THE SERIALIZATION MEETING EARLIER THAN THE 26TH....
ALL RIGHT, LET'S GO DOWN TO NIZUMA'S PLACE TO MAKE THE TRANSFER.
GREAT.
EIJI NIZUMA... I CAN'T BELIEVE I'VE BECOME THE EDITOR OF SUCH A BIG-TIME MANGA ARTIST. IT'S PRETTY EXCITING.
BE CAREFUL. YOU'LL BECOME NOTHING BUT A PICK-UP MAN FOR HIS FINAL DRAFTS IF YOU DON'T WATCH OUT.
JUST A PICK-UP MAN?
HE DOESN'T GIVE EDITORS MUCH OF A CHANCE TO GIVE THEIR INPUT...
I SEE... SOUNDS LIKE I MIGHT LEARN A THING OR TWO FROM HIM.
THAT'S RIGHT! JUST WATCH AND LEARN.
...!
ALL RIGHT...

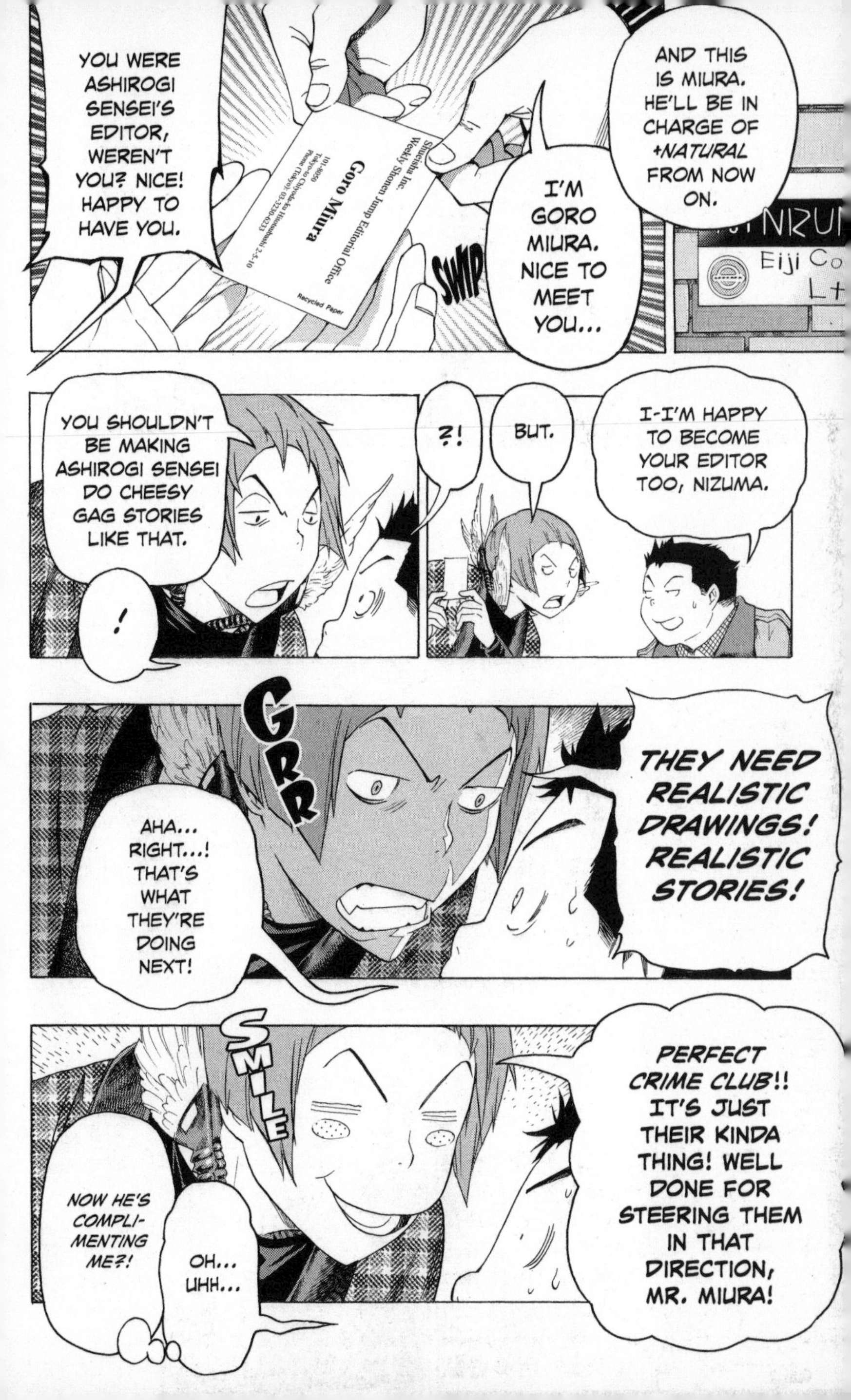
AND THIS IS MIURA. HE'LL BE IN CHARGE OF +NATURAL FROM NOW ON.
I'M GORO MIURA. NICE TO MEET YOU...
SWIP
Shueisha Inc. Weekly Shonen Jump Editorial Office
Goro Miura
101-8050 Tokyo-to Chiyoda-ku Hitotsubashi 2-5-10
Phone (Tokyo) 03-3230-6233
Recycled Paper
YOU WERE ASHIROGI SENSEI'S EDITOR, WEREN'T YOU? NICE! HAPPY TO HAVE YOU.
I-I'M HAPPY TO BECOME YOUR EDITOR TOO, NIZUMA.
BUT.
?!
YOU SHOULDN'T BE MAKING ASHIROGI SENSEI DO CHEESY GAG STORIES LIKE THAT.
!
THEY NEED REALISTIC DRAWINGS! REALISTIC STORIES!
GRR
AHA... RIGHT...! THAT'S WHAT THEY'RE DOING NEXT!
PERFECT CRIME CLUB!! IT'S JUST THEIR KINDA THING! WELL DONE FOR STEERING THEM IN THAT DIRECTION, MR. MIURA!
SMILE
OH... UHH...
NOW HE'S COMPLI-MENTING ME?!

READ THIS WAY

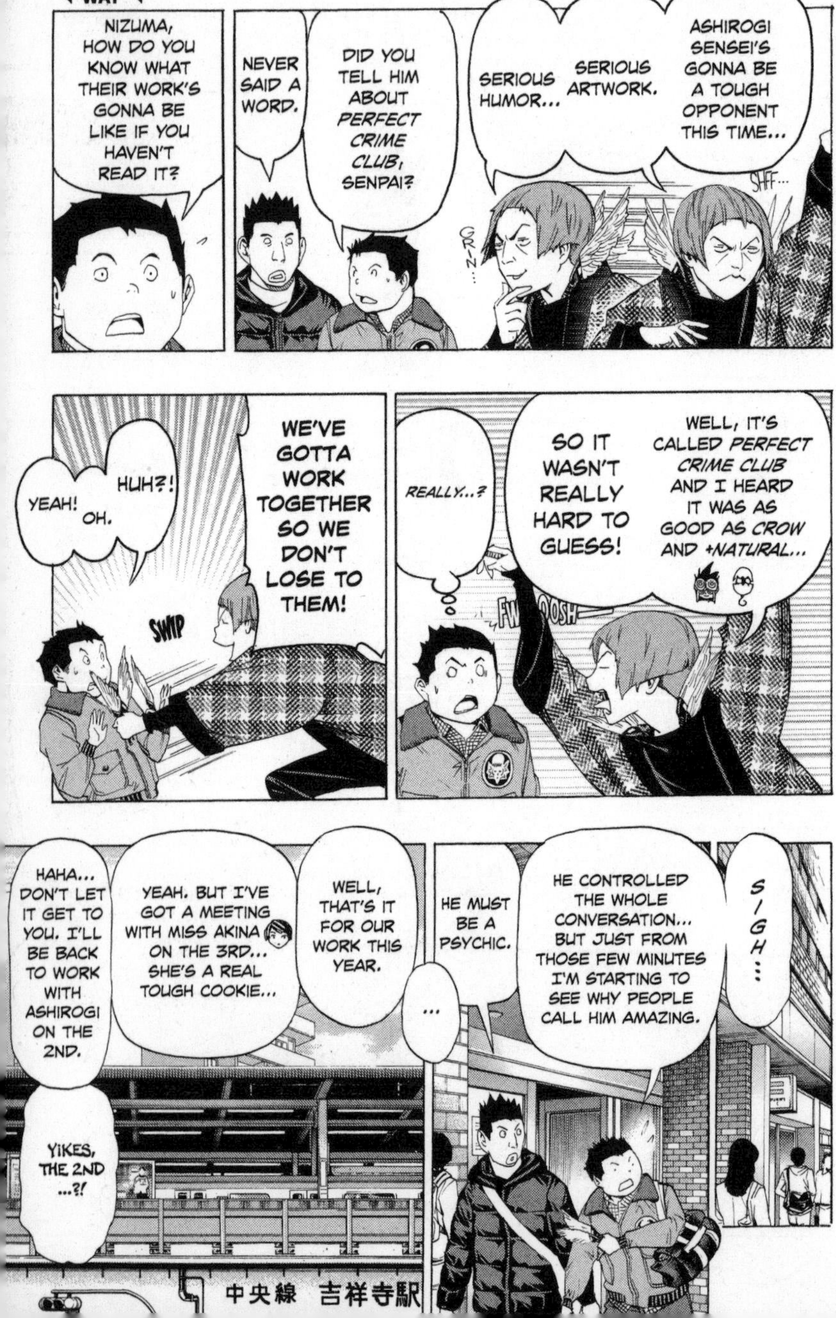

ASHIROGI SENSEI'S GONNA BE A TOUGH OPPONENT THIS TIME...
SERIOUS ARTWORK.
SERIOUS HUMOR...
SHFF...
GRIN...
DID YOU TELL HIM ABOUT *PERFECT CRIME CLUB*, SENPAI?
NEVER SAID A WORD.
NIZUMA, HOW DO YOU KNOW WHAT THEIR WORK'S GONNA BE LIKE IF YOU HAVEN'T READ IT?
WELL, IT'S CALLED *PERFECT CRIME CLUB* AND I HEARD IT WAS AS GOOD AS *CROW* AND *+NATURAL*...
SO IT WASN'T REALLY HARD TO GUESS!
REALLY...?
FWOOSH
WE'VE GOTTA WORK TOGETHER SO WE DON'T LOSE TO THEM!
SWIP
HUH?! OH.
YEAH!
S I G H . . .
HE CONTROLLED THE WHOLE CONVERSATION... BUT JUST FROM THOSE FEW MINUTES I'M STARTING TO SEE WHY PEOPLE CALL HIM AMAZING.
HE MUST BE A PSYCHIC.
...
WELL, THAT'S IT FOR OUR WORK THIS YEAR.
YEAH. BUT I'VE GOT A MEETING WITH MISS AKINA ON THE 3RD... SHE'S A REAL TOUGH COOKIE...
HAHA... DON'T LET IT GET TO YOU. I'LL BE BACK TO WORK WITH ASHIROGI ON THE 2ND.
YIKES, THE 2ND ...?!
中央線　吉祥寺駅

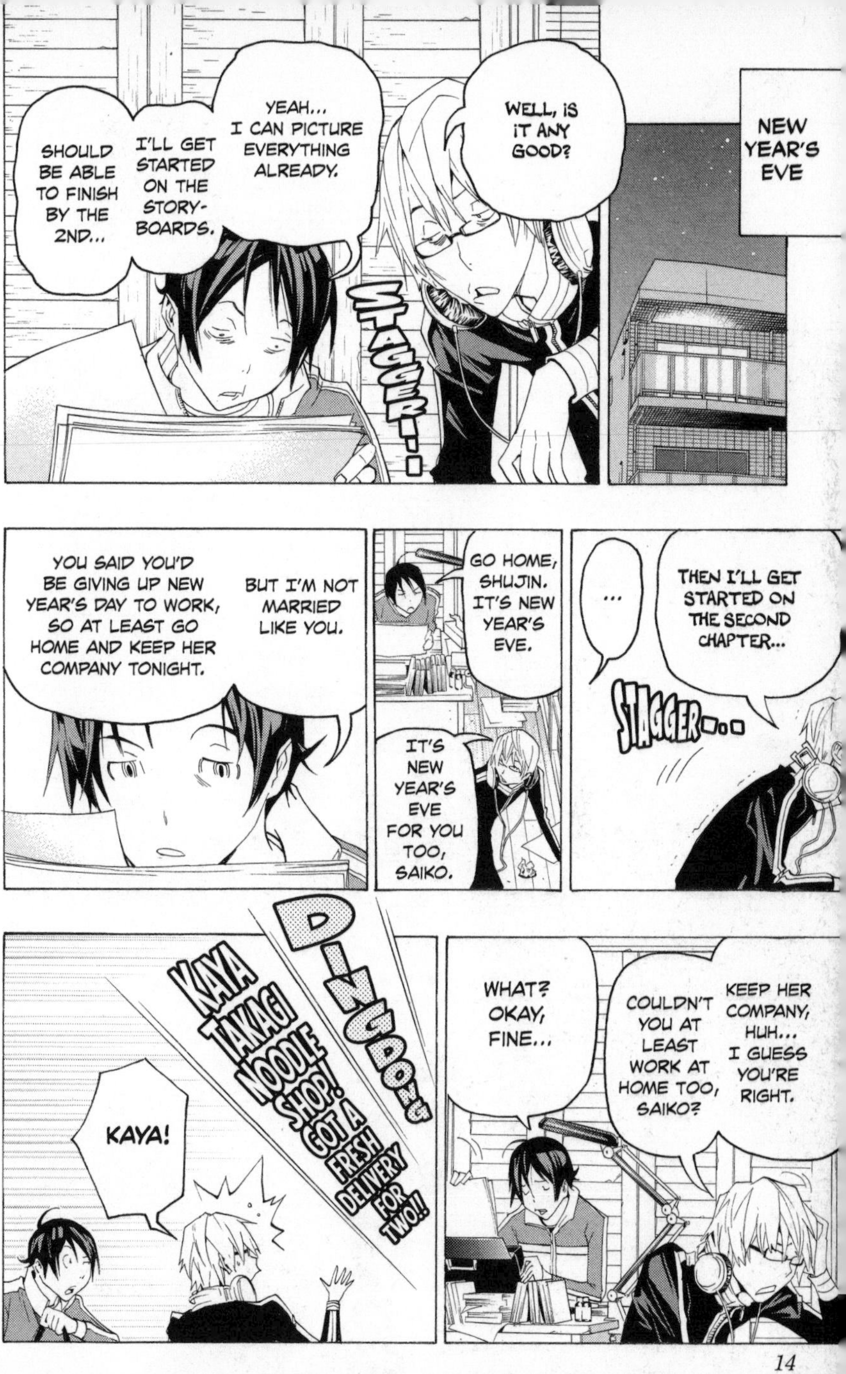
NEW YEAR'S EVE
WELL, IS IT ANY GOOD?
YEAH... I CAN PICTURE EVERYTHING ALREADY.
I'LL GET STARTED ON THE STORY-BOARDS.
SHOULD BE ABLE TO FINISH BY THE 2ND...
STAGGER...
THEN I'LL GET STARTED ON THE SECOND CHAPTER...
...
STAGGER...
GO HOME, SHUJIN. IT'S NEW YEAR'S EVE.
IT'S NEW YEAR'S EVE FOR YOU TOO, SAIKO.
BUT I'M NOT MARRIED LIKE YOU.
YOU SAID YOU'D BE GIVING UP NEW YEAR'S DAY TO WORK, SO AT LEAST GO HOME AND KEEP HER COMPANY TONIGHT.
KEEP HER COMPANY, HUH... I GUESS YOU'RE RIGHT.
COULDN'T YOU AT LEAST WORK AT HOME TOO, SAIKO?
WHAT? OKAY, FINE...
DING DONG
KAYA TAKAGI NOODLE SHOP! GOT A FRESH DELIVERY FOR TWO!!
KAYA!

READ THIS WAY

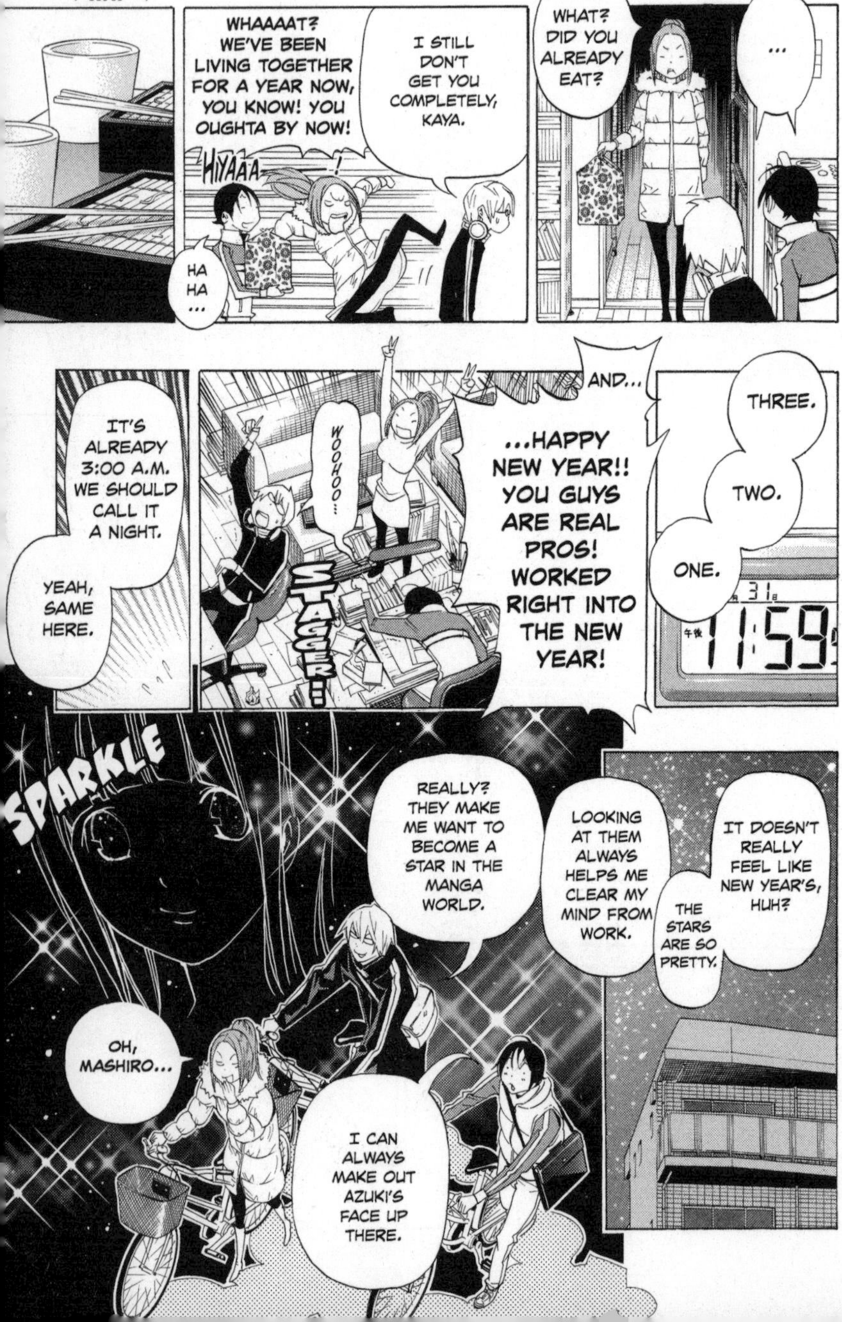
...
WHAT? DID YOU ALREADY EAT?
I STILL DON'T GET YOU COMPLETELY, KAYA.
WHAAAAT? WE'VE BEEN LIVING TOGETHER FOR A YEAR NOW, YOU KNOW! YOU OUGHTA BY NOW!
HIYAAA
HA HA ...
THREE.
TWO.
ONE.
AND...
...HAPPY NEW YEAR!! YOU GUYS ARE REAL PROS! WORKED RIGHT INTO THE NEW YEAR!
WOOHOO...
STAGGER!!
IT'S ALREADY 3:00 A.M. WE SHOULD CALL IT A NIGHT.
YEAH, SAME HERE.
IT DOESN'T REALLY FEEL LIKE NEW YEAR'S, HUH?
THE STARS ARE SO PRETTY.
LOOKING AT THEM ALWAYS HELPS ME CLEAR MY MIND FROM WORK.
REALLY? THEY MAKE ME WANT TO BECOME A STAR IN THE MANGA WORLD.
SPARKLE
OH, MASHIRO...
I CAN ALWAYS MAKE OUT AZUKI'S FACE UP THERE.

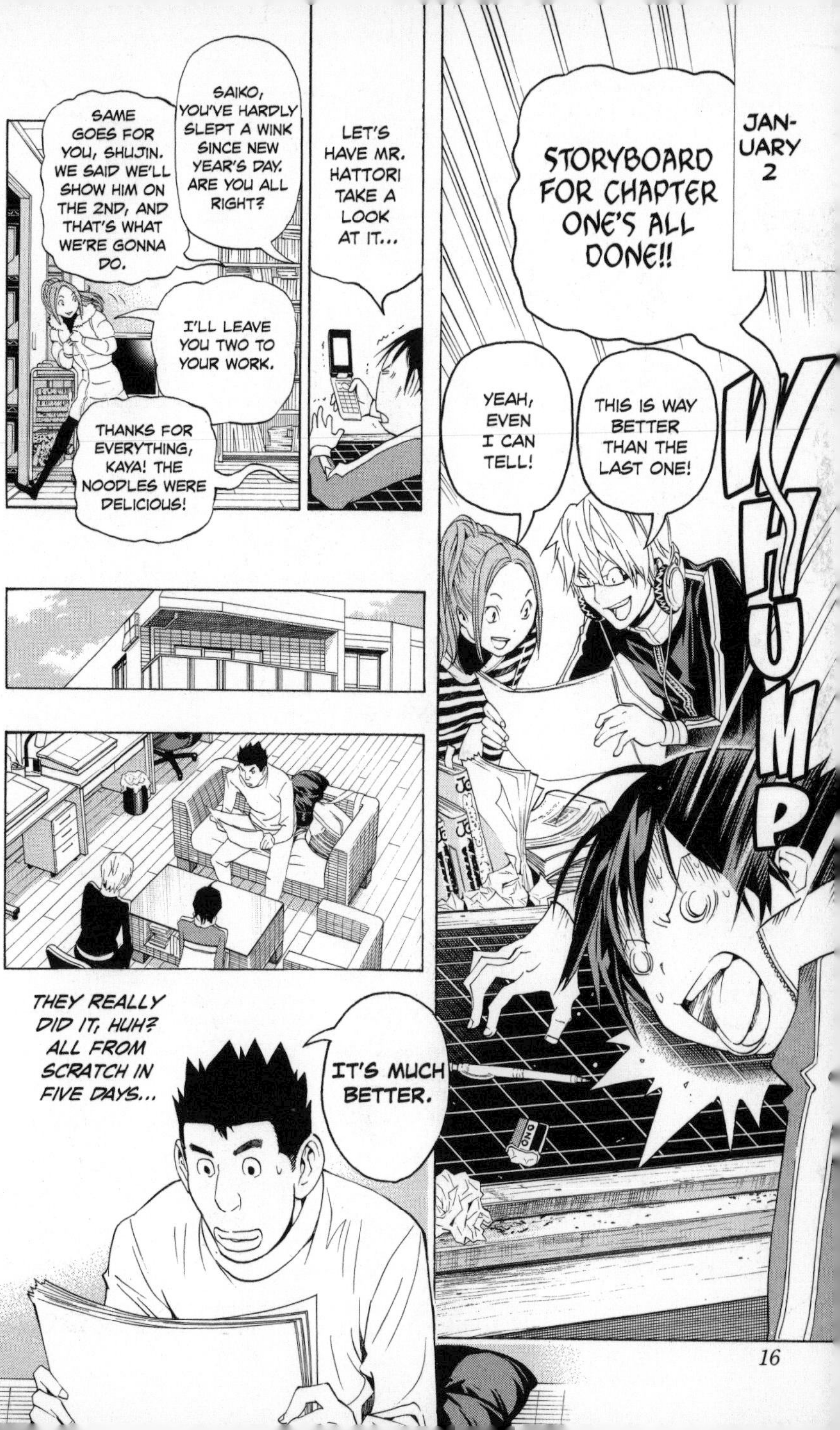
JANUARY 2
STORYBOARD FOR CHAPTER ONE'S ALL DONE!!
WHUMP
THIS IS WAY BETTER THAN THE LAST ONE!
YEAH, EVEN I CAN TELL!
LET'S HAVE MR. HATTORI TAKE A LOOK AT IT...
SAIKO, YOU'VE HARDLY SLEPT A WINK SINCE NEW YEAR'S DAY. ARE YOU ALL RIGHT?
SAME GOES FOR YOU, SHUJIN. WE SAID WE'LL SHOW HIM ON THE 2ND, AND THAT'S WHAT WE'RE GONNA DO.
I'LL LEAVE YOU TWO TO YOUR WORK.
THANKS FOR EVERYTHING, KAYA! THE NOODLES WERE DELICIOUS!
IT'S MUCH BETTER.
THEY REALLY DID IT, HUH? ALL FROM SCRATCH IN FIVE DAYS...

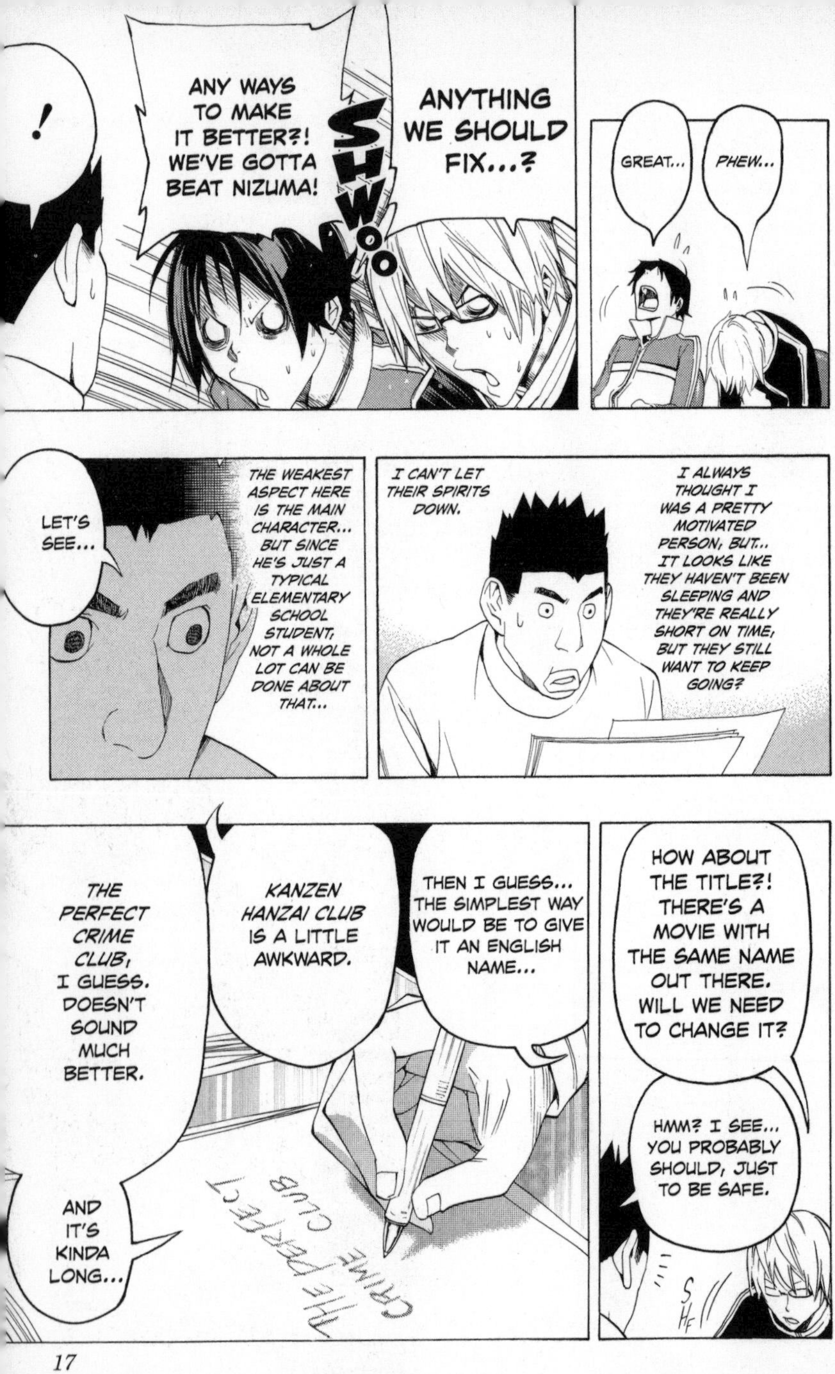
PHEW...
GREAT...
ANYTHING WE SHOULD FIX...?
SHWOO
ANY WAYS TO MAKE IT BETTER?! WE'VE GOTTA BEAT NIZUMA!
!
I ALWAYS THOUGHT I WAS A PRETTY MOTIVATED PERSON, BUT... IT LOOKS LIKE THEY HAVEN'T BEEN SLEEPING AND THEY'RE REALLY SHORT ON TIME, BUT THEY STILL WANT TO KEEP GOING?
I CAN'T LET THEIR SPIRITS DOWN.
THE WEAKEST ASPECT HERE IS THE MAIN CHARACTER... BUT SINCE HE'S JUST A TYPICAL ELEMENTARY SCHOOL STUDENT, NOT A WHOLE LOT CAN BE DONE ABOUT THAT...
LET'S SEE...
HOW ABOUT THE TITLE?! THERE'S A MOVIE WITH THE SAME NAME OUT THERE. WILL WE NEED TO CHANGE IT?
HMM? I SEE... YOU PROBABLY SHOULD, JUST TO BE SAFE.
SHF
THEN I GUESS... THE SIMPLEST WAY WOULD BE TO GIVE IT AN ENGLISH NAME...
KANZEN HANZAI CLUB IS A LITTLE AWKWARD.
THE PERFECT CRIME CLUB, I GUESS. DOESN'T SOUND MUCH BETTER.
AND IT'S KINDA LONG...
THE PERFECT CRIME CLUB

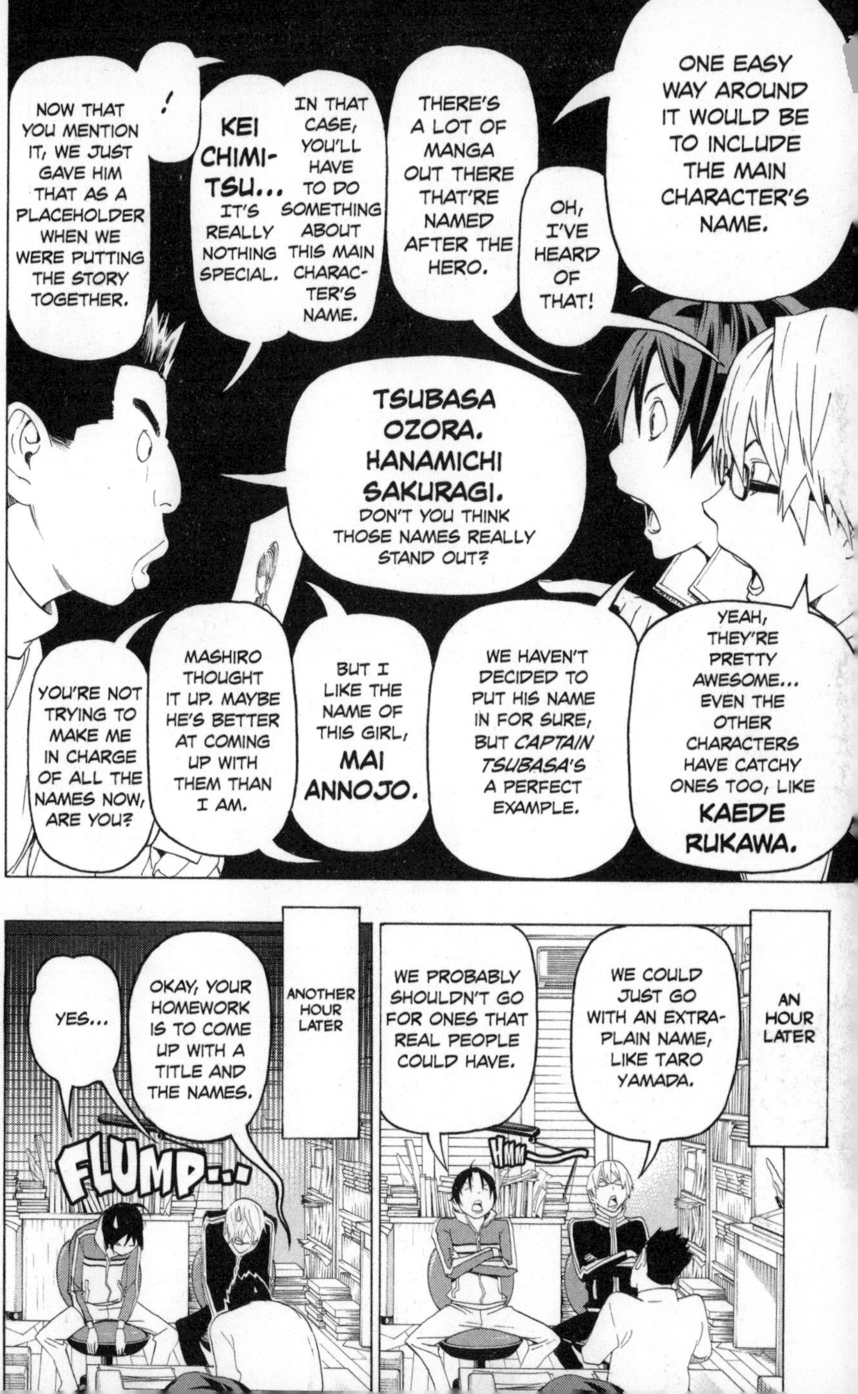
ONE EASY WAY AROUND IT WOULD BE TO INCLUDE THE MAIN CHARACTER'S NAME.
OH, I'VE HEARD OF THAT!
THERE'S A LOT OF MANGA OUT THERE THAT'RE NAMED AFTER THE HERO.
IN THAT CASE, YOU'LL HAVE TO DO SOMETHING ABOUT THIS MAIN CHARAC-TER'S NAME.
KEI CHIMI-TSU... IT'S REALLY NOTHING SPECIAL.
!
NOW THAT YOU MENTION IT, WE JUST GAVE HIM THAT AS A PLACEHOLDER WHEN WE WERE PUTTING THE STORY TOGETHER.
TSUBASA OZORA. HANAMICHI SAKURAGI. DON'T YOU THINK THOSE NAMES REALLY STAND OUT?
YEAH, THEY'RE PRETTY AWESOME... EVEN THE OTHER CHARACTERS HAVE CATCHY ONES TOO, LIKE KAEDE RUKAWA.
WE HAVEN'T DECIDED TO PUT HIS NAME IN FOR SURE, BUT *CAPTAIN TSUBASA*'S A PERFECT EXAMPLE.
BUT I LIKE THE NAME OF THIS GIRL, MAI ANNOJO.
MASHIRO THOUGHT IT UP. MAYBE HE'S BETTER AT COMING UP WITH THEM THAN I AM.
YOU'RE NOT TRYING TO MAKE ME IN CHARGE OF ALL THE NAMES NOW, ARE YOU?
AN HOUR LATER
WE COULD JUST GO WITH AN EXTRA-PLAIN NAME, LIKE TARO YAMADA.
WE PROBABLY SHOULDN'T GO FOR ONES THAT REAL PEOPLE COULD HAVE.
HMM
ANOTHER HOUR LATER
OKAY, YOUR HOMEWORK IS TO COME UP WITH A TITLE AND THE NAMES.
YES...
FLUMP...

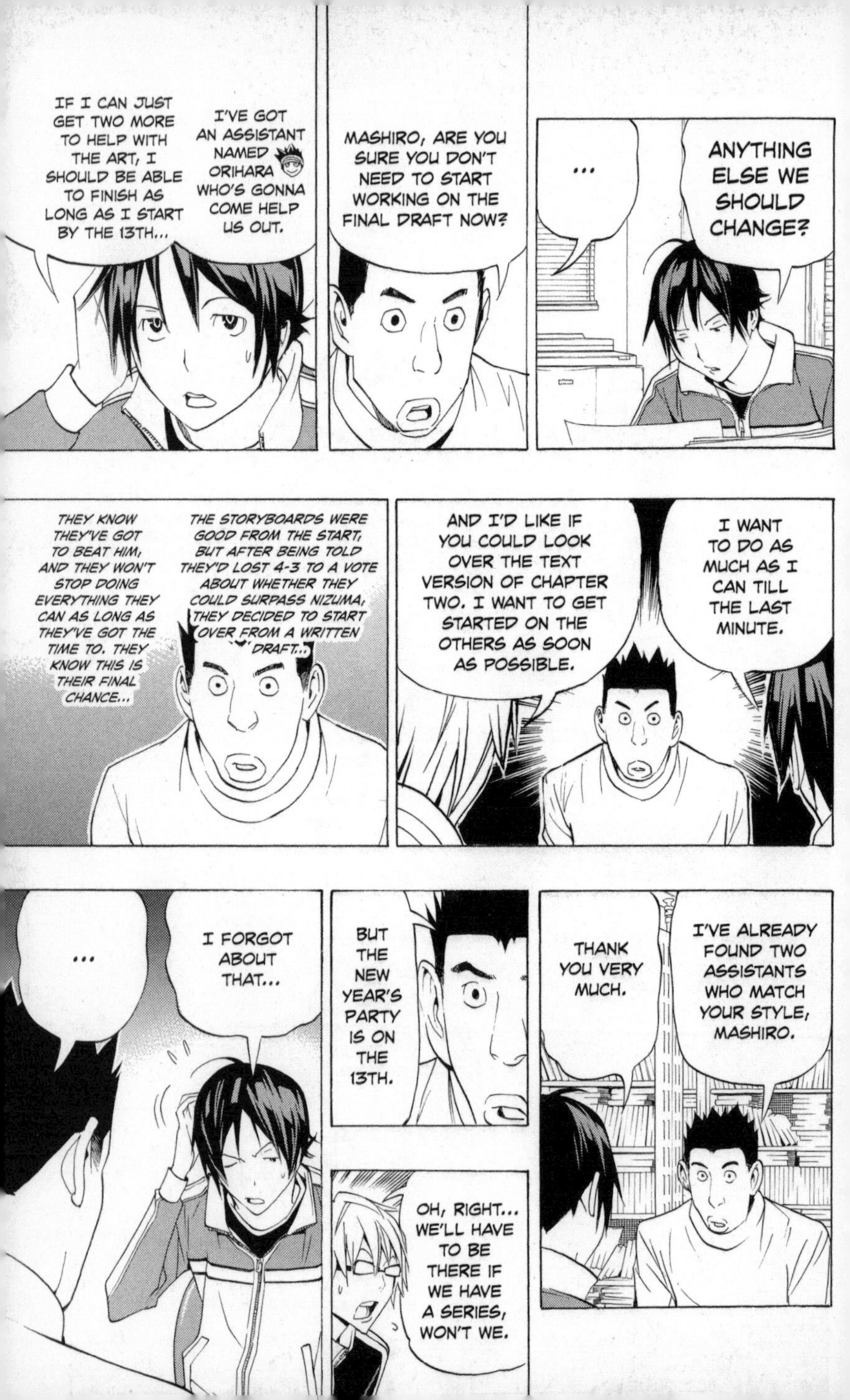
ANYTHING ELSE WE SHOULD CHANGE?
...
MASHIRO, ARE YOU SURE YOU DON'T NEED TO START WORKING ON THE FINAL DRAFT NOW?
I'VE GOT AN ASSISTANT NAMED ORIHARA WHO'S GONNA COME HELP US OUT.
IF I CAN JUST GET TWO MORE TO HELP WITH THE ART, I SHOULD BE ABLE TO FINISH AS LONG AS I START BY THE 13TH...
I WANT TO DO AS MUCH AS I CAN TILL THE LAST MINUTE.
AND I'D LIKE IF YOU COULD LOOK OVER THE TEXT VERSION OF CHAPTER TWO. I WANT TO GET STARTED ON THE OTHERS AS SOON AS POSSIBLE.
THE STORYBOARDS WERE GOOD FROM THE START, BUT AFTER BEING TOLD THEY'D LOST 4-3 TO A VOTE ABOUT WHETHER THEY COULD SURPASS NIZUMA, THEY DECIDED TO START OVER FROM A WRITTEN DRAFT...
THEY KNOW THEY'VE GOT TO BEAT HIM, AND THEY WON'T STOP DOING EVERYTHING THEY CAN AS LONG AS THEY'VE GOT THE TIME TO. THEY KNOW THIS IS THEIR FINAL CHANCE...
I'VE ALREADY FOUND TWO ASSISTANTS WHO MATCH YOUR STYLE, MASHIRO.
THANK YOU VERY MUCH.
BUT THE NEW YEAR'S PARTY IS ON THE 13TH.
OH, RIGHT... WE'LL HAVE TO BE THERE IF WE HAVE A SERIES, WON'T WE.
I FORGOT ABOUT THAT...
...

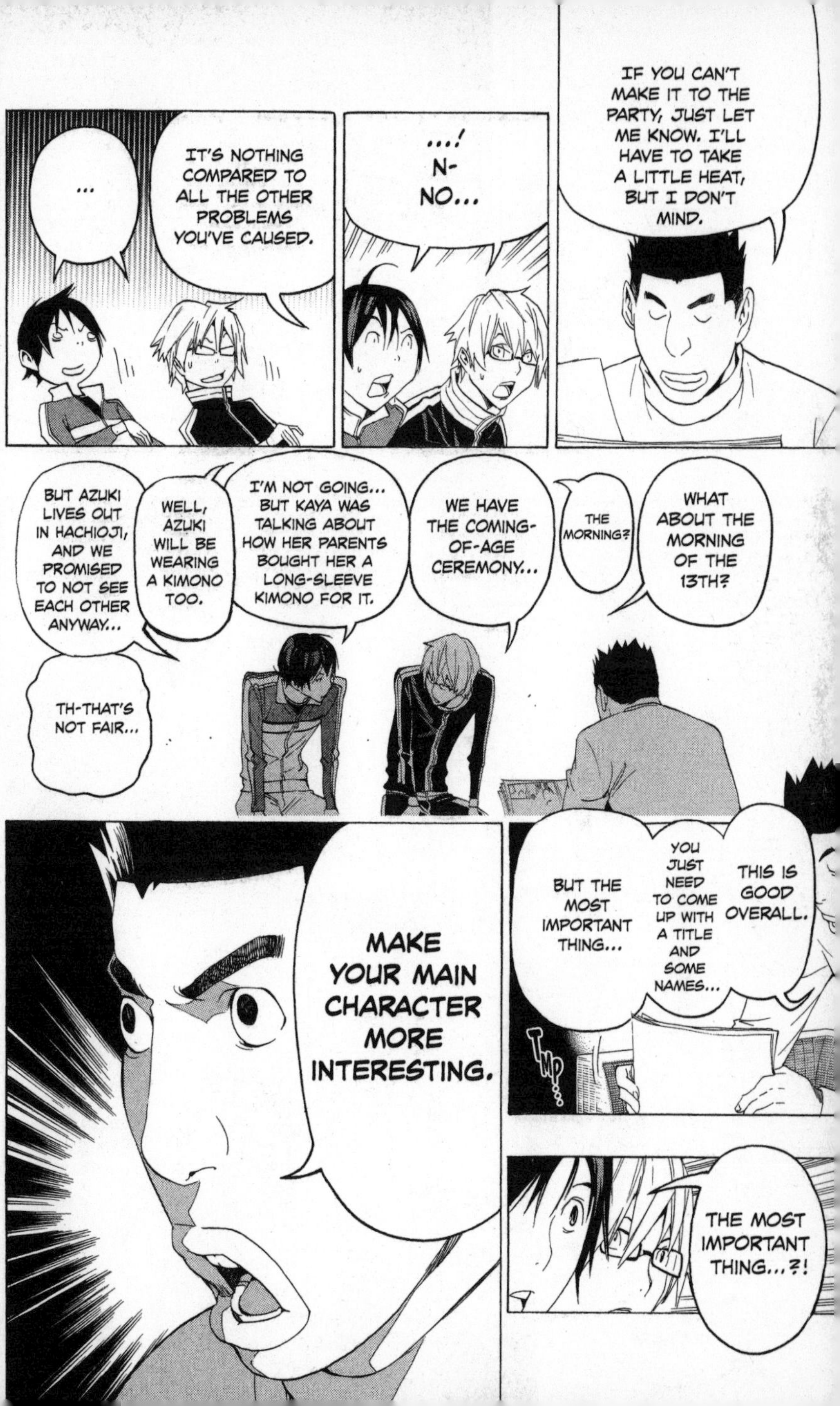
IF YOU CAN'T MAKE IT TO THE PARTY, JUST LET ME KNOW. I'LL HAVE TO TAKE A LITTLE HEAT, BUT I DON'T MIND.
...! N- NO...
IT'S NOTHING COMPARED TO ALL THE OTHER PROBLEMS YOU'VE CAUSED.
...
WHAT ABOUT THE MORNING OF THE 13TH?
THE MORNING?
WE HAVE THE COMING-OF-AGE CEREMONY...
I'M NOT GOING... BUT KAYA WAS TALKING ABOUT HOW HER PARENTS BOUGHT HER A LONG-SLEEVE KIMONO FOR IT.
WELL, AZUKI WILL BE WEARING A KIMONO TOO.
BUT AZUKI LIVES OUT IN HACHIOJI, AND WE PROMISED TO NOT SEE EACH OTHER ANYWAY...
TH-THAT'S NOT FAIR...
THIS IS GOOD OVERALL.
YOU JUST NEED TO COME UP WITH A TITLE AND SOME NAMES...
BUT THE MOST IMPORTANT THING...
TMP...
THE MOST IMPORTANT THING...?!
MAKE YOUR MAIN CHARACTER MORE INTERESTING.

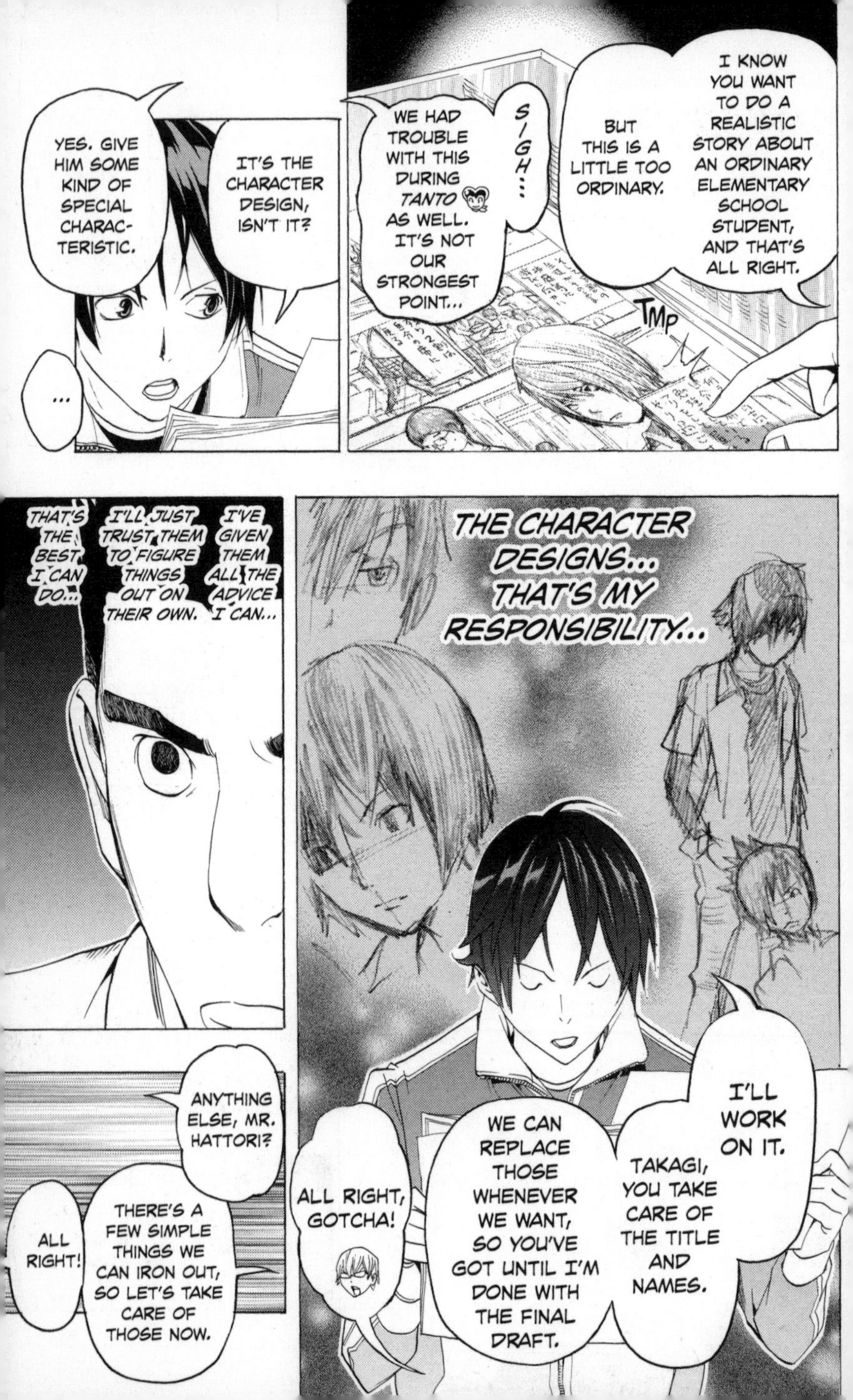
I KNOW YOU WANT TO DO A REALISTIC STORY ABOUT AN ORDINARY ELEMENTARY SCHOOL STUDENT, AND THAT'S ALL RIGHT.
BUT THIS IS A LITTLE TOO ORDINARY.
SIGH...
WE HAD TROUBLE WITH THIS DURING *TANTO* AS WELL. IT'S NOT OUR STRONGEST POINT...
TMP
IT'S THE CHARACTER DESIGN, ISN'T IT?
YES. GIVE HIM SOME KIND OF SPECIAL CHARACTERISTIC.
...
THE CHARACTER DESIGNS... THAT'S MY RESPONSIBILITY...
I'LL WORK ON IT.
TAKAGI, YOU TAKE CARE OF THE TITLE AND NAMES.
WE CAN REPLACE THOSE WHENEVER WE WANT, SO YOU'VE GOT UNTIL I'M DONE WITH THE FINAL DRAFT.
ALL RIGHT, GOTCHA!
I'VE GIVEN THEM ALL THE ADVICE I CAN...
I'LL JUST TRUST THEM TO FIGURE THINGS OUT ON THEIR OWN.
THAT'S THE BEST I CAN DO...
ANYTHING ELSE, MR. HATTORI?
THERE'S A FEW SIMPLE THINGS WE CAN IRON OUT, SO LET'S TAKE CARE OF THOSE NOW.
ALL RIGHT!

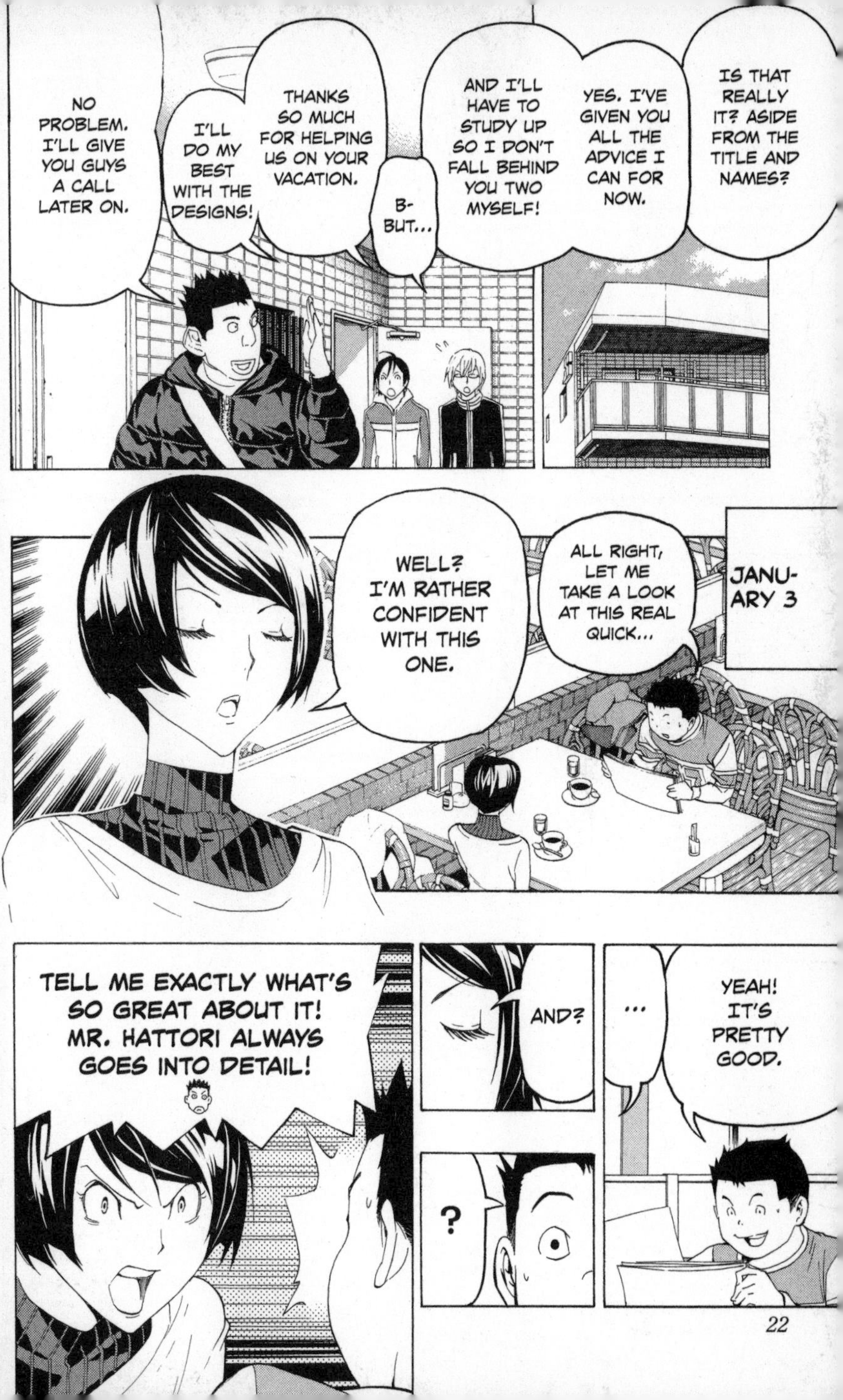
IS THAT REALLY IT? ASIDE FROM THE TITLE AND NAMES?
YES. I'VE GIVEN YOU ALL THE ADVICE I CAN FOR NOW.
AND I'LL HAVE TO STUDY UP SO I DON'T FALL BEHIND YOU TWO MYSELF!
B-BUT...
THANKS SO MUCH FOR HELPING US ON YOUR VACATION.
I'LL DO MY BEST WITH THE DESIGNS!
NO PROBLEM. I'LL GIVE YOU GUYS A CALL LATER ON.
JANUARY 3
ALL RIGHT, LET ME TAKE A LOOK AT THIS REAL QUICK...
WELL? I'M RATHER CONFIDENT WITH THIS ONE.
YEAH! IT'S PRETTY GOOD.
...
AND?
?
TELL ME EXACTLY WHAT'S SO GREAT ABOUT IT! MR. HATTORI ALWAYS GOES INTO DETAIL!

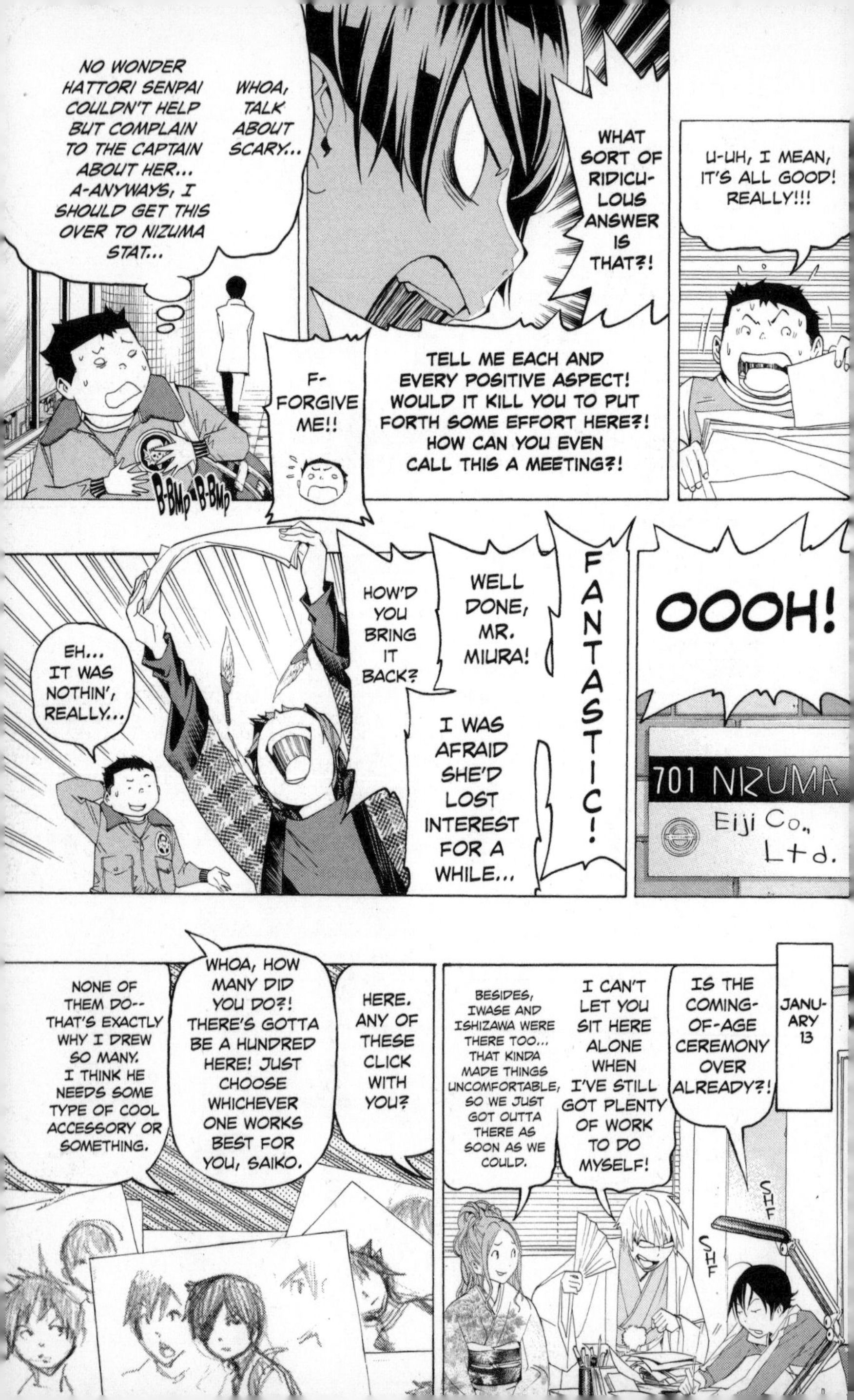
U-UH, I MEAN, IT'S ALL GOOD! REALLY!!!
WHAT SORT OF RIDICULOUS ANSWER IS THAT?!
TELL ME EACH AND EVERY POSITIVE ASPECT! WOULD IT KILL YOU TO PUT FORTH SOME EFFORT HERE?! HOW CAN YOU EVEN CALL THIS A MEETING?!
F-FORGIVE ME!!
WHOA, TALK ABOUT SCARY...
NO WONDER HATTORI SENPAI COULDN'T HELP BUT COMPLAIN TO THE CAPTAIN ABOUT HER... A-ANYWAYS, I SHOULD GET THIS OVER TO NIZUMA STAT...
B-BMP B-BMP
OOOH!
701 NIZUMA
Eiji Co., Ltd.
FANTASTIC!
WELL DONE, MR. MIURA!
HOW'D YOU BRING IT BACK?
I WAS AFRAID SHE'D LOST INTEREST FOR A WHILE...
EH... IT WAS NOTHIN', REALLY...
JANUARY 13
IS THE COMING-OF-AGE CEREMONY OVER ALREADY?!
I CAN'T LET YOU SIT HERE ALONE WHEN I'VE STILL GOT PLENTY OF WORK TO DO MYSELF!
BESIDES, IWASE AND ISHIZAWA WERE THERE TOO... THAT KINDA MADE THINGS UNCOMFORTABLE, SO WE JUST GOT OUTTA THERE AS SOON AS WE COULD.
SHF
SHF
HERE. ANY OF THESE CLICK WITH YOU?
WHOA, HOW MANY DID YOU DO?! THERE'S GOTTA BE A HUNDRED HERE! JUST CHOOSE WHICHEVER ONE WORKS BEST FOR YOU, SAIKO.
NONE OF THEM DO--THAT'S EXACTLY WHY I DREW SO MANY. I THINK HE NEEDS SOME TYPE OF COOL ACCESSORY OR SOMETHING.

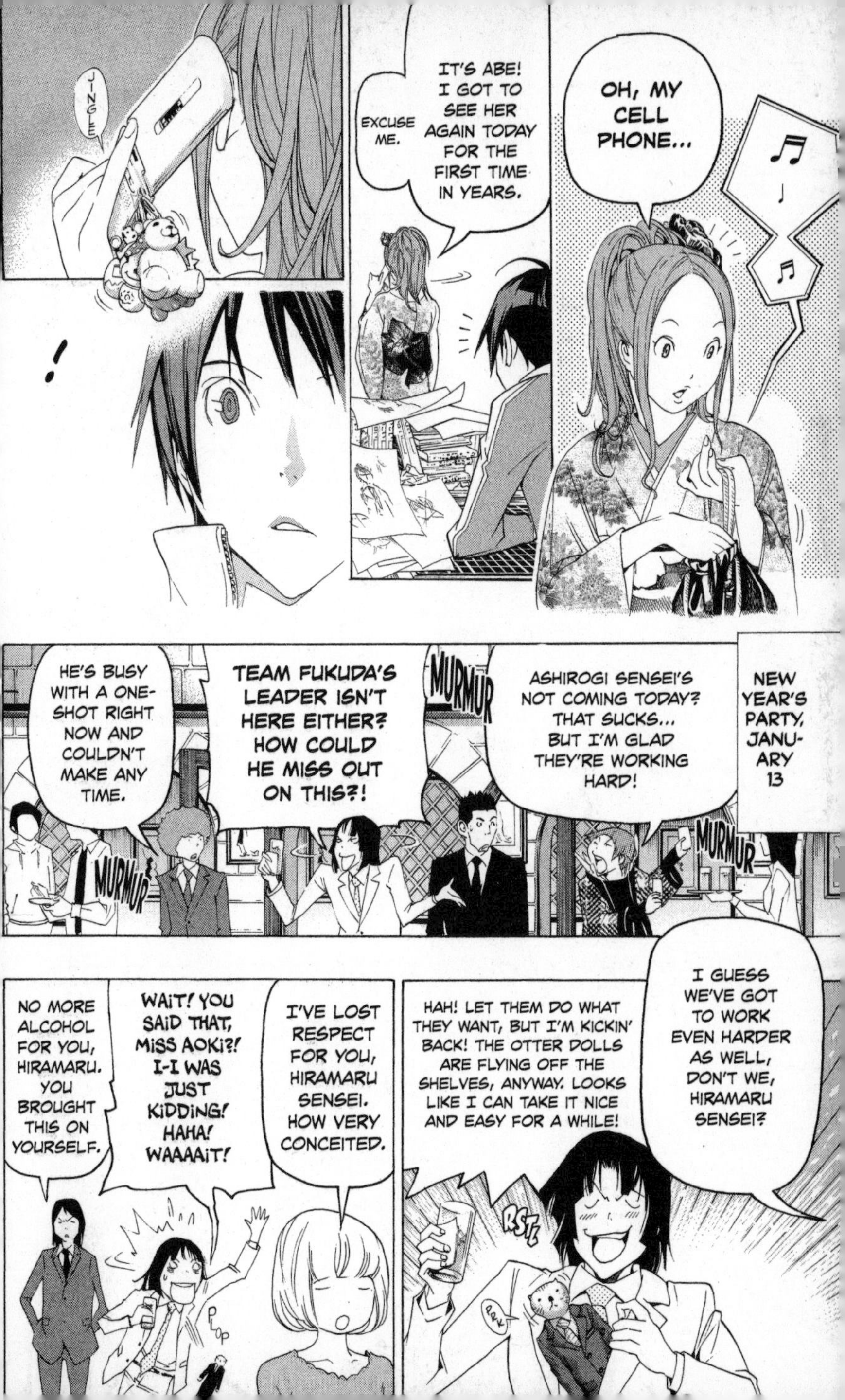
OH, MY CELL PHONE...
IT'S ABE! I GOT TO SEE HER AGAIN TODAY FOR THE FIRST TIME IN YEARS.
EXCUSE ME.
JINGLE
!
NEW YEAR'S PARTY, JANUARY 13
MURMUR
ASHIROGI SENSEI'S NOT COMING TODAY? THAT SUCKS... BUT I'M GLAD THEY'RE WORKING HARD!
MURMUR
TEAM FUKUDA'S LEADER ISN'T HERE EITHER? HOW COULD HE MISS OUT ON THIS?!
HE'S BUSY WITH A ONE-SHOT RIGHT NOW AND COULDN'T MAKE ANY TIME.
MURMUR
I GUESS WE'VE GOT TO WORK EVEN HARDER AS WELL, DON'T WE, HIRAMARU SENSEI?
HAH! LET THEM DO WHAT THEY WANT, BUT I'M KICKIN' BACK! THE OTTER DOLLS ARE FLYING OFF THE SHELVES, ANYWAY. LOOKS LIKE I CAN TAKE IT NICE AND EASY FOR A WHILE!
RSTL
I'VE LOST RESPECT FOR YOU, HIRAMARU SENSEI. HOW VERY CONCEITED.
WAIT! YOU SAID THAT, MISS AOKI?! I-I WAS JUST KIDDING! HAHA! WAAAAIT!
NO MORE ALCOHOL FOR YOU, HIRAMARU. YOU BROUGHT THIS ON YOURSELF.
PLOP

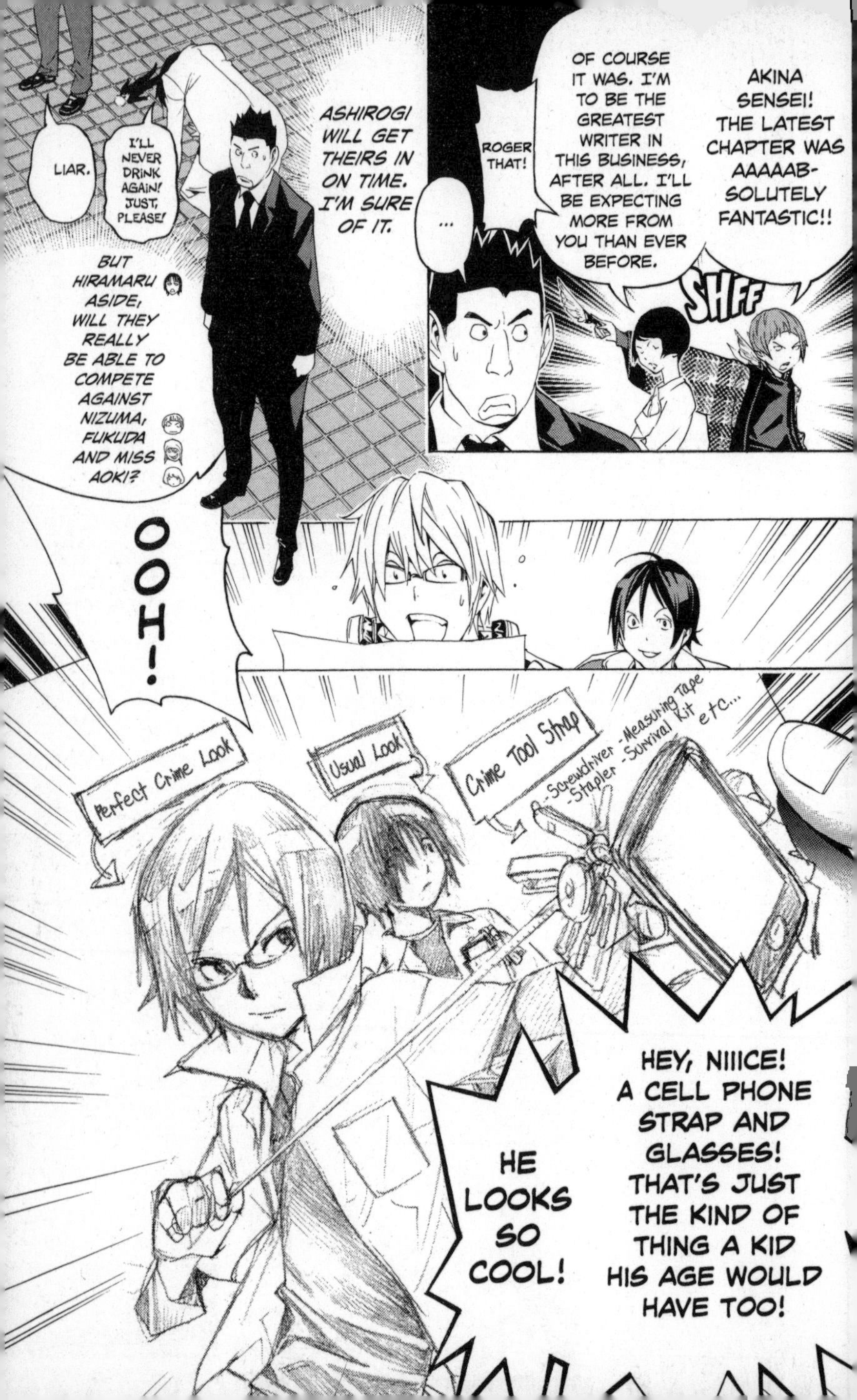

AKINA SENSEI! THE LATEST CHAPTER WAS AAAAAB-SOLUTELY FANTASTIC!!
SHFF
OF COURSE IT WAS. I'M TO BE THE GREATEST WRITER IN THIS BUSINESS, AFTER ALL. I'LL BE EXPECTING MORE FROM YOU THAN EVER BEFORE.
ROGER THAT!
...
ASHIROGI WILL GET THEIRS IN ON TIME. I'M SURE OF IT.
I'LL NEVER DRINK AGAIN! JUST, PLEASE!
LIAR.
BUT HIRAMARU ASIDE, WILL THEY REALLY BE ABLE TO COMPETE AGAINST NIZUMA, FUKUDA AND MISS AOKI?
OOH!
Crime Tool Strap
-Screwdriver -Measuring Tape
-Stapler -Survival Kit
etc...
Usual Look
Perfect Crime Look
HEY, NIIICE! A CELL PHONE STRAP AND GLASSES! THAT'S JUST THE KIND OF THING A KID HIS AGE WOULD HAVE TOO!
HE LOOKS SO COOL!

OHBA'S STORYBOARD

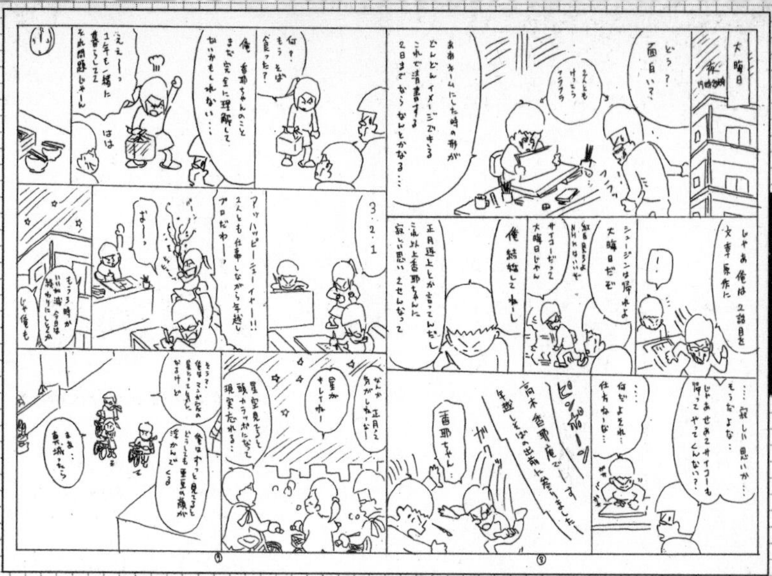
大晦日
どう? 面白いて?
2人とも けっこう フラフラ
ああネームにした時の形が どんどんイメージできる これで清書する 2日までならなんとかなる…
じゃあ俺は 2話目を 文庫原作に
!
シュージンは帰れよ 大晦日だぞ
サイコーだって 大晦日じゃん
俺 結婚してねーし
正月返上とか言ってんだし これ以上香耶ちゃんに 寂しい思いさせんなって
…寂しい思いか…
じゃあせめてサイコーも 帰ってやってくんない?
何だよそれ… 仕方ねーな…
ピンポーン
高木香耶でーす 年越しそばの出前に参りました
ガチャ
香耶ちゃん…
何? もうそば 食った?
俺 香耶ちゃんのこと まだ完全に理解して ないかもしれない…
ええー!? 2年も一緒に 暮らしてて それ問題じゃーん
はは
3.2.1
ハッピーニューイヤー!! 2人とも仕事しながら年越し プロだわー
おー
もう3時か いい加減 今日は 終わりにしとくか
じゃ俺も
なんか 正月って 気がしねーなー
星が キレイだー
星空見てると 頭カラッポになって 現実忘れる…
俺はずっと見てると どうしても亜豆の顔が 浮かんでくる
まぁ… 真城ったら

OBATA'S STORYBOARD

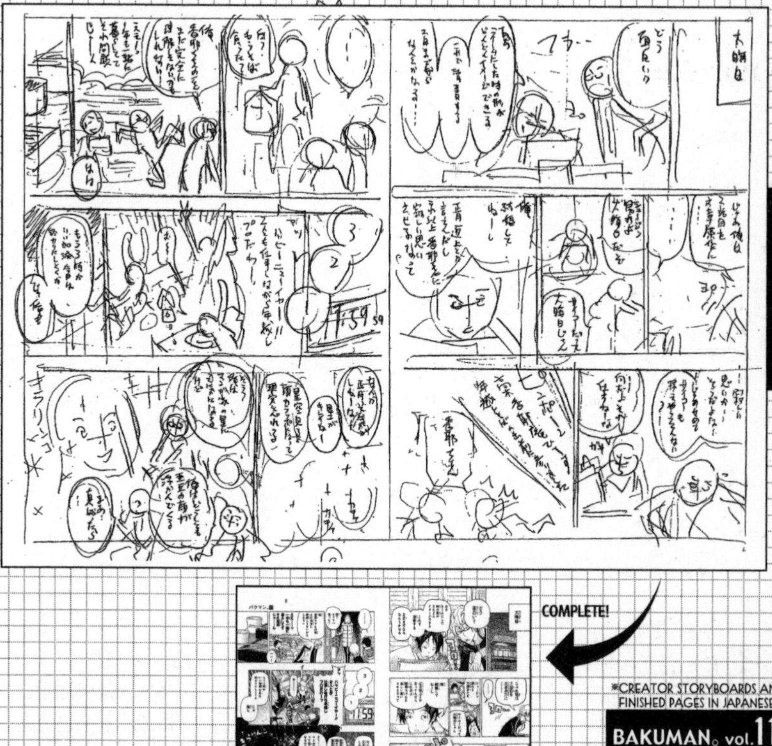

COMPLETE!

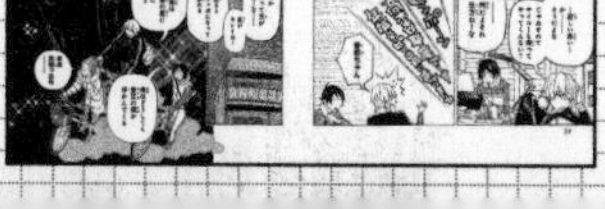

※CREATOR STORYBOARDS AND FINISHED PAGES IN JAPANESE

BAKUMAN。 vol.11

"Until the Final Draft Is Complete"

Chapter 89, pp. 14-15

CHAPTER 90
ART AND MERCHANDISE

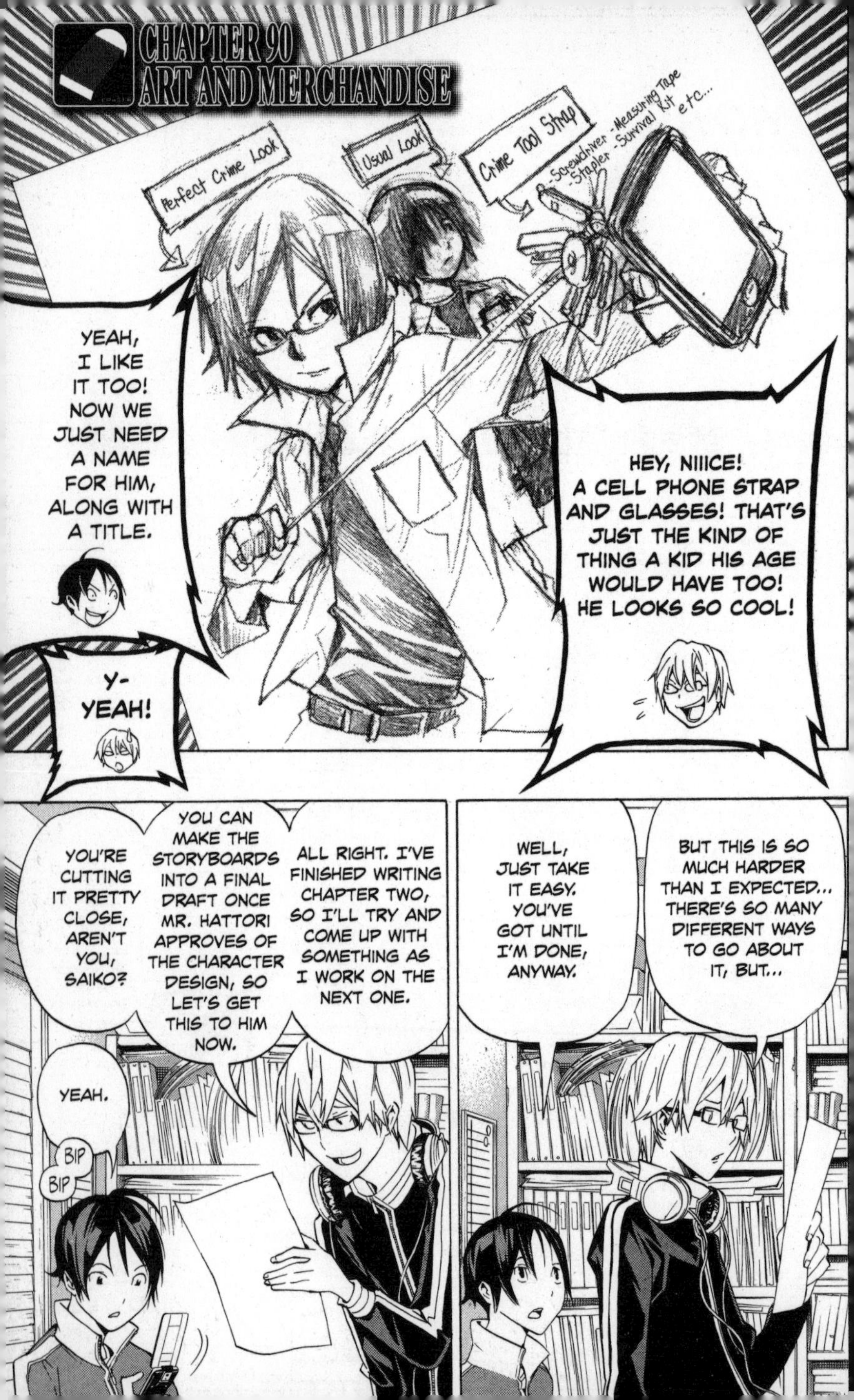
Perfect Crime Look
Usual Look
Crime Tool Strap
-Screwdriver -Measuring Tape
-Stapler -Survival Kit
etc...
HEY, NIIICE! A CELL PHONE STRAP AND GLASSES! THAT'S JUST THE KIND OF THING A KID HIS AGE WOULD HAVE TOO! HE LOOKS SO COOL!
YEAH, I LIKE IT TOO! NOW WE JUST NEED A NAME FOR HIM, ALONG WITH A TITLE.
Y-YEAH!
BUT THIS IS SO MUCH HARDER THAN I EXPECTED... THERE'S SO MANY DIFFERENT WAYS TO GO ABOUT IT, BUT...
WELL, JUST TAKE IT EASY. YOU'VE GOT UNTIL I'M DONE, ANYWAY.
ALL RIGHT. I'VE FINISHED WRITING CHAPTER TWO, SO I'LL TRY AND COME UP WITH SOMETHING AS I WORK ON THE NEXT ONE.
YOU CAN MAKE THE STORYBOARDS INTO A FINAL DRAFT ONCE MR. HATTORI APPROVES OF THE CHARACTER DESIGN, SO LET'S GET THIS TO HIM NOW.
YOU'RE CUTTING IT PRETTY CLOSE, AREN'T YOU, SAIKO?
YEAH.
BIP
BIP

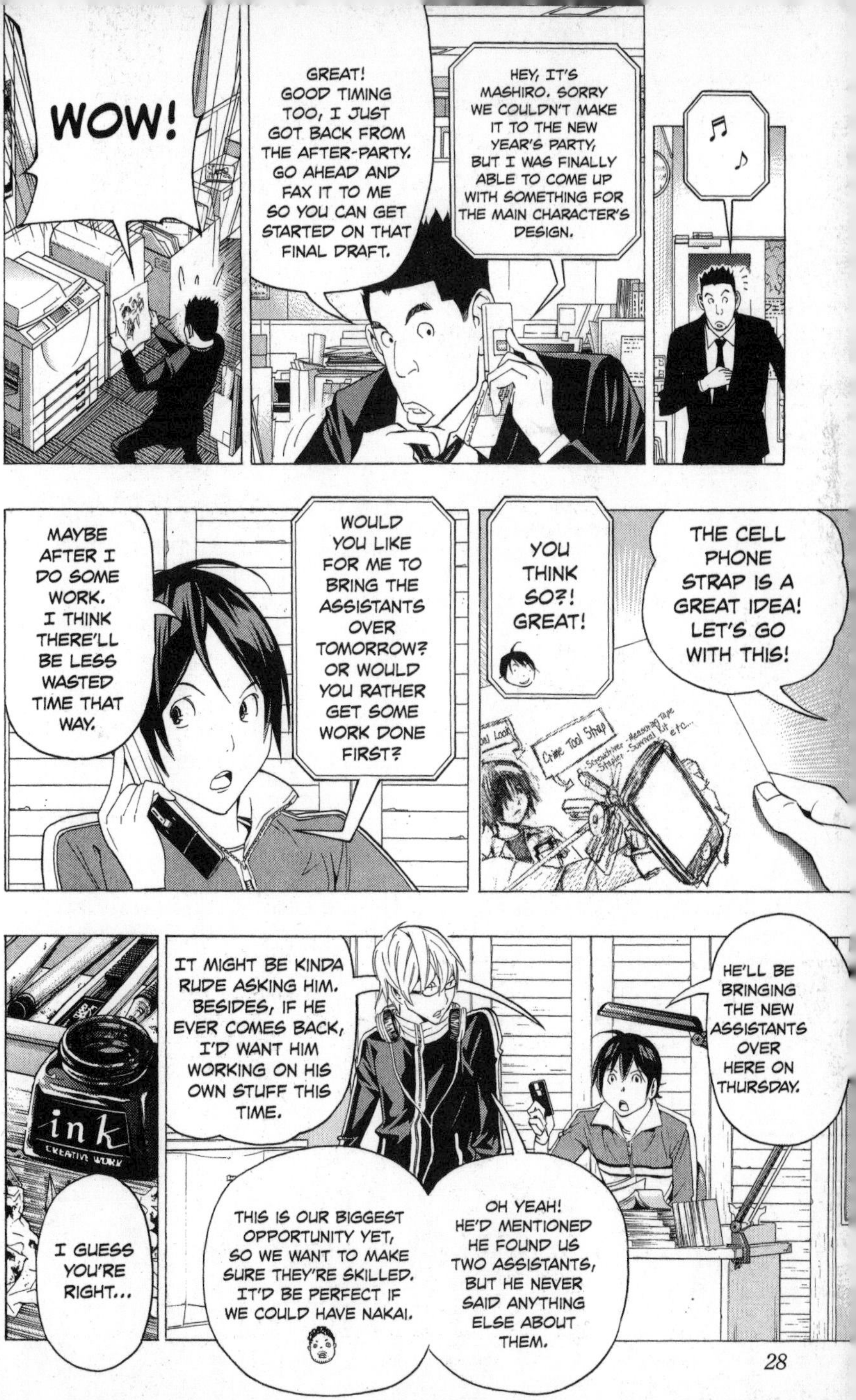
♫ ♪
HEY, IT'S MASHIRO. SORRY WE COULDN'T MAKE IT TO THE NEW YEAR'S PARTY, BUT I WAS FINALLY ABLE TO COME UP WITH SOMETHING FOR THE MAIN CHARACTER'S DESIGN.
GREAT! GOOD TIMING TOO, I JUST GOT BACK FROM THE AFTER-PARTY. GO AHEAD AND FAX IT TO ME SO YOU CAN GET STARTED ON THAT FINAL DRAFT.
WOW!
THE CELL PHONE STRAP IS A GREAT IDEA! LET'S GO WITH THIS!
YOU THINK SO?! GREAT!
Crime Tool Strap
WOULD YOU LIKE FOR ME TO BRING THE ASSISTANTS OVER TOMORROW? OR WOULD YOU RATHER GET SOME WORK DONE FIRST?
MAYBE AFTER I DO SOME WORK. I THINK THERE'LL BE LESS WASTED TIME THAT WAY.
HE'LL BE BRINGING THE NEW ASSISTANTS OVER HERE ON THURSDAY.
OH YEAH! HE'D MENTIONED HE FOUND US TWO ASSISTANTS, BUT HE NEVER SAID ANYTHING ELSE ABOUT THEM.
THIS IS OUR BIGGEST OPPORTUNITY YET, SO WE WANT TO MAKE SURE THEY'RE SKILLED. IT'D BE PERFECT IF WE COULD HAVE NAKAI.
IT MIGHT BE KINDA RUDE ASKING HIM. BESIDES, IF HE EVER COMES BACK, I'D WANT HIM WORKING ON HIS OWN STUFF THIS TIME.
ink CREATIVE WORK
I GUESS YOU'RE RIGHT...

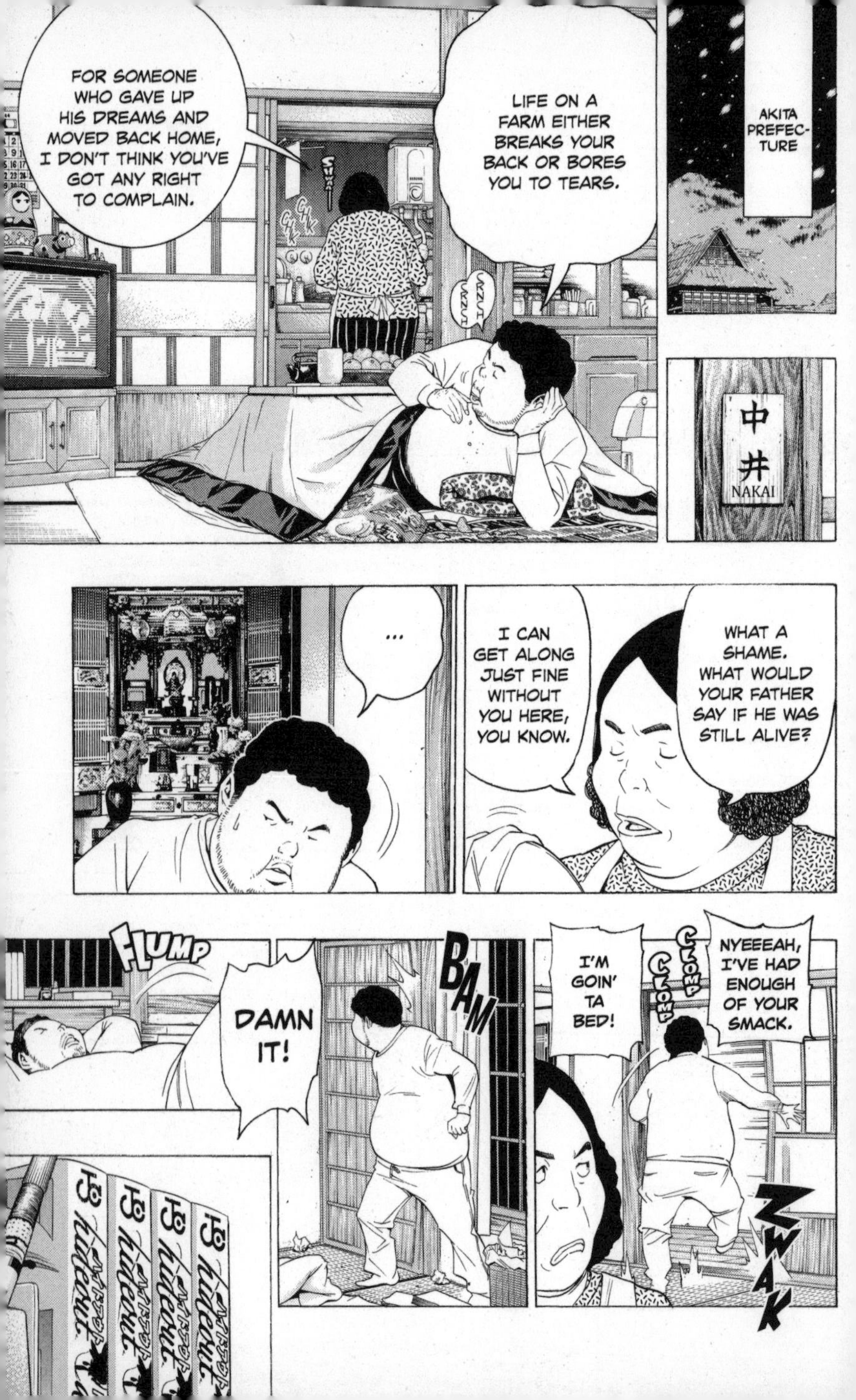
AKITA PREFEC-TURE
中
井
NAKAI
LIFE ON A FARM EITHER BREAKS YOUR BACK OR BORES YOU TO TEARS.
FOR SOMEONE WHO GAVE UP HIS DREAMS AND MOVED BACK HOME, I DON'T THINK YOU'VE GOT ANY RIGHT TO COMPLAIN.
WHAT A SHAME. WHAT WOULD YOUR FATHER SAY IF HE WAS STILL ALIVE?
I CAN GET ALONG JUST FINE WITHOUT YOU HERE, YOU KNOW.
...
NYEEEAH, I'VE HAD ENOUGH OF YOUR SMACK.
CLOMP
CLOMP
I'M GOIN' TA BED!
ZWAK
BAM
FLUMP
DAMN IT!

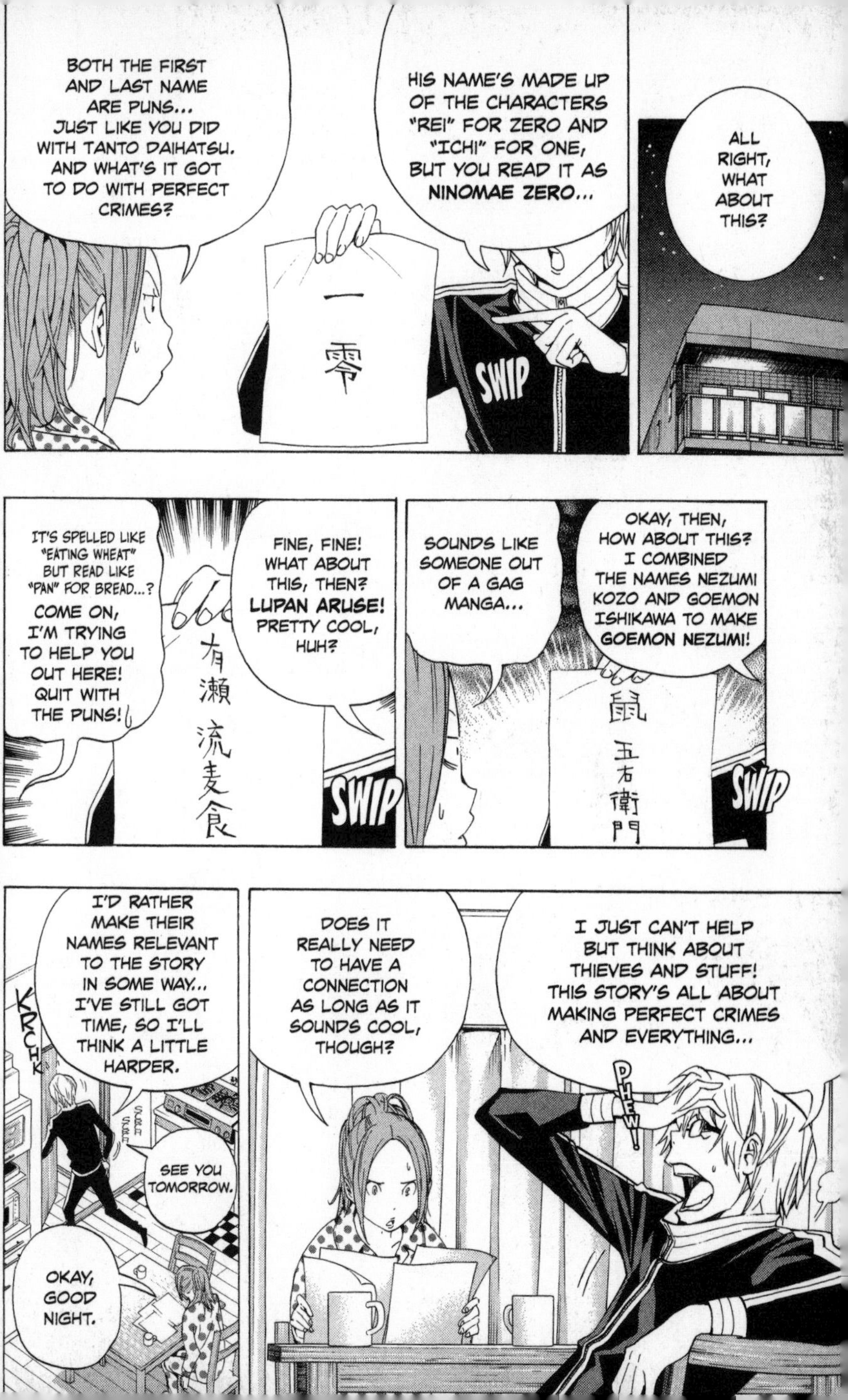
ALL RIGHT, WHAT ABOUT THIS?
HIS NAME'S MADE UP OF THE CHARACTERS "REI" FOR ZERO AND "ICHI" FOR ONE, BUT YOU READ IT AS **NINOMAE ZERO...**
SWIP
一
零
BOTH THE FIRST AND LAST NAME ARE PUNS... JUST LIKE YOU DID WITH TANTO DAIHATSU. AND WHAT'S IT GOT TO DO WITH PERFECT CRIMES?
OKAY, THEN, HOW ABOUT THIS? I COMBINED THE NAMES NEZUMI KOZO AND GOEMON ISHIKAWA TO MAKE **GOEMON NEZUMI!**
SWIP
鼠
五右衛門
SOUNDS LIKE SOMEONE OUT OF A GAG MANGA...
FINE, FINE! WHAT ABOUT THIS, THEN? **LUPAN ARUSE!** PRETTY COOL, HUH?
SWIP
有瀬
流麦食
IT'S SPELLED LIKE "EATING WHEAT" BUT READ LIKE "PAN" FOR BREAD...?
COME ON, I'M TRYING TO HELP YOU OUT HERE! QUIT WITH THE PUNS!
I JUST CAN'T HELP BUT THINK ABOUT THIEVES AND STUFF! THIS STORY'S ALL ABOUT MAKING PERFECT CRIMES AND EVERYTHING...
PHEW
DOES IT REALLY NEED TO HAVE A CONNECTION AS LONG AS IT SOUNDS COOL, THOUGH?
I'D RATHER MAKE THEIR NAMES RELEVANT TO THE STORY IN SOME WAY... I'VE STILL GOT TIME, SO I'LL THINK A LITTLE HARDER.
KRCHK
SEE YOU TOMORROW.
OKAY, GOOD NIGHT.

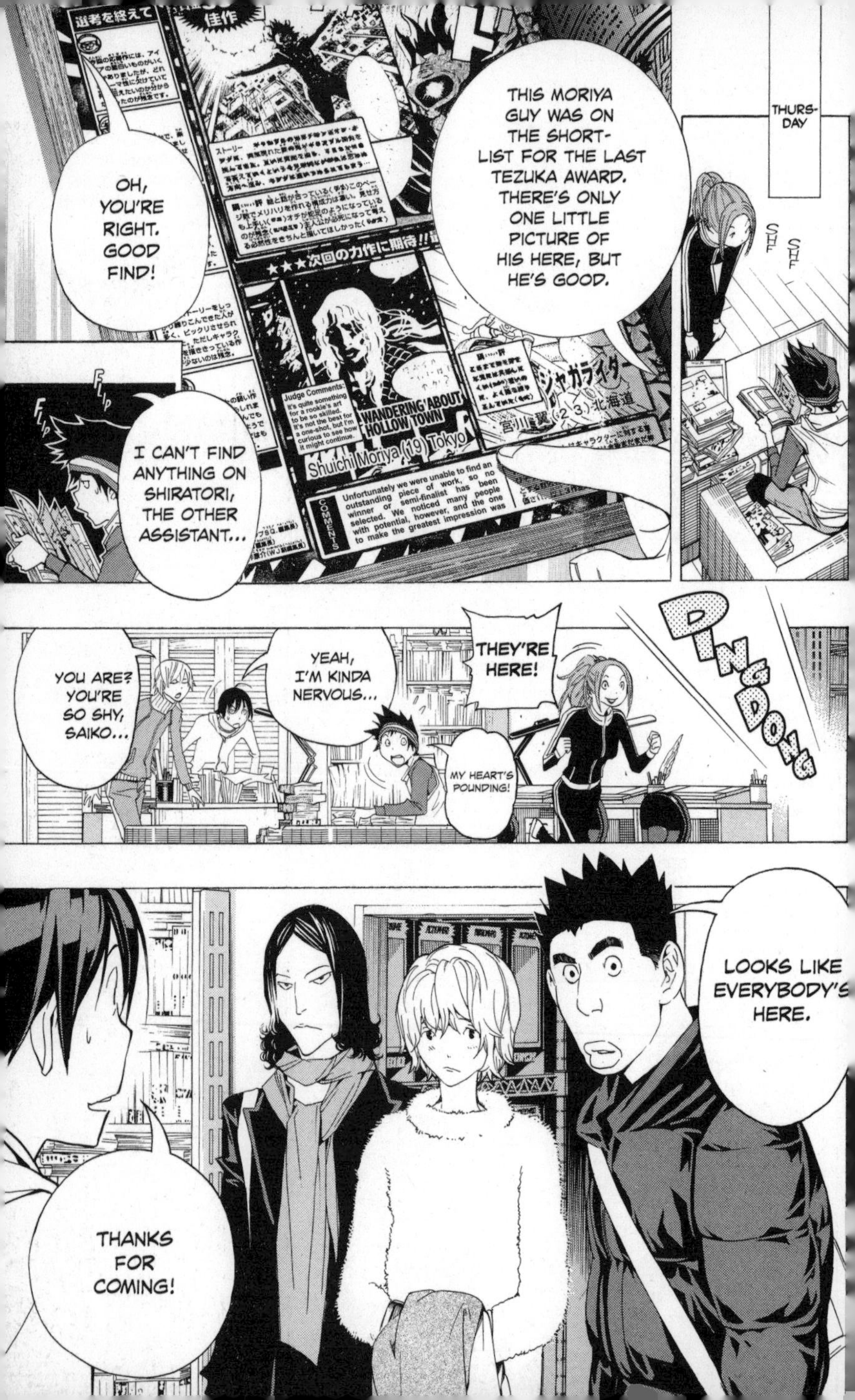
THURS-DAY
SHF SHF
THIS MORIYA GUY WAS ON THE SHORT-LIST FOR THE LAST TEZUKA AWARD. THERE'S ONLY ONE LITTLE PICTURE OF HIS HERE, BUT HE'S GOOD.
選考を終えて
佳作
★★★次回の力作に期待!!
Judge Comments: It's quite something for a rookie's art to be so skilled. It's not the best for a one-shot, but I'm curious to see how it might continue.
WANDERING ABOUT HOLLOW TOWN
Shuichi Moriya (19) Tokyo
COMMENTS
Unfortunately we were unable to find an outstanding piece of work, so no winner or semi-finalist has been selected. We noticed many people with potential, however, and the one to make the greatest impression was
OH, YOU'RE RIGHT. GOOD FIND!
FLIP FLIP
I CAN'T FIND ANYTHING ON SHIRATORI, THE OTHER ASSISTANT...
DING DONG
THEY'RE HERE!
MY HEART'S POUNDING!
YEAH, I'M KINDA NERVOUS...
YOU ARE? YOU'RE SO SHY, SAIKO...
LOOKS LIKE EVERYBODY'S HERE.
THANKS FOR COMING!

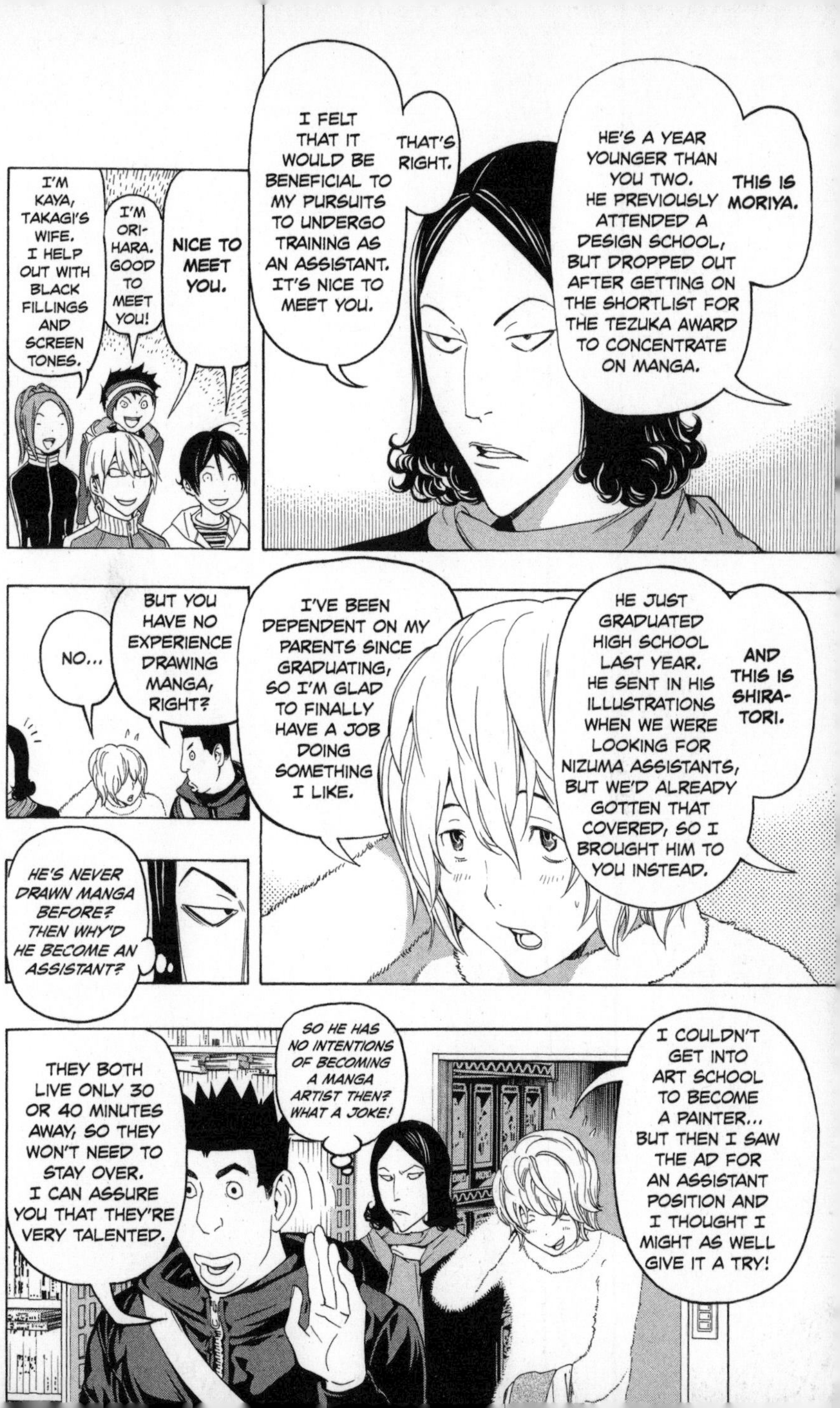
THIS IS MORIYA.
HE'S A YEAR YOUNGER THAN YOU TWO. HE PREVIOUSLY ATTENDED A DESIGN SCHOOL, BUT DROPPED OUT AFTER GETTING ON THE SHORTLIST FOR THE TEZUKA AWARD TO CONCENTRATE ON MANGA.
THAT'S RIGHT.
I FELT THAT IT WOULD BE BENEFICIAL TO MY PURSUITS TO UNDERGO TRAINING AS AN ASSISTANT. IT'S NICE TO MEET YOU.
NICE TO MEET YOU.
I'M ORI-HARA. GOOD TO MEET YOU!
I'M KAYA, TAKAGI'S WIFE. I HELP OUT WITH BLACK FILLINGS AND SCREEN TONES.
AND THIS IS SHIRA-TORI.
HE JUST GRADUATED HIGH SCHOOL LAST YEAR. HE SENT IN HIS ILLUSTRATIONS WHEN WE WERE LOOKING FOR NIZUMA ASSISTANTS, BUT WE'D ALREADY GOTTEN THAT COVERED, SO I BROUGHT HIM TO YOU INSTEAD.
I'VE BEEN DEPENDENT ON MY PARENTS SINCE GRADUATING, SO I'M GLAD TO FINALLY HAVE A JOB DOING SOMETHING I LIKE.
BUT YOU HAVE NO EXPERIENCE DRAWING MANGA, RIGHT?
NO...
HE'S NEVER DRAWN MANGA BEFORE? THEN WHY'D HE BECOME AN ASSISTANT?
I COULDN'T GET INTO ART SCHOOL TO BECOME A PAINTER... BUT THEN I SAW THE AD FOR AN ASSISTANT POSITION AND I THOUGHT I MIGHT AS WELL GIVE IT A TRY!
SO HE HAS NO INTENTIONS OF BECOMING A MANGA ARTIST THEN? WHAT A JOKE!
THEY BOTH LIVE ONLY 30 OR 40 MINUTES AWAY, SO THEY WON'T NEED TO STAY OVER. I CAN ASSURE YOU THAT THEY'RE VERY TALENTED.

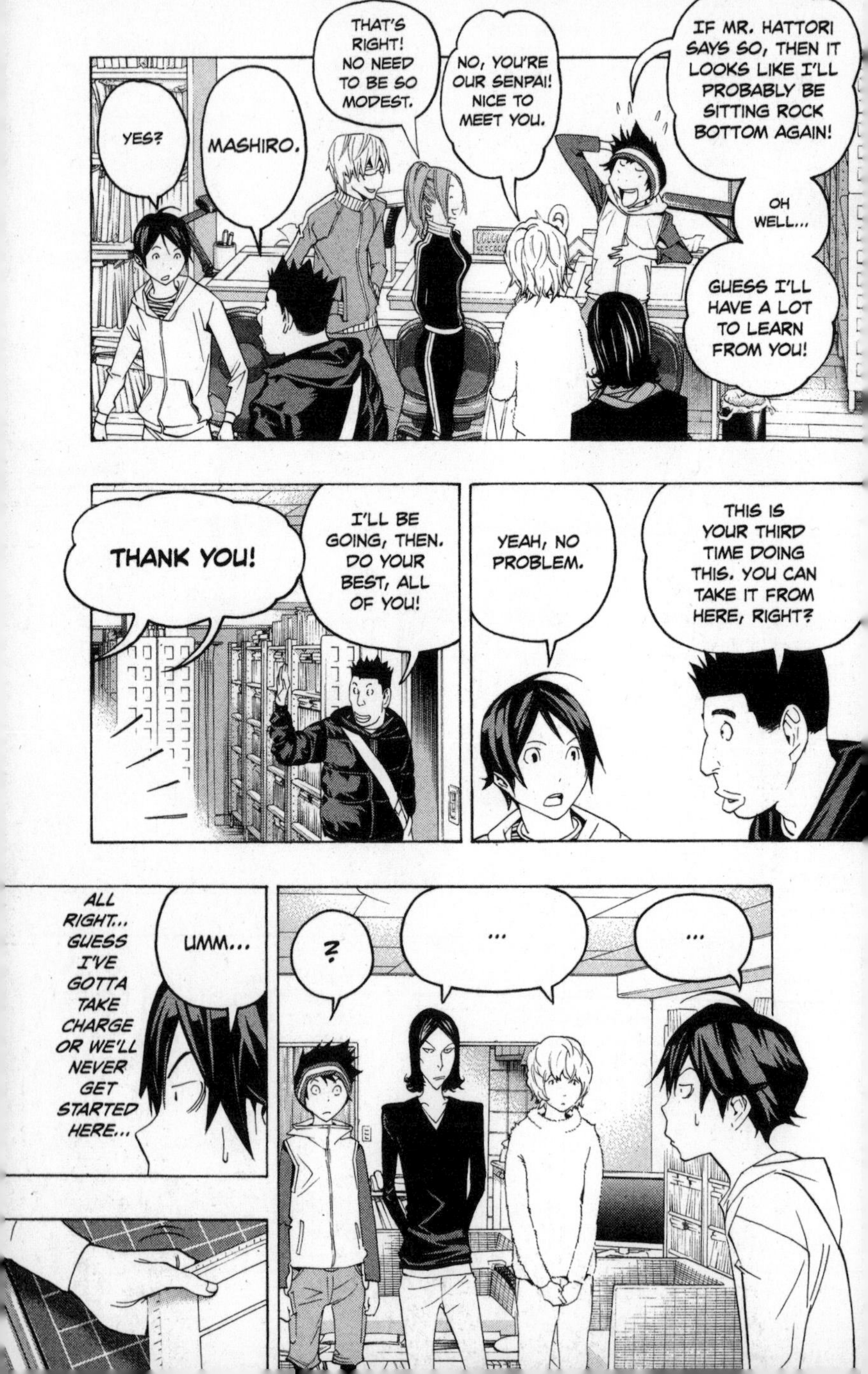
IF MR. HATTORI SAYS SO, THEN IT LOOKS LIKE I'LL PROBABLY BE SITTING ROCK BOTTOM AGAIN!
OH WELL...
GUESS I'LL HAVE A LOT TO LEARN FROM YOU!
NO, YOU'RE OUR SENPAI! NICE TO MEET YOU.
THAT'S RIGHT! NO NEED TO BE SO MODEST.
MASHIRO.
YES?
THIS IS YOUR THIRD TIME DOING THIS. YOU CAN TAKE IT FROM HERE, RIGHT?
YEAH, NO PROBLEM.
I'LL BE GOING, THEN. DO YOUR BEST, ALL OF YOU!
THANK YOU!
...
...
?
UMM...
ALL RIGHT... GUESS I'VE GOTTA TAKE CHARGE OR WE'LL NEVER GET STARTED HERE...

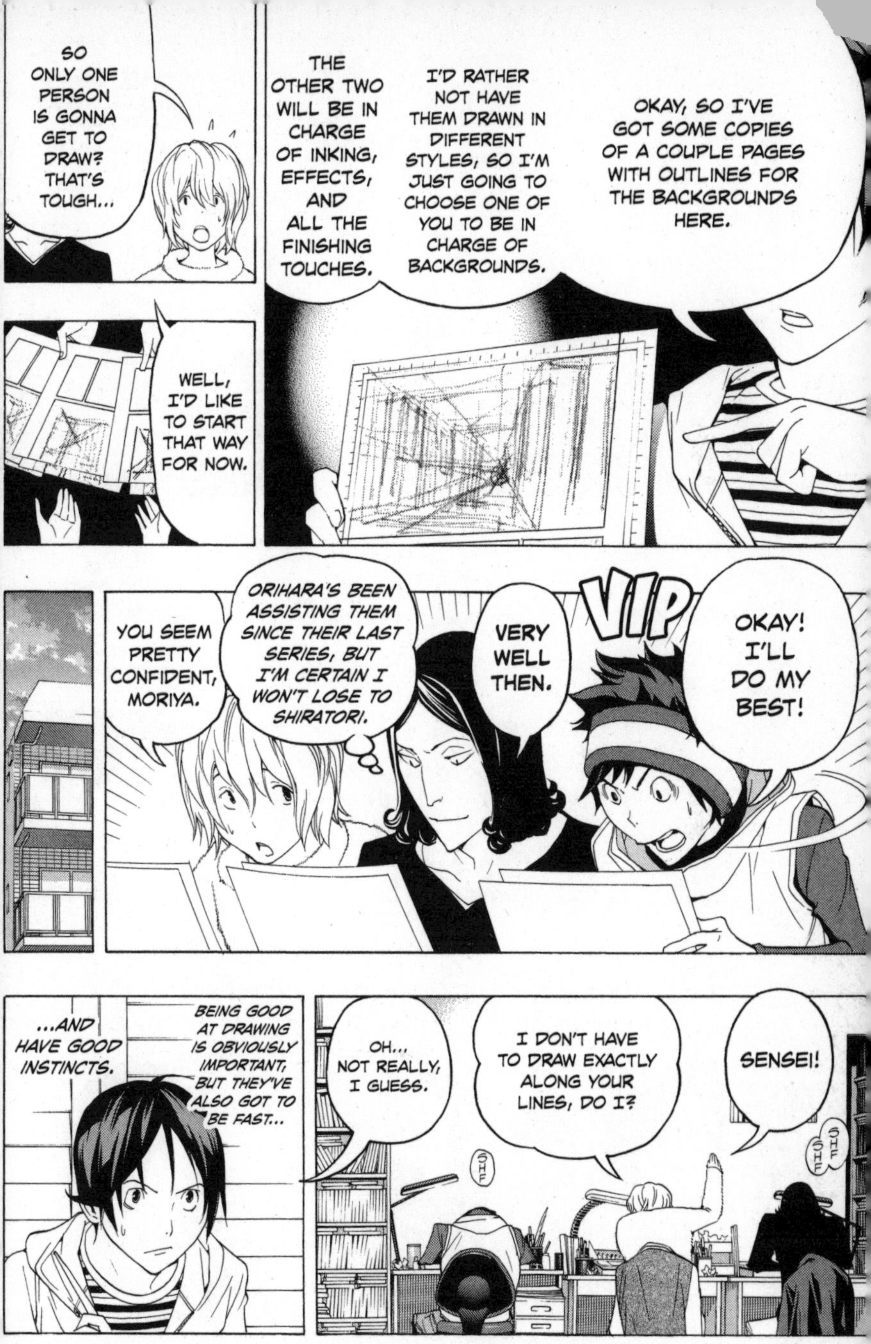
OKAY, SO I'VE GOT SOME COPIES OF A COUPLE PAGES WITH OUTLINES FOR THE BACKGROUNDS HERE.
I'D RATHER NOT HAVE THEM DRAWN IN DIFFERENT STYLES, SO I'M JUST GOING TO CHOOSE ONE OF YOU TO BE IN CHARGE OF BACKGROUNDS.
THE OTHER TWO WILL BE IN CHARGE OF INKING, EFFECTS, AND ALL THE FINISHING TOUCHES.
SO ONLY ONE PERSON IS GONNA GET TO DRAW? THAT'S TOUGH...
WELL, I'D LIKE TO START THAT WAY FOR NOW.
OKAY! I'LL DO MY BEST!
VIP
VERY WELL THEN.
ORIHARA'S BEEN ASSISTING THEM SINCE THEIR LAST SERIES, BUT I'M CERTAIN I WON'T LOSE TO SHIRATORI.
YOU SEEM PRETTY CONFIDENT, MORIYA.
SENSEI!
SHF SHF
I DON'T HAVE TO DRAW EXACTLY ALONG YOUR LINES, DO I?
SHF
OH... NOT REALLY, I GUESS.
BEING GOOD AT DRAWING IS OBVIOUSLY IMPORTANT, BUT THEY'VE ALSO GOT TO BE FAST...
...AND HAVE GOOD INSTINCTS.

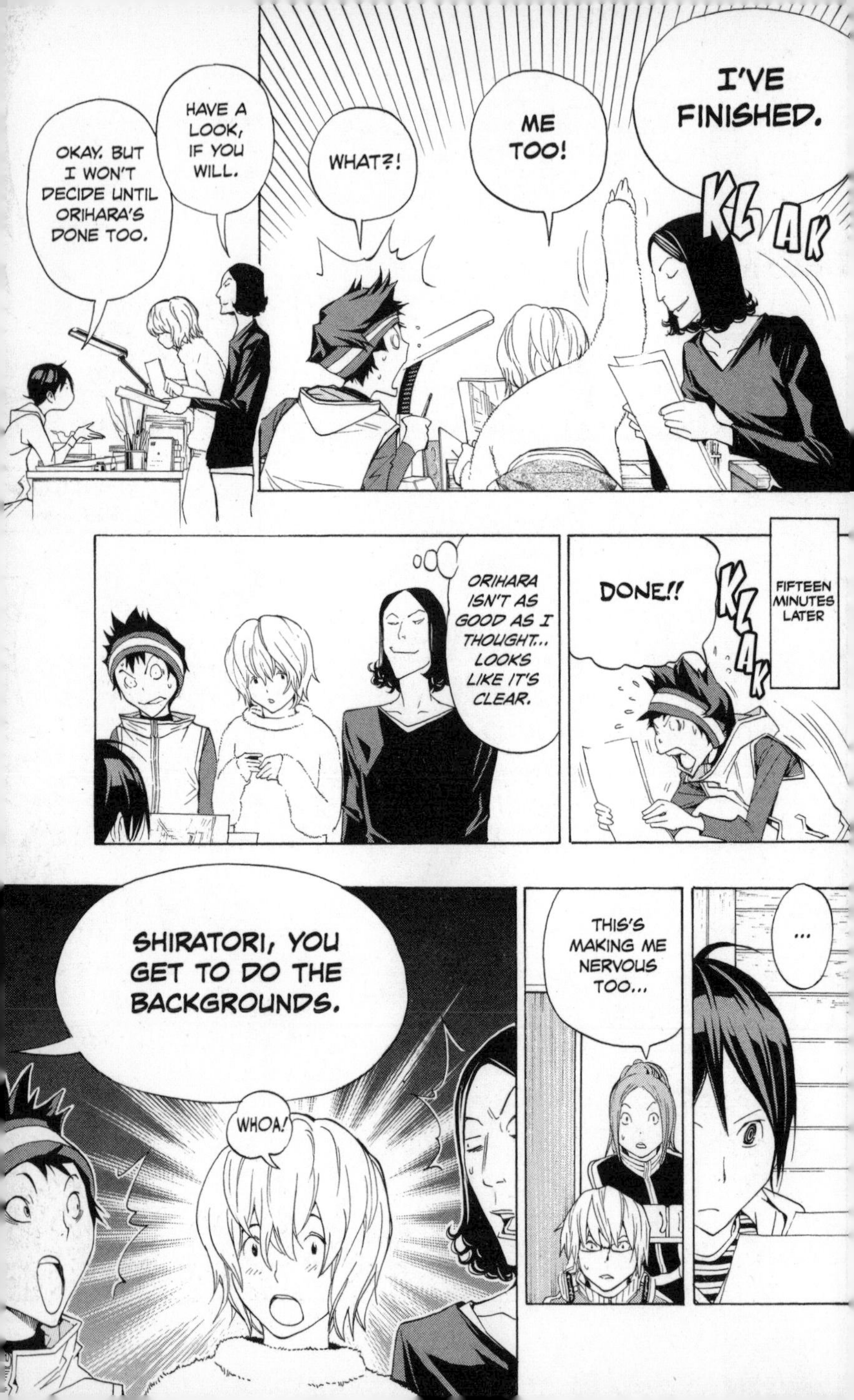
I'VE FINISHED.
KLAK
ME TOO!
WHAT?!
HAVE A LOOK, IF YOU WILL.
OKAY. BUT I WON'T DECIDE UNTIL ORIHARA'S DONE TOO.
FIFTEEN MINUTES LATER
KLAK
DONE!!
ORIHARA ISN'T AS GOOD AS I THOUGHT... LOOKS LIKE IT'S CLEAR.
...
THIS'S MAKING ME NERVOUS TOO...
SHIRATORI, YOU GET TO DO THE BACKGROUNDS.
WHOA!

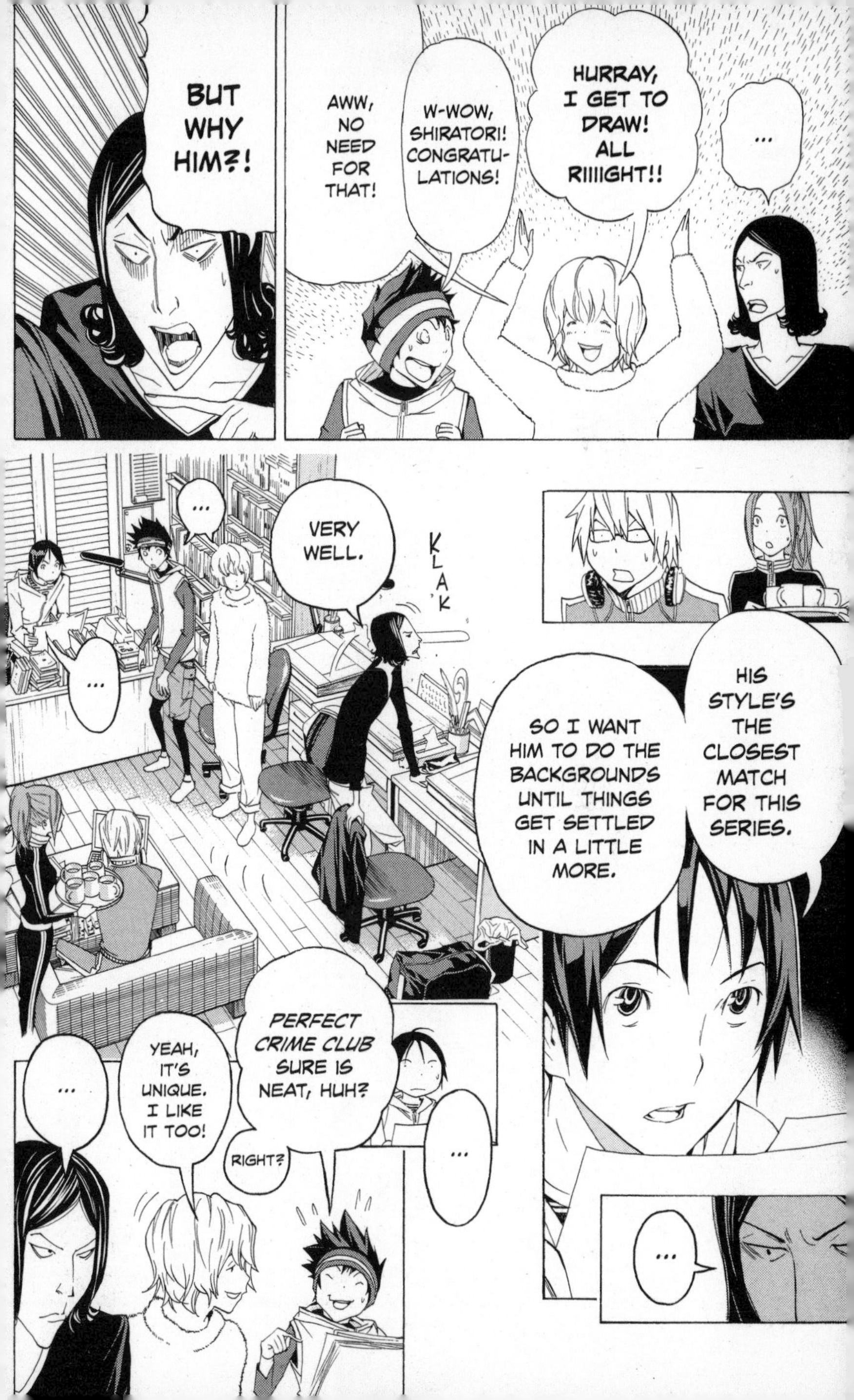
...
HURRAY, I GET TO DRAW! ALL RIIIIGHT!!
W-WOW, SHIRATORI! CONGRATU-LATIONS!
AWW, NO NEED FOR THAT!
BUT WHY HIM?!
HIS STYLE'S THE CLOSEST MATCH FOR THIS SERIES.
SO I WANT HIM TO DO THE BACKGROUNDS UNTIL THINGS GET SETTLED IN A LITTLE MORE.
...
VERY WELL.
KLAK
...
...
PERFECT CRIME CLUB SURE IS NEAT, HUH?
...
RIGHT?
YEAH, IT'S UNIQUE. I LIKE IT TOO!
...

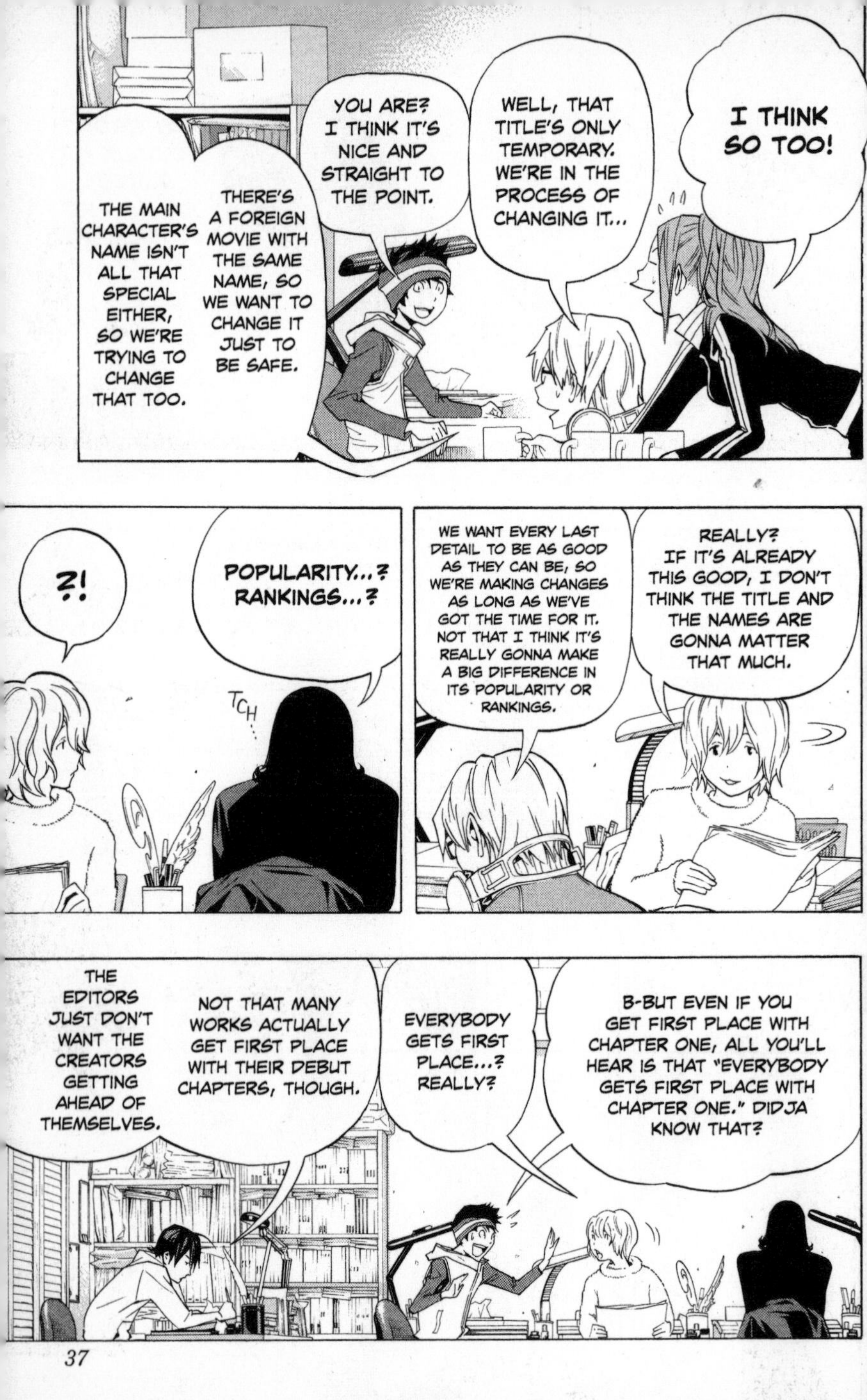
I THINK SO TOO!
WELL, THAT TITLE'S ONLY TEMPORARY. WE'RE IN THE PROCESS OF CHANGING IT...
YOU ARE? I THINK IT'S NICE AND STRAIGHT TO THE POINT.
THERE'S A FOREIGN MOVIE WITH THE SAME NAME, SO WE WANT TO CHANGE IT JUST TO BE SAFE.
THE MAIN CHARACTER'S NAME ISN'T ALL THAT SPECIAL EITHER, SO WE'RE TRYING TO CHANGE THAT TOO.
REALLY? IF IT'S ALREADY THIS GOOD, I DON'T THINK THE TITLE AND THE NAMES ARE GONNA MATTER THAT MUCH.
WE WANT EVERY LAST DETAIL TO BE AS GOOD AS THEY CAN BE, SO WE'RE MAKING CHANGES AS LONG AS WE'VE GOT THE TIME FOR IT. NOT THAT I THINK IT'S REALLY GONNA MAKE A BIG DIFFERENCE IN ITS POPULARITY OR RANKINGS.
POPULARITY...? RANKINGS...?
TCH...
?!
B-BUT EVEN IF YOU GET FIRST PLACE WITH CHAPTER ONE, ALL YOU'LL HEAR IS THAT "EVERYBODY GETS FIRST PLACE WITH CHAPTER ONE." DIDJA KNOW THAT?
EVERYBODY GETS FIRST PLACE...? REALLY?
NOT THAT MANY WORKS ACTUALLY GET FIRST PLACE WITH THEIR DEBUT CHAPTERS, THOUGH.
THE EDITORS JUST DON'T WANT THE CREATORS GETTING AHEAD OF THEMSELVES.

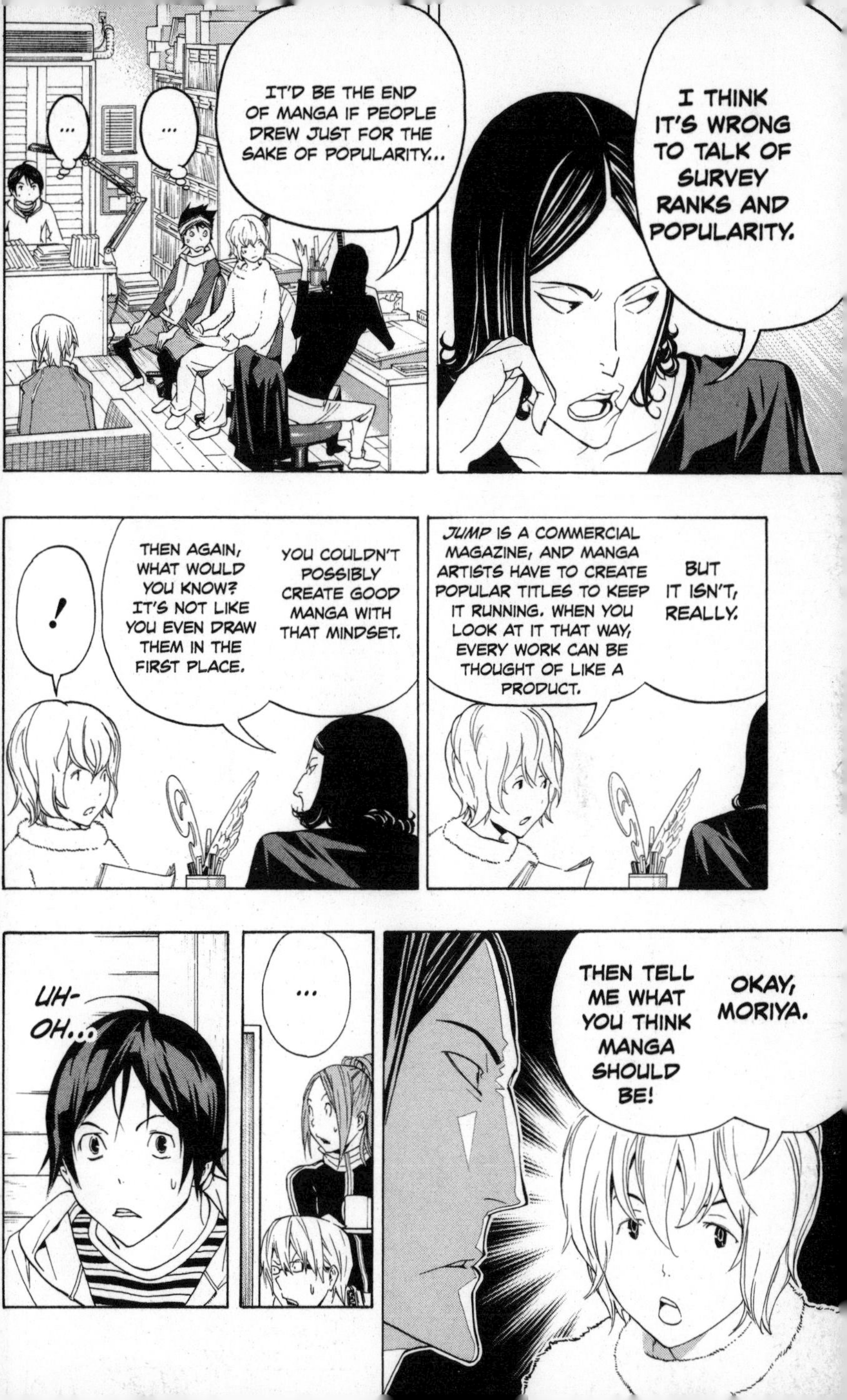
I THINK IT'S WRONG TO TALK OF SURVEY RANKS AND POPULARITY.
IT'D BE THE END OF MANGA IF PEOPLE DREW JUST FOR THE SAKE OF POPULARITY...
...
...
BUT IT ISN'T, REALLY.
JUMP IS A COMMERCIAL MAGAZINE, AND MANGA ARTISTS HAVE TO CREATE POPULAR TITLES TO KEEP IT RUNNING. WHEN YOU LOOK AT IT THAT WAY, EVERY WORK CAN BE THOUGHT OF LIKE A PRODUCT.
YOU COULDN'T POSSIBLY CREATE GOOD MANGA WITH THAT MINDSET.
THEN AGAIN, WHAT WOULD YOU KNOW? IT'S NOT LIKE YOU EVEN DRAW THEM IN THE FIRST PLACE.
!
OKAY, MORIYA.
THEN TELL ME WHAT YOU THINK MANGA SHOULD BE!
...
UH-OH...

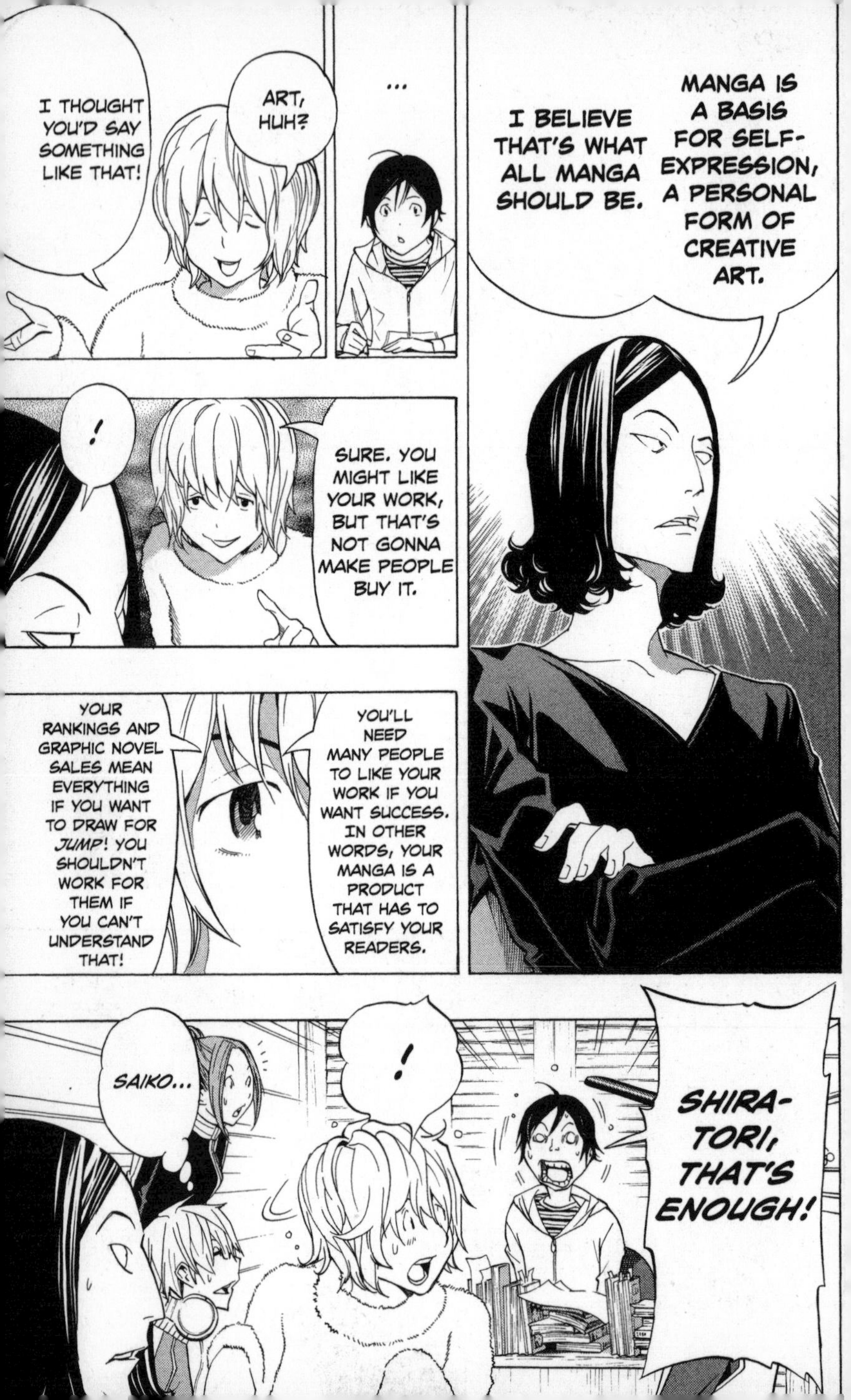
MANGA IS A BASIS FOR SELF-EXPRESSION, A PERSONAL FORM OF CREATIVE ART.
I BELIEVE THAT'S WHAT ALL MANGA SHOULD BE.
...
ART, HUH?
I THOUGHT YOU'D SAY SOMETHING LIKE THAT!
SURE. YOU MIGHT LIKE YOUR WORK, BUT THAT'S NOT GONNA MAKE PEOPLE BUY IT.
!
YOU'LL NEED MANY PEOPLE TO LIKE YOUR WORK IF YOU WANT SUCCESS. IN OTHER WORDS, YOUR MANGA IS A PRODUCT THAT HAS TO SATISFY YOUR READERS.
YOUR RANKINGS AND GRAPHIC NOVEL SALES MEAN EVERYTHING IF YOU WANT TO DRAW FOR *JUMP*! YOU SHOULDN'T WORK FOR THEM IF YOU CAN'T UNDERSTAND THAT!
SHIRATORI, THAT'S ENOUGH!
!
SAIKO...

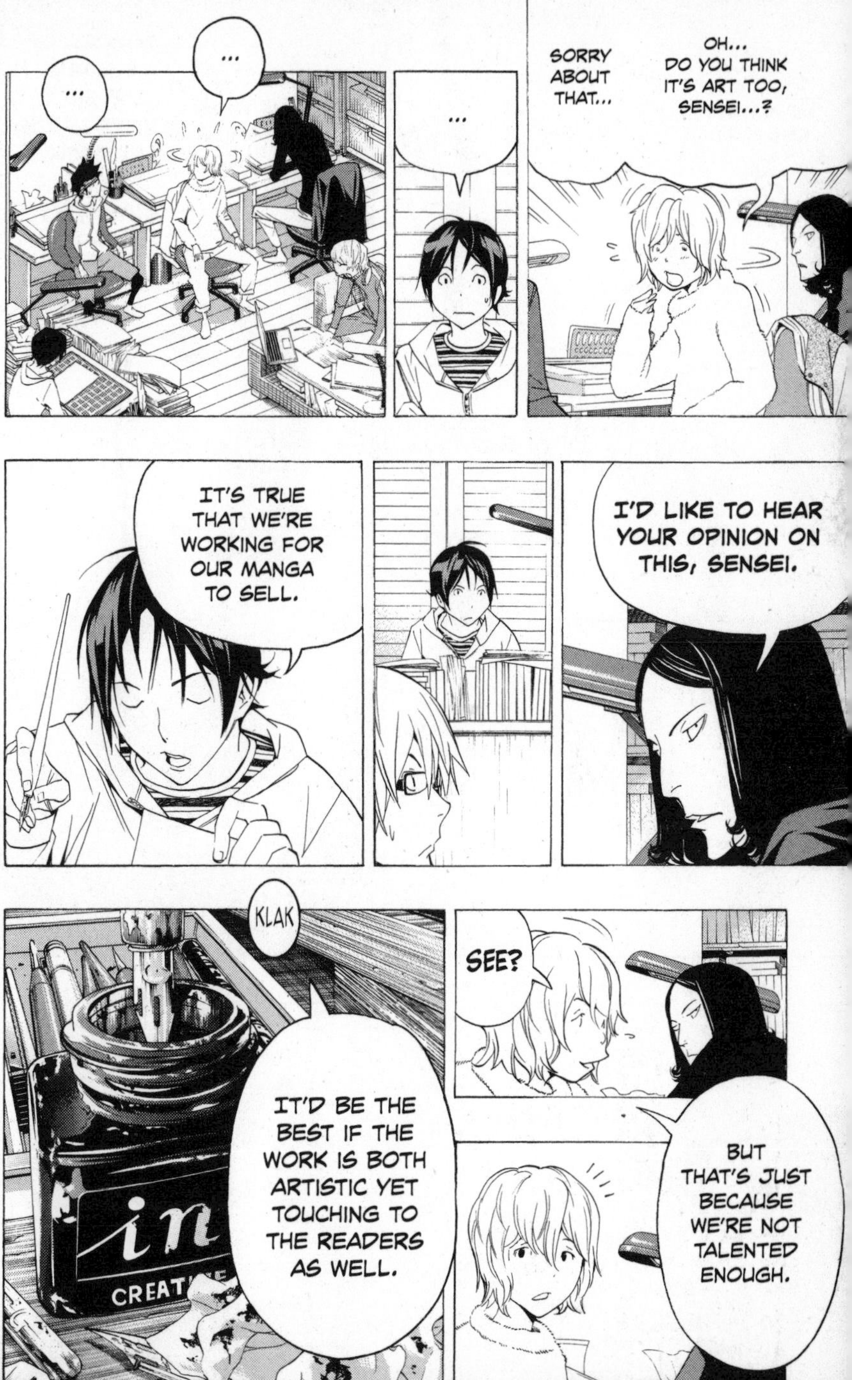
OH... DO YOU THINK IT'S ART TOO, SENSEI...?
SORRY ABOUT THAT...
...
...
...
I'D LIKE TO HEAR YOUR OPINION ON THIS, SENSEI.
IT'S TRUE THAT WE'RE WORKING FOR OUR MANGA TO SELL.
SEE?
BUT THAT'S JUST BECAUSE WE'RE NOT TALENTED ENOUGH.
KLAK
IT'D BE THE BEST IF THE WORK IS BOTH ARTISTIC YET TOUCHING TO THE READERS AS WELL.
CREAT

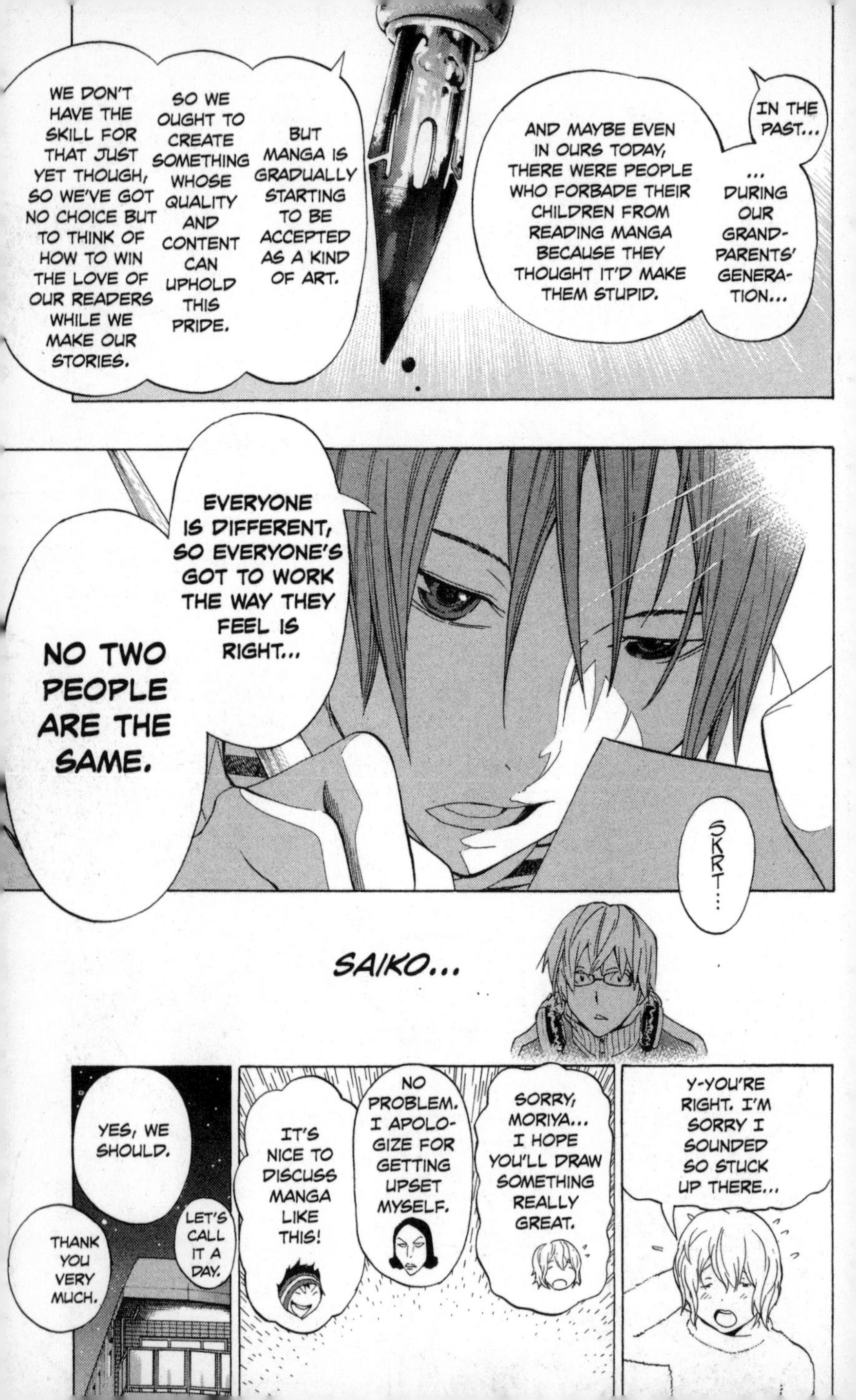
IN THE PAST... ...DURING OUR GRANDPARENTS' GENERATION...
AND MAYBE EVEN IN OURS TODAY, THERE WERE PEOPLE WHO FORBADE THEIR CHILDREN FROM READING MANGA BECAUSE THEY THOUGHT IT'D MAKE THEM STUPID.
BUT MANGA IS GRADUALLY STARTING TO BE ACCEPTED AS A KIND OF ART.
SO WE OUGHT TO CREATE SOMETHING WHOSE QUALITY AND CONTENT CAN UPHOLD THIS PRIDE.
WE DON'T HAVE THE SKILL FOR THAT JUST YET THOUGH, SO WE'VE GOT NO CHOICE BUT TO THINK OF HOW TO WIN THE LOVE OF OUR READERS WHILE WE MAKE OUR STORIES.
EVERYONE IS DIFFERENT, SO EVERYONE'S GOT TO WORK THE WAY THEY FEEL IS RIGHT...
SKRT...
NO TWO PEOPLE ARE THE SAME.
SAIKO...
Y-YOU'RE RIGHT. I'M SORRY I SOUNDED SO STUCK UP THERE...
SORRY, MORIYA... I HOPE YOU'LL DRAW SOMETHING REALLY GREAT.
NO PROBLEM. I APOLOGIZE FOR GETTING UPSET MYSELF.
IT'S NICE TO DISCUSS MANGA LIKE THIS!
YES, WE SHOULD.
LET'S CALL IT A DAY.
THANK YOU VERY MUCH.

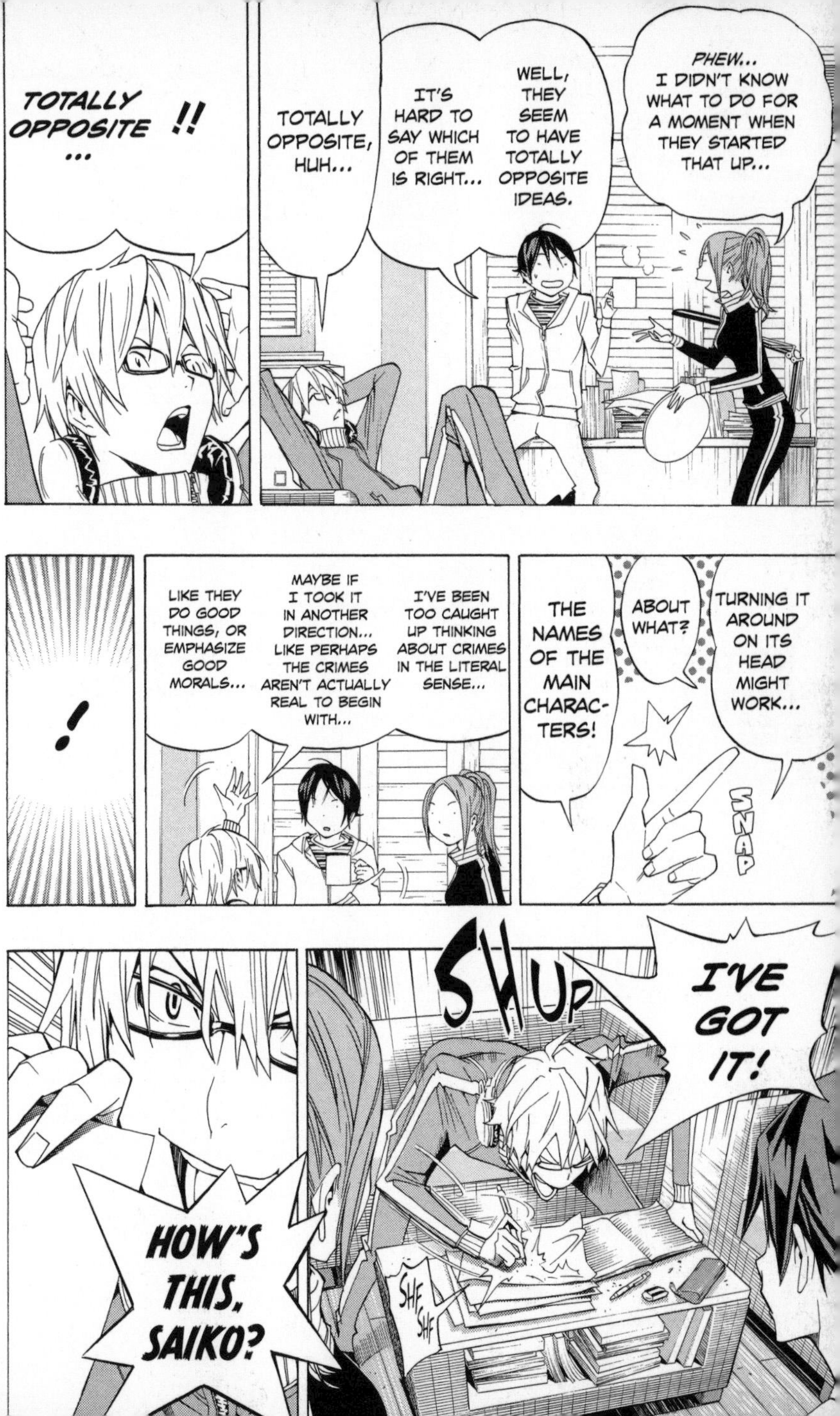
PHEW... I DIDN'T KNOW WHAT TO DO FOR A MOMENT WHEN THEY STARTED THAT UP...
WELL, THEY SEEM TO HAVE TOTALLY OPPOSITE IDEAS.
IT'S HARD TO SAY WHICH OF THEM IS RIGHT...
TOTALLY OPPOSITE, HUH...
TOTALLY OPPOSITE ...!!
TURNING IT AROUND ON ITS HEAD MIGHT WORK...
ABOUT WHAT?
THE NAMES OF THE MAIN CHARACTERS!
SNAP
I'VE BEEN TOO CAUGHT UP THINKING ABOUT CRIMES IN THE LITERAL SENSE...
MAYBE IF I TOOK IT IN ANOTHER DIRECTION... LIKE PERHAPS THE CRIMES AREN'T ACTUALLY REAL TO BEGIN WITH...
LIKE THEY DO GOOD THINGS, OR EMPHASIZE GOOD MORALS...
!
I'VE GOT IT!
SHUP
SHF SHF
HOW'S THIS, SAIKO?

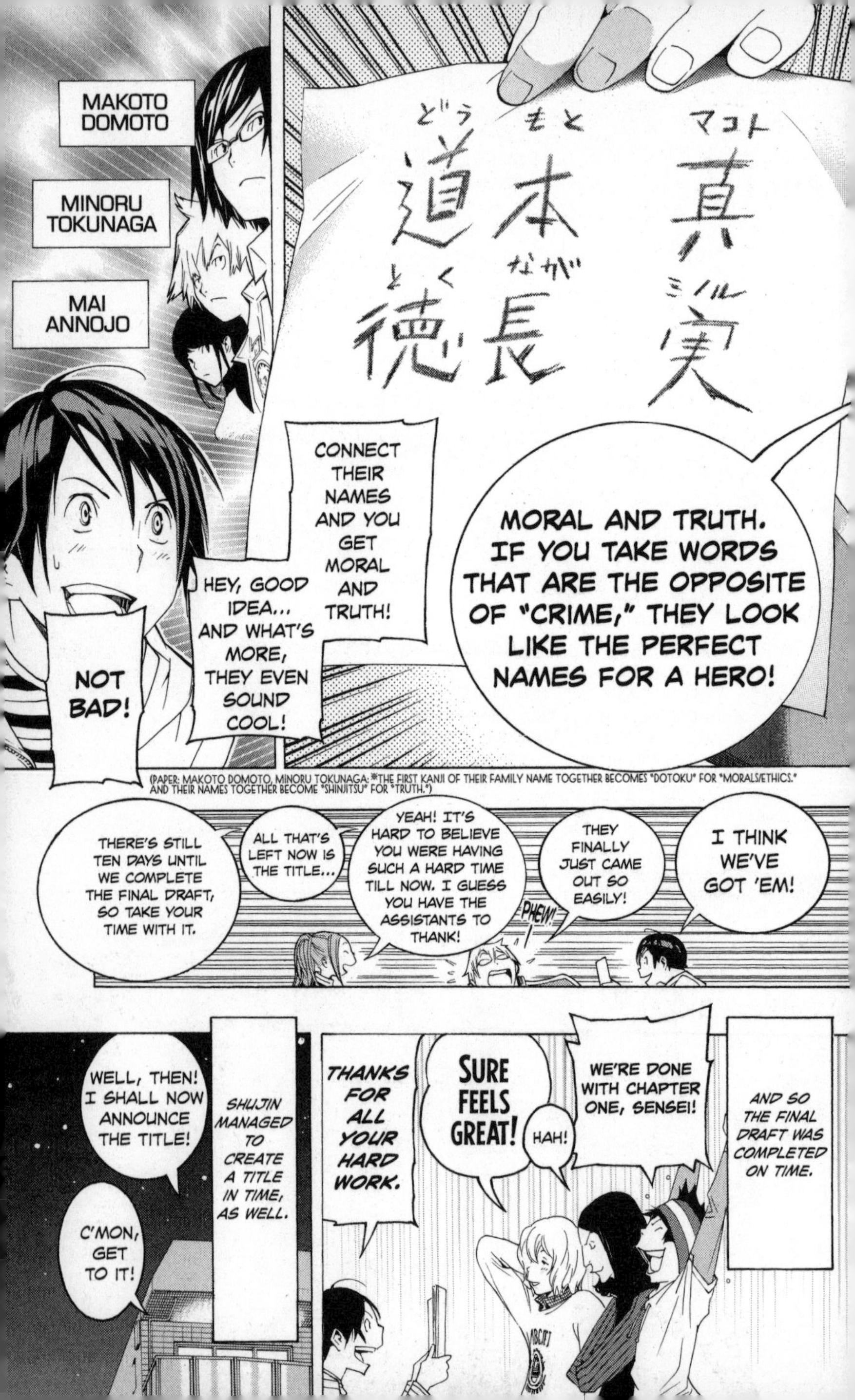
どうもと マコト
道本真
とくなが ミノル
徳長実
MAKOTO DOMOTO
MINORU TOKUNAGA
MAI ANNOJO
MORAL AND TRUTH. IF YOU TAKE WORDS THAT ARE THE OPPOSITE OF "CRIME," THEY LOOK LIKE THE PERFECT NAMES FOR A HERO!
CONNECT THEIR NAMES AND YOU GET MORAL AND TRUTH!
HEY, GOOD IDEA... AND WHAT'S MORE, THEY EVEN SOUND COOL!
NOT BAD!
(PAPER: MAKOTO DOMOTO, MINORU TOKUNAGA: *THE FIRST KANJI OF THEIR FAMILY NAME TOGETHER BECOMES "DOTOKU" FOR "MORALS/ETHICS." AND THEIR NAMES TOGETHER BECOME "SHINJITSU" FOR "TRUTH.")
I THINK WE'VE GOT 'EM!
THEY FINALLY JUST CAME OUT SO EASILY!
PHEW!
YEAH! IT'S HARD TO BELIEVE YOU WERE HAVING SUCH A HARD TIME TILL NOW. I GUESS YOU HAVE THE ASSISTANTS TO THANK!
ALL THAT'S LEFT NOW IS THE TITLE...
THERE'S STILL TEN DAYS UNTIL WE COMPLETE THE FINAL DRAFT, SO TAKE YOUR TIME WITH IT.
AND SO THE FINAL DRAFT WAS COMPLETED ON TIME.
WE'RE DONE WITH CHAPTER ONE, SENSEI!
HAH!
SURE FEELS GREAT!
THANKS FOR ALL YOUR HARD WORK.
SHUJIN MANAGED TO CREATE A TITLE IN TIME, AS WELL.
WELL, THEN! I SHALL NOW ANNOUNCE THE TITLE!
C'MON, GET TO IT!

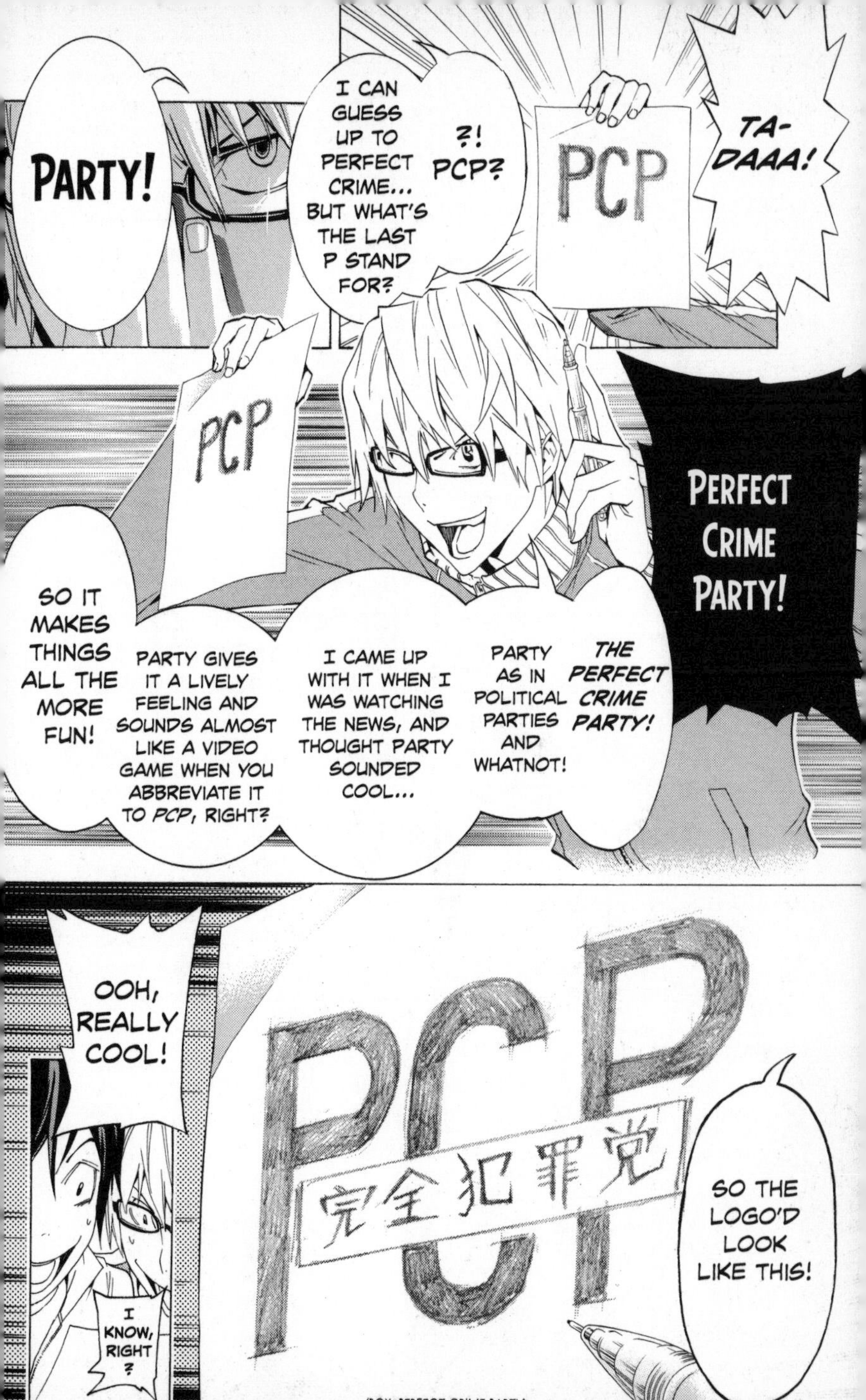
TA-DAAA!
PCP
?! PCP?
I CAN GUESS UP TO PERFECT CRIME... BUT WHAT'S THE LAST P STAND FOR?
PARTY!
PERFECT CRIME PARTY!
PCP
THE PERFECT CRIME PARTY!
PARTY AS IN POLITICAL PARTIES AND WHATNOT!
I CAME UP WITH IT WHEN I WAS WATCHING THE NEWS, AND THOUGHT PARTY SOUNDED COOL...
PARTY GIVES IT A LIVELY FEELING AND SOUNDS ALMOST LIKE A VIDEO GAME WHEN YOU ABBREVIATE IT TO *PCP*, RIGHT?
SO IT MAKES THINGS ALL THE MORE FUN!
SO THE LOGO'D LOOK LIKE THIS!
PCP
完全犯罪党
OOH, REALLY COOL!
I KNOW, RIGHT?

(BOX: PERFECT CRIME PARTY)

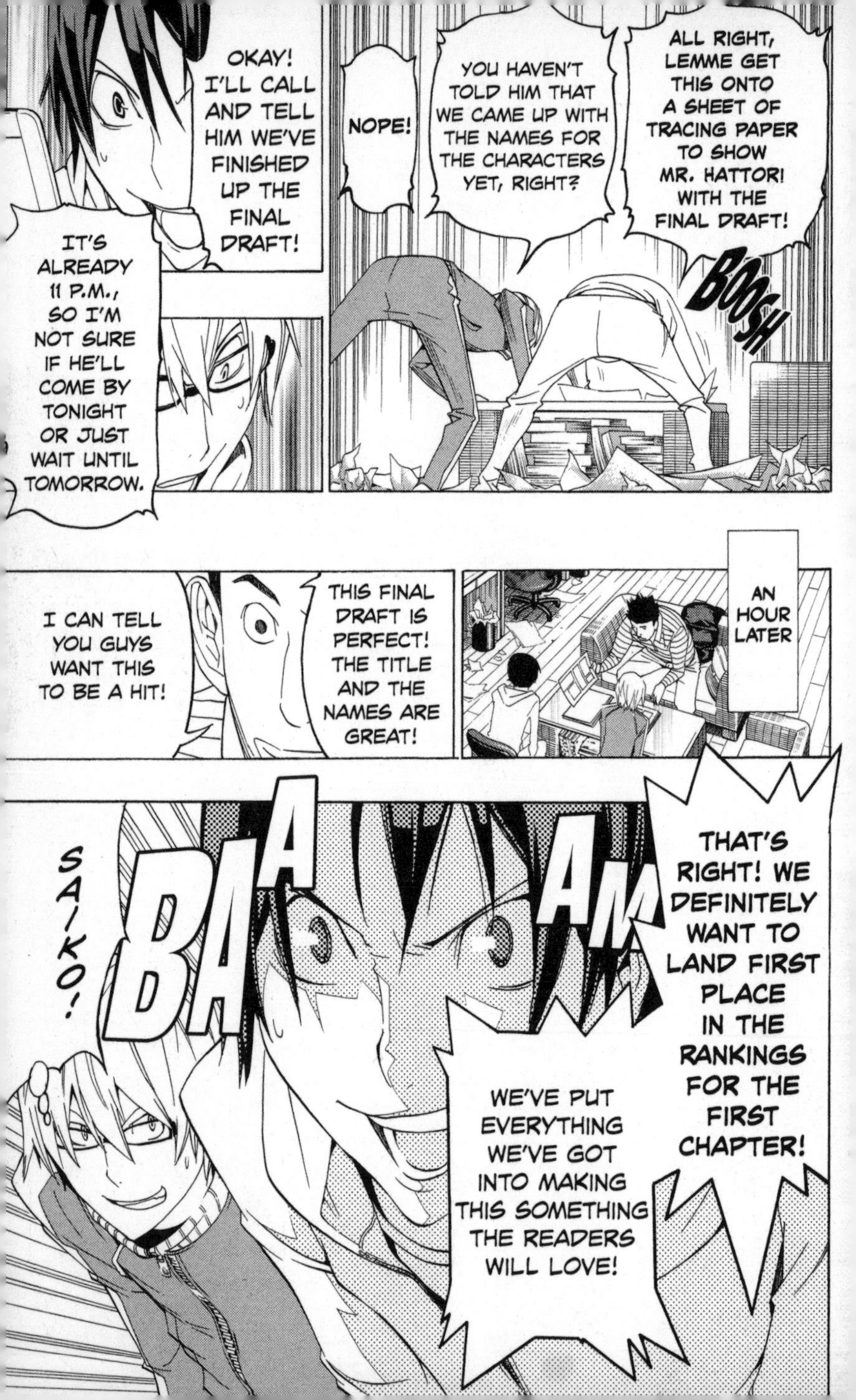
ALL RIGHT, LEMME GET THIS ONTO A SHEET OF TRACING PAPER TO SHOW MR. HATTORI WITH THE FINAL DRAFT!
YOU HAVEN'T TOLD HIM THAT WE CAME UP WITH THE NAMES FOR THE CHARACTERS YET, RIGHT?
NOPE!
BOOSH
OKAY! I'LL CALL AND TELL HIM WE'VE FINISHED UP THE FINAL DRAFT!
IT'S ALREADY 11 P.M., SO I'M NOT SURE IF HE'LL COME BY TONIGHT OR JUST WAIT UNTIL TOMORROW.
AN HOUR LATER
THIS FINAL DRAFT IS PERFECT! THE TITLE AND THE NAMES ARE GREAT!
I CAN TELL YOU GUYS WANT THIS TO BE A HIT!
THAT'S RIGHT! WE DEFINITELY WANT TO LAND FIRST PLACE IN THE RANKINGS FOR THE FIRST CHAPTER!
BAAAM
WE'VE PUT EVERYTHING WE'VE GOT INTO MAKING THIS SOMETHING THE READERS WILL LOVE!
SAIKO!

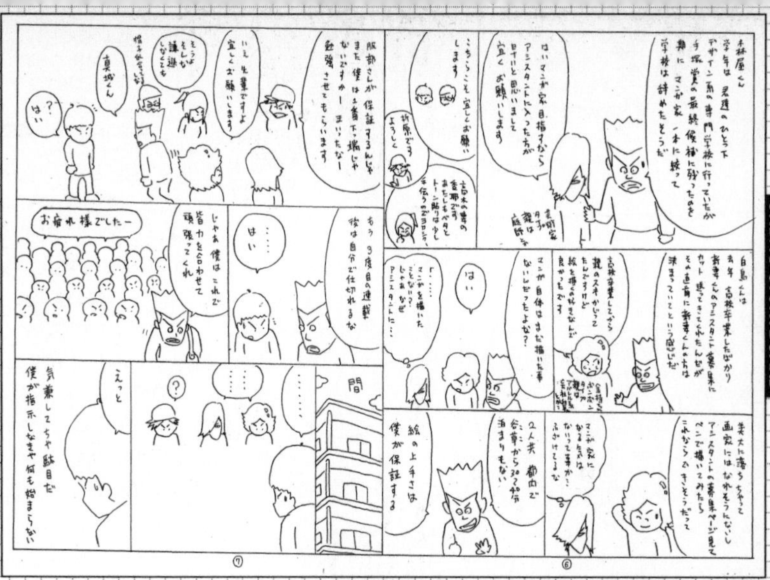
木林屋くん 学年は君達のひとつ下 デザイン系の専門学校に行っていたが 手塚賞の最終候補に残ったのを期に マンガ家一本に絞って 学校は辞めたそうだ
はいマンガ家目指すなら アシスタントに入った方が早いと思いまして 宜しくお願いします
こちらこそ 宜しくお願いします
折原です よろしく
高木の妻の香耶です あたしもベタとトーン貼りは少し手伝うのでヨロシク
白鳥くんは 去年高校卒業したばかり 新妻くんのアシスタント募集にカット送ってきてくれたんだが その直前に新妻くんの方は決まっていてという感じだ
高校卒業してから 親のスネかじってたんですけど 絵を描くのが好きなんで 良かったです
マンガ自体はまだ描いた事ないんだったよな?
はい
マンガを描いたことない? じゃあなぜアシスタントに…
美大に落ちちゃって 画家にはなれそうにないし アシスタントの募集ページ見て ペンで描いてみたら これならいけそうだって
マンガ家になる気はないって事か… ふざけてるな
2人共 都内で 仕事場から30分 泊まりもない
絵の上手さは 僕が保証する
⑥
服部さんが保証するんじゃ また僕は一番下っ端じゃないですか〜 まいったな〜 勉強させてもらいます
いえ 先輩ですよ 宜しくお願いします
そうよ そんな謙遜しなくても
真城くん
はい?
もう9度目の連載 後は自分で仕切れるな
……はい
じゃあ僕はこれで 皆力を合わせて頑張ってくれ
お疲れ様でした〜
間
……
……
?
えっと
気兼ねしてちゃ駄目だ 僕が指示しなきゃ何も始まらない
⑦

OHBA'S STORYBOARD

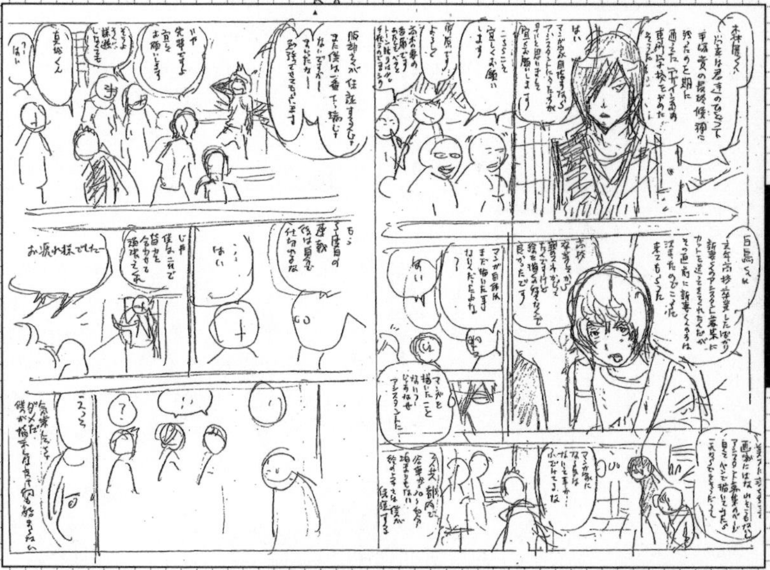

OBATA'S STORYBOARD

COMPLETE!

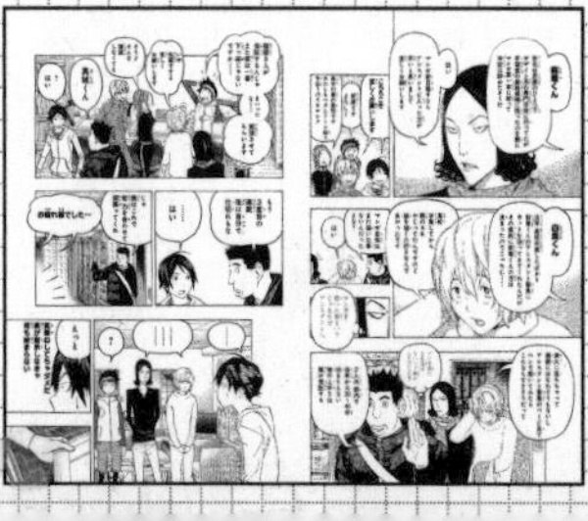

※CREATOR STORYBOARDS AND FINISHED PAGES IN JAPANESE

BAKUMAN。vol.11

"Until the Final Draft Is Complete"

Chapter 90, pp. 32-33

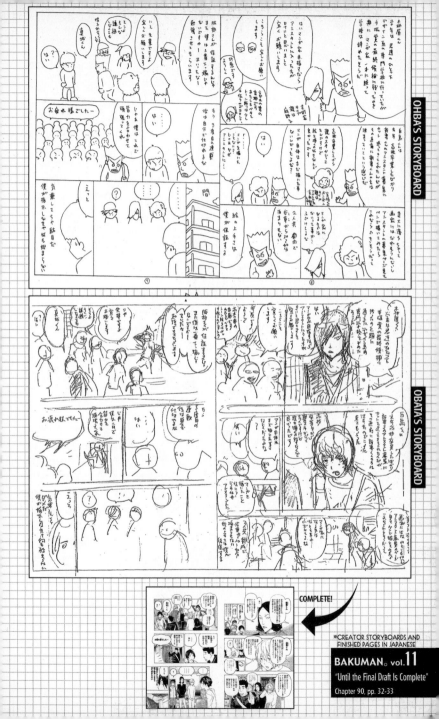

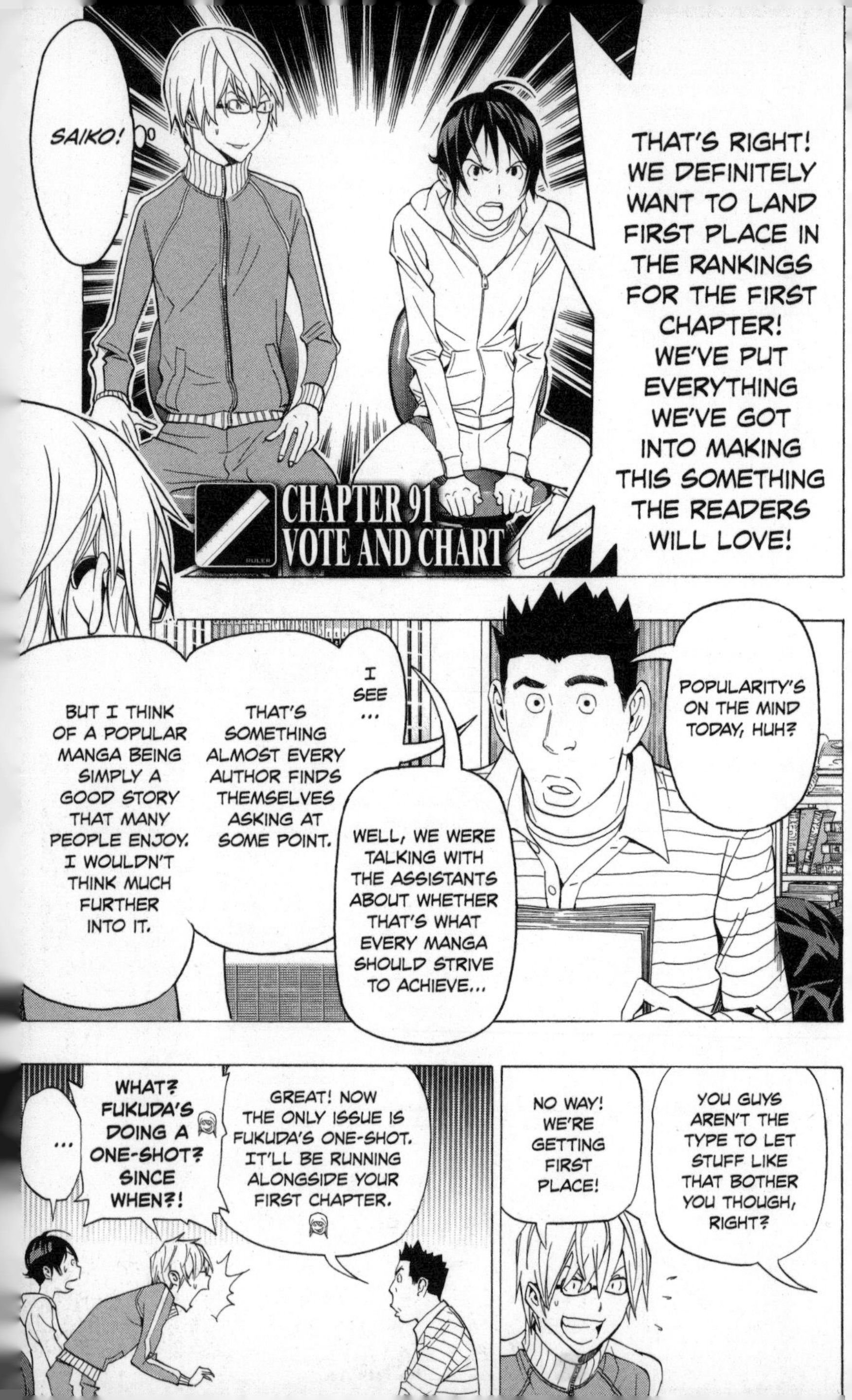
THAT'S RIGHT! WE DEFINITELY WANT TO LAND FIRST PLACE IN THE RANKINGS FOR THE FIRST CHAPTER! WE'VE PUT EVERYTHING WE'VE GOT INTO MAKING THIS SOMETHING THE READERS WILL LOVE!
SAIKO!
CHAPTER 91
VOTE AND CHART
POPULARITY'S ON THE MIND TODAY, HUH?
WELL, WE WERE TALKING WITH THE ASSISTANTS ABOUT WHETHER THAT'S WHAT EVERY MANGA SHOULD STRIVE TO ACHIEVE...
I SEE...
THAT'S SOMETHING ALMOST EVERY AUTHOR FINDS THEMSELVES ASKING AT SOME POINT.
BUT I THINK OF A POPULAR MANGA BEING SIMPLY A GOOD STORY THAT MANY PEOPLE ENJOY. I WOULDN'T THINK MUCH FURTHER INTO IT.
YOU GUYS AREN'T THE TYPE TO LET STUFF LIKE THAT BOTHER YOU THOUGH, RIGHT?
NO WAY! WE'RE GETTING FIRST PLACE!
GREAT! NOW THE ONLY ISSUE IS FUKUDA'S ONE-SHOT. IT'LL BE RUNNING ALONGSIDE YOUR FIRST CHAPTER.
WHAT? FUKUDA'S DOING A ONE-SHOT? SINCE WHEN?!
...

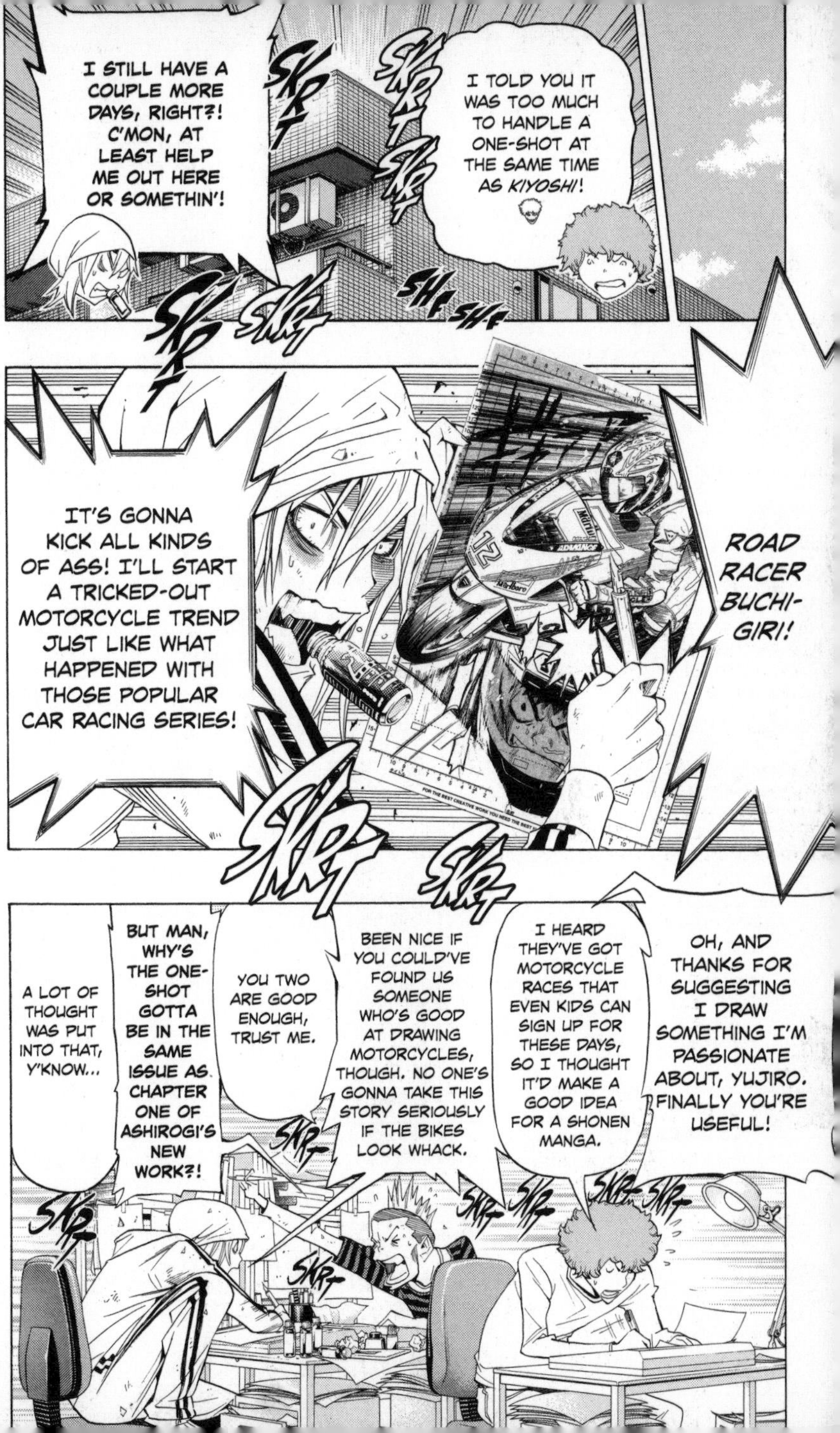
SKRT SKRT
I TOLD YOU IT WAS TOO MUCH TO HANDLE A ONE-SHOT AT THE SAME TIME AS KIYOSHI!
SKRT
I STILL HAVE A COUPLE MORE DAYS, RIGHT?! C'MON, AT LEAST HELP ME OUT HERE OR SOMETHIN'!
SHF SHF
SKRT SKRT
ROAD RACER BUCHI-GIRI!
IT'S GONNA KICK ALL KINDS OF ASS! I'LL START A TRICKED-OUT MOTORCYCLE TREND JUST LIKE WHAT HAPPENED WITH THOSE POPULAR CAR RACING SERIES!
SKRT SKRT
OH, AND THANKS FOR SUGGESTING I DRAW SOMETHING I'M PASSIONATE ABOUT, YUJIRO. FINALLY YOU'RE USEFUL!
I HEARD THEY'VE GOT MOTORCYCLE RACES THAT EVEN KIDS CAN SIGN UP FOR THESE DAYS, SO I THOUGHT IT'D MAKE A GOOD IDEA FOR A SHONEN MANGA.
BEEN NICE IF YOU COULD'VE FOUND US SOMEONE WHO'S GOOD AT DRAWING MOTORCYCLES, THOUGH. NO ONE'S GONNA TAKE THIS STORY SERIOUSLY IF THE BIKES LOOK WHACK.
YOU TWO ARE GOOD ENOUGH, TRUST ME.
BUT MAN, WHY'S THE ONE-SHOT GOTTA BE IN THE SAME ISSUE AS CHAPTER ONE OF ASHIROGI'S NEW WORK?!
A LOT OF THOUGHT WAS PUT INTO THAT, Y'KNOW...
SKRT SKRT SKRT SKRT SKRT SKRT

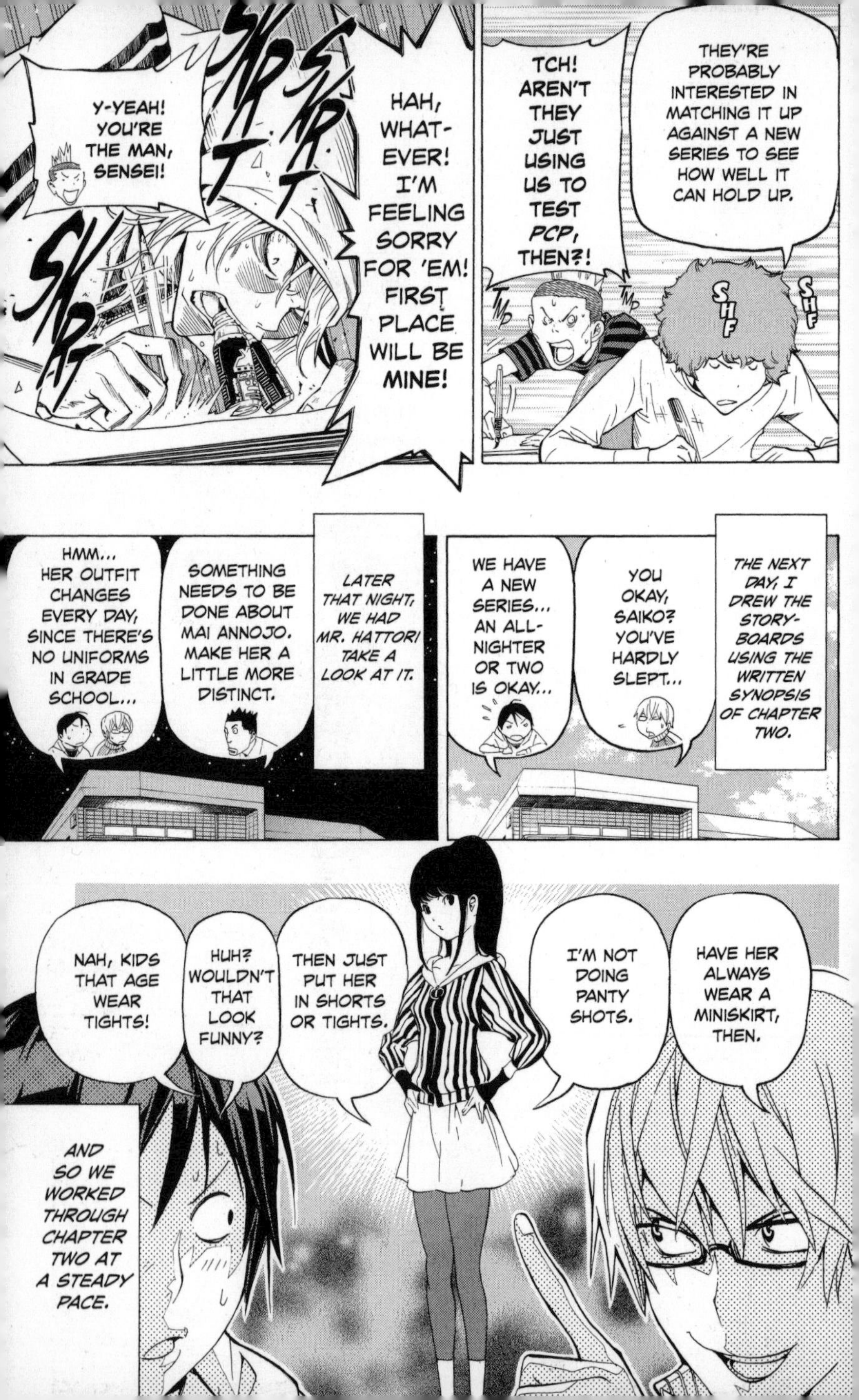
THEY'RE PROBABLY INTERESTED IN MATCHING IT UP AGAINST A NEW SERIES TO SEE HOW WELL IT CAN HOLD UP.
SHF
SHF
TCH! AREN'T THEY JUST USING US TO TEST PCP, THEN?!
TMP
TMP
HAH, WHAT-EVER! I'M FEELING SORRY FOR 'EM! FIRST PLACE WILL BE MINE!
SKRT
SKRT
Y-YEAH! YOU'RE THE MAN, SENSEI!
SKRT
THE NEXT DAY, I DREW THE STORY-BOARDS USING THE WRITTEN SYNOPSIS OF CHAPTER TWO.
YOU OKAY, SAIKO? YOU'VE HARDLY SLEPT...
WE HAVE A NEW SERIES... AN ALL-NIGHTER OR TWO IS OKAY...
LATER THAT NIGHT, WE HAD MR. HATTORI TAKE A LOOK AT IT.
SOMETHING NEEDS TO BE DONE ABOUT MAI ANNOJO. MAKE HER A LITTLE MORE DISTINCT.
HMM... HER OUTFIT CHANGES EVERY DAY, SINCE THERE'S NO UNIFORMS IN GRADE SCHOOL...
HAVE HER ALWAYS WEAR A MINISKIRT, THEN.
I'M NOT DOING PANTY SHOTS.
THEN JUST PUT HER IN SHORTS OR TIGHTS.
HUH? WOULDN'T THAT LOOK FUNNY?
NAH, KIDS THAT AGE WEAR TIGHTS!
AND SO WE WORKED THROUGH CHAPTER TWO AT A STEADY PACE.

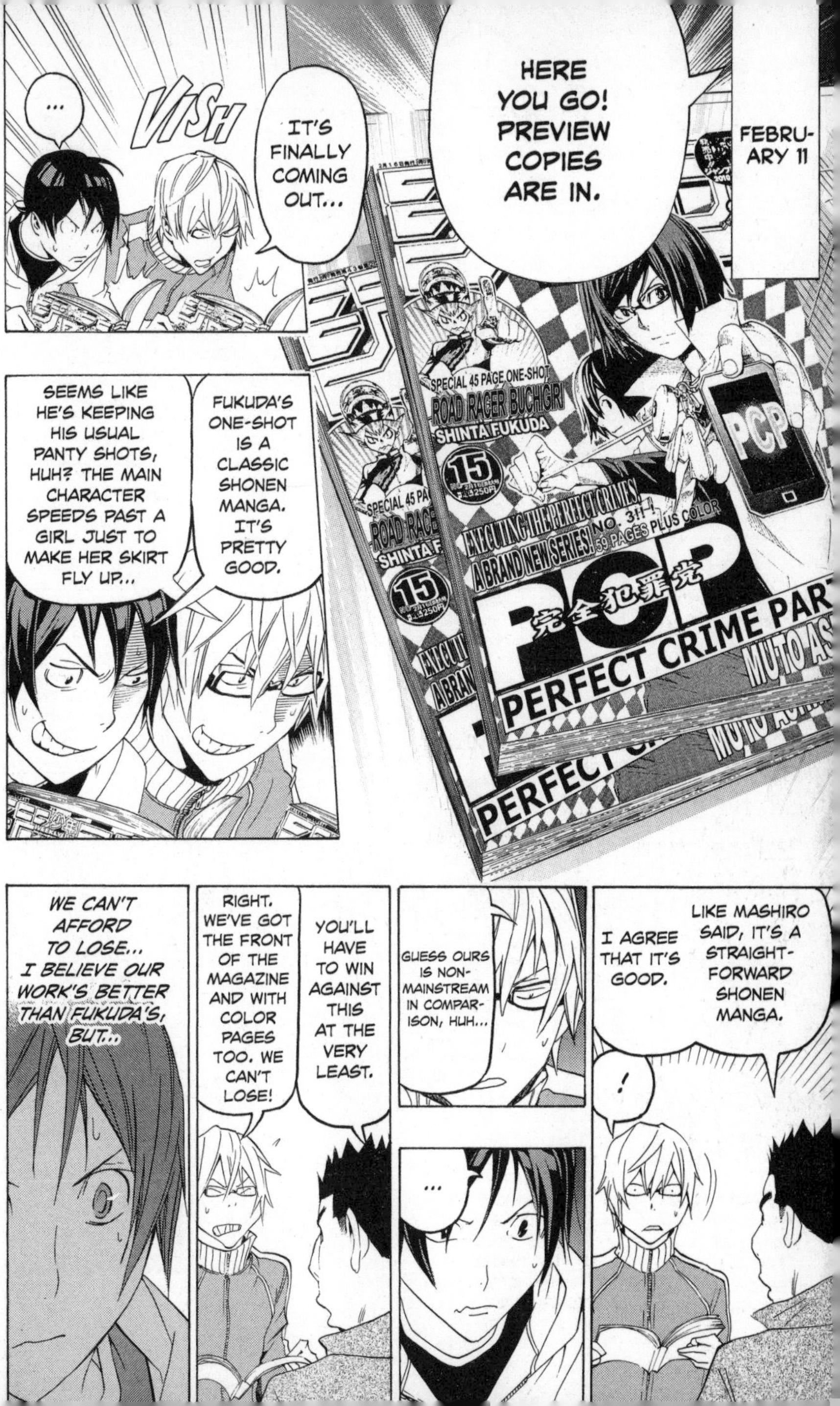
FEBRUARY 11
HERE YOU GO! PREVIEW COPIES ARE IN.
IT'S FINALLY COMING OUT...
VISH
...
SPECIAL 45 PAGE ONE-SHOT
ROAD RACER BUCHIGIRI
SHINTA FUKUDA
EXECUTING THE PERFECT CRIMES. A BRAND NEW SERIES! NO. 3!!-! 59 PAGES PLUS COLOR
PCP
完全犯罪党
PERFECT CRIME PART
FUKUDA'S ONE-SHOT IS A CLASSIC SHONEN MANGA. IT'S PRETTY GOOD.
SEEMS LIKE HE'S KEEPING HIS USUAL PANTY SHOTS, HUH? THE MAIN CHARACTER SPEEDS PAST A GIRL JUST TO MAKE HER SKIRT FLY UP...
LIKE MASHIRO SAID, IT'S A STRAIGHT-FORWARD SHONEN MANGA.
I AGREE THAT IT'S GOOD.
!
GUESS OURS IS NON-MAINSTREAM IN COMPARISON, HUH...
...
YOU'LL HAVE TO WIN AGAINST THIS AT THE VERY LEAST.
RIGHT. WE'VE GOT THE FRONT OF THE MAGAZINE AND WITH COLOR PAGES TOO. WE CAN'T LOSE!
WE CAN'T AFFORD TO LOSE... I BELIEVE OUR WORK'S BETTER THAN FUKUDA'S, BUT...

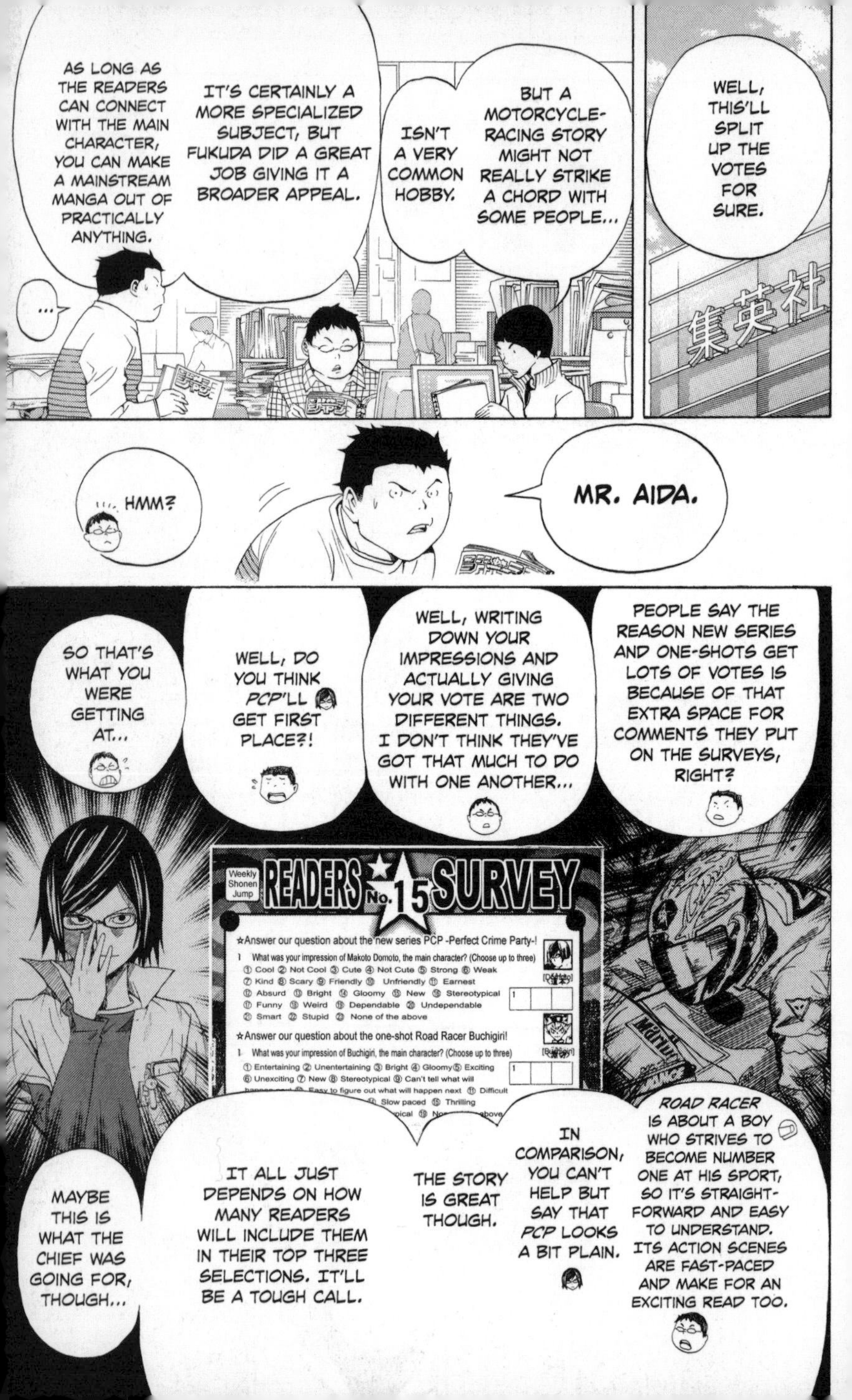
WELL, THIS'LL SPLIT UP THE VOTES FOR SURE.
集英社
BUT A MOTORCYCLE-RACING STORY MIGHT NOT REALLY STRIKE A CHORD WITH SOME PEOPLE...
ISN'T A VERY COMMON HOBBY.
IT'S CERTAINLY A MORE SPECIALIZED SUBJECT, BUT FUKUDA DID A GREAT JOB GIVING IT A BROADER APPEAL.
AS LONG AS THE READERS CAN CONNECT WITH THE MAIN CHARACTER, YOU CAN MAKE A MAINSTREAM MANGA OUT OF PRACTICALLY ANYTHING.
...
MR. AIDA.
HMM?
PEOPLE SAY THE REASON NEW SERIES AND ONE-SHOTS GET LOTS OF VOTES IS BECAUSE OF THAT EXTRA SPACE FOR COMMENTS THEY PUT ON THE SURVEYS, RIGHT?
WELL, WRITING DOWN YOUR IMPRESSIONS AND ACTUALLY GIVING YOUR VOTE ARE TWO DIFFERENT THINGS. I DON'T THINK THEY'VE GOT THAT MUCH TO DO WITH ONE ANOTHER...
WELL, DO YOU THINK *PCP*'LL GET FIRST PLACE?!
SO THAT'S WHAT YOU WERE GETTING AT...
Weekly Shonen Jump READERS No. 15 SURVEY
☆Answer our question about the new series PCP -Perfect Crime Party-!
1 What was your impression of Makoto Domoto, the main character? (Choose up to three)
① Cool ② Not Cool ③ Cute ④ Not Cute ⑤ Strong ⑥ Weak ⑦ Kind ⑧ Scary ⑨ Friendly ⑩ Unfriendly ⑪ Earnest ⑫ Absurd ⑬ Bright ⑭ Gloomy ⑮ New ⑯ Stereotypical ⑰ Funny ⑱ Weird ⑲ Dependable ⑳ Undependable ㉑ Smart ㉒ Stupid ㉓ None of the above
☆Answer our question about the one-shot Road Racer Buchigiri!
1 What was your impression of Buchigiri, the main character? (Choose up to three)
① Entertaining ② Unentertaining ③ Bright ④ Gloomy ⑤ Exciting ⑥ Unexciting ⑦ New ⑧ Stereotypical ⑨ Can't tell what will
ROAD RACER IS ABOUT A BOY WHO STRIVES TO BECOME NUMBER ONE AT HIS SPORT, SO IT'S STRAIGHT-FORWARD AND EASY TO UNDERSTAND. ITS ACTION SCENES ARE FAST-PACED AND MAKE FOR AN EXCITING READ TOO.
IN COMPARISON, YOU CAN'T HELP BUT SAY THAT *PCP* LOOKS A BIT PLAIN.
THE STORY IS GREAT THOUGH.
IT ALL JUST DEPENDS ON HOW MANY READERS WILL INCLUDE THEM IN THEIR TOP THREE SELECTIONS. IT'LL BE A TOUGH CALL.
MAYBE THIS IS WHAT THE CHIEF WAS GOING FOR, THOUGH...

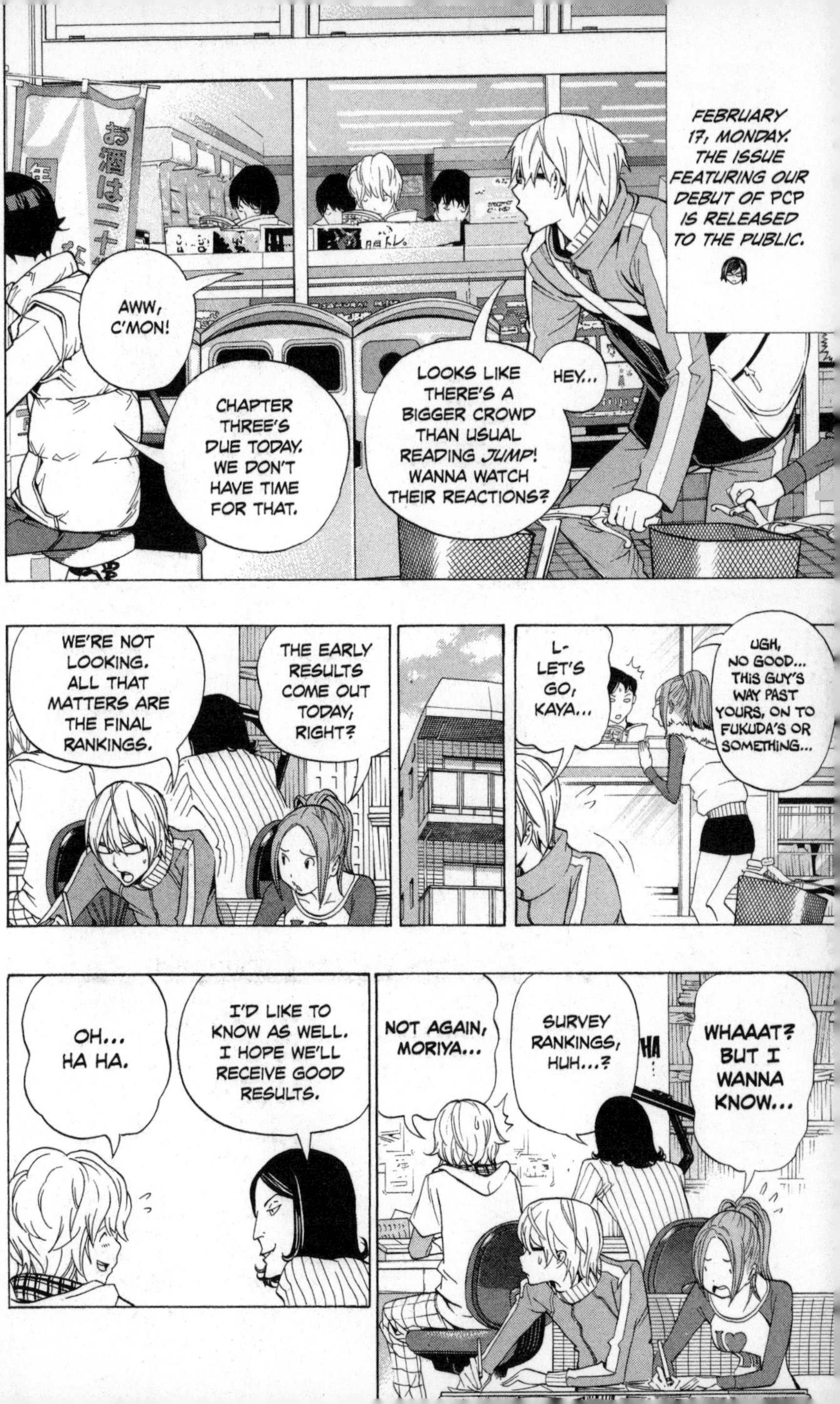
FEBRUARY 17, MONDAY. THE ISSUE FEATURING OUR DEBUT OF PCP IS RELEASED TO THE PUBLIC.
HEY...
LOOKS LIKE THERE'S A BIGGER CROWD THAN USUAL READING *JUMP*! WANNA WATCH THEIR REACTIONS?
AWW, C'MON!
CHAPTER THREE'S DUE TODAY. WE DON'T HAVE TIME FOR THAT.
UGH, NO GOOD... THIS GUY'S WAY PAST YOURS, ON TO FUKUDA'S OR SOMETHING...
L-LET'S GO, KAYA...
THE EARLY RESULTS COME OUT TODAY, RIGHT?
WE'RE NOT LOOKING. ALL THAT MATTERS ARE THE FINAL RANKINGS.
WHAAAT? BUT I WANNA KNOW...
HA
SURVEY RANKINGS, HUH...?
NOT AGAIN, MORIYA...
I'D LIKE TO KNOW AS WELL. I HOPE WE'LL RECEIVE GOOD RESULTS.
OH... HA HA.

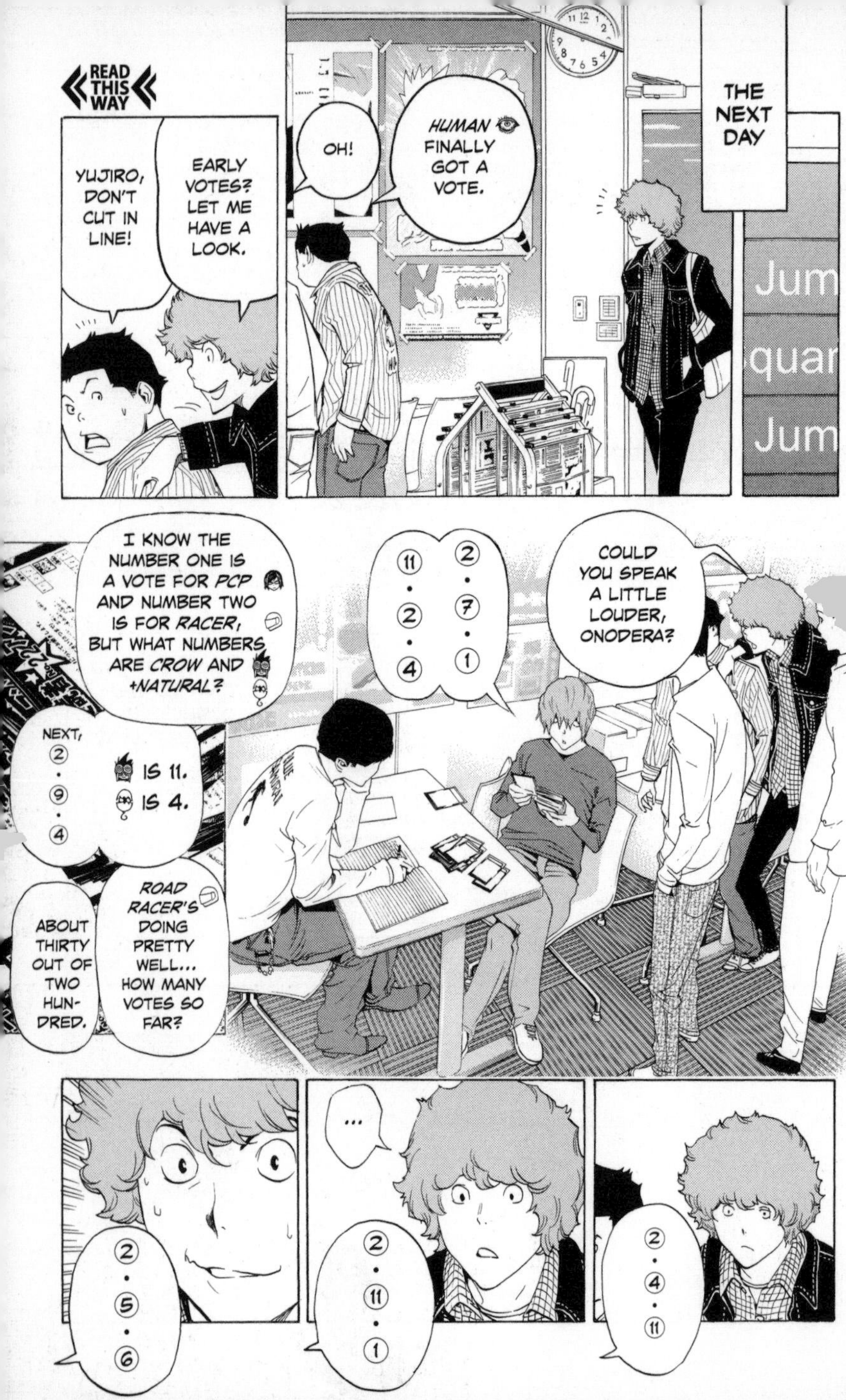
READ THIS WAY
THE NEXT DAY
HUMAN FINALLY GOT A VOTE.
OH!
EARLY VOTES? LET ME HAVE A LOOK.
YUJIRO, DON'T CUT IN LINE!
COULD YOU SPEAK A LITTLE LOUDER, ONODERA?
2 · 7 · 1
11 · 2 · 4
I KNOW THE NUMBER ONE IS A VOTE FOR PCP AND NUMBER TWO IS FOR RACER, BUT WHAT NUMBERS ARE CROW AND +NATURAL?
IS 11. IS 4.
NEXT, 2 · 9 · 4
ROAD RACER'S DOING PRETTY WELL... HOW MANY VOTES SO FAR?
ABOUT THIRTY OUT OF TWO HUN-DRED.
2 · 4 · 11
...
2 · 11 · 1
2 · 5 · 6

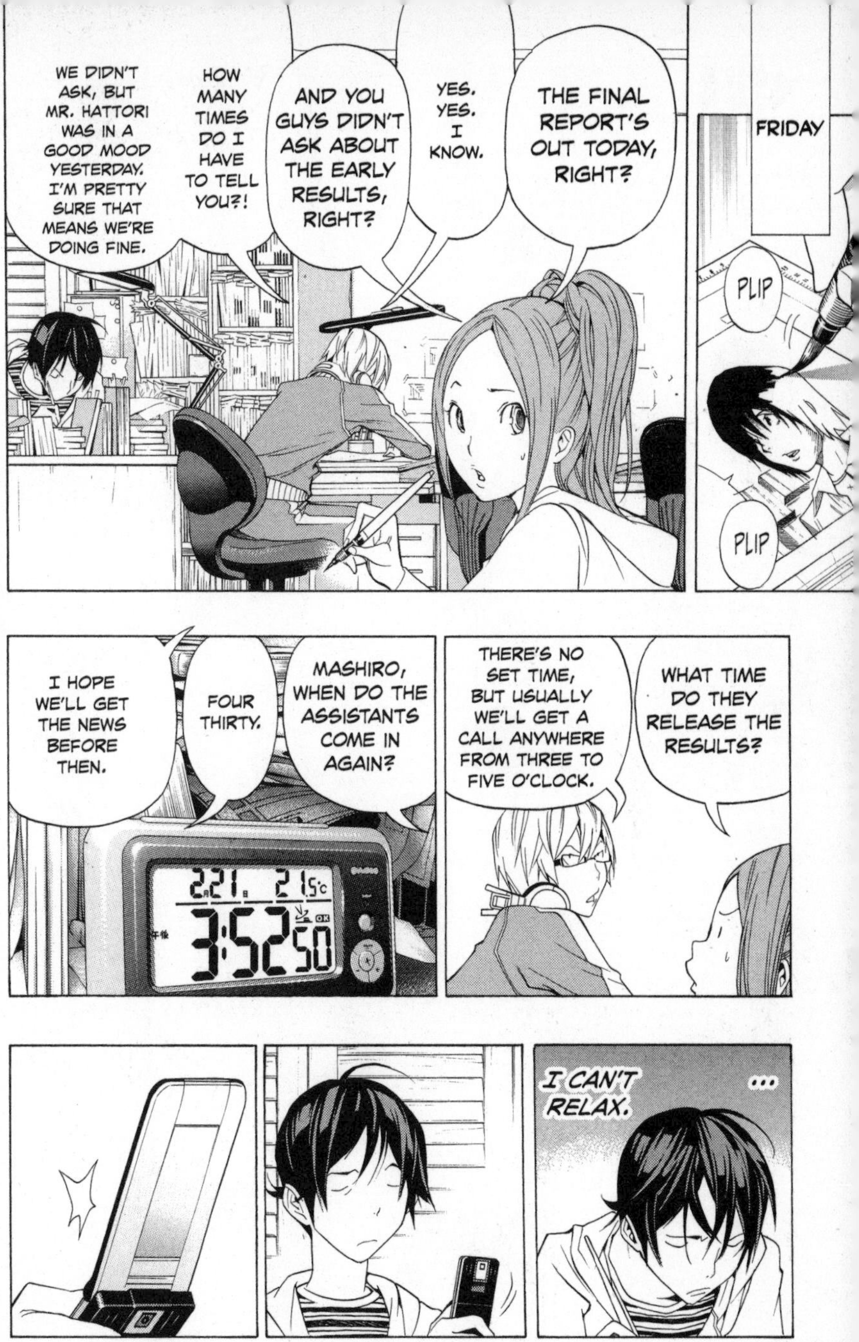
FRIDAY
PLIP
PLIP
THE FINAL REPORT'S OUT TODAY, RIGHT?
YES. YES. I KNOW.
AND YOU GUYS DIDN'T ASK ABOUT THE EARLY RESULTS, RIGHT?
HOW MANY TIMES DO I HAVE TO TELL YOU?!
WE DIDN'T ASK, BUT MR. HATTORI WAS IN A GOOD MOOD YESTERDAY. I'M PRETTY SURE THAT MEANS WE'RE DOING FINE.
WHAT TIME DO THEY RELEASE THE RESULTS?
THERE'S NO SET TIME, BUT USUALLY WE'LL GET A CALL ANYWHERE FROM THREE TO FIVE O'CLOCK.
MASHIRO, WHEN DO THE ASSISTANTS COME IN AGAIN?
FOUR THIRTY.
I HOPE WE'LL GET THE NEWS BEFORE THEN.
...
I CAN'T RELAX.

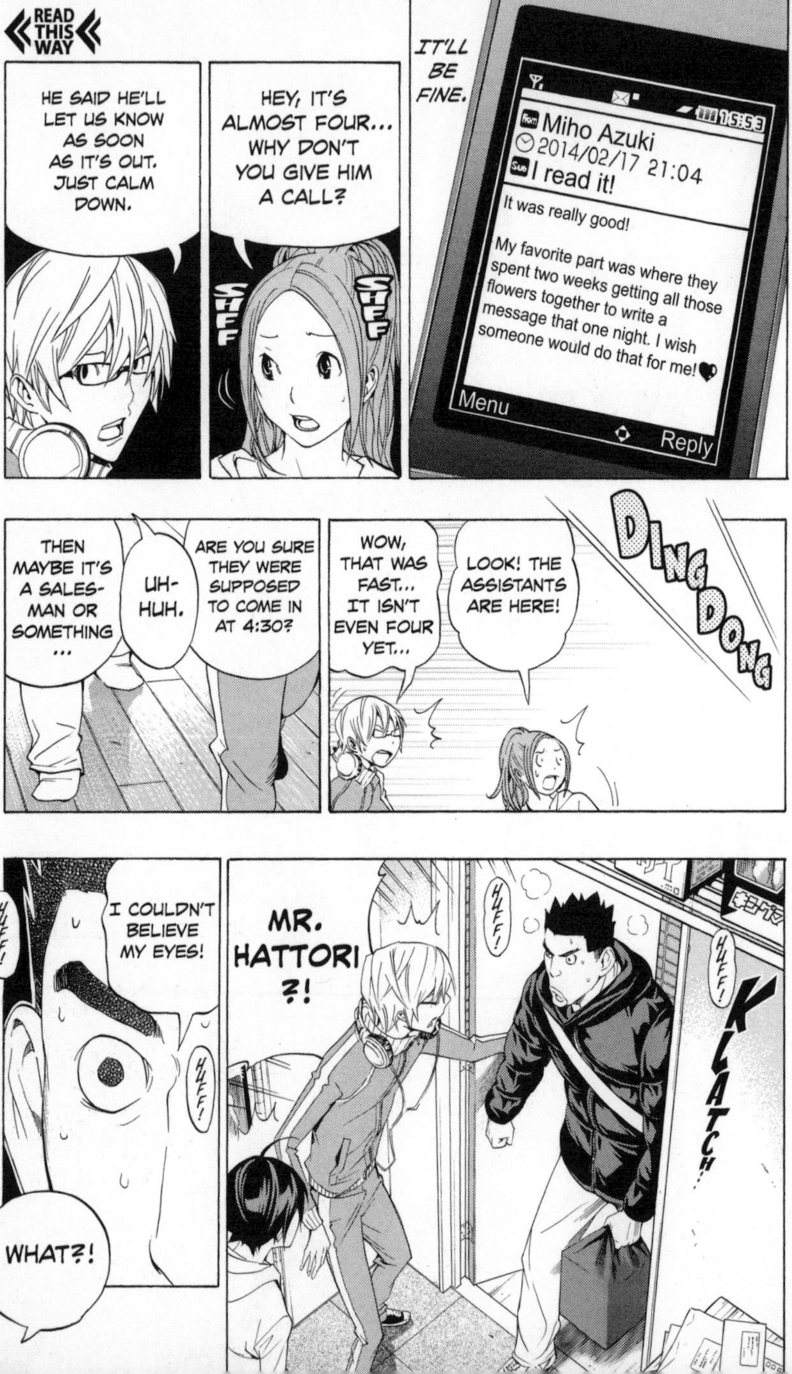
READ THIS WAY
IT'LL BE FINE.
15:53
Miho Azuki
2014/02/17 21:04
I read it!
It was really good!
My favorite part was where they spent two weeks getting all those flowers together to write a message that one night. I wish someone would do that for me!
Menu
Reply
HEY, IT'S ALMOST FOUR... WHY DON'T YOU GIVE HIM A CALL?
SHEFF
SHEFF
HE SAID HE'LL LET US KNOW AS SOON AS IT'S OUT. JUST CALM DOWN.
DING DONG
LOOK! THE ASSISTANTS ARE HERE!
WOW, THAT WAS FAST... IT ISN'T EVEN FOUR YET...
ARE YOU SURE THEY WERE SUPPOSED TO COME IN AT 4:30?
UH-HUH.
THEN MAYBE IT'S A SALES-MAN OR SOMETHING...
KLATCH
HUFF!
HUFF!
MR. HATTORI?!
I COULDN'T BELIEVE MY EYES!
HUFF!
HUFF!
WHAT?!

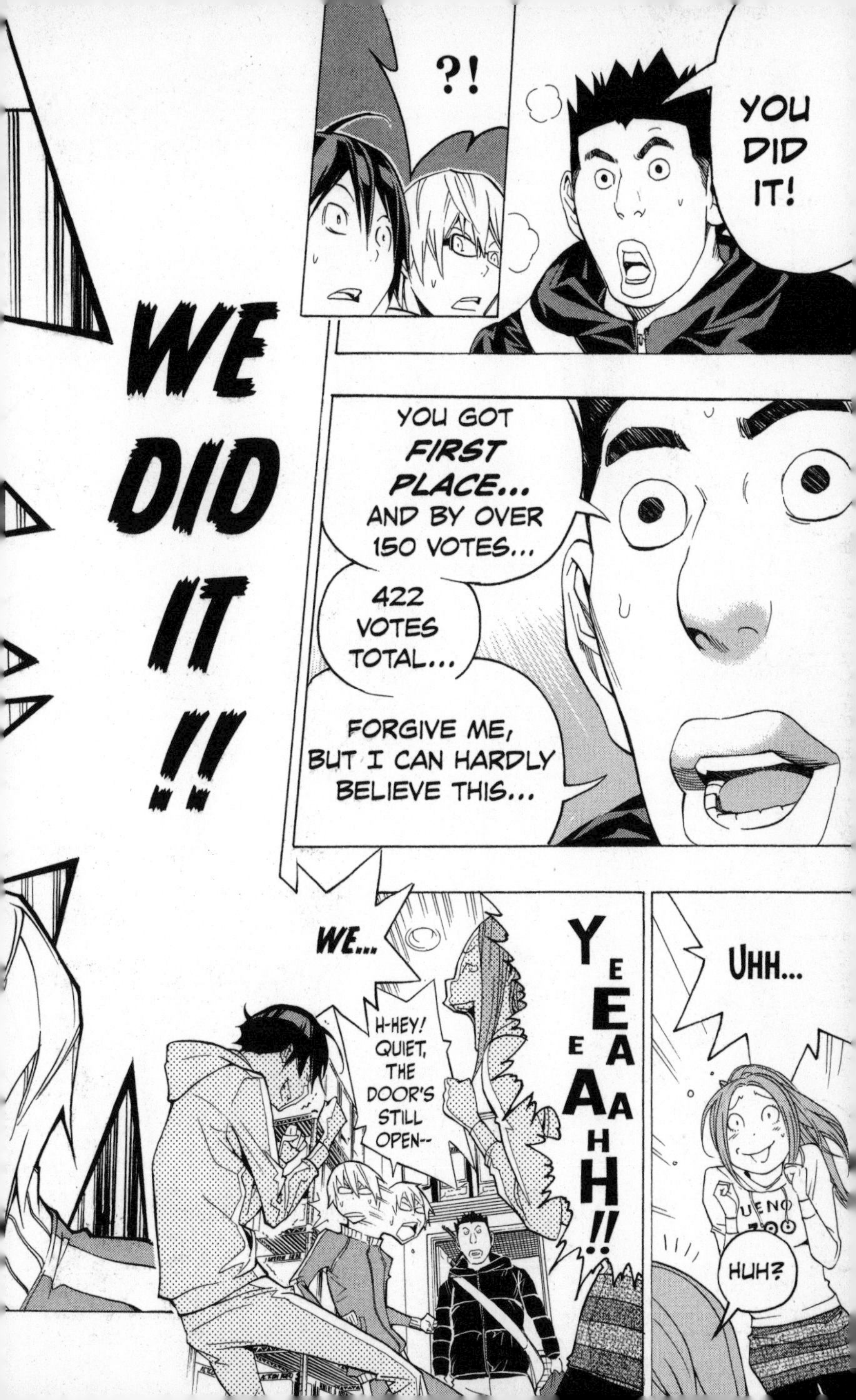
YOU DID IT!
?!
YOU GOT *FIRST PLACE...* AND BY OVER 150 VOTES...
422 VOTES TOTAL...
FORGIVE ME, BUT I CAN HARDLY BELIEVE THIS...
WE DID IT!!
UHH...
HUH?
WE...
YEEEAAAHH!!
H-HEY! QUIET, THE DOOR'S STILL OPEN--

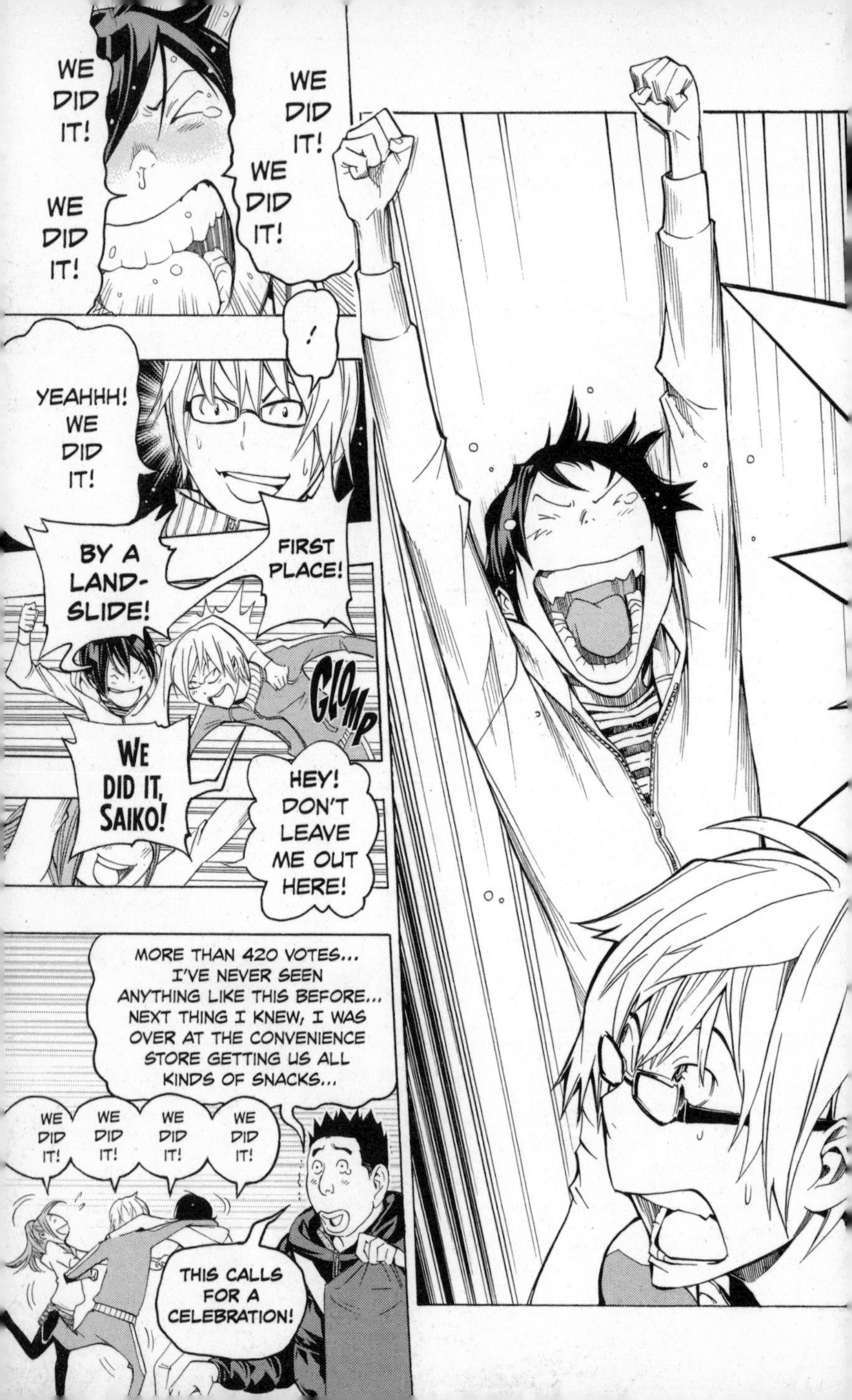
WE DID IT!
WE DID IT!
WE DID IT!
WE DID IT!
!
YEAHHH! WE DID IT!
FIRST PLACE!
BY A LAND-SLIDE!
GLOMP
HEY! DON'T LEAVE ME OUT HERE!
WE DID IT, SAIKO!
MORE THAN 420 VOTES... I'VE NEVER SEEN ANYTHING LIKE THIS BEFORE... NEXT THING I KNEW, I WAS OVER AT THE CONVENIENCE STORE GETTING US ALL KINDS OF SNACKS...
WE DID IT!
WE DID IT!
WE DID IT!
WE DID IT!
THIS CALLS FOR A CELEBRATION!

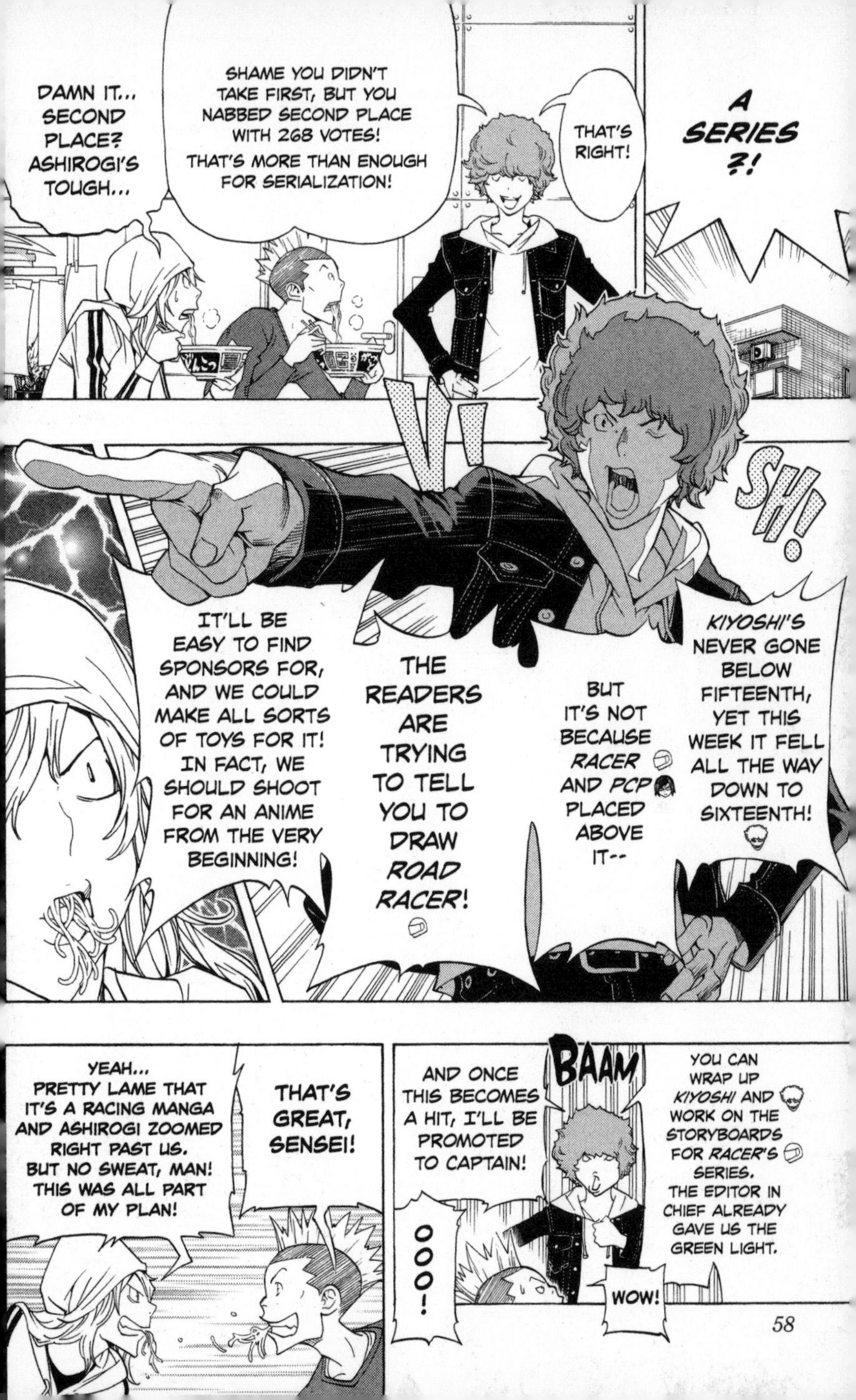
A SERIES?!
THAT'S RIGHT!
SHAME YOU DIDN'T TAKE FIRST, BUT YOU NABBED SECOND PLACE WITH 268 VOTES! THAT'S MORE THAN ENOUGH FOR SERIALIZATION!
DAMN IT... SECOND PLACE? ASHIROGI'S TOUGH...
SH!
KIYOSHI'S NEVER GONE BELOW FIFTEENTH, YET THIS WEEK IT FELL ALL THE WAY DOWN TO SIXTEENTH!
BUT IT'S NOT BECAUSE RACER AND PCP PLACED ABOVE IT--
THE READERS ARE TRYING TO TELL YOU TO DRAW ROAD RACER!
IT'LL BE EASY TO FIND SPONSORS FOR, AND WE COULD MAKE ALL SORTS OF TOYS FOR IT! IN FACT, WE SHOULD SHOOT FOR AN ANIME FROM THE VERY BEGINNING!
YOU CAN WRAP UP KIYOSHI AND WORK ON THE STORYBOARDS FOR RACER'S SERIES. THE EDITOR IN CHIEF ALREADY GAVE US THE GREEN LIGHT.
BAAM
AND ONCE THIS BECOMES A HIT, I'LL BE PROMOTED TO CAPTAIN!
WOW!
OOO!
THAT'S GREAT, SENSEI!
YEAH... PRETTY LAME THAT IT'S A RACING MANGA AND ASHIROGI ZOOMED RIGHT PAST US. BUT NO SWEAT, MAN! THIS WAS ALL PART OF MY PLAN!

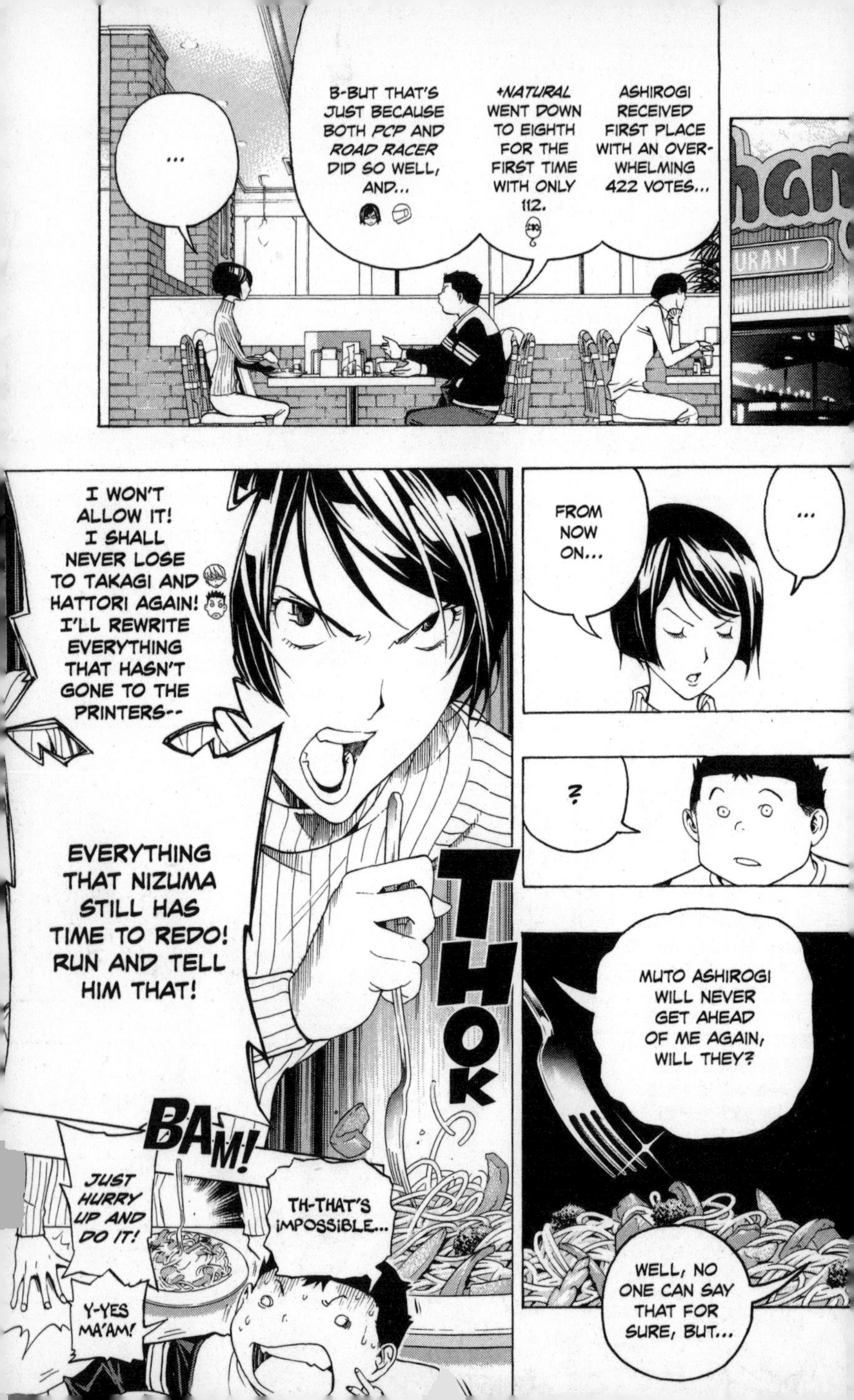
ASHIROGI RECEIVED FIRST PLACE WITH AN OVERWHELMING 422 VOTES...
+NATURAL WENT DOWN TO EIGHTH FOR THE FIRST TIME WITH ONLY 112.
B-BUT THAT'S JUST BECAUSE BOTH PCP AND ROAD RACER DID SO WELL, AND...
...
...
FROM NOW ON...
?
MUTO ASHIROGI WILL NEVER GET AHEAD OF ME AGAIN, WILL THEY?
WELL, NO ONE CAN SAY THAT FOR SURE, BUT...
I WON'T ALLOW IT! I SHALL NEVER LOSE TO TAKAGI AND HATTORI AGAIN! I'LL REWRITE EVERYTHING THAT HASN'T GONE TO THE PRINTERS--
EVERYTHING THAT NIZUMA STILL HAS TIME TO REDO! RUN AND TELL HIM THAT!
THOK
BAM!
TH-THAT'S IMPOSSIBLE...
JUST HURRY UP AND DO IT!
Y-YES MA'AM!

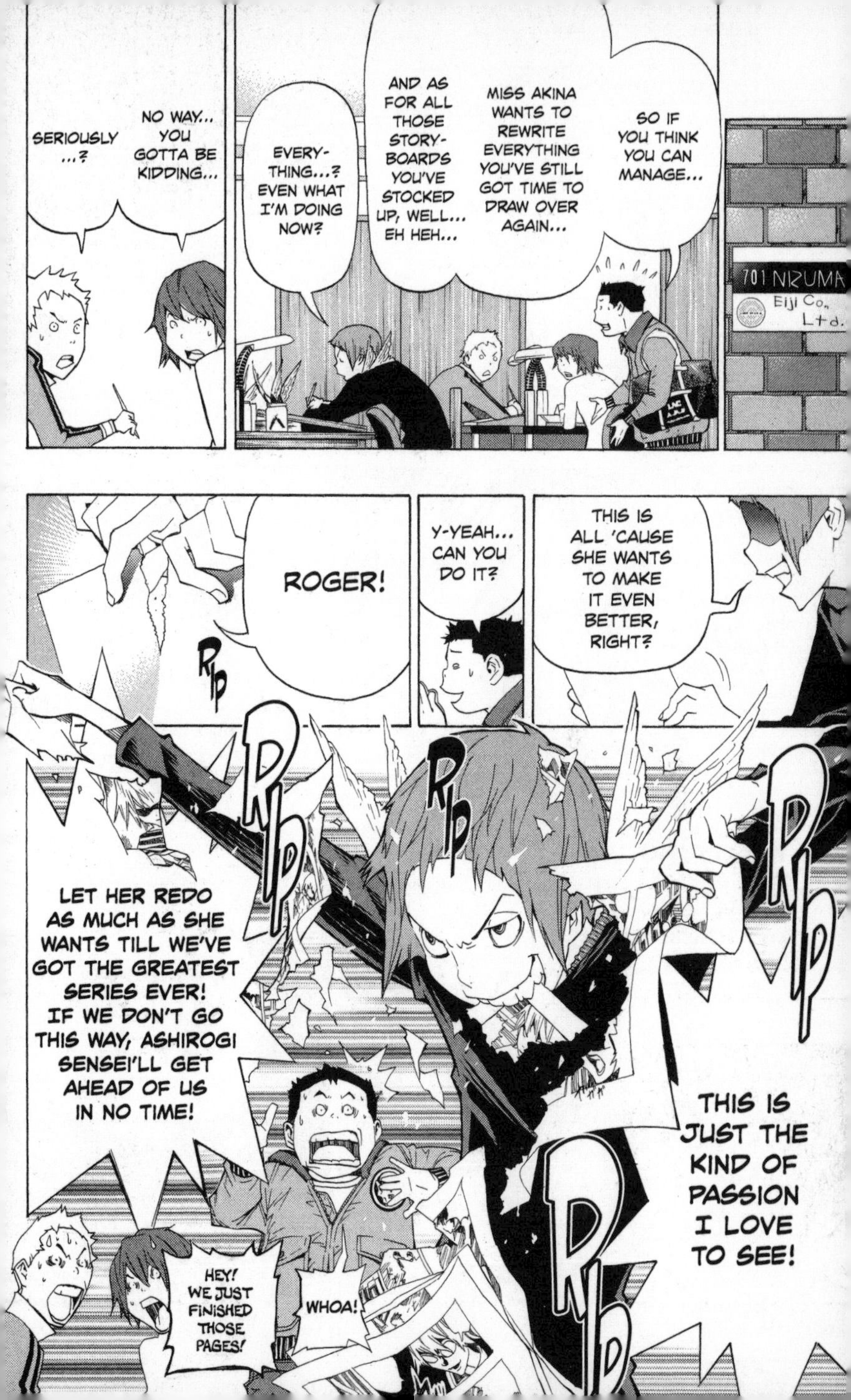
701 NIZUMA
Eiji Co., Ltd.
SO IF YOU THINK YOU CAN MANAGE...
MISS AKINA WANTS TO REWRITE EVERYTHING YOU'VE STILL GOT TIME TO DRAW OVER AGAIN...
AND AS FOR ALL THOSE STORY-BOARDS YOU'VE STOCKED UP, WELL... EH HEH...
EVERY-THING...? EVEN WHAT I'M DOING NOW?
NO WAY... YOU GOTTA BE KIDDING...
SERIOUSLY ...?
THIS IS ALL 'CAUSE SHE WANTS TO MAKE IT EVEN BETTER, RIGHT?
Y-YEAH... CAN YOU DO IT?
ROGER!
RIP
RIP
RIP
THIS IS JUST THE KIND OF PASSION I LOVE TO SEE!
RIP
RIP
LET HER REDO AS MUCH AS SHE WANTS TILL WE'VE GOT THE GREATEST SERIES EVER! IF WE DON'T GO THIS WAY, ASHIROGI SENSEI'LL GET AHEAD OF US IN NO TIME!
WHOA!
HEY! WE JUST FINISHED THOSE PAGES!

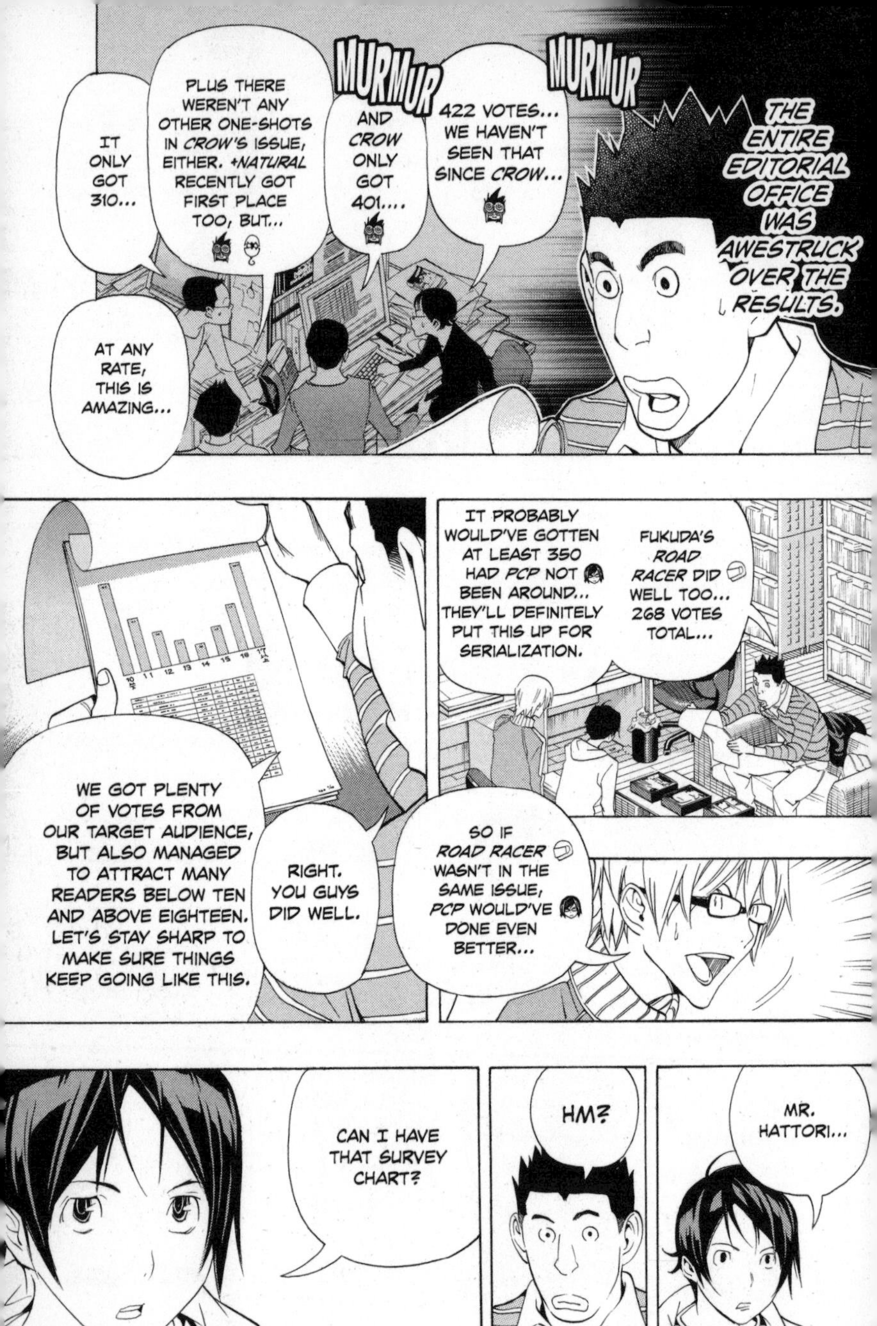
THE ENTIRE EDITORIAL OFFICE WAS AWESTRUCK OVER THE RESULTS.
MURMUR
422 VOTES... WE HAVEN'T SEEN THAT SINCE *CROW*...
MURMUR
AND *CROW* ONLY GOT 401....
PLUS THERE WEREN'T ANY OTHER ONE-SHOTS IN *CROW'S* ISSUE, EITHER. *+NATURAL* RECENTLY GOT FIRST PLACE TOO, BUT...
IT ONLY GOT 310...
AT ANY RATE, THIS IS AMAZING...
FUKUDA'S *ROAD RACER* DID WELL TOO... 268 VOTES TOTAL...
IT PROBABLY WOULD'VE GOTTEN AT LEAST 350 HAD *PCP* NOT BEEN AROUND... THEY'LL DEFINITELY PUT THIS UP FOR SERIALIZATION.
SO IF *ROAD RACER* WASN'T IN THE SAME ISSUE, *PCP* WOULD'VE DONE EVEN BETTER...
RIGHT. YOU GUYS DID WELL.
WE GOT PLENTY OF VOTES FROM OUR TARGET AUDIENCE, BUT ALSO MANAGED TO ATTRACT MANY READERS BELOW TEN AND ABOVE EIGHTEEN. LET'S STAY SHARP TO MAKE SURE THINGS KEEP GOING LIKE THIS.
MR. HATTORI...
HM?
CAN I HAVE THAT SURVEY CHART?

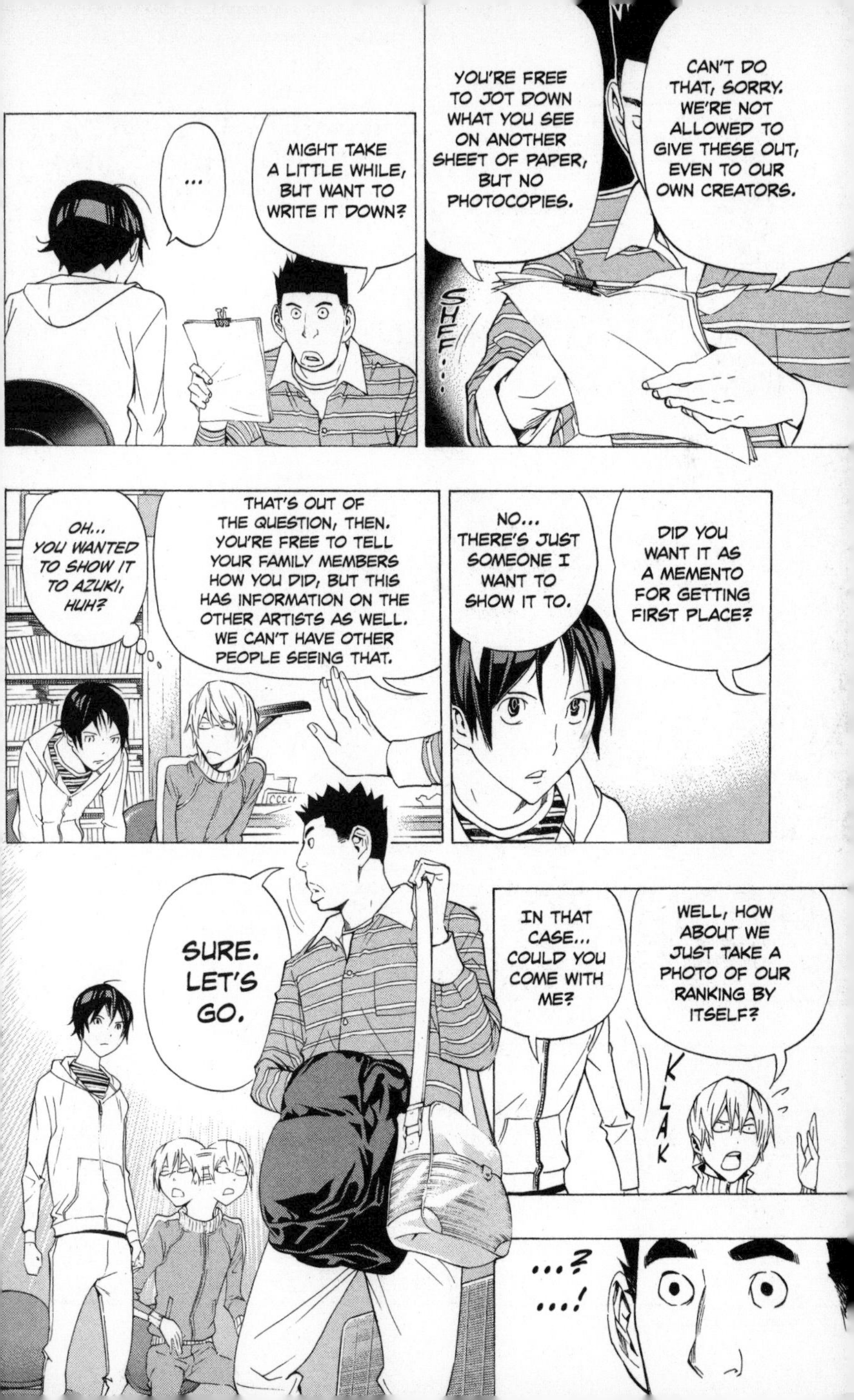
CAN'T DO THAT, SORRY. WE'RE NOT ALLOWED TO GIVE THESE OUT, EVEN TO OUR OWN CREATORS.
YOU'RE FREE TO JOT DOWN WHAT YOU SEE ON ANOTHER SHEET OF PAPER, BUT NO PHOTOCOPIES.
SHEF...
MIGHT TAKE A LITTLE WHILE, BUT WANT TO WRITE IT DOWN?
...
DID YOU WANT IT AS A MEMENTO FOR GETTING FIRST PLACE?
NO... THERE'S JUST SOMEONE I WANT TO SHOW IT TO.
THAT'S OUT OF THE QUESTION, THEN. YOU'RE FREE TO TELL YOUR FAMILY MEMBERS HOW YOU DID, BUT THIS HAS INFORMATION ON THE OTHER ARTISTS AS WELL. WE CAN'T HAVE OTHER PEOPLE SEEING THAT.
OH... YOU WANTED TO SHOW IT TO AZUKI, HUH?
WELL, HOW ABOUT WE JUST TAKE A PHOTO OF OUR RANKING BY ITSELF?
KLAK
IN THAT CASE... COULD YOU COME WITH ME?
...?
...!
SURE. LET'S GO.

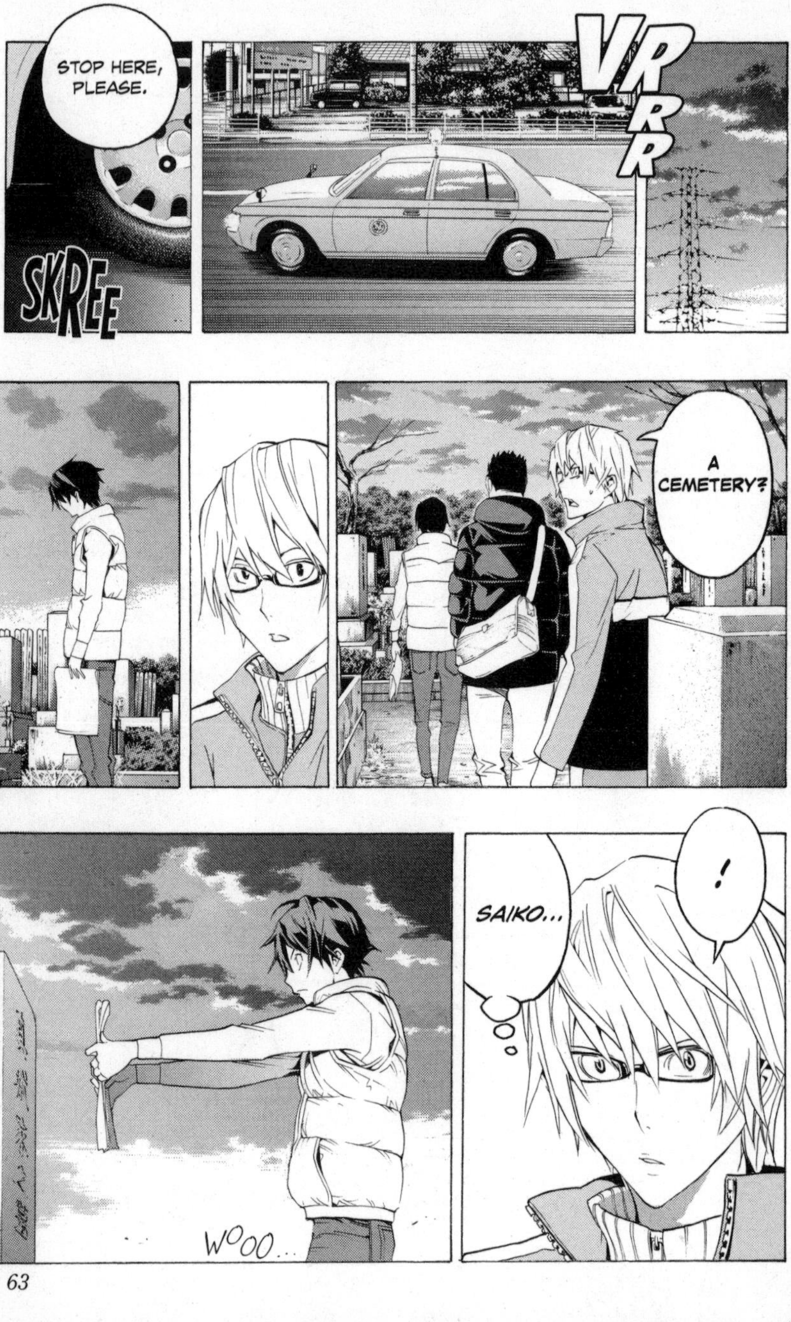
VRRR
STOP HERE, PLEASE.
SKREE
A CEMETERY?
!
SAIKO...
WOOO...

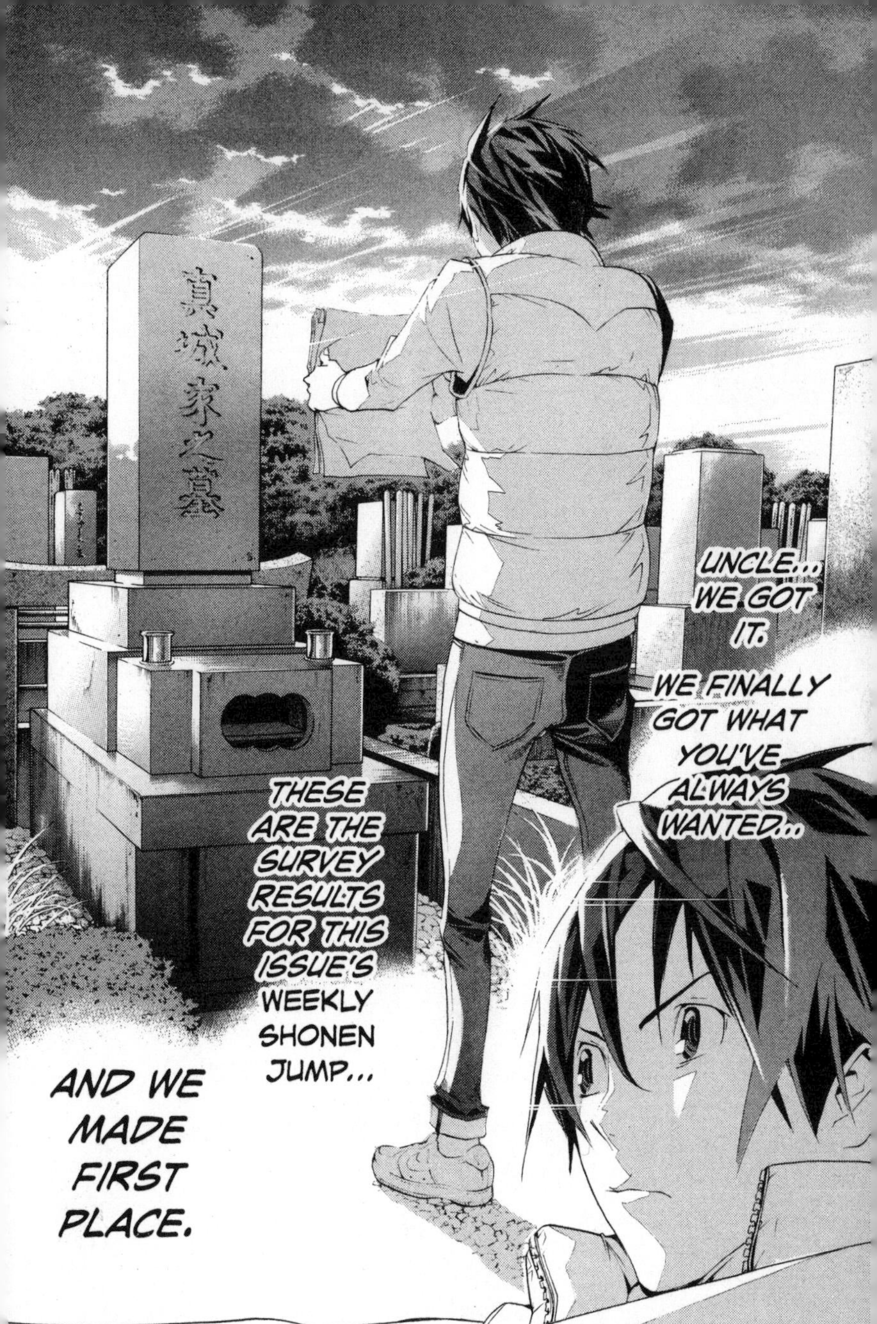
UNCLE... WE GOT IT.
WE FINALLY GOT WHAT YOU'VE ALWAYS WANTED...
THESE ARE THE SURVEY RESULTS FOR THIS ISSUE'S WEEKLY SHONEN JUMP...
AND WE MADE FIRST PLACE.
真城家之墓

(ON GRAVE: MASHIRO FAMILY GRAVE)

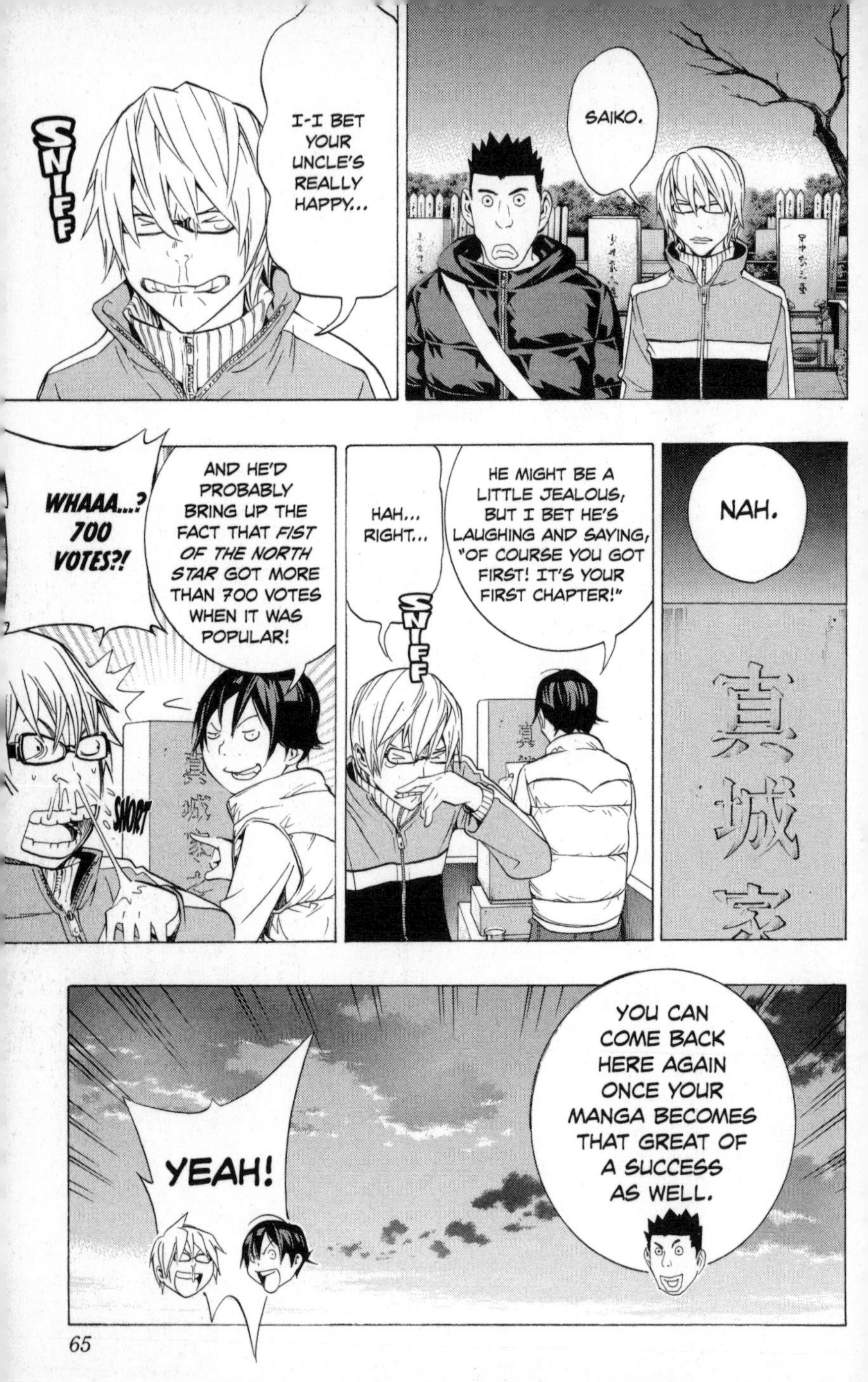
SAIKO.
I-I BET YOUR UNCLE'S REALLY HAPPY...
SNIFF
NAH.
HE MIGHT BE A LITTLE JEALOUS, BUT I BET HE'S LAUGHING AND SAYING, "OF COURSE YOU GOT FIRST! IT'S YOUR FIRST CHAPTER!"
HAH... RIGHT...
SNIFF
AND HE'D PROBABLY BRING UP THE FACT THAT *FIST OF THE NORTH STAR* GOT MORE THAN 700 VOTES WHEN IT WAS POPULAR!
WHAAA...? 700 VOTES?!
SHORT
YOU CAN COME BACK HERE AGAIN ONCE YOUR MANGA BECOMES THAT GREAT OF A SUCCESS AS WELL.
YEAH!

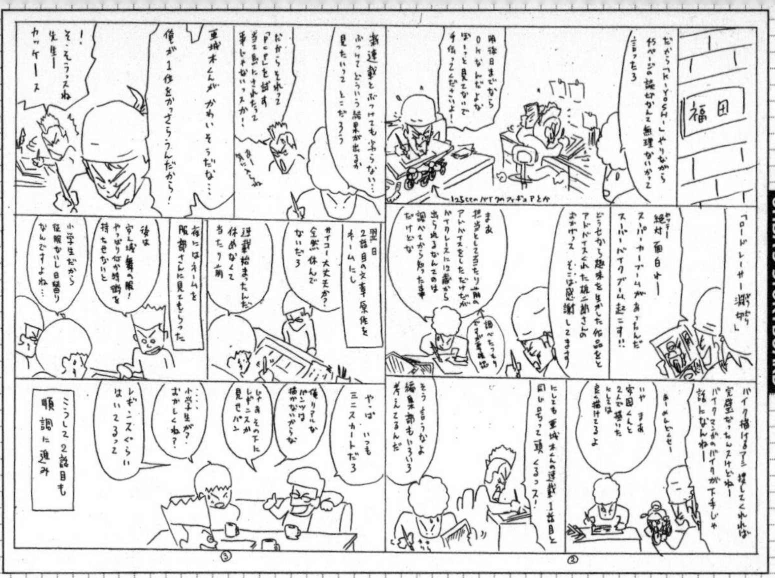

OHBA'S STORYBOARD

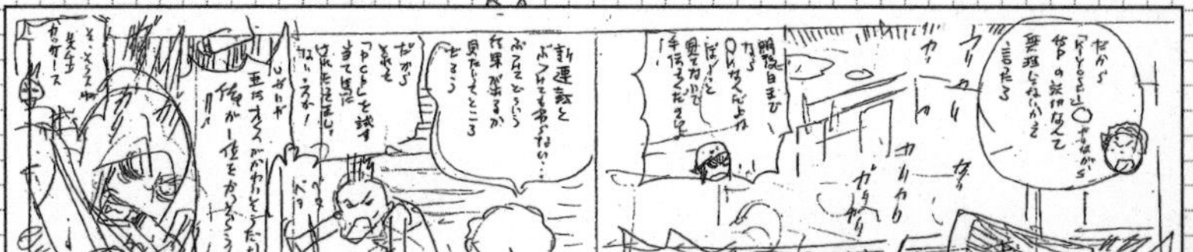

OBATA'S STORYBOARD

COMPLETE!

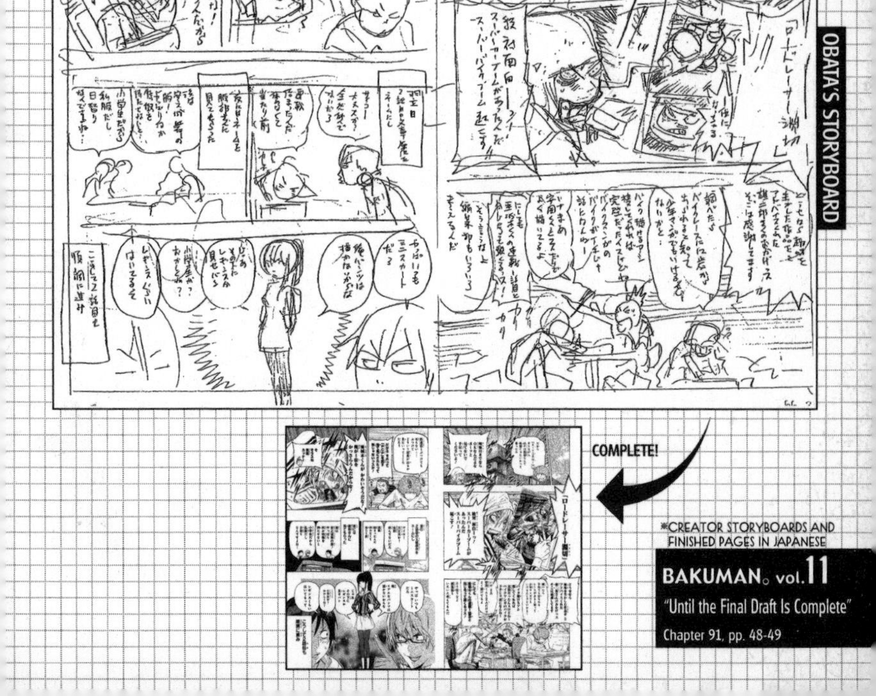

*CREATOR STORYBOARDS AND FINISHED PAGES IN JAPANESE

BAKUMAN。 vol.11

"Until the Final Draft Is Complete"

Chapter 91, pp. 48-49

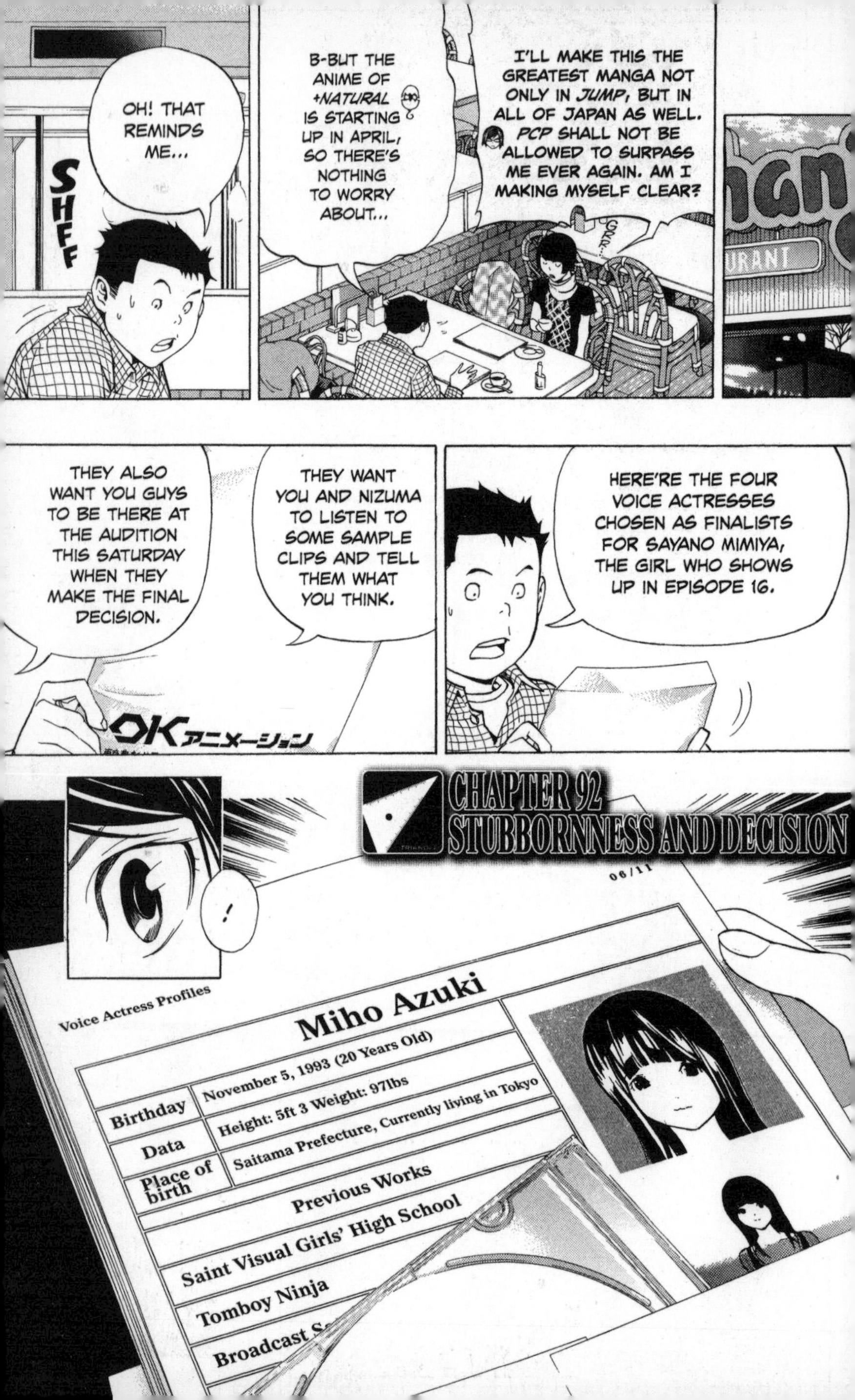
I'LL MAKE THIS THE GREATEST MANGA NOT ONLY IN *JUMP*, BUT IN ALL OF JAPAN AS WELL. *PCP* SHALL NOT BE ALLOWED TO SURPASS ME EVER AGAIN. AM I MAKING MYSELF CLEAR?
GRR...
B-BUT THE ANIME OF *+NATURAL* IS STARTING UP IN APRIL, SO THERE'S NOTHING TO WORRY ABOUT...
OH! THAT REMINDS ME...
SHFF
HERE'RE THE FOUR VOICE ACTRESSES CHOSEN AS FINALISTS FOR SAYANO MIMIYA, THE GIRL WHO SHOWS UP IN EPISODE 16.
THEY WANT YOU AND NIZUMA TO LISTEN TO SOME SAMPLE CLIPS AND TELL THEM WHAT YOU THINK.
THEY ALSO WANT YOU GUYS TO BE THERE AT THE AUDITION THIS SATURDAY WHEN THEY MAKE THE FINAL DECISION.
OKアニメーション
CHAPTER 92
STUBBORNNESS AND DECISION
!
06/11
Voice Actress Profiles
Miho Azuki
Birthday November 5, 1993 (20 Years Old)
Data Height: 5ft 3 Weight: 97lbs
Place of birth Saitama Prefecture, Currently living in Tokyo
Previous Works
Saint Visual Girls' High School
Tomboy Ninja

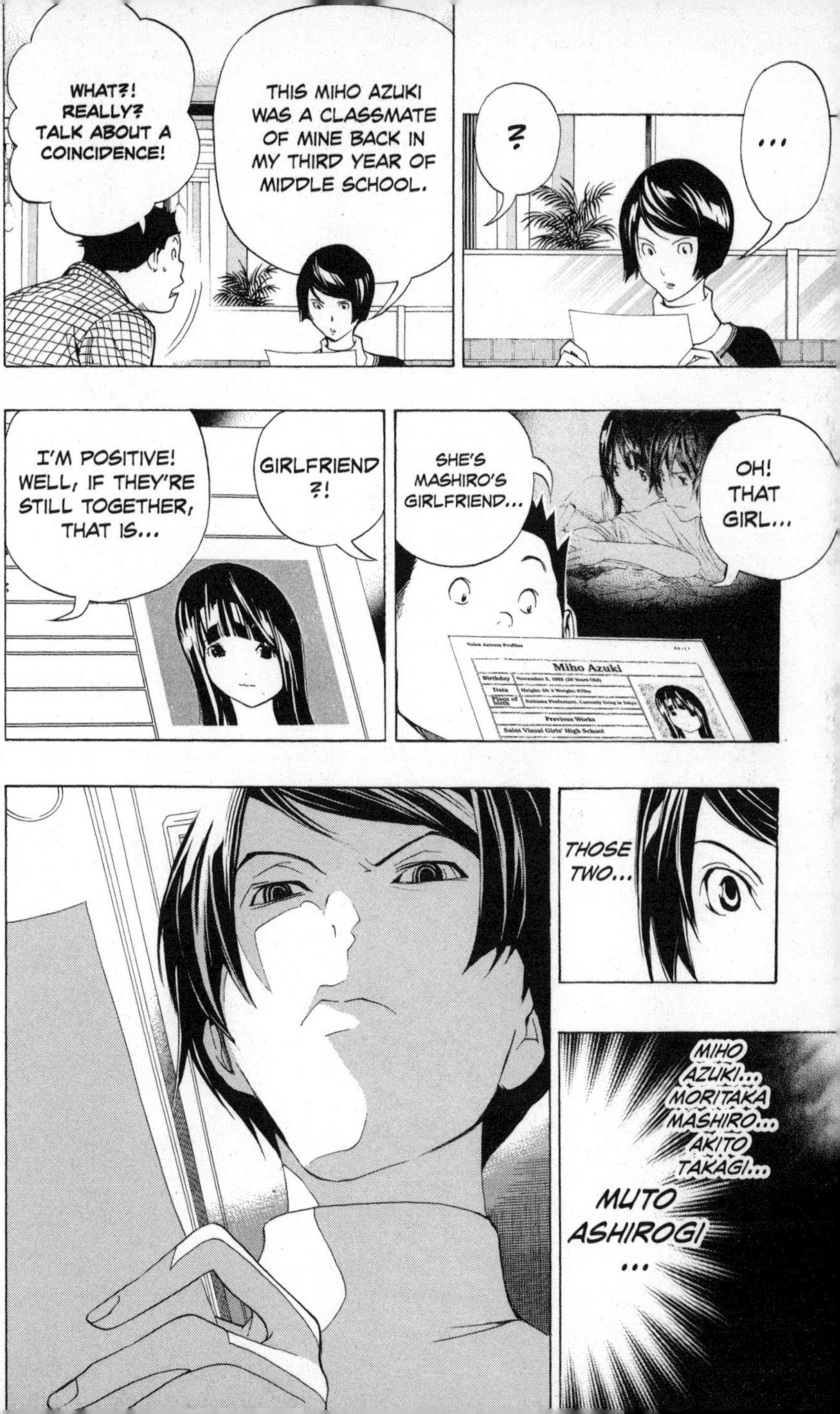
...
?
THIS MIHO AZUKI WAS A CLASSMATE OF MINE BACK IN MY THIRD YEAR OF MIDDLE SCHOOL.
WHAT?! REALLY? TALK ABOUT A COINCIDENCE!
OH! THAT GIRL...
SHE'S MASHIRO'S GIRLFRIEND...
Voice Actress Profiles
Miho Azuki
Birthday
Data
Place of birth
Saitama Prefecture, Currently living in Tokyo
Previous Works
Saint Visual Girls' High School
GIRLFRIEND?!
I'M POSITIVE! WELL, IF THEY'RE STILL TOGETHER, THAT IS...
THOSE TWO...
MIHO AZUKI... MORITAKA MASHIRO... AKITO TAKAGI...
MUTO ASHIROGI ...

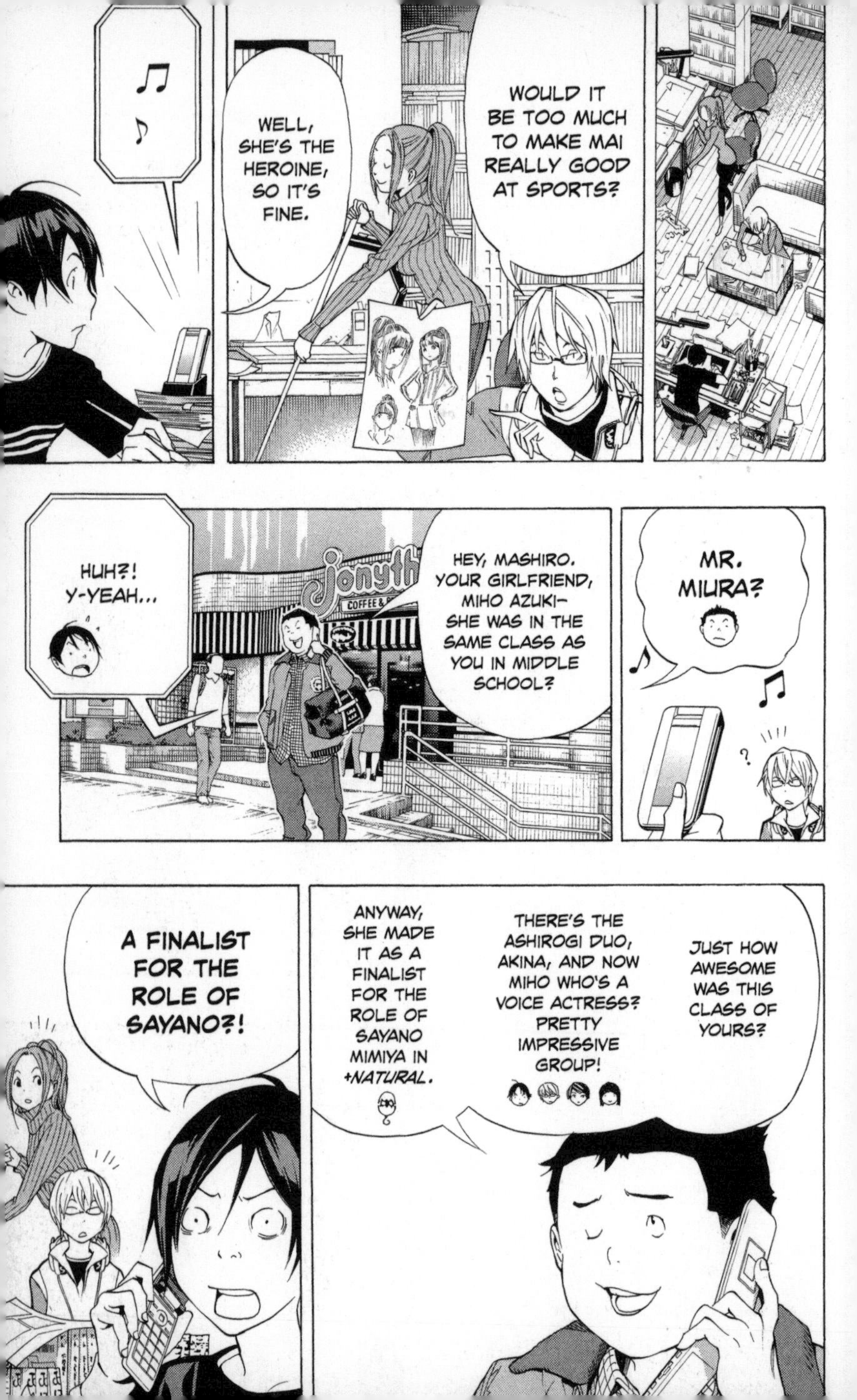
WOULD IT BE TOO MUCH TO MAKE MAI REALLY GOOD AT SPORTS?
WELL, SHE'S THE HEROINE, SO IT'S FINE.
MR. MIURA?
HEY, MASHIRO. YOUR GIRLFRIEND, MIHO AZUKI– SHE WAS IN THE SAME CLASS AS YOU IN MIDDLE SCHOOL?
HUH?! Y-YEAH...
JUST HOW AWESOME WAS THIS CLASS OF YOURS?
THERE'S THE ASHIROGI DUO, AKINA, AND NOW MIHO WHO'S A VOICE ACTRESS? PRETTY IMPRESSIVE GROUP!
ANYWAY, SHE MADE IT AS A FINALIST FOR THE ROLE OF SAYANO MIMIYA IN +NATURAL.
A FINALIST FOR THE ROLE OF SAYANO?!

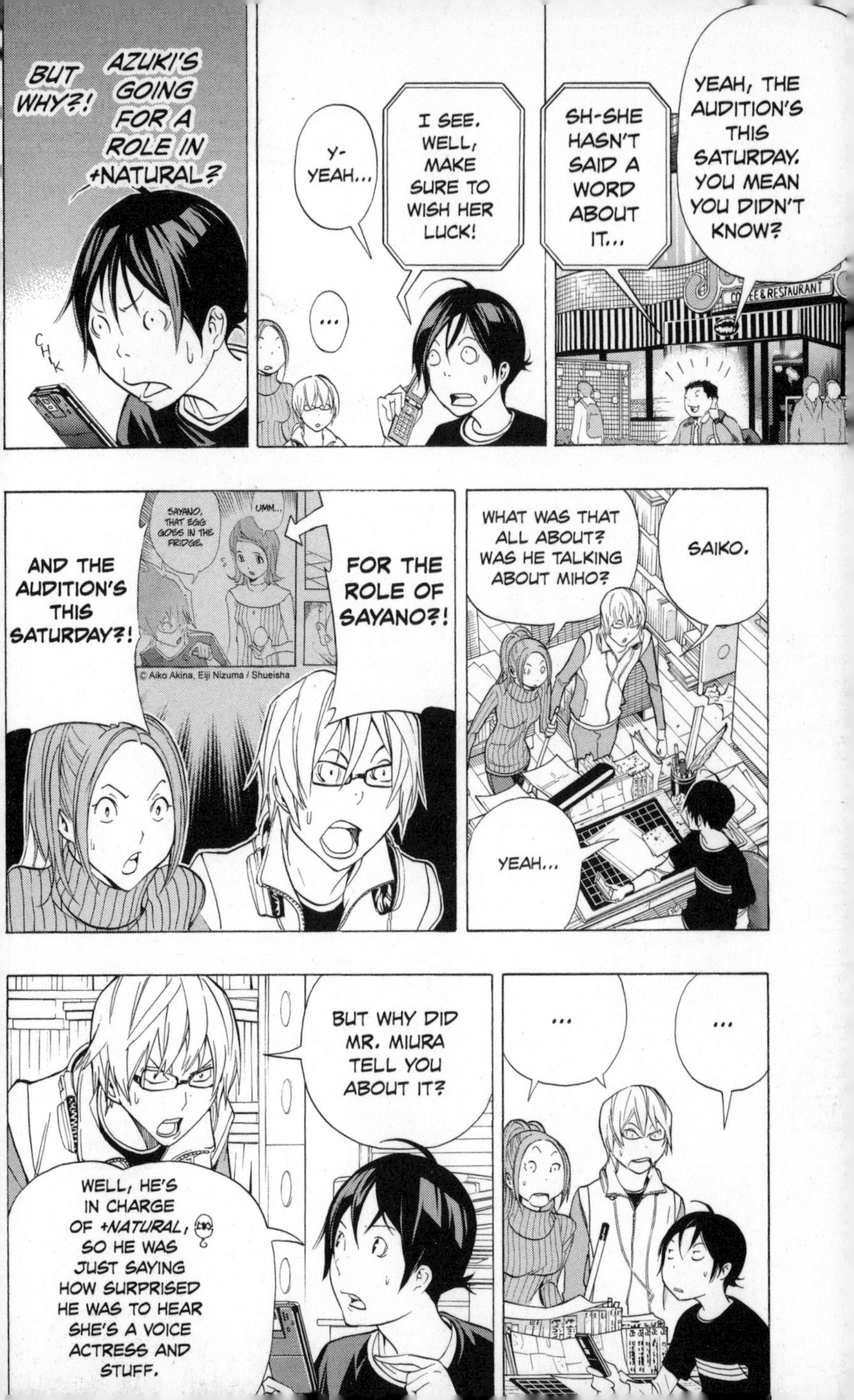
YEAH, THE AUDITION'S THIS SATURDAY. YOU MEAN YOU DIDN'T KNOW?
SH-SHE HASN'T SAID A WORD ABOUT IT...
CO EE&RESTAURANT
I SEE. WELL, MAKE SURE TO WISH HER LUCK!
Y-YEAH...
...
AZUKI'S GOING FOR A ROLE IN +NATURAL?
BUT WHY?!
CHIK
SAIKO.
WHAT WAS THAT ALL ABOUT? WAS HE TALKING ABOUT MIHO?
YEAH...
FOR THE ROLE OF SAYANO?!
UMM...
SAYANO, THAT EGG GOES IN THE FRIDGE.
AND THE AUDITION'S THIS SATURDAY?!
© Aiko Akina, Eiji Nizuma / Shueisha
...
...
BUT WHY DID MR. MIURA TELL YOU ABOUT IT?
WELL, HE'S IN CHARGE OF +NATURAL, SO HE WAS JUST SAYING HOW SURPRISED HE WAS TO HEAR SHE'S A VOICE ACTRESS AND STUFF.

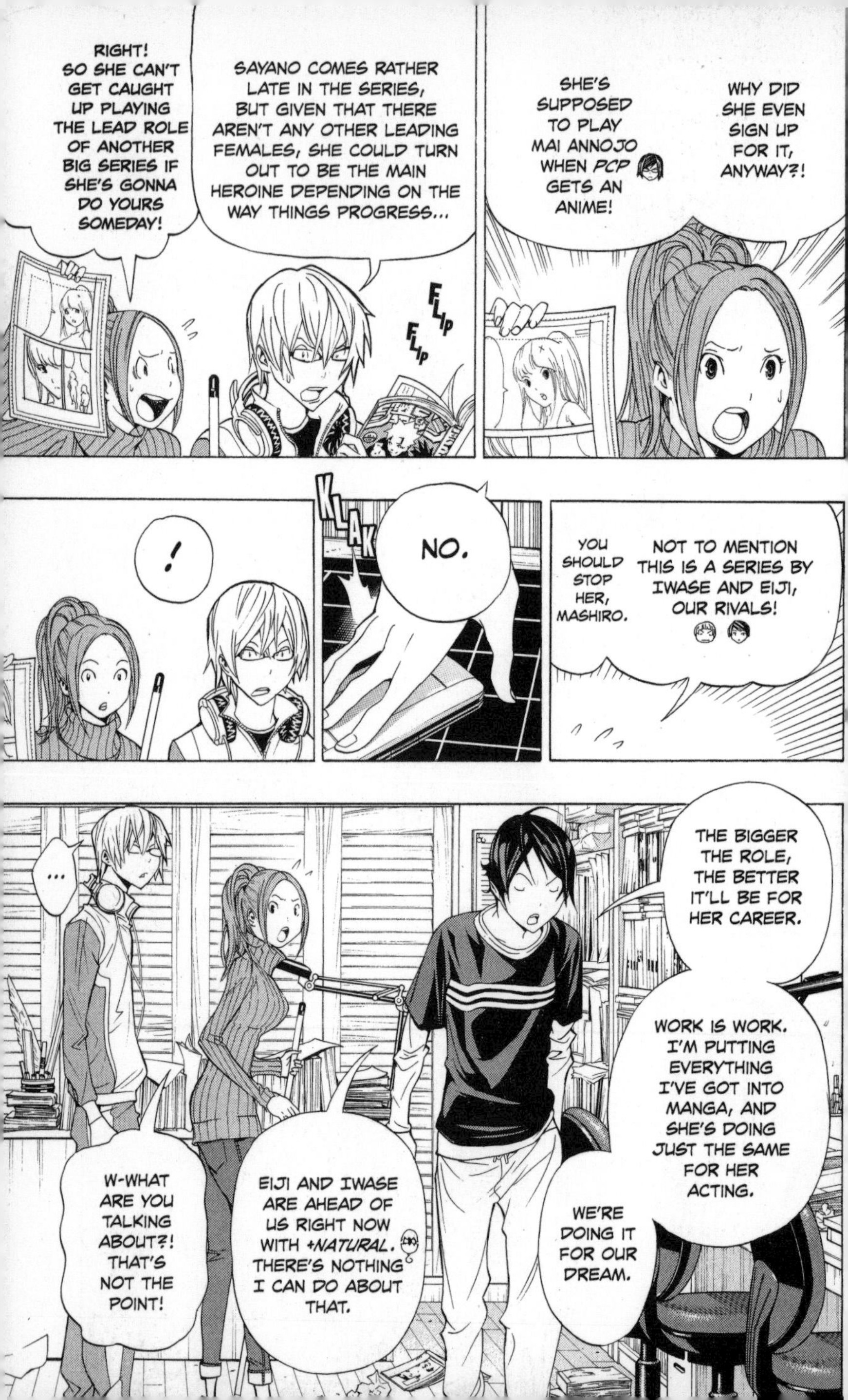

WHY DID SHE EVEN SIGN UP FOR IT, ANYWAY?!
SHE'S SUPPOSED TO PLAY MAI ANNOJO WHEN *PCP* GETS AN ANIME!
SAYANO COMES RATHER LATE IN THE SERIES, BUT GIVEN THAT THERE AREN'T ANY OTHER LEADING FEMALES, SHE COULD TURN OUT TO BE THE MAIN HEROINE DEPENDING ON THE WAY THINGS PROGRESS...
FLIP
FLIP
RIGHT! SO SHE CAN'T GET CAUGHT UP PLAYING THE LEAD ROLE OF ANOTHER BIG SERIES IF SHE'S GONNA DO YOURS SOMEDAY!
NOT TO MENTION THIS IS A SERIES BY IWASE AND EIJI, OUR RIVALS!
YOU SHOULD STOP HER, MASHIRO.
KLAK
NO.
!
THE BIGGER THE ROLE, THE BETTER IT'LL BE FOR HER CAREER.
WORK IS WORK. I'M PUTTING EVERYTHING I'VE GOT INTO MANGA, AND SHE'S DOING JUST THE SAME FOR HER ACTING.
WE'RE DOING IT FOR OUR DREAM.
W-WHAT ARE YOU TALKING ABOUT?! THAT'S NOT THE POINT!
EIJI AND IWASE ARE AHEAD OF US RIGHT NOW WITH *+NATURAL*. THERE'S NOTHING I CAN DO ABOUT THAT.
...

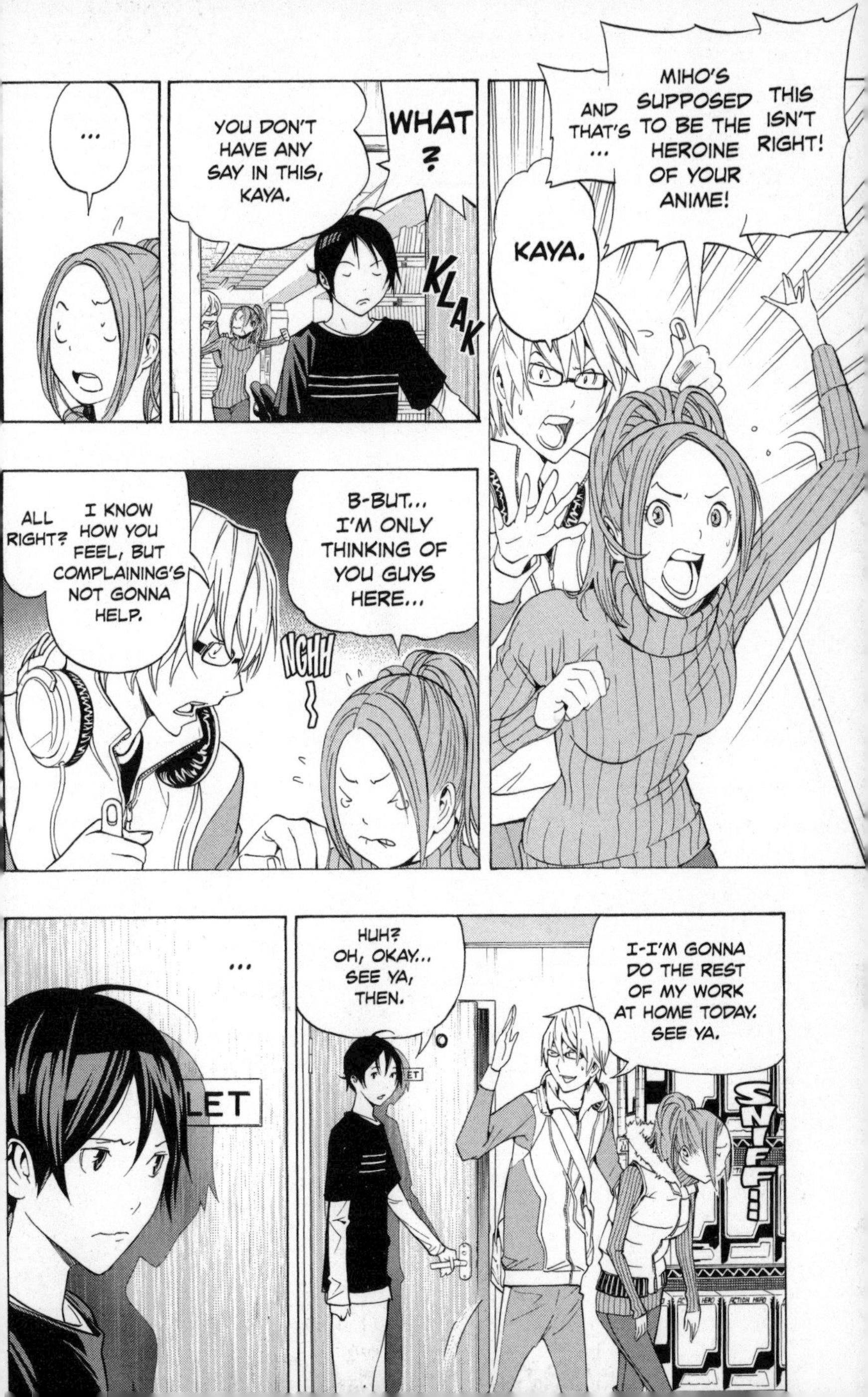
THIS ISN'T RIGHT!
MIHO'S SUPPOSED TO BE THE HEROINE OF YOUR ANIME!
AND THAT'S ...
KAYA.
WHAT?
KLAK
YOU DON'T HAVE ANY SAY IN THIS, KAYA.
...
B-BUT... I'M ONLY THINKING OF YOU GUYS HERE...
NGHH~
I KNOW HOW YOU FEEL, BUT COMPLAINING'S NOT GONNA HELP.
ALL RIGHT?
I-I'M GONNA DO THE REST OF MY WORK AT HOME TODAY. SEE YA.
SNIF...
HUH? OH, OKAY... SEE YA, THEN.
...
LET

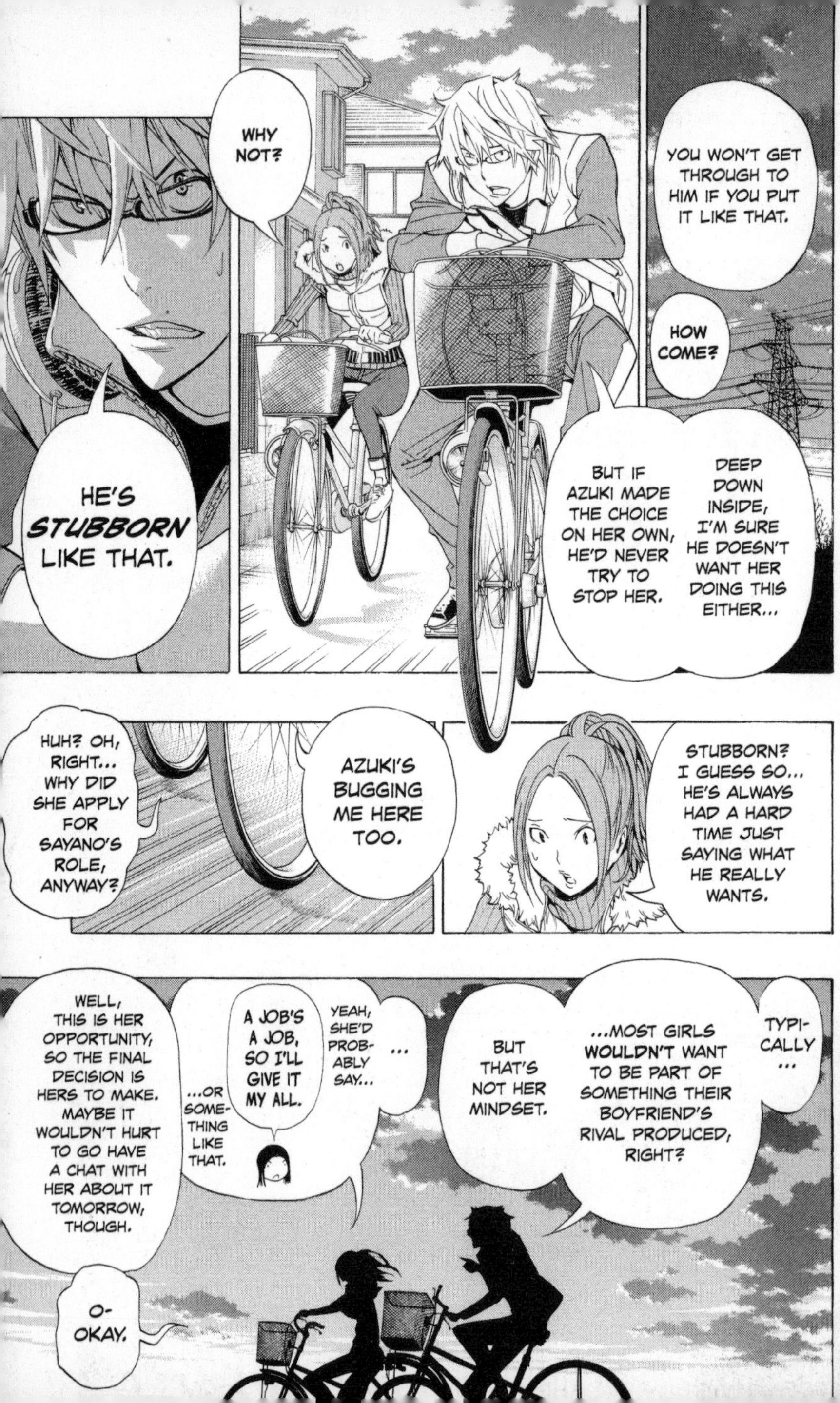
YOU WON'T GET THROUGH TO HIM IF YOU PUT IT LIKE THAT.
HOW COME?
DEEP DOWN INSIDE, I'M SURE HE DOESN'T WANT HER DOING THIS EITHER...
BUT IF AZUKI MADE THE CHOICE ON HER OWN, HE'D NEVER TRY TO STOP HER.
WHY NOT?
HE'S *STUBBORN* LIKE THAT.
STUBBORN? I GUESS SO... HE'S ALWAYS HAD A HARD TIME JUST SAYING WHAT HE REALLY WANTS.
AZUKI'S BUGGING ME HERE TOO.
HUH? OH, RIGHT... WHY DID SHE APPLY FOR SAYANO'S ROLE, ANYWAY?
TYPI-CALLY...
...MOST GIRLS **WOULDN'T** WANT TO BE PART OF SOMETHING THEIR BOYFRIEND'S RIVAL PRODUCED, RIGHT?
BUT THAT'S NOT HER MINDSET.
...
YEAH, SHE'D PROB-ABLY SAY...
A JOB'S A JOB, SO I'LL GIVE IT MY ALL.
...OR SOME-THING LIKE THAT.
WELL, THIS IS HER OPPORTUNITY, SO THE FINAL DECISION IS HERS TO MAKE. MAYBE IT WOULDN'T HURT TO GO HAVE A CHAT WITH HER ABOUT IT TOMORROW, THOUGH.
O-OKAY.

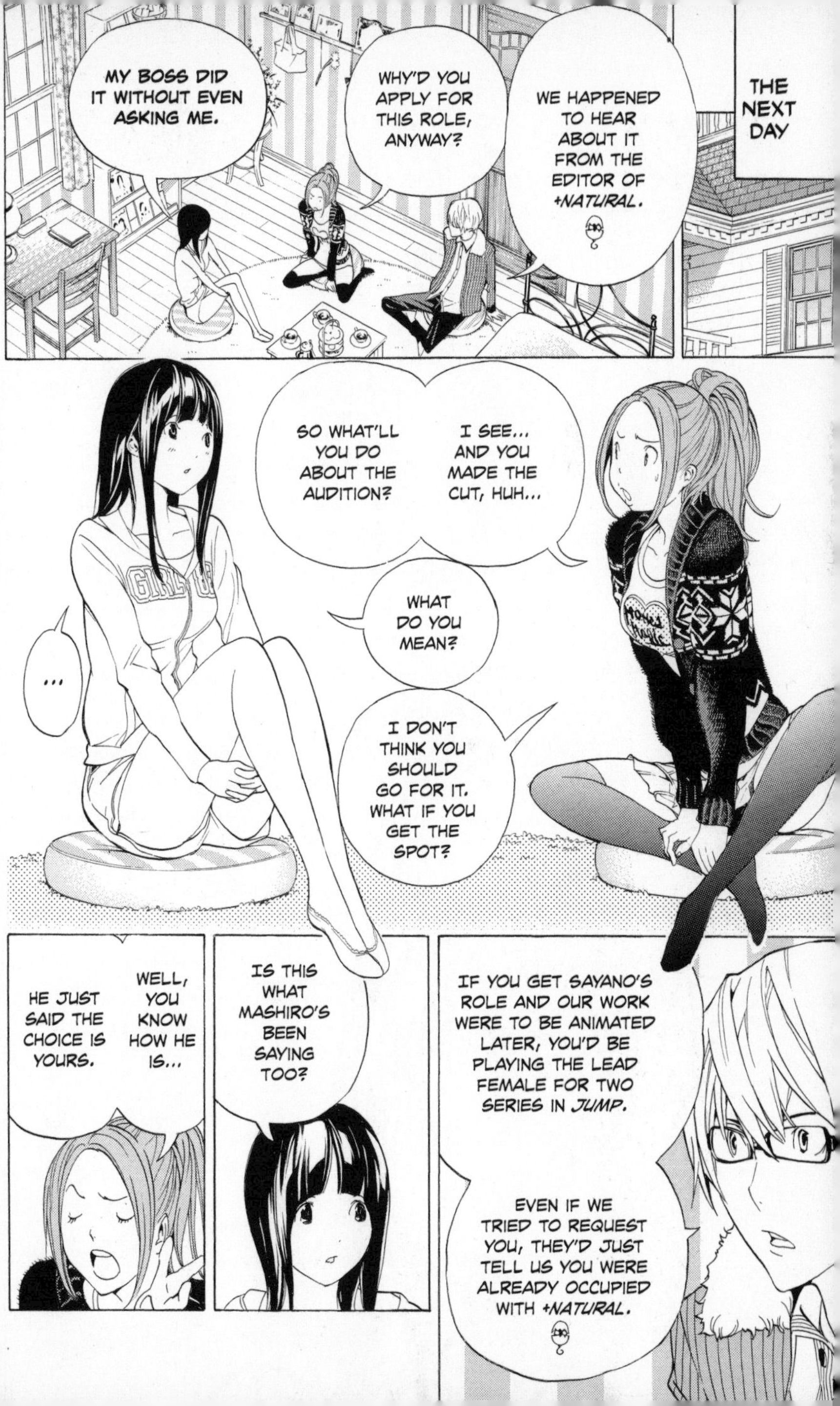
THE NEXT DAY
WE HAPPENED TO HEAR ABOUT IT FROM THE EDITOR OF *+NATURAL*.
WHY'D YOU APPLY FOR THIS ROLE, ANYWAY?
MY BOSS DID IT WITHOUT EVEN ASKING ME.
I SEE... AND YOU MADE THE CUT, HUH...
SO WHAT'LL YOU DO ABOUT THE AUDITION?
WHAT DO YOU MEAN?
I DON'T THINK YOU SHOULD GO FOR IT. WHAT IF YOU GET THE SPOT?
...
IF YOU GET SAYANO'S ROLE AND OUR WORK WERE TO BE ANIMATED LATER, YOU'D BE PLAYING THE LEAD FEMALE FOR TWO SERIES IN *JUMP*.
EVEN IF WE TRIED TO REQUEST YOU, THEY'D JUST TELL US YOU WERE ALREADY OCCUPIED WITH *+NATURAL*.
IS THIS WHAT MASHIRO'S BEEN SAYING TOO?
WELL, YOU KNOW HOW HE IS...
HE JUST SAID THE CHOICE IS YOURS.

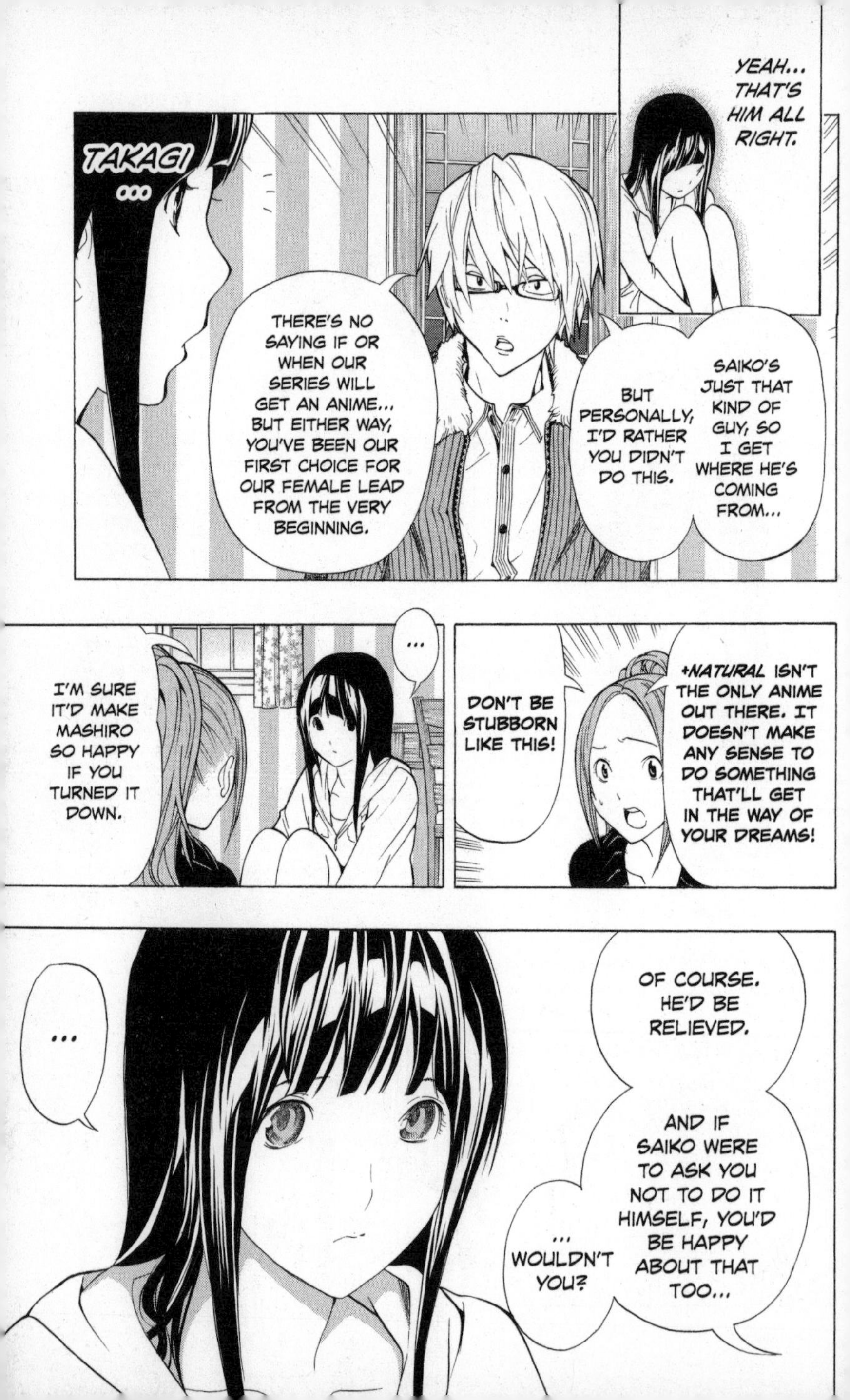
YEAH... THAT'S HIM ALL RIGHT.
TAKAGI ...
THERE'S NO SAYING IF OR WHEN OUR SERIES WILL GET AN ANIME... BUT EITHER WAY, YOU'VE BEEN OUR FIRST CHOICE FOR OUR FEMALE LEAD FROM THE VERY BEGINNING.
SAIKO'S JUST THAT KIND OF GUY, SO I GET WHERE HE'S COMING FROM...
BUT PERSONALLY, I'D RATHER YOU DIDN'T DO THIS.
+NATURAL ISN'T THE ONLY ANIME OUT THERE. IT DOESN'T MAKE ANY SENSE TO DO SOMETHING THAT'LL GET IN THE WAY OF YOUR DREAMS!
DON'T BE STUBBORN LIKE THIS!
...
I'M SURE IT'D MAKE MASHIRO SO HAPPY IF YOU TURNED IT DOWN.
OF COURSE. HE'D BE RELIEVED.
AND IF SAIKO WERE TO ASK YOU NOT TO DO IT HIMSELF, YOU'D BE HAPPY ABOUT THAT TOO...
... WOULDN'T YOU?
...

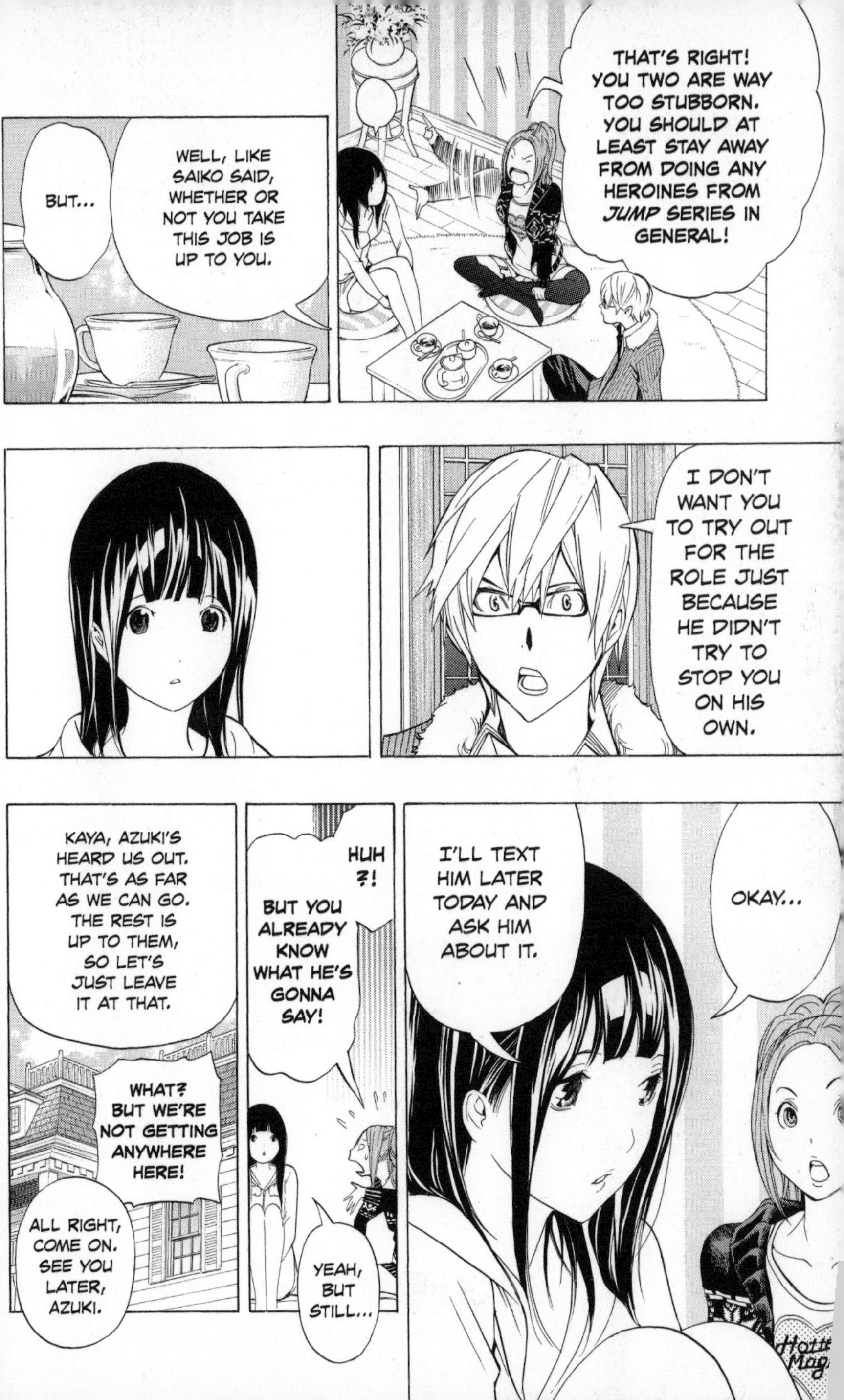
THAT'S RIGHT! YOU TWO ARE WAY TOO STUBBORN. YOU SHOULD AT LEAST STAY AWAY FROM DOING ANY HEROINES FROM *JUMP* SERIES IN GENERAL!
WELL, LIKE SAIKO SAID, WHETHER OR NOT YOU TAKE THIS JOB IS UP TO YOU.
BUT...
I DON'T WANT YOU TO TRY OUT FOR THE ROLE JUST BECAUSE HE DIDN'T TRY TO STOP YOU ON HIS OWN.
OKAY...
I'LL TEXT HIM LATER TODAY AND ASK HIM ABOUT IT.
HUH ?!
BUT YOU ALREADY KNOW WHAT HE'S GONNA SAY!
YEAH, BUT STILL...
KAYA, AZUKI'S HEARD US OUT. THAT'S AS FAR AS WE CAN GO. THE REST IS UP TO THEM, SO LET'S JUST LEAVE IT AT THAT.
WHAT? BUT WE'RE NOT GETTING ANYWHERE HERE!
ALL RIGHT, COME ON. SEE YOU LATER, AZUKI.

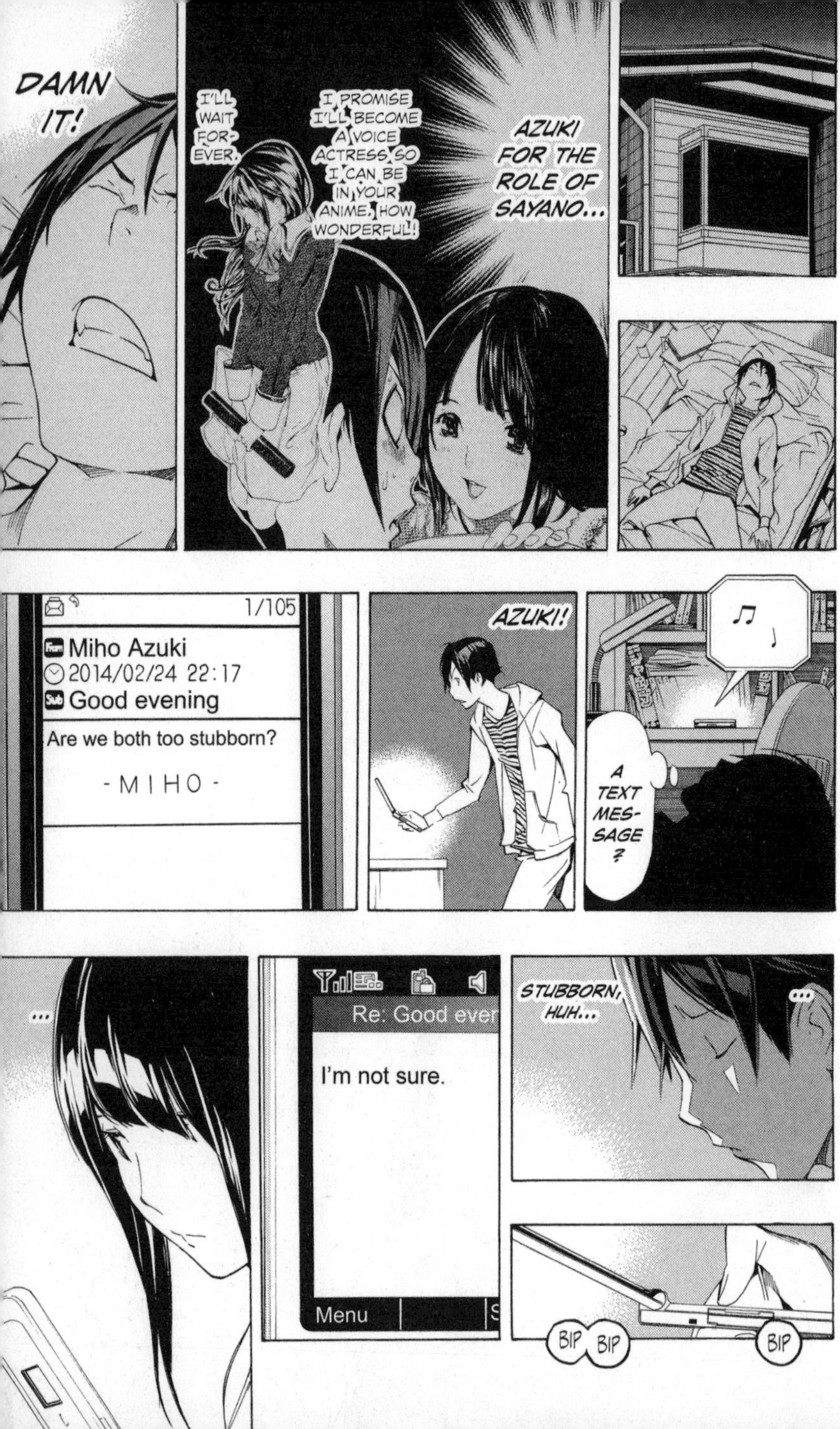
AZUKI FOR THE ROLE OF SAYANO...
I PROMISE I'LL BECOME A VOICE ACTRESS SO I CAN BE IN YOUR ANIME. HOW WONDERFUL!
I'LL WAIT FOREVER.
DAMN IT!
♫ ♩
A TEXT MESSAGE?
AZUKI!
1/105
Miho Azuki
2014/02/24 22:17
Good evening
Are we both too stubborn?
-MIHO-
...
STUBBORN, HUH...
BIP BIP
BIP
Re: Good ever
I'm not sure.
Menu
...

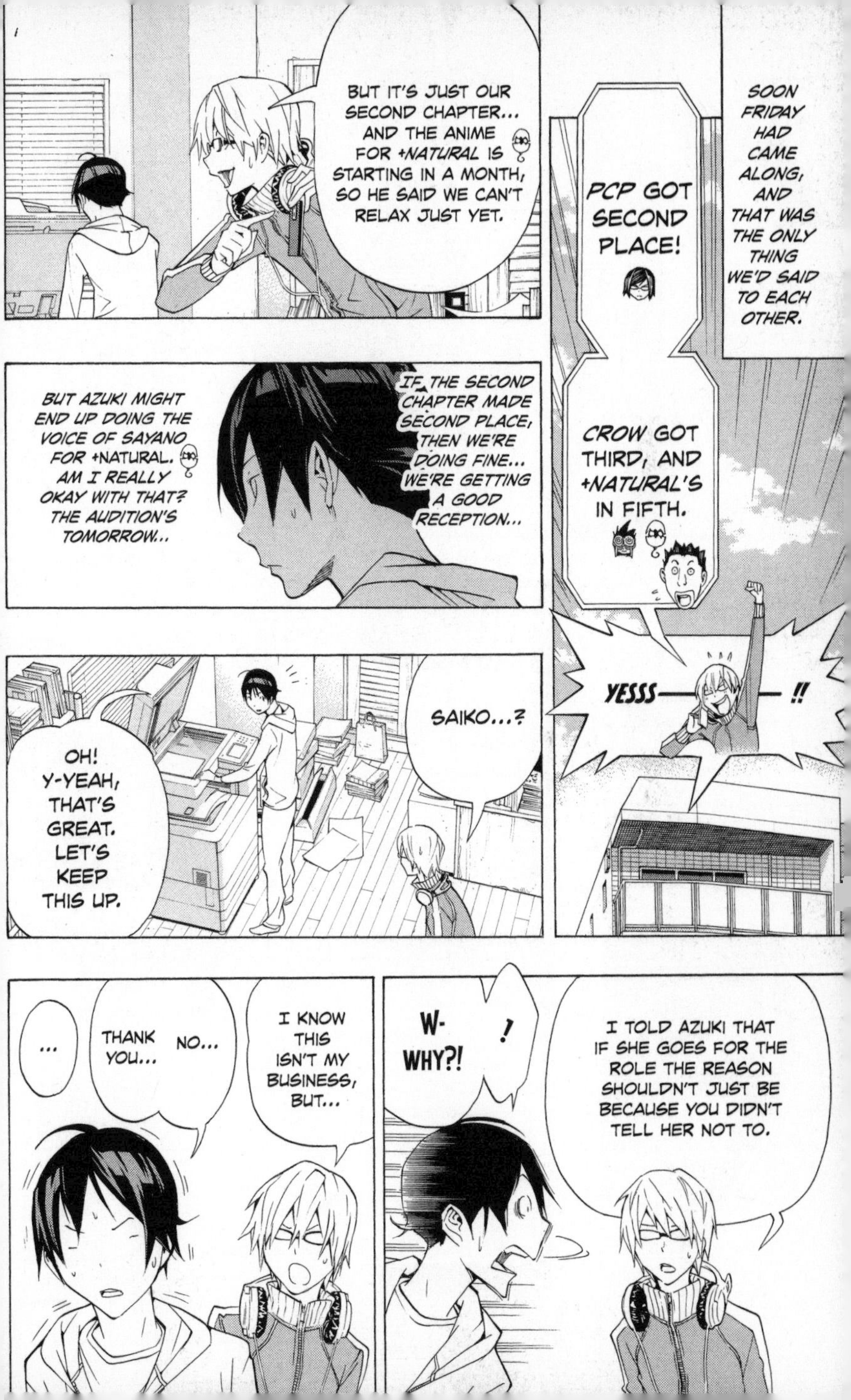
SOON FRIDAY HAD CAME ALONG, AND THAT WAS THE ONLY THING WE'D SAID TO EACH OTHER.
PCP GOT SECOND PLACE!
CROW GOT THIRD, AND +NATURAL'S IN FIFTH.
YESSS—!!
BUT IT'S JUST OUR SECOND CHAPTER... AND THE ANIME FOR +NATURAL IS STARTING IN A MONTH, SO HE SAID WE CAN'T RELAX JUST YET.
IF THE SECOND CHAPTER MADE SECOND PLACE, THEN WE'RE DOING FINE... WE'RE GETTING A GOOD RECEPTION...
BUT AZUKI MIGHT END UP DOING THE VOICE OF SAYANO FOR +NATURAL. AM I REALLY OKAY WITH THAT? THE AUDITION'S TOMORROW...
SAIKO...?
OH! Y-YEAH, THAT'S GREAT. LET'S KEEP THIS UP.
I TOLD AZUKI THAT IF SHE GOES FOR THE ROLE THE REASON SHOULDN'T JUST BE BECAUSE YOU DIDN'T TELL HER NOT TO.
!
W- WHY?!
I KNOW THIS ISN'T MY BUSINESS, BUT...
NO...
THANK YOU...
...

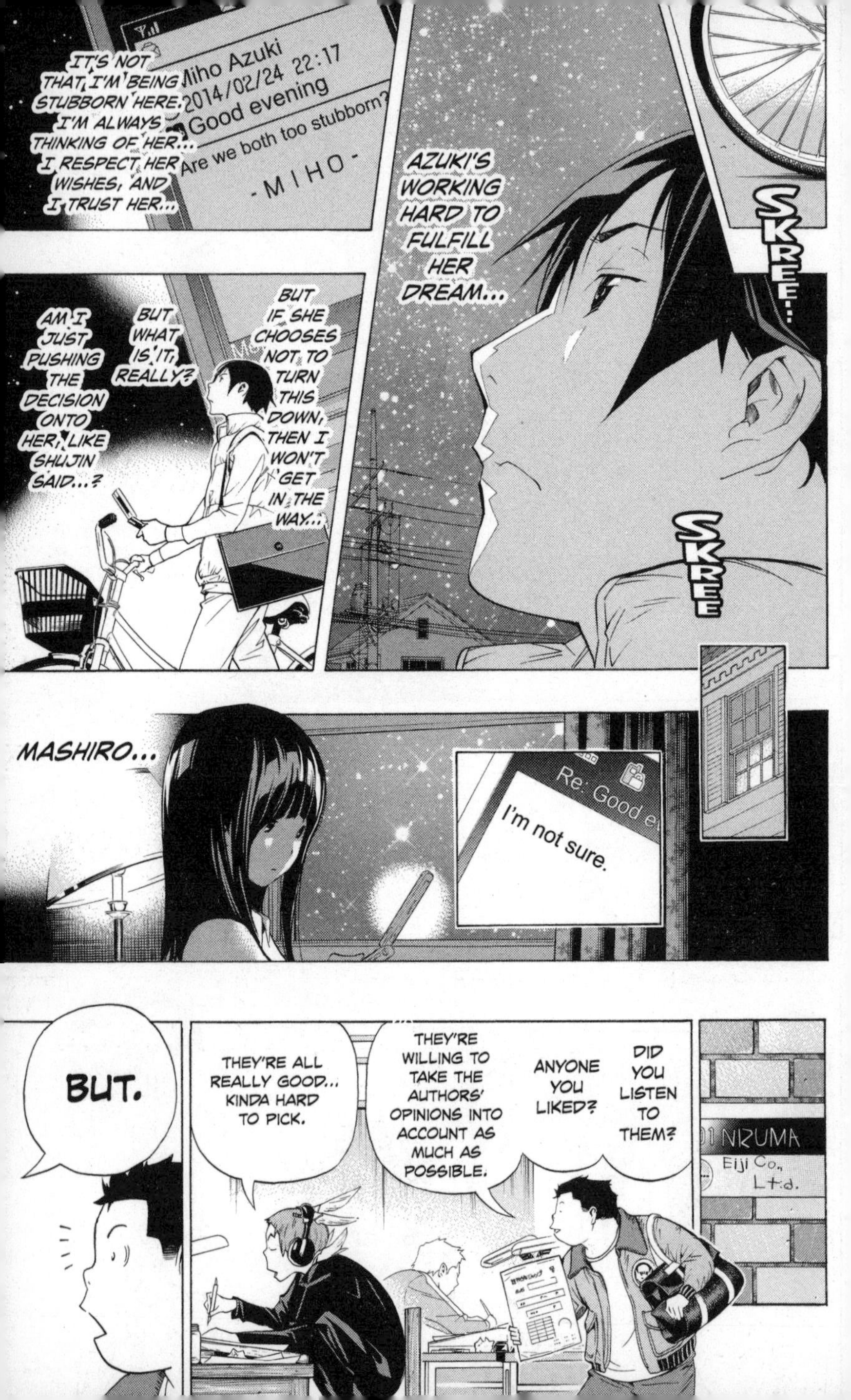
SKREE...
AZUKI'S WORKING HARD TO FULFILL HER DREAM...
SKREE
Miho Azuki
2014/02/24 22:17
Good evening
Are we both too stubborn?
-MIHO-
IT'S NOT THAT I'M BEING STUBBORN HERE. I'M ALWAYS THINKING OF HER... I RESPECT HER WISHES, AND I TRUST HER...
BUT IF SHE CHOOSES NOT TO TURN THIS DOWN, THEN I WON'T GET IN THE WAY...
BUT WHAT IS IT, REALLY?
AM I JUST PUSHING THE DECISION ONTO HER, LIKE SHUJIN SAID...?
Re: Good e
I'm not sure.
MASHIRO...
01 NIZUMA
Eiji Co., Ltd.
DID YOU LISTEN TO THEM?
ANYONE YOU LIKED?
THEY'RE WILLING TO TAKE THE AUTHORS' OPINIONS INTO ACCOUNT AS MUCH AS POSSIBLE.
THEY'RE ALL REALLY GOOD... KINDA HARD TO PICK.
BUT.

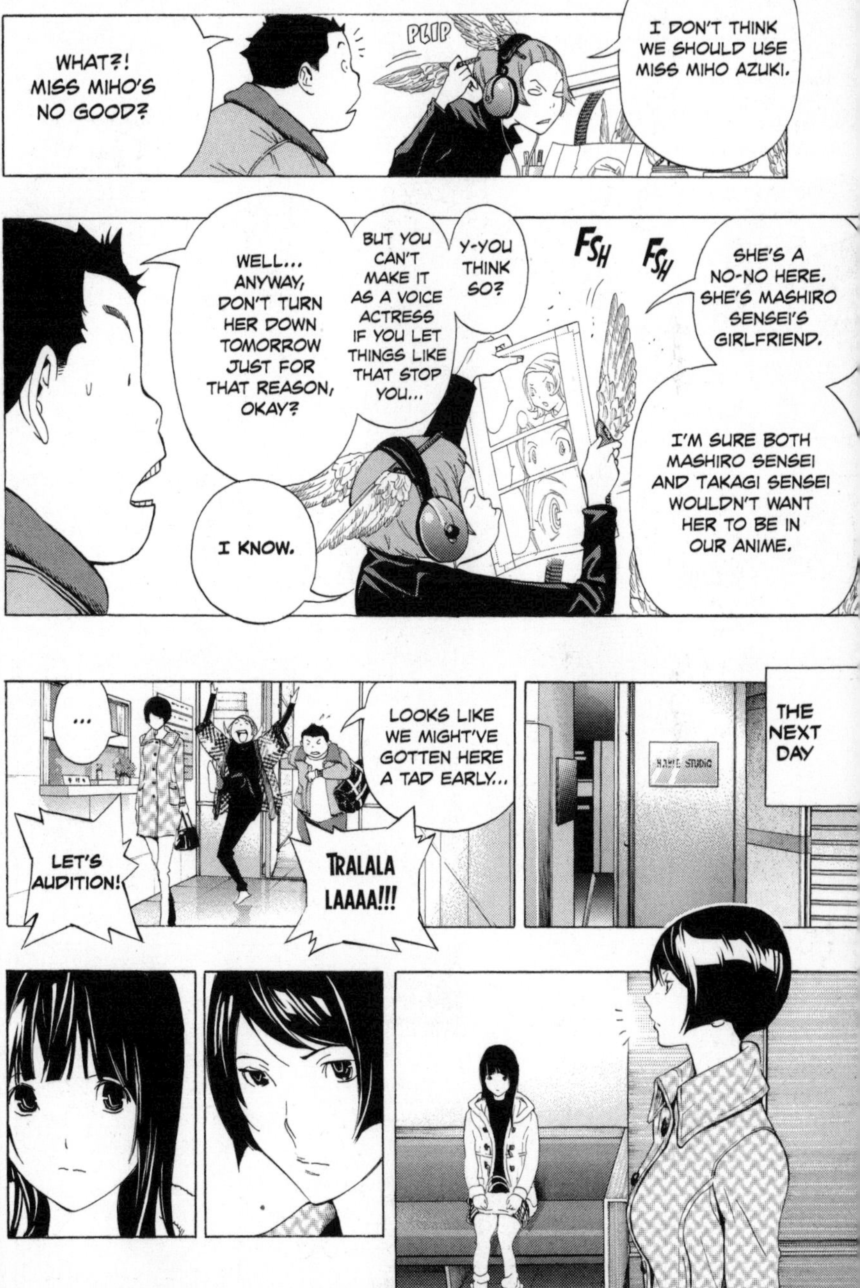
I DON'T THINK WE SHOULD USE MISS MIHO AZUKI.
PLIP
WHAT?! MISS MIHO'S NO GOOD?
SHE'S A NO-NO HERE. SHE'S MASHIRO SENSEI'S GIRLFRIEND.
FSH
FSH
I'M SURE BOTH MASHIRO SENSEI AND TAKAGI SENSEI WOULDN'T WANT HER TO BE IN OUR ANIME.
Y-YOU THINK SO?
BUT YOU CAN'T MAKE IT AS A VOICE ACTRESS IF YOU LET THINGS LIKE THAT STOP YOU...
I KNOW.
WELL... ANYWAY, DON'T TURN HER DOWN TOMORROW JUST FOR THAT REASON, OKAY?
THE NEXT DAY
LOOKS LIKE WE MIGHT'VE GOTTEN HERE A TAD EARLY...
TRALALA LAAAA!!!
...
LET'S AUDITION!

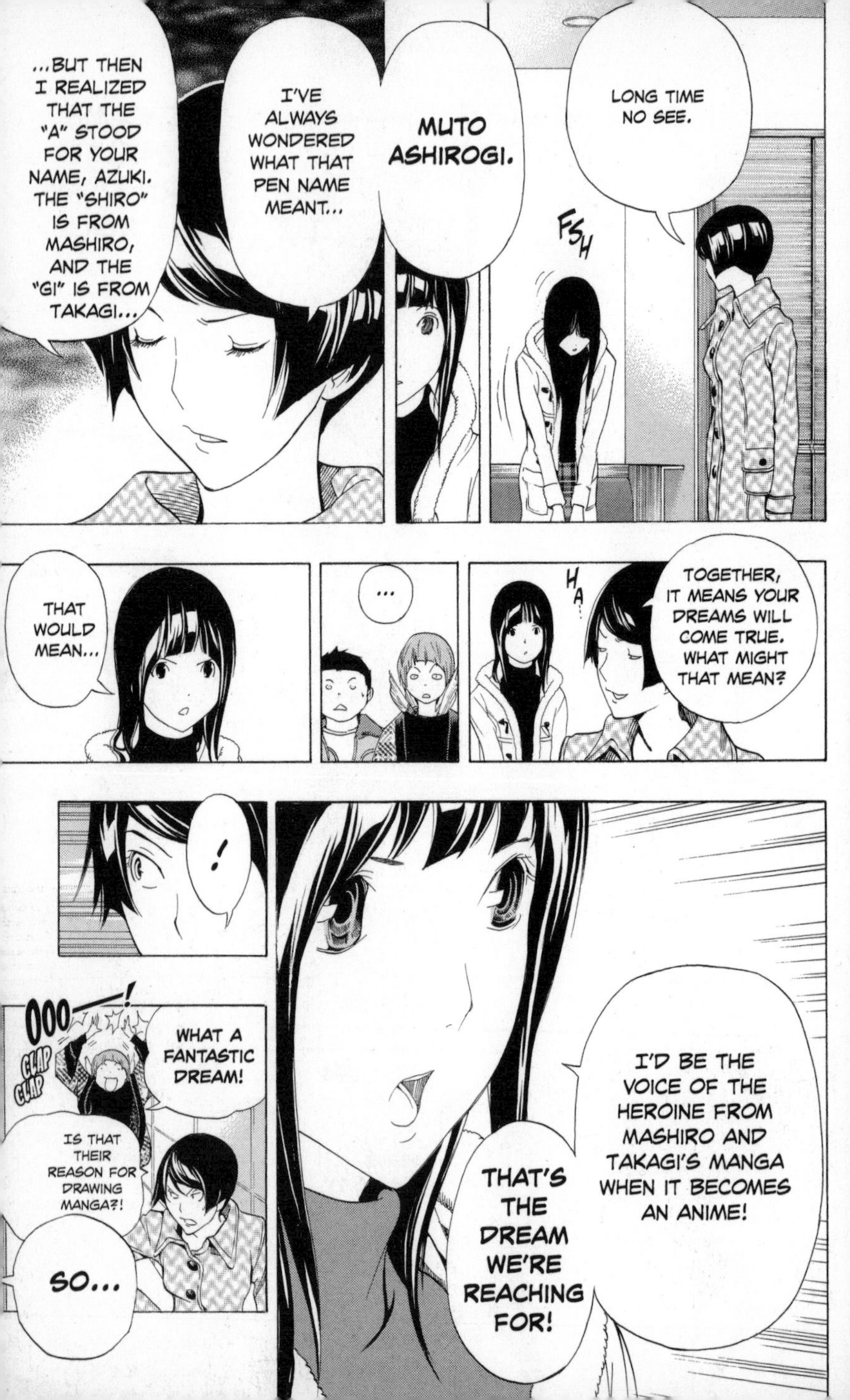
LONG TIME NO SEE.
FSH
MUTO ASHIROGI.
I'VE ALWAYS WONDERED WHAT THAT PEN NAME MEANT...
...BUT THEN I REALIZED THAT THE "A" STOOD FOR YOUR NAME, AZUKI. THE "SHIRO" IS FROM MASHIRO, AND THE "GI" IS FROM TAKAGI...
HA...
TOGETHER, IT MEANS YOUR DREAMS WILL COME TRUE. WHAT MIGHT THAT MEAN?
...
THAT WOULD MEAN...
I'D BE THE VOICE OF THE HEROINE FROM MASHIRO AND TAKAGI'S MANGA WHEN IT BECOMES AN ANIME!
THAT'S THE DREAM WE'RE REACHING FOR!
!
OOO—!
CLAP CLAP
WHAT A FANTASTIC DREAM!
IS THAT THEIR REASON FOR DRAWING MANGA?!
SO...

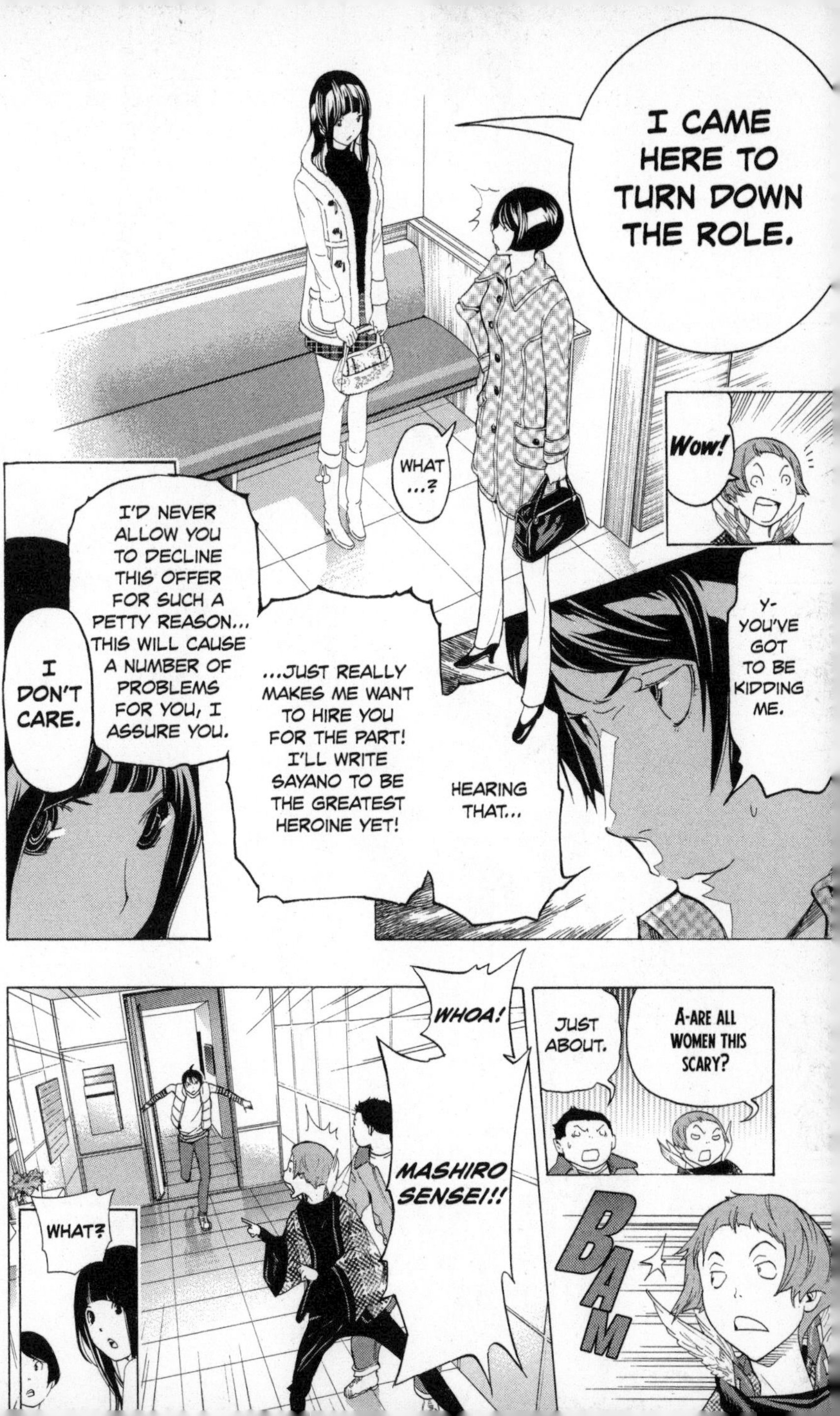
I CAME HERE TO TURN DOWN THE ROLE.
Wow!
WHAT ...?
Y-YOU'VE GOT TO BE KIDDING ME.
HEARING THAT...
...JUST REALLY MAKES ME WANT TO HIRE YOU FOR THE PART! I'LL WRITE SAYANO TO BE THE GREATEST HEROINE YET!
I'D NEVER ALLOW YOU TO DECLINE THIS OFFER FOR SUCH A PETTY REASON... THIS WILL CAUSE A NUMBER OF PROBLEMS FOR YOU, I ASSURE YOU.
I DON'T CARE.
A-ARE ALL WOMEN THIS SCARY?
JUST ABOUT.
BAM
WHOA!
MASHIRO SENSEI!!
WHAT?

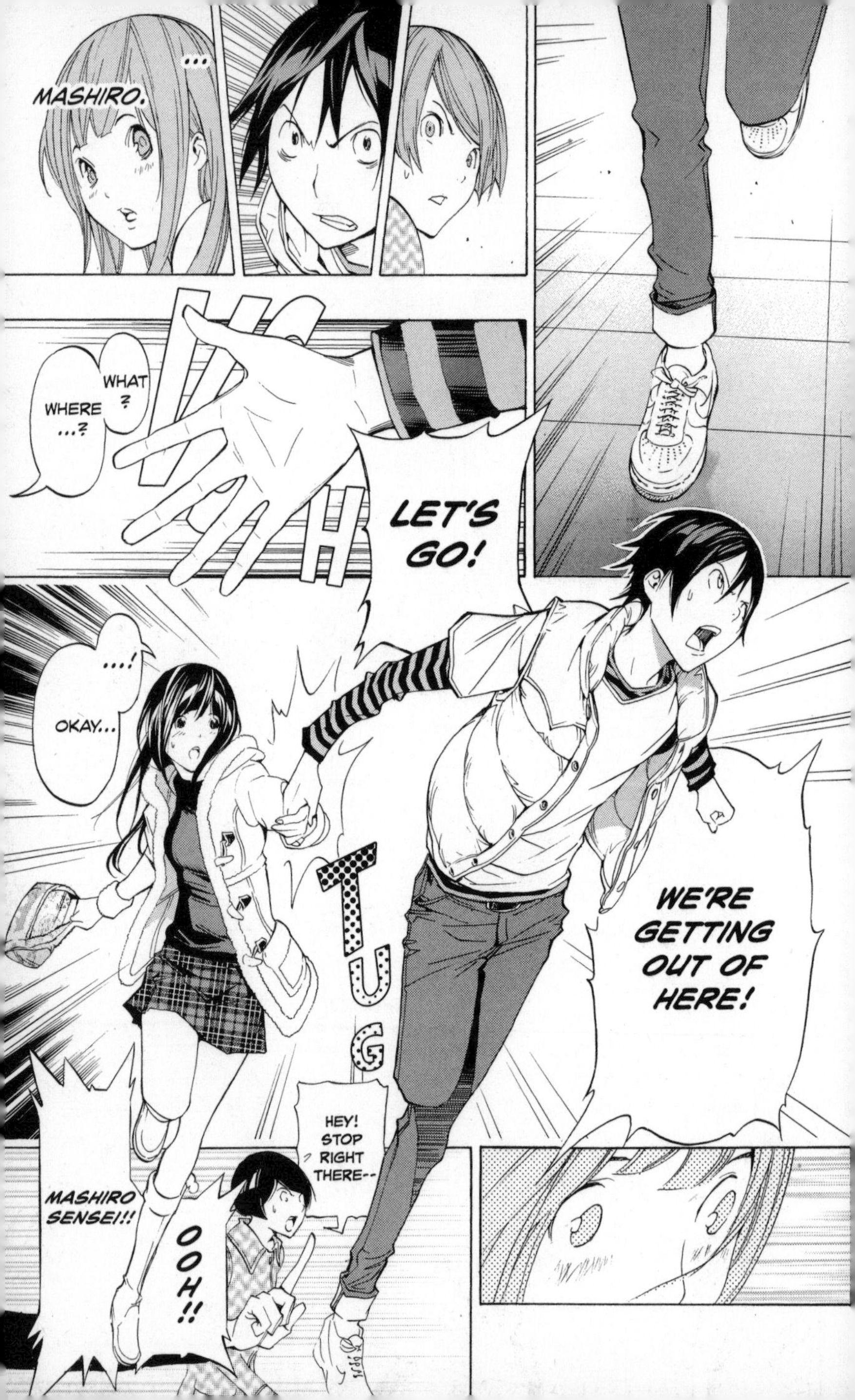
...
MASHIRO.
LET'S GO!
WHAT? WHERE...?
WE'RE GETTING OUT OF HERE!
TUG
...! OKAY...
HEY! STOP RIGHT THERE--
OOH!!
MASHIRO SENSEI!!

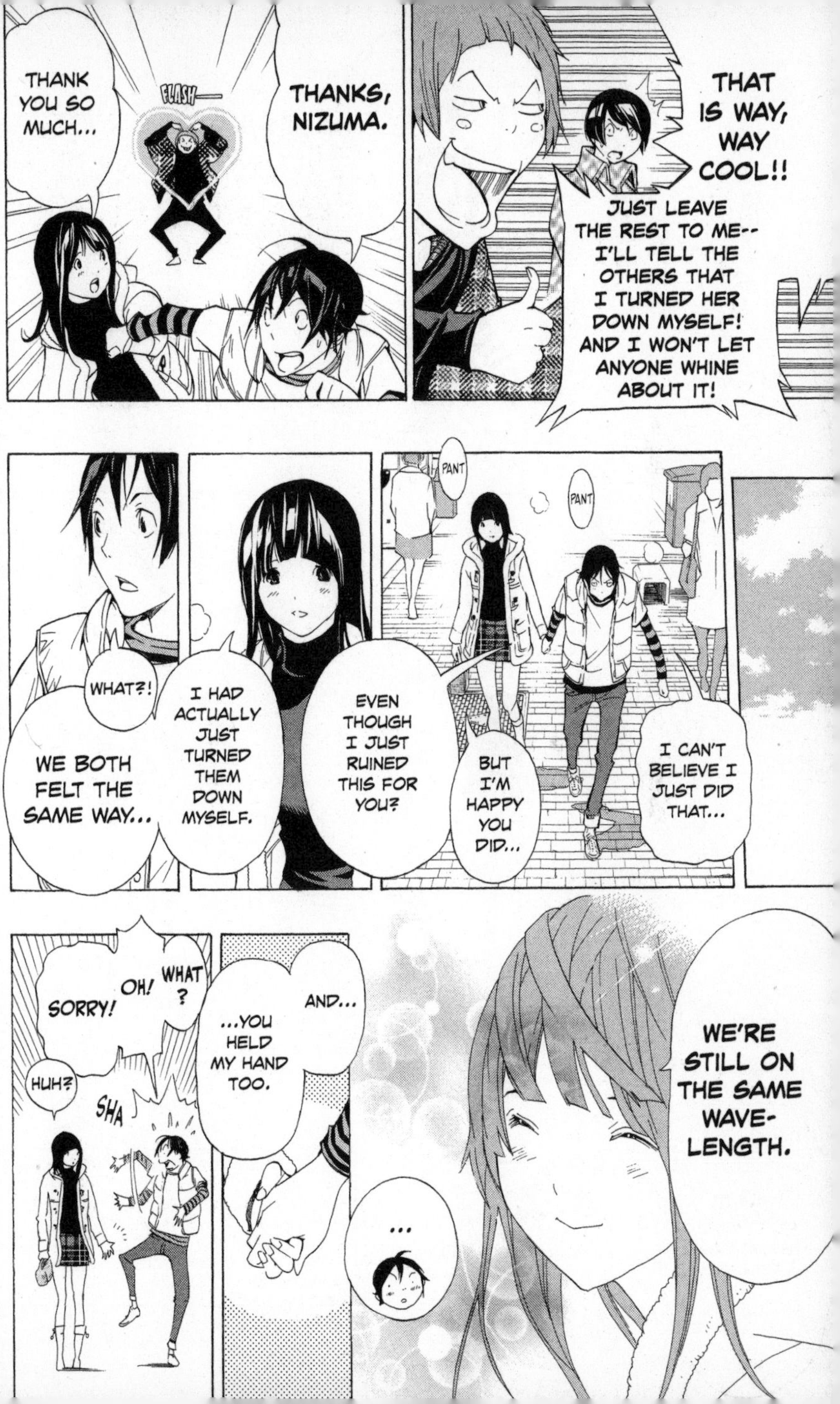
THAT IS WAY, WAY COOL!!
JUST LEAVE THE REST TO ME-- I'LL TELL THE OTHERS THAT I TURNED HER DOWN MYSELF! AND I WON'T LET ANYONE WHINE ABOUT IT!
THANKS, NIZUMA.
FLASH—
THANK YOU SO MUCH...
PANT
PANT
I CAN'T BELIEVE I JUST DID THAT...
BUT I'M HAPPY YOU DID...
EVEN THOUGH I JUST RUINED THIS FOR YOU?
I HAD ACTUALLY JUST TURNED THEM DOWN MYSELF.
WHAT?!
WE BOTH FELT THE SAME WAY...
WE'RE STILL ON THE SAME WAVE-LENGTH.
...
AND...
...YOU HELD MY HAND TOO.
WHAT?
OH!
SORRY!
HUH?
SHA

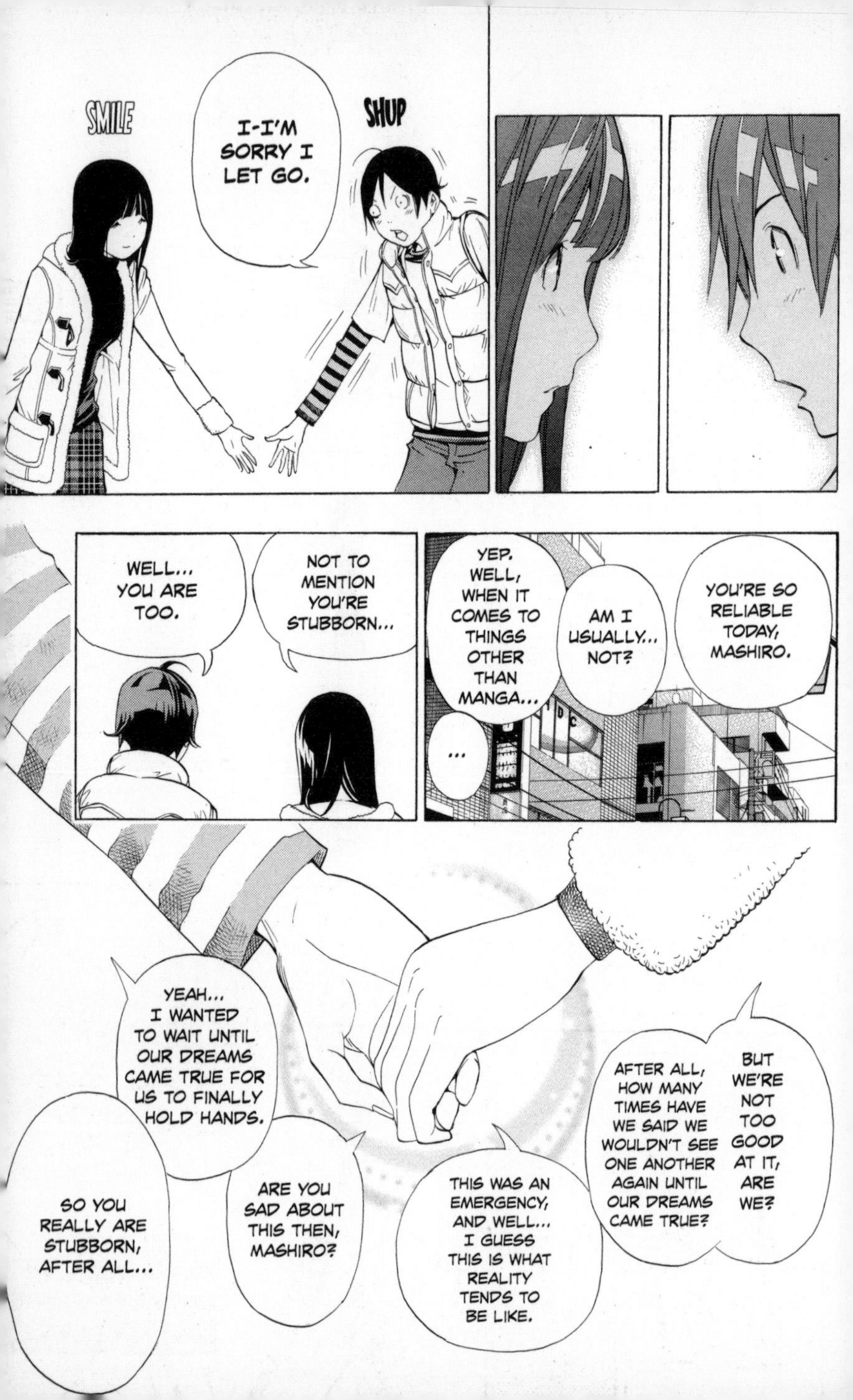
SHUP
I-I'M SORRY I LET GO.
SMILE
YOU'RE SO RELIABLE TODAY, MASHIRO.
AM I USUALLY... NOT?
YEP. WELL, WHEN IT COMES TO THINGS OTHER THAN MANGA...
...
NOT TO MENTION YOU'RE STUBBORN...
WELL... YOU ARE TOO.
BUT WE'RE NOT TOO GOOD AT IT, ARE WE?
AFTER ALL, HOW MANY TIMES HAVE WE SAID WE WOULDN'T SEE ONE ANOTHER AGAIN UNTIL OUR DREAMS CAME TRUE?
THIS WAS AN EMERGENCY, AND WELL... I GUESS THIS IS WHAT REALITY TENDS TO BE LIKE.
ARE YOU SAD ABOUT THIS THEN, MASHIRO?
YEAH... I WANTED TO WAIT UNTIL OUR DREAMS CAME TRUE FOR US TO FINALLY HOLD HANDS.
SO YOU REALLY ARE STUBBORN, AFTER ALL...

OHBA'S STORYBOARD

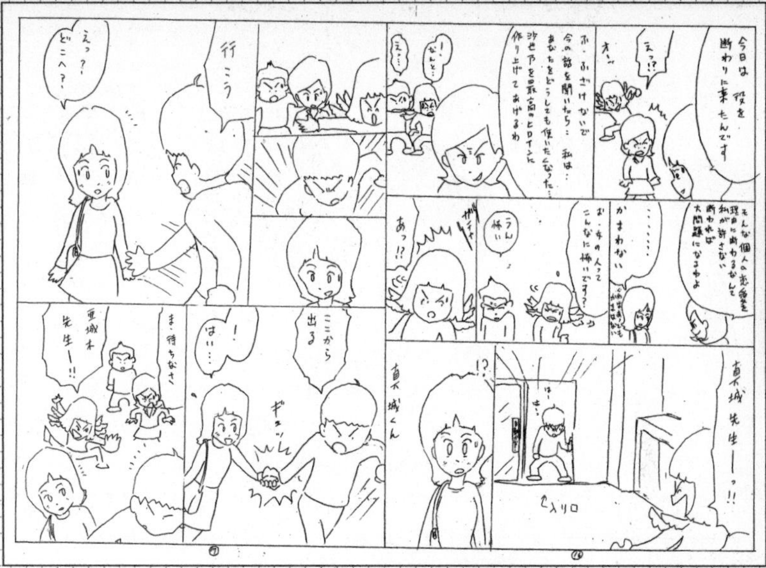

今日は役を断わりに来たんです
えっ!?
オー
ふ・ふざけないで 今の話を聞いたら… 私は… あなたをどうしても使いたくなった… 沙也乃を最高のヒロインに作り上げてあげるわ
!なんと…
え…
そんな個人の恋愛を理由に断わるなんて私が許さない 断われば大問題になるわよ
……かまわない
お・女の人ってこんなに怖いです?
うん 怖い
ガチャ
あっ!?
行こう
えっ?どこへ?
ここから出る
!はい…
ま・待ちなさい
亜城木先生ー!!
ギュッ
亜城木先生ーっ!!
は…
入り口
!?
亜城木くん

OBATA'S STORYBOARD

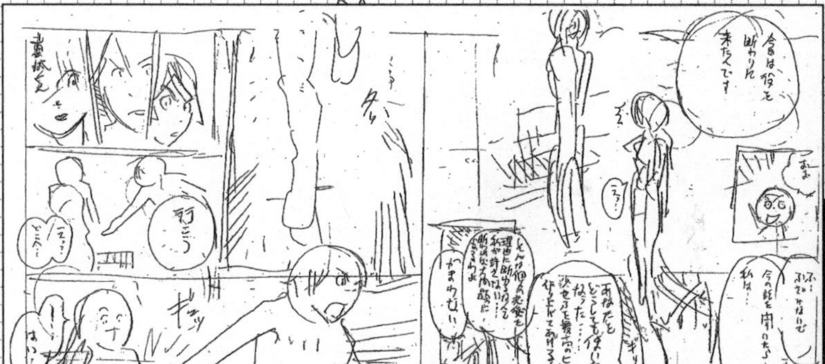

今日は役を断わりに来たんです
えっ…
ふ・ふざけないで 今の話を聞いたら 私は…
あなたをどうしてもほしくなった… 沙也乃を最高のヒロインに作り上げてあげるわ
ギリ…
かまわない!!
行こう
えっ…どこへ…
ギュッ
!はい…!!

COMPLETE!

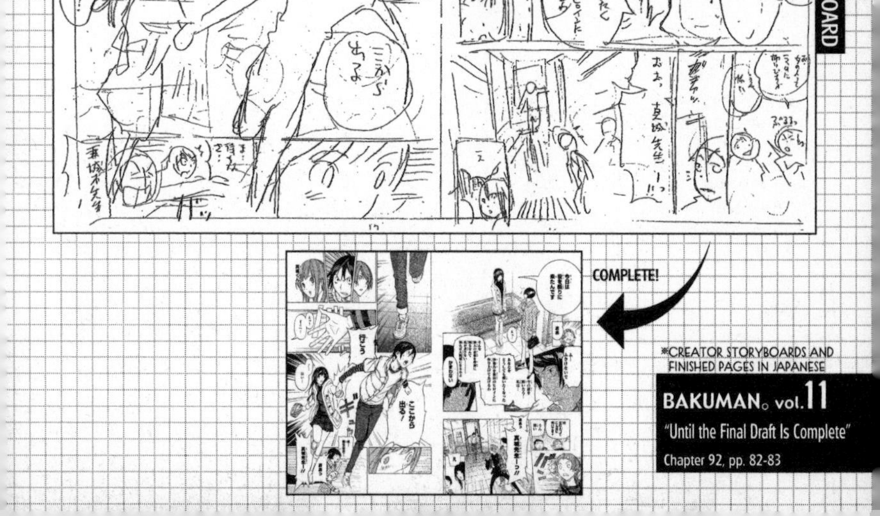

※CREATOR STORYBOARDS AND FINISHED PAGES IN JAPANESE

BAKUMAN。 vol.11

"Until the Final Draft Is Complete"

Chapter 92, pp. 82-83

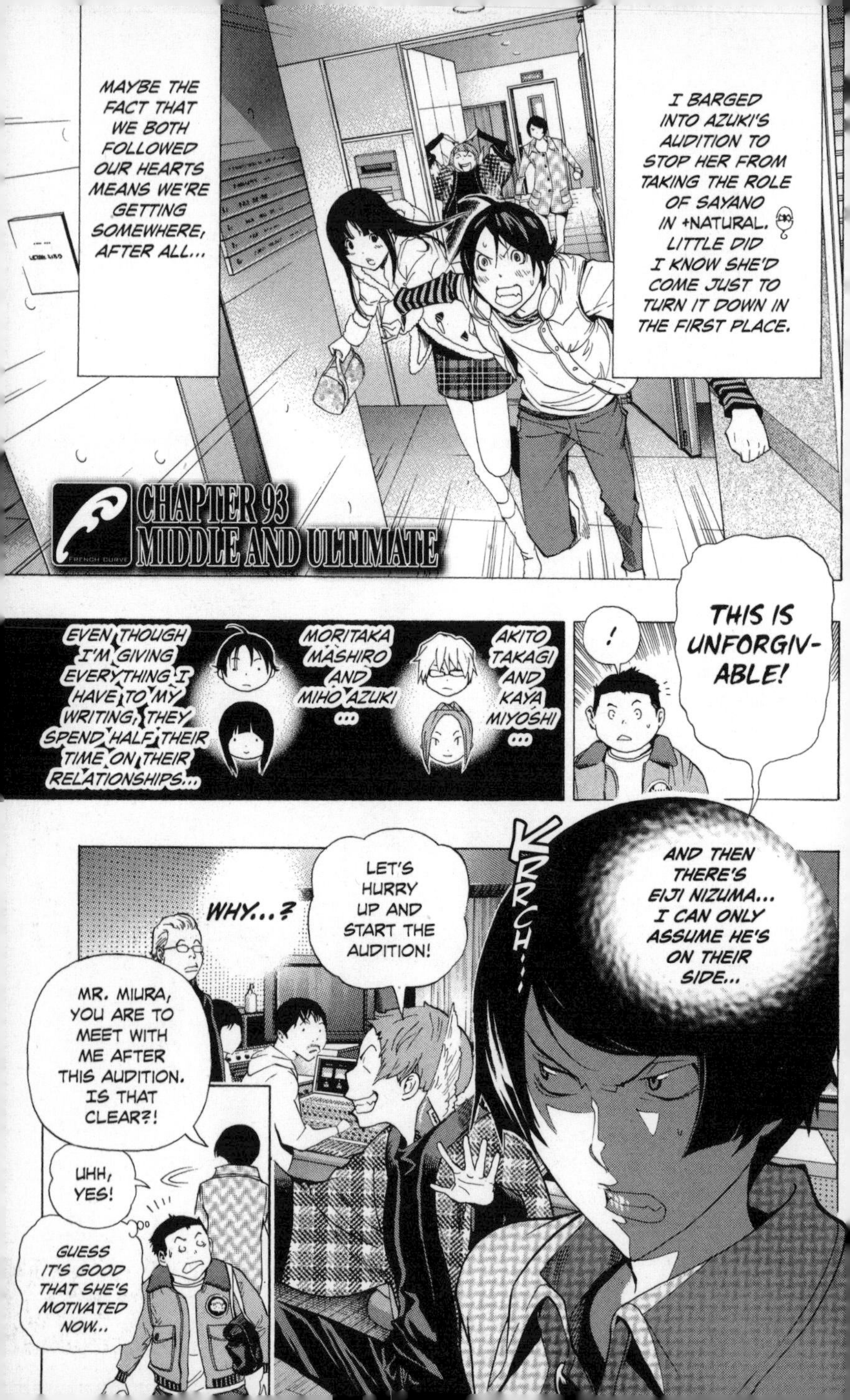
I BARGED INTO AZUKI'S AUDITION TO STOP HER FROM TAKING THE ROLE OF SAYANO IN +NATURAL. LITTLE DID I KNOW SHE'D COME JUST TO TURN IT DOWN IN THE FIRST PLACE.
MAYBE THE FACT THAT WE BOTH FOLLOWED OUR HEARTS MEANS WE'RE GETTING SOMEWHERE, AFTER ALL...
CHAPTER 93
MIDDLE AND ULTIMATE
!
THIS IS UNFORGIVABLE!
EVEN THOUGH I'M GIVING EVERYTHING I HAVE TO MY WRITING, THEY SPEND HALF THEIR TIME ON THEIR RELATIONSHIPS...
MORITAKA MASHIRO AND MIHO AZUKI...
AKITO TAKAGI AND KAYA MIYOSHI...
AND THEN THERE'S EIJI NIZUMA... I CAN ONLY ASSUME HE'S ON THEIR SIDE...
KRRCH...
LET'S HURRY UP AND START THE AUDITION!
WHY...?
MR. MIURA, YOU ARE TO MEET WITH ME AFTER THIS AUDITION. IS THAT CLEAR?!
UHH, YES!
GUESS IT'S GOOD THAT SHE'S MOTIVATED NOW...

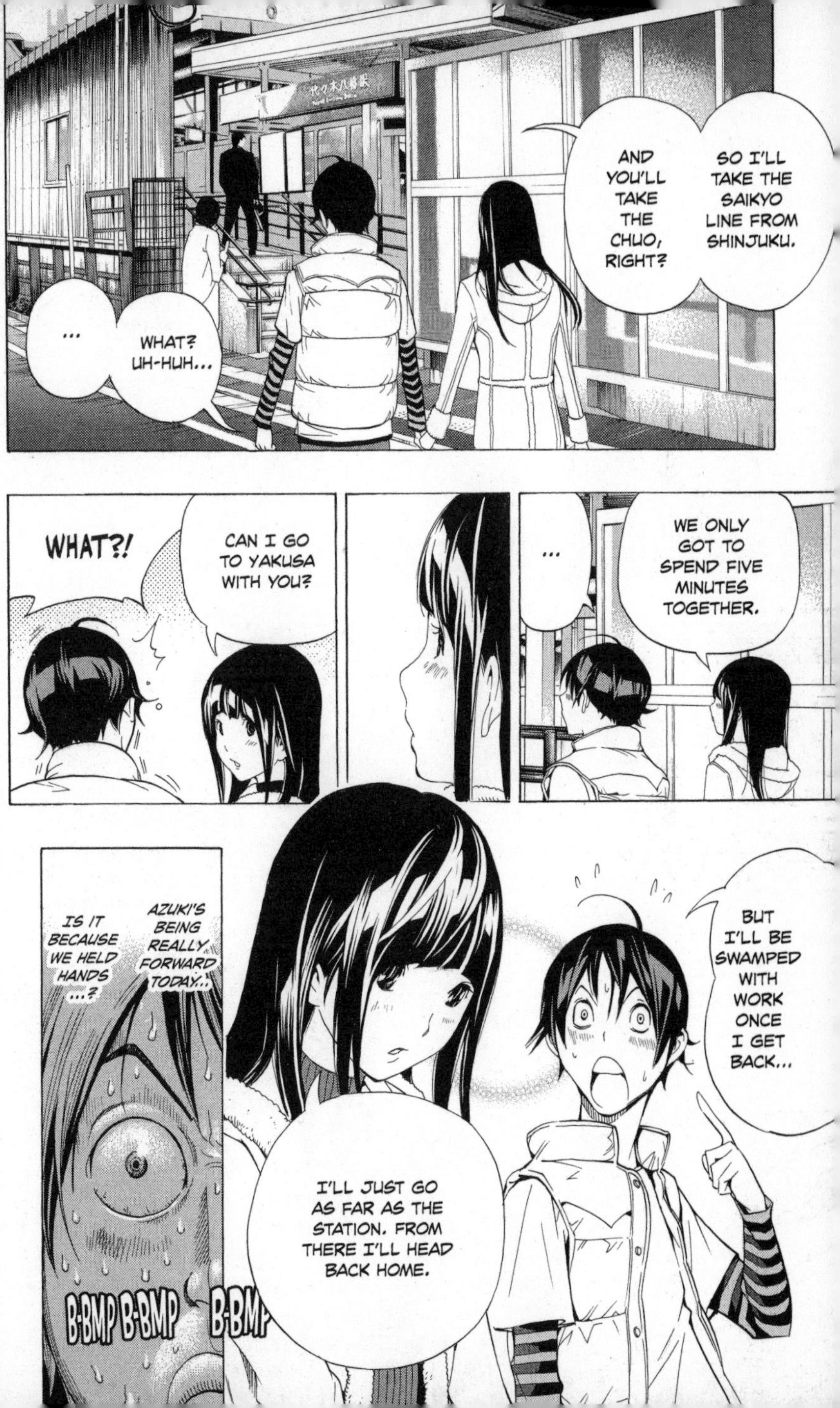
SO I'LL TAKE THE SAIKYO LINE FROM SHINJUKU.
AND YOU'LL TAKE THE CHUO, RIGHT?
WHAT? UH-HUH...
...
WE ONLY GOT TO SPEND FIVE MINUTES TOGETHER.
...
CAN I GO TO YAKUSA WITH YOU?
WHAT?!
BUT I'LL BE SWAMPED WITH WORK ONCE I GET BACK...
I'LL JUST GO AS FAR AS THE STATION. FROM THERE I'LL HEAD BACK HOME.
AZUKI'S BEING REALLY FORWARD TODAY...
IS IT BECAUSE WE HELD HANDS ...?
B-BMP B-BMP B-BMP

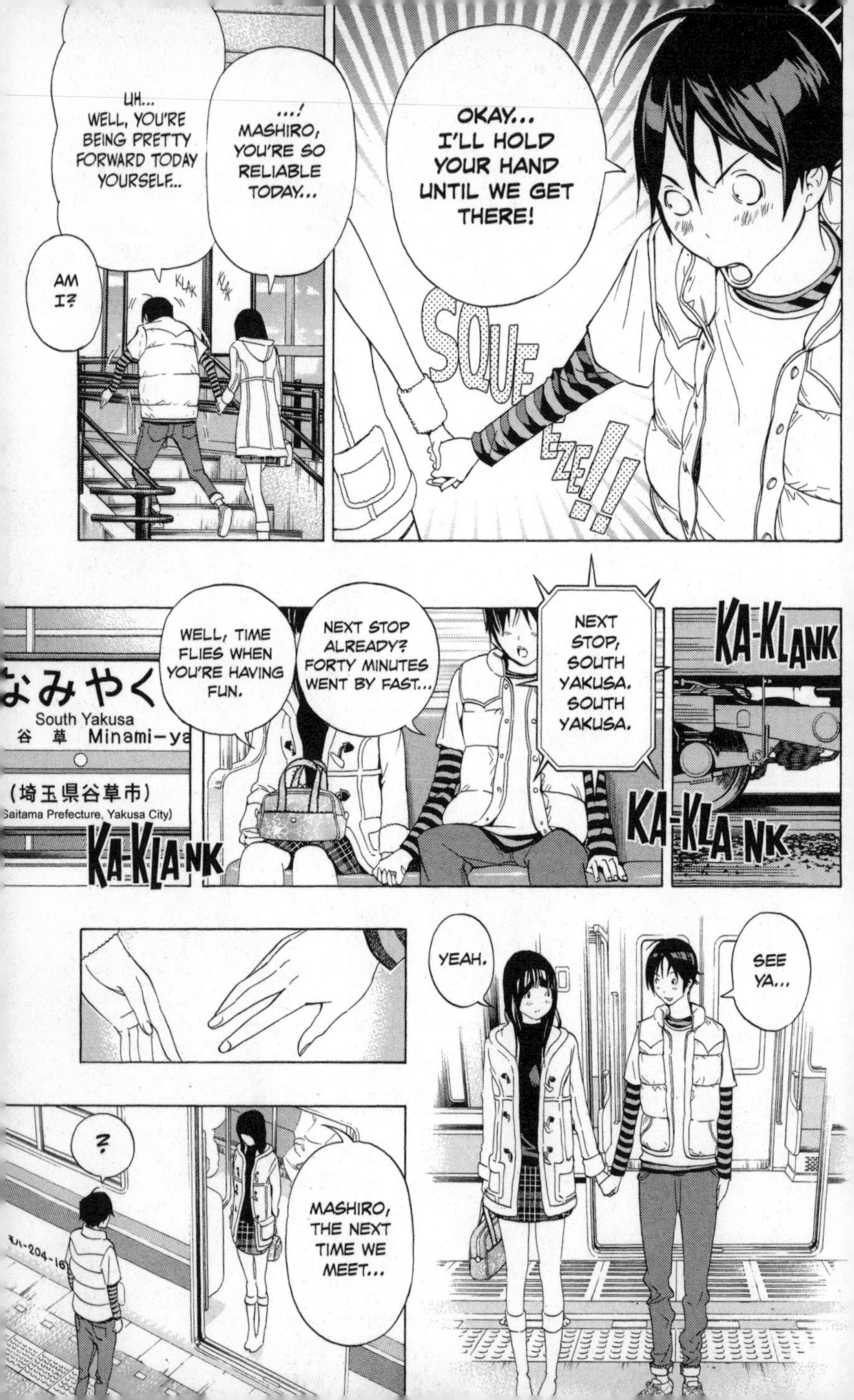
OKAY... I'LL HOLD YOUR HAND UNTIL WE GET THERE!
SQUEEZE!!
...! MASHIRO, YOU'RE SO RELIABLE TODAY...
UH... WELL, YOU'RE BEING PRETTY FORWARD TODAY YOURSELF...
AM I?
KLAK
KLAK
KA-KLANK
KA-KLANK
NEXT STOP, SOUTH YAKUSA. SOUTH YAKUSA.
NEXT STOP ALREADY? FORTY MINUTES WENT BY FAST...
WELL, TIME FLIES WHEN YOU'RE HAVING FUN.
なみやく
South Yakusa
谷 草 Minami-ya
(埼玉県谷草市)
aitama Prefecture, Yakusa City)
KA-KLANK
SEE YA...
YEAH.
MASHIRO, THE NEXT TIME WE MEET...
?
モハ-204-16

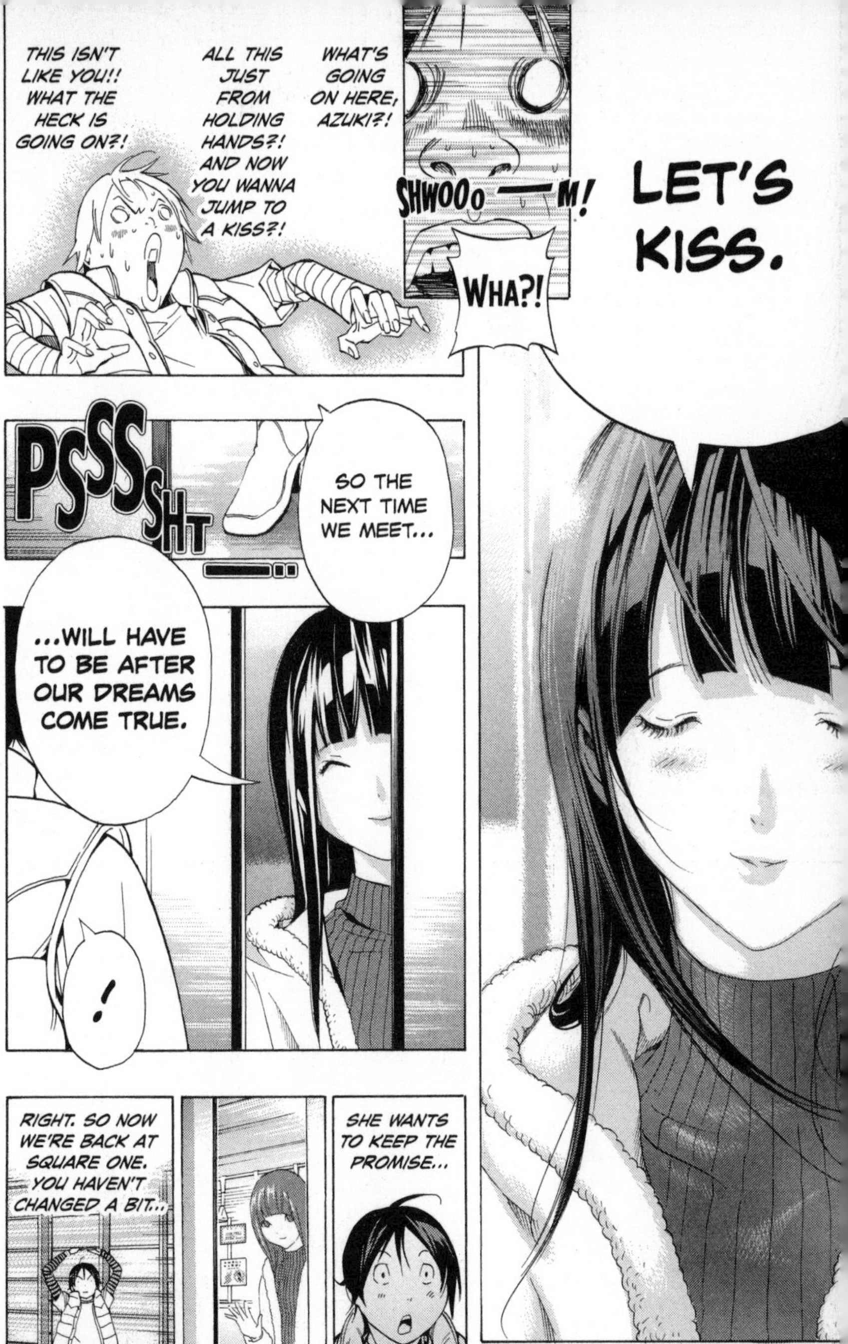
LET'S KISS.
SHWOOo—M!
WHA?!
WHAT'S GOING ON HERE, AZUKI?!
ALL THIS JUST FROM HOLDING HANDS?! AND NOW YOU WANNA JUMP TO A KISS?!
THIS ISN'T LIKE YOU!! WHAT THE HECK IS GOING ON?!
PSSSSHT
SO THE NEXT TIME WE MEET...
...WILL HAVE TO BE AFTER OUR DREAMS COME TRUE.
!
SHE WANTS TO KEEP THE PROMISE...
RIGHT. SO NOW WE'RE BACK AT SQUARE ONE. YOU HAVEN'T CHANGED A BIT...

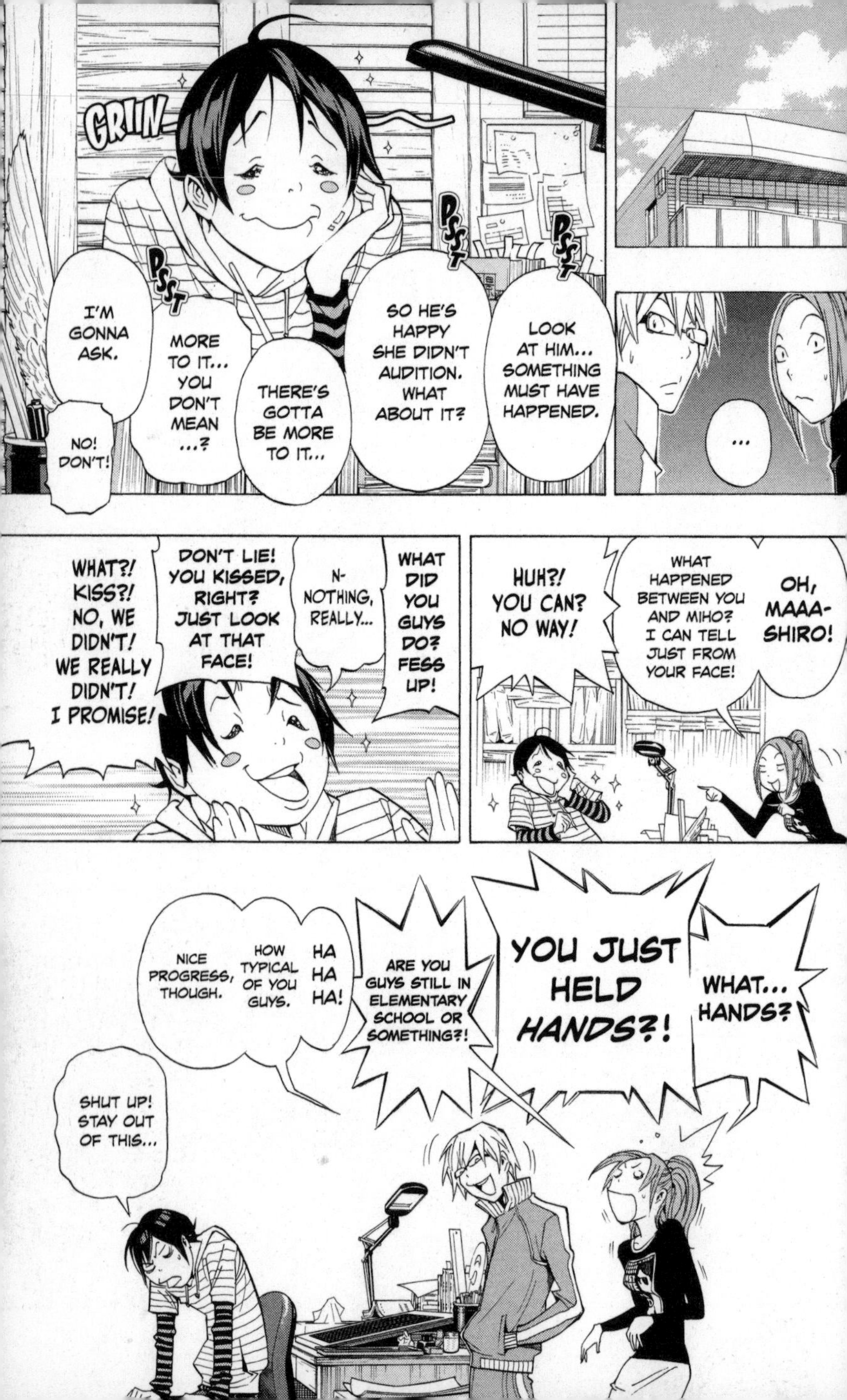
...
LOOK AT HIM... SOMETHING MUST HAVE HAPPENED.
PSST
SO HE'S HAPPY SHE DIDN'T AUDITION. WHAT ABOUT IT?
PSST
THERE'S GOTTA BE MORE TO IT...
MORE TO IT... YOU DON'T MEAN ...?
PSST
I'M GONNA ASK.
NO! DON'T!
GRIIN
OH, MAAA-SHIRO!
WHAT HAPPENED BETWEEN YOU AND MIHO? I CAN TELL JUST FROM YOUR FACE!
HUH?! YOU CAN? NO WAY!
WHAT DID YOU GUYS DO? FESS UP!
N-NOTHING, REALLY...
DON'T LIE! YOU KISSED, RIGHT? JUST LOOK AT THAT FACE!
WHAT?! KISS?! NO, WE DIDN'T! WE REALLY DIDN'T! I PROMISE!
WHAT... HANDS?
YOU JUST HELD HANDS?!
ARE YOU GUYS STILL IN ELEMENTARY SCHOOL OR SOMETHING?!
HA HA HA!
HOW TYPICAL OF YOU GUYS.
NICE PROGRESS, THOUGH.
SHUT UP! STAY OUT OF THIS...

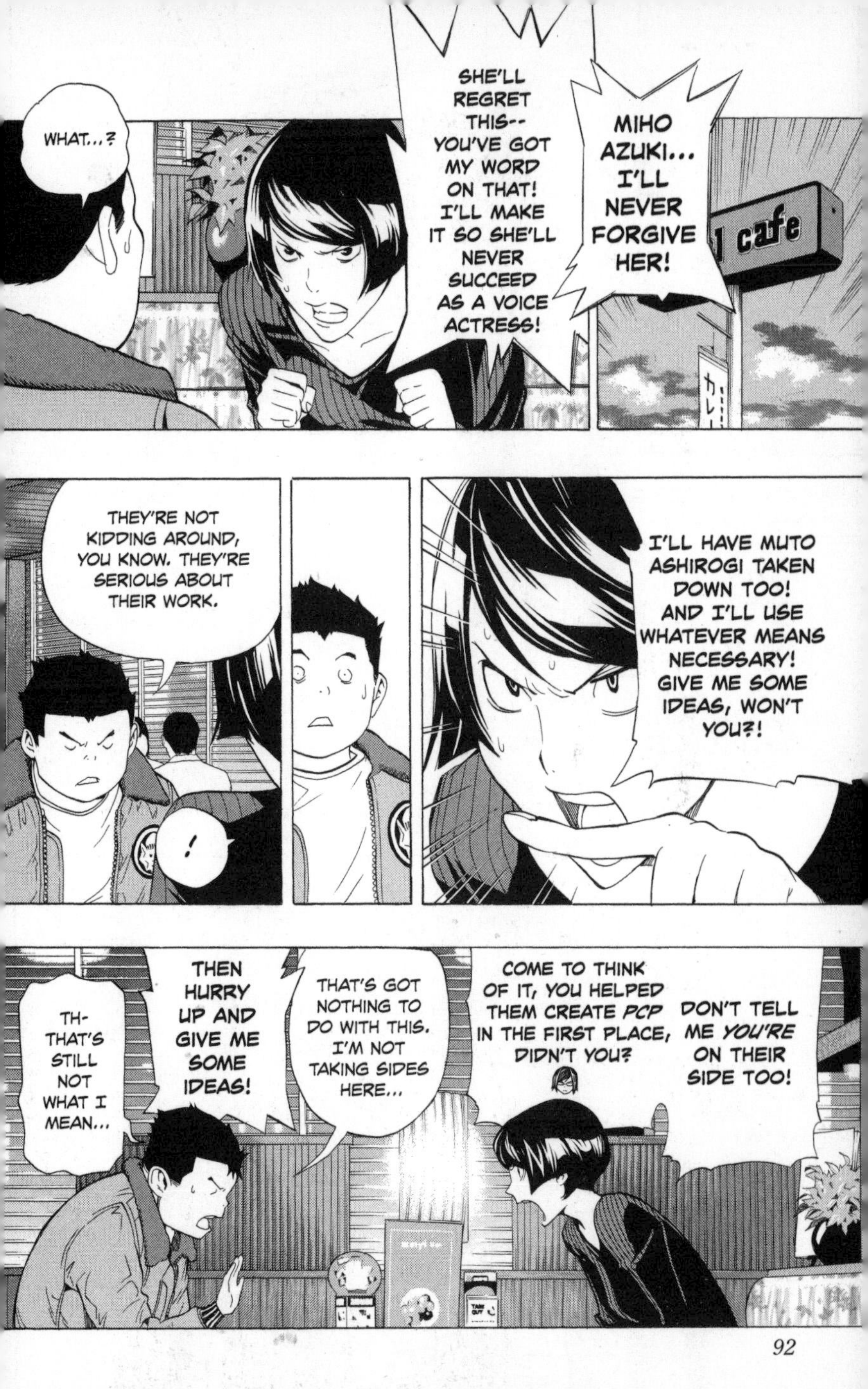
MIHO AZUKI... I'LL NEVER FORGIVE HER!
SHE'LL REGRET THIS-- YOU'VE GOT MY WORD ON THAT! I'LL MAKE IT SO SHE'LL NEVER SUCCEED AS A VOICE ACTRESS!
cafe
WHAT...?
I'LL HAVE MUTO ASHIROGI TAKEN DOWN TOO! AND I'LL USE WHATEVER MEANS NECESSARY! GIVE ME SOME IDEAS, WON'T YOU?!
THEY'RE NOT KIDDING AROUND, YOU KNOW. THEY'RE SERIOUS ABOUT THEIR WORK.
!
DON'T TELL ME *YOU'RE* ON THEIR SIDE TOO!
COME TO THINK OF IT, YOU HELPED THEM CREATE *PCP* IN THE FIRST PLACE, DIDN'T YOU?
THAT'S GOT NOTHING TO DO WITH THIS. I'M NOT TAKING SIDES HERE...
THEN HURRY UP AND GIVE ME SOME IDEAS!
TH-THAT'S STILL NOT WHAT I MEAN...

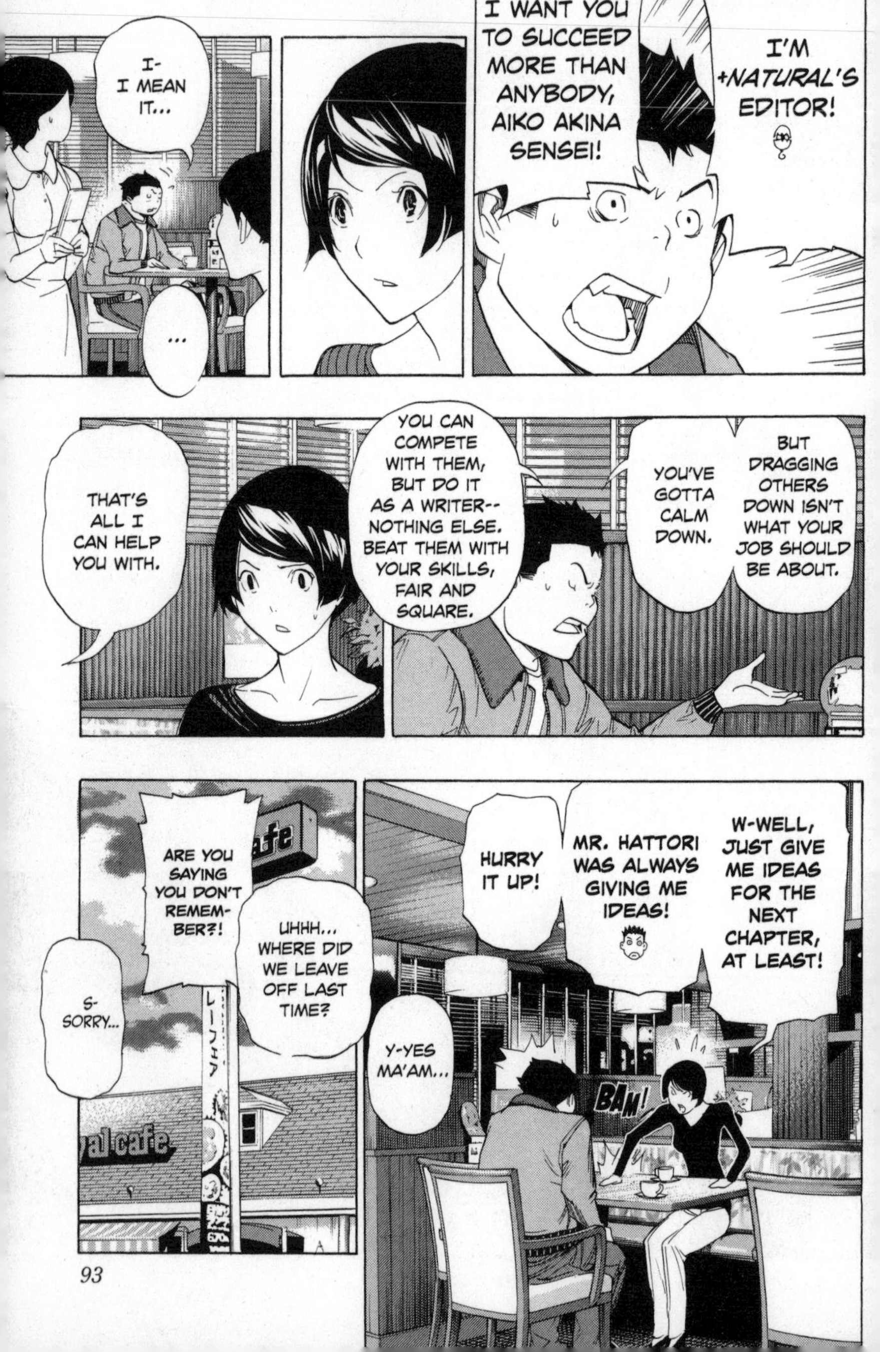
I'M +NATURAL'S EDITOR!
I WANT YOU TO SUCCEED MORE THAN ANYBODY, AIKO AKINA SENSEI!
I- I MEAN IT...
...
YOU'VE GOTTA CALM DOWN.
BUT DRAGGING OTHERS DOWN ISN'T WHAT YOUR JOB SHOULD BE ABOUT.
YOU CAN COMPETE WITH THEM, BUT DO IT AS A WRITER--NOTHING ELSE. BEAT THEM WITH YOUR SKILLS, FAIR AND SQUARE.
THAT'S ALL I CAN HELP YOU WITH.
W-WELL, JUST GIVE ME IDEAS FOR THE NEXT CHAPTER, AT LEAST!
MR. HATTORI WAS ALWAYS GIVING ME IDEAS!
HURRY IT UP!
BAM!
Y-YES MA'AM...
ARE YOU SAYING YOU DON'T REMEMBER?!
UHHH... WHERE DID WE LEAVE OFF LAST TIME?
S-SORRY...

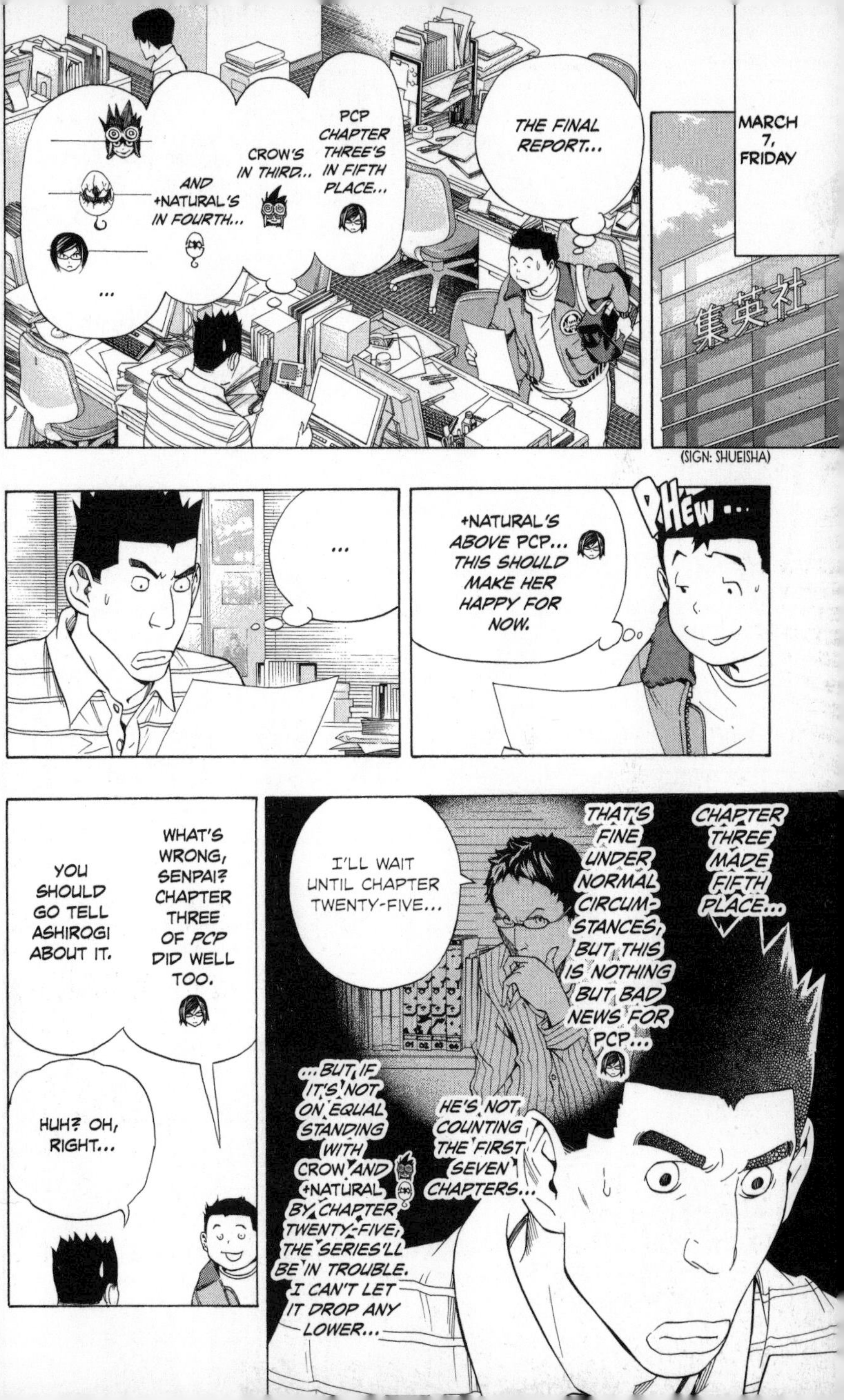
MARCH 7, FRIDAY
集英社
(SIGN: SHUEISHA)
THE FINAL REPORT...
PCP CHAPTER THREE'S IN FIFTH PLACE...
CROW'S IN THIRD...
AND +NATURAL'S IN FOURTH...
...
PHEW...
+NATURAL'S ABOVE PCP... THIS SHOULD MAKE HER HAPPY FOR NOW.
...
CHAPTER THREE MADE FIFTH PLACE...
THAT'S FINE UNDER NORMAL CIRCUM-STANCES, BUT THIS IS NOTHING BUT BAD NEWS FOR PCP...
I'LL WAIT UNTIL CHAPTER TWENTY-FIVE...
HE'S NOT COUNTING THE FIRST SEVEN CHAPTERS...
...BUT IF IT'S NOT ON EQUAL STANDING WITH CROW AND +NATURAL BY CHAPTER TWENTY-FIVE, THE SERIES'LL BE IN TROUBLE. I CAN'T LET IT DROP ANY LOWER...
WHAT'S WRONG, SENPAI? CHAPTER THREE OF PCP DID WELL TOO.
YOU SHOULD GO TELL ASHIROGI ABOUT IT.
HUH? OH, RIGHT...

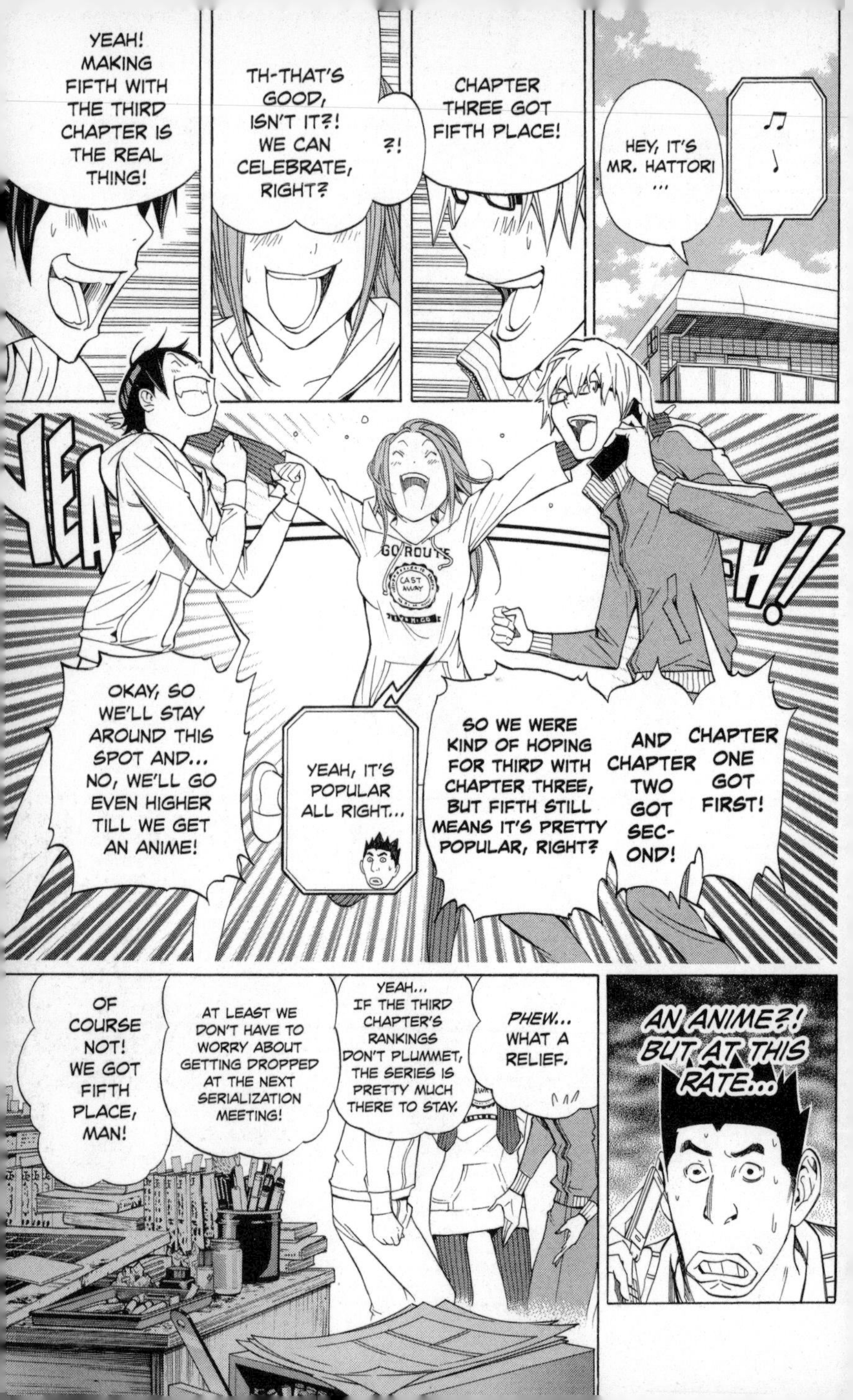
♪ ♪
HEY, IT'S MR. HATTORI ...
CHAPTER THREE GOT FIFTH PLACE!
?!
TH-THAT'S GOOD, ISN'T IT?! WE CAN CELEBRATE, RIGHT?
YEAH! MAKING FIFTH WITH THE THIRD CHAPTER IS THE REAL THING!
H!!
YEA
CHAPTER ONE GOT FIRST!
AND CHAPTER TWO GOT SEC-OND!
SO WE WERE KIND OF HOPING FOR THIRD WITH CHAPTER THREE, BUT FIFTH STILL MEANS IT'S PRETTY POPULAR, RIGHT?
YEAH, IT'S POPULAR ALL RIGHT...
OKAY, SO WE'LL STAY AROUND THIS SPOT AND... NO, WE'LL GO EVEN HIGHER TILL WE GET AN ANIME!
AN ANIME?! BUT AT THIS RATE...
PHEW... WHAT A RELIEF.
YEAH... IF THE THIRD CHAPTER'S RANKINGS DON'T PLUMMET, THE SERIES IS PRETTY MUCH THERE TO STAY.
AT LEAST WE DON'T HAVE TO WORRY ABOUT GETTING DROPPED AT THE NEXT SERIALIZATION MEETING!
OF COURSE NOT! WE GOT FIFTH PLACE, MAN!

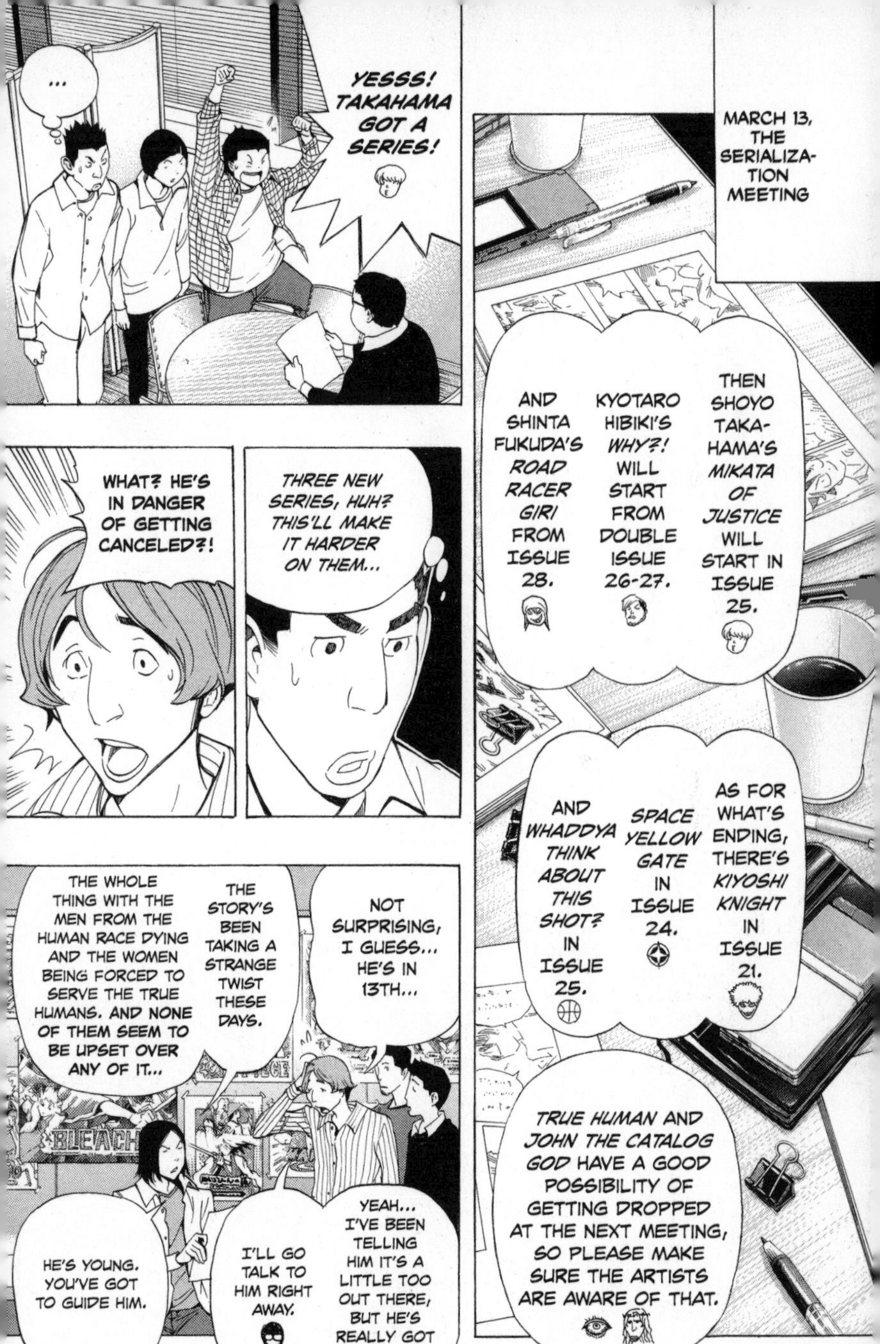
MARCH 13, THE SERIALIZATION MEETING
THEN SHOYO TAKAHAMA'S *MIKATA OF JUSTICE* WILL START IN ISSUE 25.
KYOTARO HIBIKI'S *WHY?!* WILL START FROM DOUBLE ISSUE 26-27.
AND SHINTA FUKUDA'S *ROAD RACER GIRI* FROM ISSUE 28.
AS FOR WHAT'S ENDING, THERE'S *KIYOSHI KNIGHT* IN ISSUE 21.
SPACE YELLOW GATE IN ISSUE 24.
AND *WHADDYA THINK ABOUT THIS SHOT?* IN ISSUE 25.
TRUE HUMAN AND *JOHN THE CATALOG GOD* HAVE A GOOD POSSIBILITY OF GETTING DROPPED AT THE NEXT MEETING, SO PLEASE MAKE SURE THE ARTISTS ARE AWARE OF THAT.
YESSS! TAKAHAMA GOT A SERIES!
...
THREE NEW SERIES, HUH? THIS'LL MAKE IT HARDER ON THEM...
WHAT? HE'S IN DANGER OF GETTING CANCELED?!
NOT SURPRISING, I GUESS... HE'S IN 13TH...
THE STORY'S BEEN TAKING A STRANGE TWIST THESE DAYS.
THE WHOLE THING WITH THE MEN FROM THE HUMAN RACE DYING AND THE WOMEN BEING FORCED TO SERVE THE TRUE HUMANS. AND NONE OF THEM SEEM TO BE UPSET OVER ANY OF IT...
YEAH... I'VE BEEN TELLING HIM IT'S A LITTLE TOO OUT THERE, BUT HE'S REALLY GOT HIS SIGHTS SET.
I'LL GO TALK TO HIM RIGHT AWAY.
HE'S YOUNG. YOU'VE GOT TO GUIDE HIM.

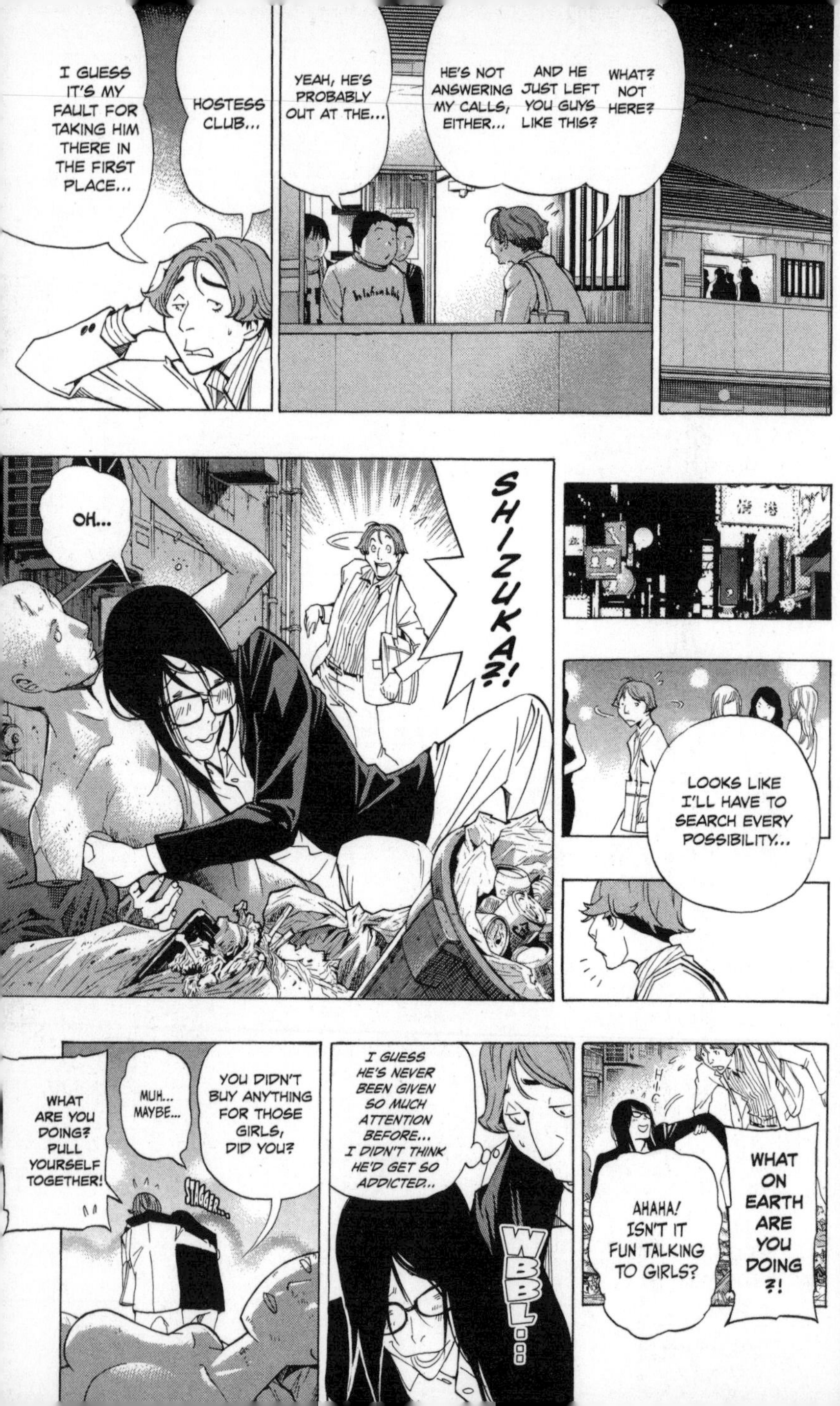
WHAT? NOT HERE?
AND HE JUST LEFT YOU GUYS LIKE THIS?
HE'S NOT ANSWERING MY CALLS, EITHER...
YEAH, HE'S PROBABLY OUT AT THE...
HOSTESS CLUB...
I GUESS IT'S MY FAULT FOR TAKING HIM THERE IN THE FIRST PLACE...
LOOKS LIKE I'LL HAVE TO SEARCH EVERY POSSIBILITY...
SHIZUKA?!
OH...
WHAT ON EARTH ARE YOU DOING?!
HIC
AHAHA! ISN'T IT FUN TALKING TO GIRLS?
I GUESS HE'S NEVER BEEN GIVEN SO MUCH ATTENTION BEFORE... I DIDN'T THINK HE'D GET SO ADDICTED...
WBBL...
YOU DIDN'T BUY ANYTHING FOR THOSE GIRLS, DID YOU?
MUH... MAYBE...
STAGGER...
WHAT ARE YOU DOING? PULL YOURSELF TOGETHER!

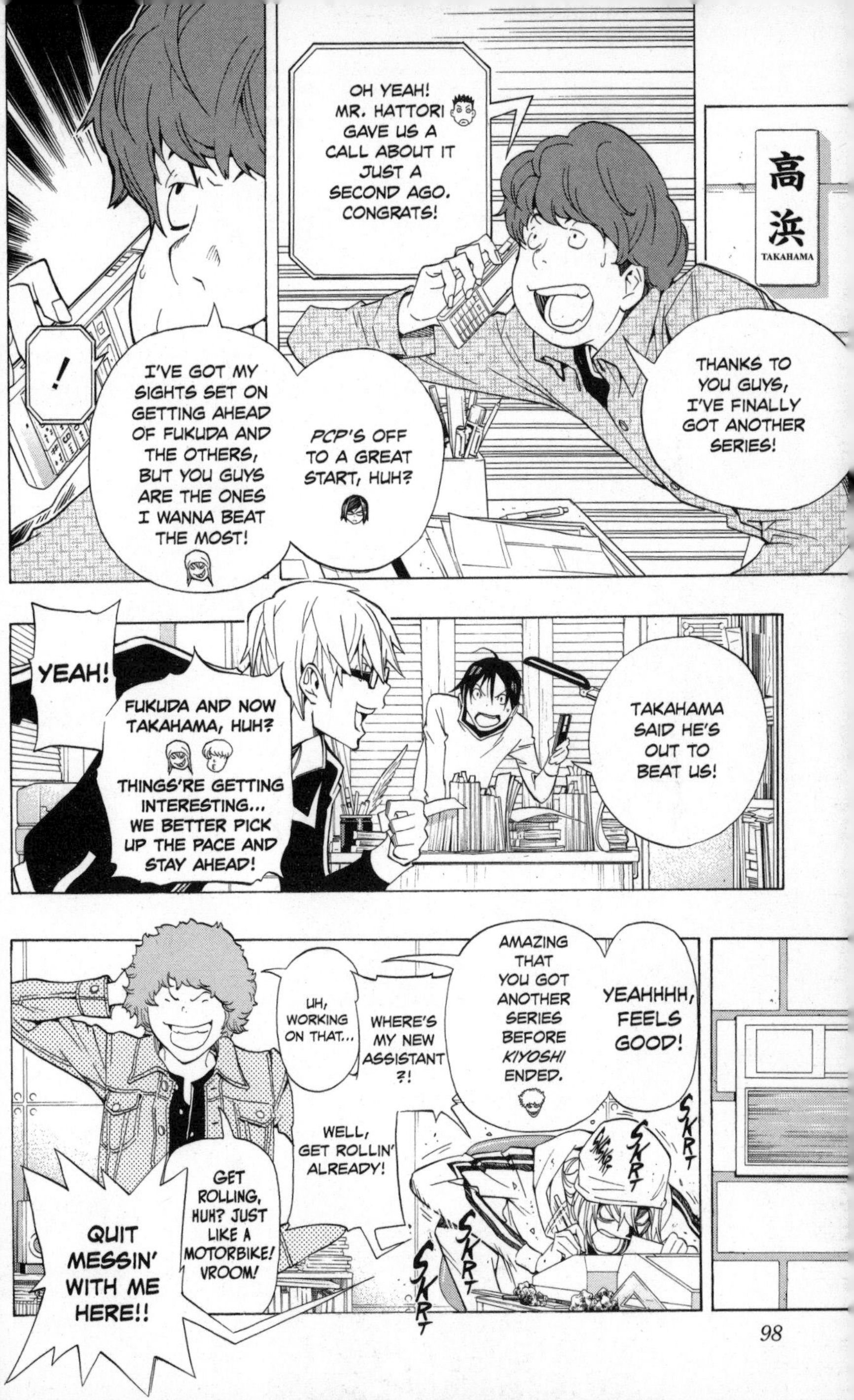
高浜
TAKAHAMA
THANKS TO YOU GUYS, I'VE FINALLY GOT ANOTHER SERIES!
OH YEAH! MR. HATTORI GAVE US A CALL ABOUT IT JUST A SECOND AGO. CONGRATS!
PCP'S OFF TO A GREAT START, HUH?
I'VE GOT MY SIGHTS SET ON GETTING AHEAD OF FUKUDA AND THE OTHERS, BUT YOU GUYS ARE THE ONES I WANNA BEAT THE MOST!
!
TAKAHAMA SAID HE'S OUT TO BEAT US!
YEAH!
FUKUDA AND NOW TAKAHAMA, HUH?
THINGS'RE GETTING INTERESTING... WE BETTER PICK UP THE PACE AND STAY AHEAD!
YEAHHHH, FEELS GOOD!
AMAZING THAT YOU GOT ANOTHER SERIES BEFORE *KIYOSHI* ENDED.
WHERE'S MY NEW ASSISTANT ?!
UH, WORKING ON THAT...
SKRT
SKRT
WELL, GET ROLLIN' ALREADY!
GET ROLLING, HUH? JUST LIKE A MOTORBIKE! VROOM!
SKRT
SKRT
QUIT MESSIN' WITH ME HERE!!

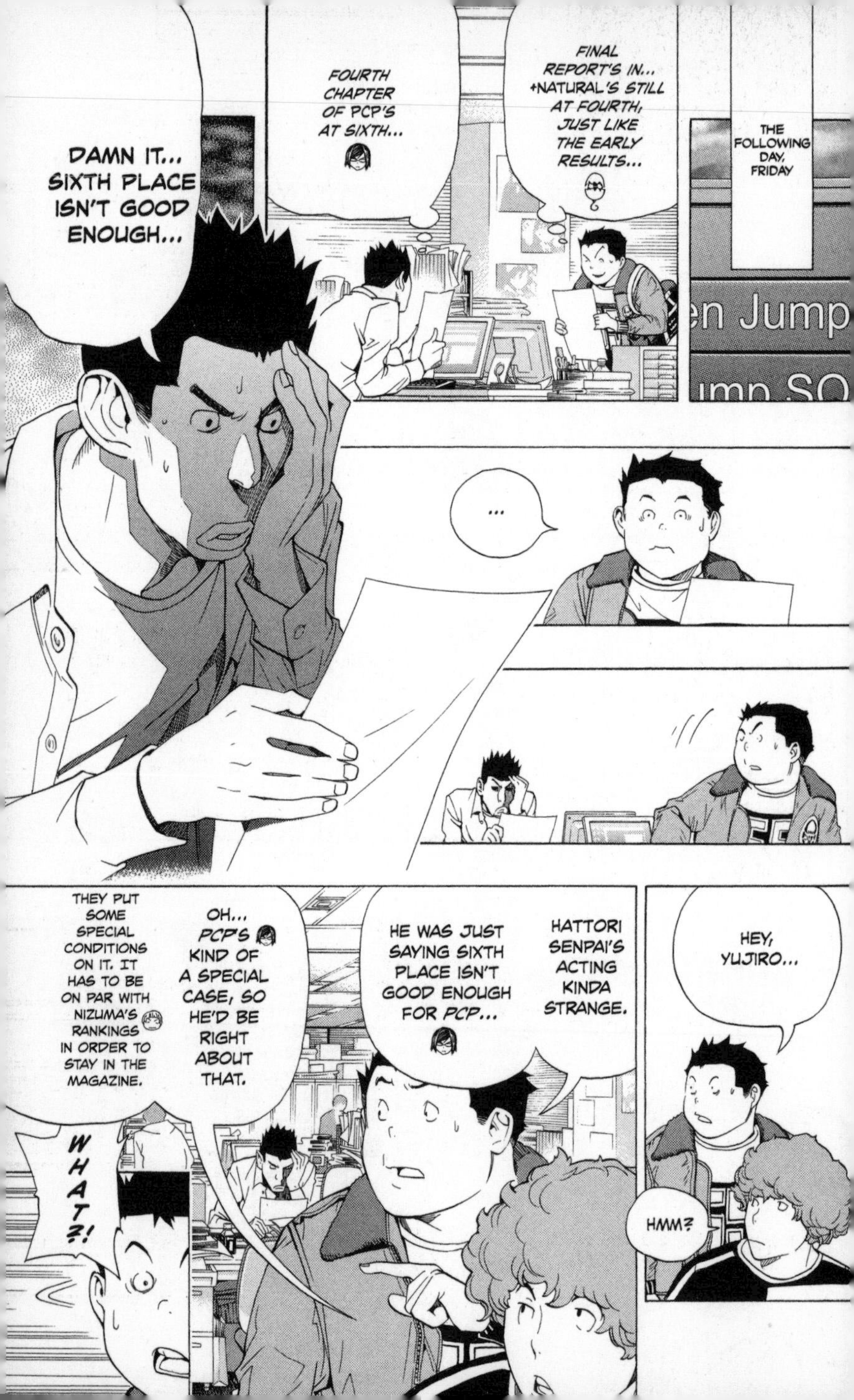
THE FOLLOWING DAY, FRIDAY
en Jump
FINAL REPORT'S IN... +NATURAL'S STILL AT FOURTH, JUST LIKE THE EARLY RESULTS...
FOURTH CHAPTER OF PCP'S AT SIXTH...
...
DAMN IT... SIXTH PLACE ISN'T GOOD ENOUGH...
HEY, YUJIRO...
HMM?
HATTORI SENPAI'S ACTING KINDA STRANGE.
HE WAS JUST SAYING SIXTH PLACE ISN'T GOOD ENOUGH FOR PCP...
OH... PCP'S KIND OF A SPECIAL CASE, SO HE'D BE RIGHT ABOUT THAT.
THEY PUT SOME SPECIAL CONDITIONS ON IT. IT HAS TO BE ON PAR WITH NIZUMA'S RANKINGS IN ORDER TO STAY IN THE MAGAZINE.
WHAT?!

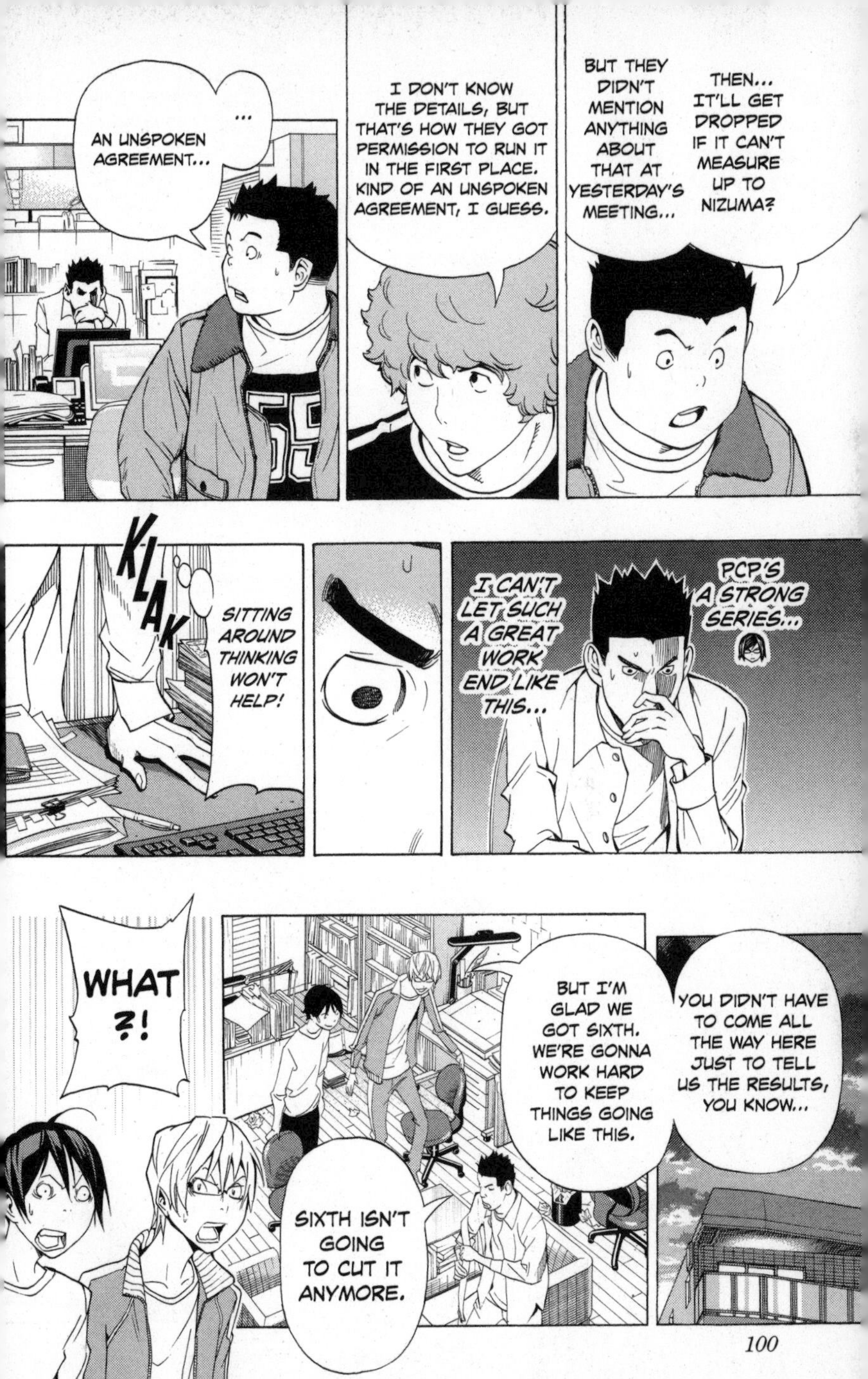
THEN... IT'LL GET DROPPED IF IT CAN'T MEASURE UP TO NIZUMA?
BUT THEY DIDN'T MENTION ANYTHING ABOUT THAT AT YESTERDAY'S MEETING...
I DON'T KNOW THE DETAILS, BUT THAT'S HOW THEY GOT PERMISSION TO RUN IT IN THE FIRST PLACE. KIND OF AN UNSPOKEN AGREEMENT, I GUESS.
...
AN UNSPOKEN AGREEMENT...
PCP'S A STRONG SERIES...
I CAN'T LET SUCH A GREAT WORK END LIKE THIS...
KLAK
SITTING AROUND THINKING WON'T HELP!
YOU DIDN'T HAVE TO COME ALL THE WAY HERE JUST TO TELL US THE RESULTS, YOU KNOW...
BUT I'M GLAD WE GOT SIXTH. WE'RE GONNA WORK HARD TO KEEP THINGS GOING LIKE THIS.
SIXTH ISN'T GOING TO CUT IT ANYMORE.
WHAT?!

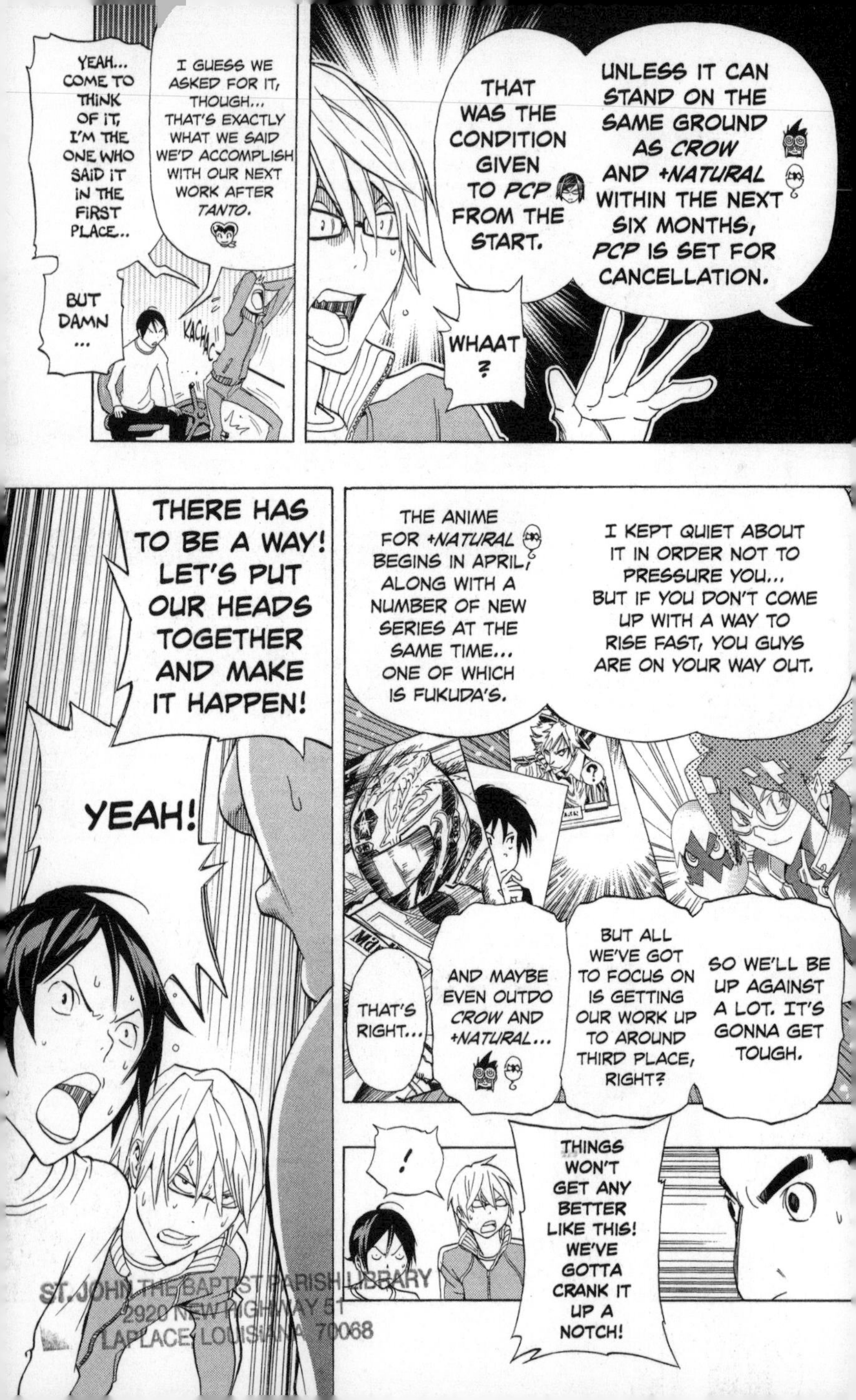
UNLESS IT CAN STAND ON THE SAME GROUND AS *CROW* AND *+NATURAL* WITHIN THE NEXT SIX MONTHS, *PCP* IS SET FOR CANCELLATION.
THAT WAS THE CONDITION GIVEN TO *PCP* FROM THE START.
WHAAT?
I GUESS WE ASKED FOR IT, THOUGH... THAT'S EXACTLY WHAT WE SAID WE'D ACCOMPLISH WITH OUR NEXT WORK AFTER *TANTO*.
YEAH... COME TO THINK OF IT, I'M THE ONE WHO SAID IT IN THE FIRST PLACE...
KACHAC
BUT DAMN...
THE ANIME FOR *+NATURAL* BEGINS IN APRIL, ALONG WITH A NUMBER OF NEW SERIES AT THE SAME TIME... ONE OF WHICH IS FUKUDA'S.
I KEPT QUIET ABOUT IT IN ORDER NOT TO PRESSURE YOU... BUT IF YOU DON'T COME UP WITH A WAY TO RISE FAST, YOU GUYS ARE ON YOUR WAY OUT.
SO WE'LL BE UP AGAINST A LOT. IT'S GONNA GET TOUGH.
BUT ALL WE'VE GOT TO FOCUS ON IS GETTING OUR WORK UP TO AROUND THIRD PLACE, RIGHT?
AND MAYBE EVEN OUTDO *CROW* AND *+NATURAL*...
THAT'S RIGHT...
THINGS WON'T GET ANY BETTER LIKE THIS! WE'VE GOTTA CRANK IT UP A NOTCH!
!
THERE HAS TO BE A WAY! LET'S PUT OUR HEADS TOGETHER AND MAKE IT HAPPEN!
YEAH!

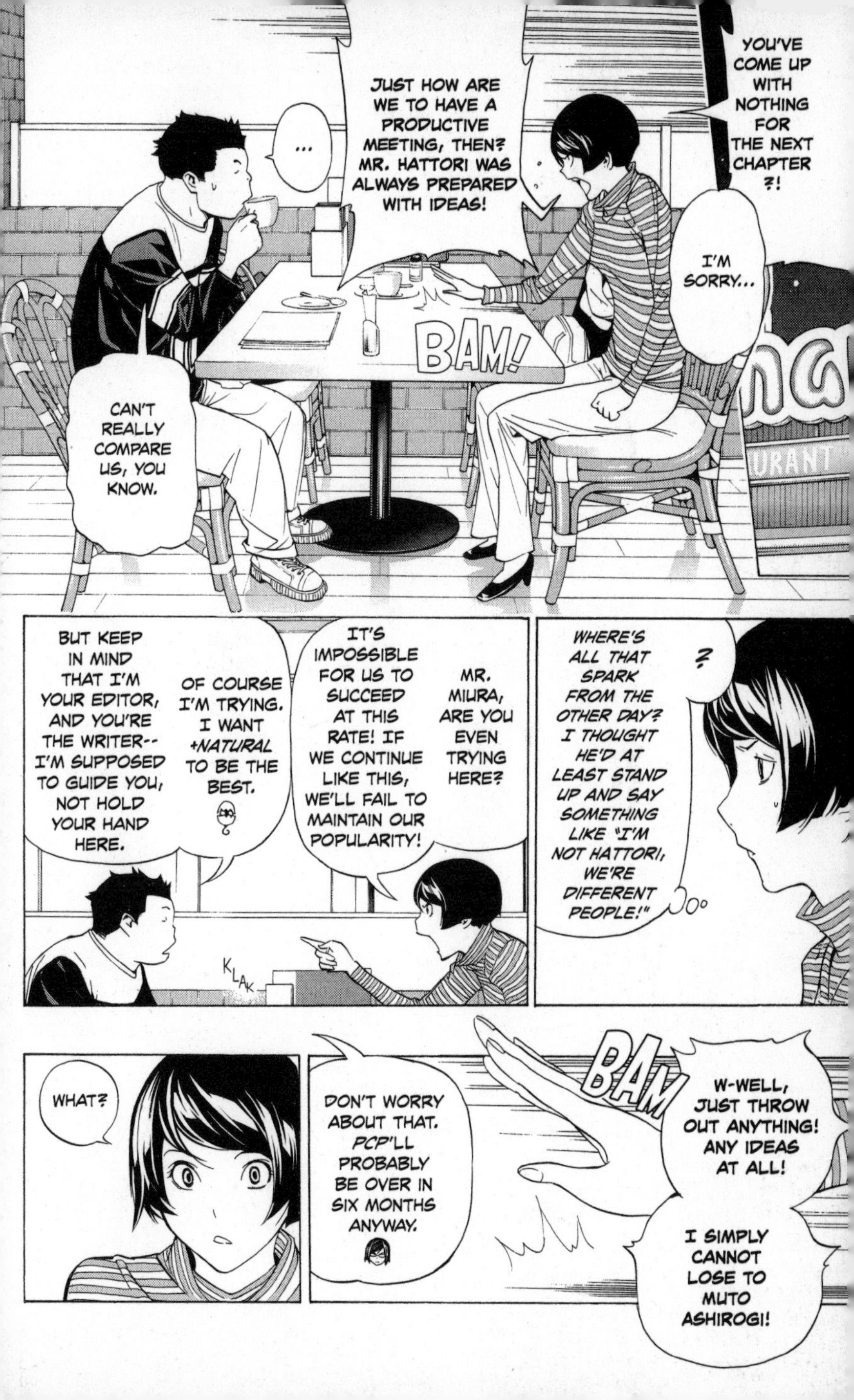
YOU'VE COME UP WITH NOTHING FOR THE NEXT CHAPTER?!
JUST HOW ARE WE TO HAVE A PRODUCTIVE MEETING, THEN? MR. HATTORI WAS ALWAYS PREPARED WITH IDEAS!
...
I'M SORRY...
BAM!
CAN'T REALLY COMPARE US, YOU KNOW.
?
WHERE'S ALL THAT SPARK FROM THE OTHER DAY? I THOUGHT HE'D AT LEAST STAND UP AND SAY SOMETHING LIKE "I'M NOT HATTORI, WE'RE DIFFERENT PEOPLE!"
MR. MIURA, ARE YOU EVEN TRYING HERE?
IT'S IMPOSSIBLE FOR US TO SUCCEED AT THIS RATE! IF WE CONTINUE LIKE THIS, WE'LL FAIL TO MAINTAIN OUR POPULARITY!
OF COURSE I'M TRYING. I WANT +NATURAL TO BE THE BEST.
BUT KEEP IN MIND THAT I'M YOUR EDITOR, AND YOU'RE THE WRITER-- I'M SUPPOSED TO GUIDE YOU, NOT HOLD YOUR HAND HERE.
KLAK
BAM
W-WELL, JUST THROW OUT ANYTHING! ANY IDEAS AT ALL!
I SIMPLY CANNOT LOSE TO MUTO ASHIROGI!
DON'T WORRY ABOUT THAT. PCP'LL PROBABLY BE OVER IN SIX MONTHS ANYWAY.
WHAT?

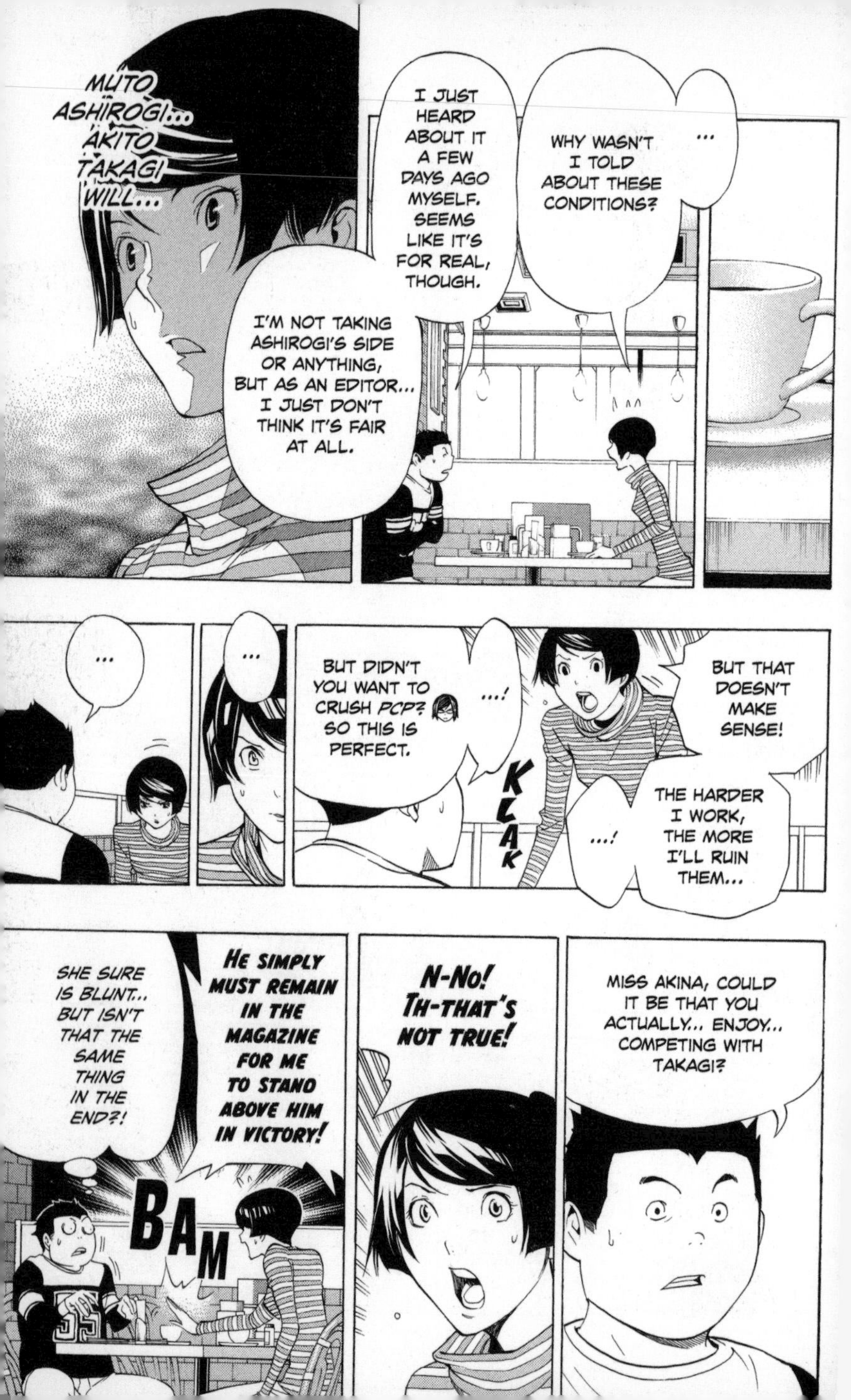
...
WHY WASN'T I TOLD ABOUT THESE CONDITIONS?
I JUST HEARD ABOUT IT A FEW DAYS AGO MYSELF. SEEMS LIKE IT'S FOR REAL, THOUGH.
I'M NOT TAKING ASHIROGI'S SIDE OR ANYTHING, BUT AS AN EDITOR... I JUST DON'T THINK IT'S FAIR AT ALL.
MUTO ASHIROGI... AKITO TAKAGI WILL...
BUT THAT DOESN'T MAKE SENSE!
THE HARDER I WORK, THE MORE I'LL RUIN THEM...
...!
KLAK
...!
BUT DIDN'T YOU WANT TO CRUSH *PCP*? SO THIS IS PERFECT.
...
...
MISS AKINA, COULD IT BE THAT YOU ACTUALLY... ENJOY... COMPETING WITH TAKAGI?
N-NO! TH-THAT'S NOT TRUE!
HE SIMPLY MUST REMAIN IN THE MAGAZINE FOR ME TO STAND ABOVE HIM IN VICTORY!
BAM
SHE SURE IS BLUNT... BUT ISN'T THAT THE SAME THING IN THE END?!

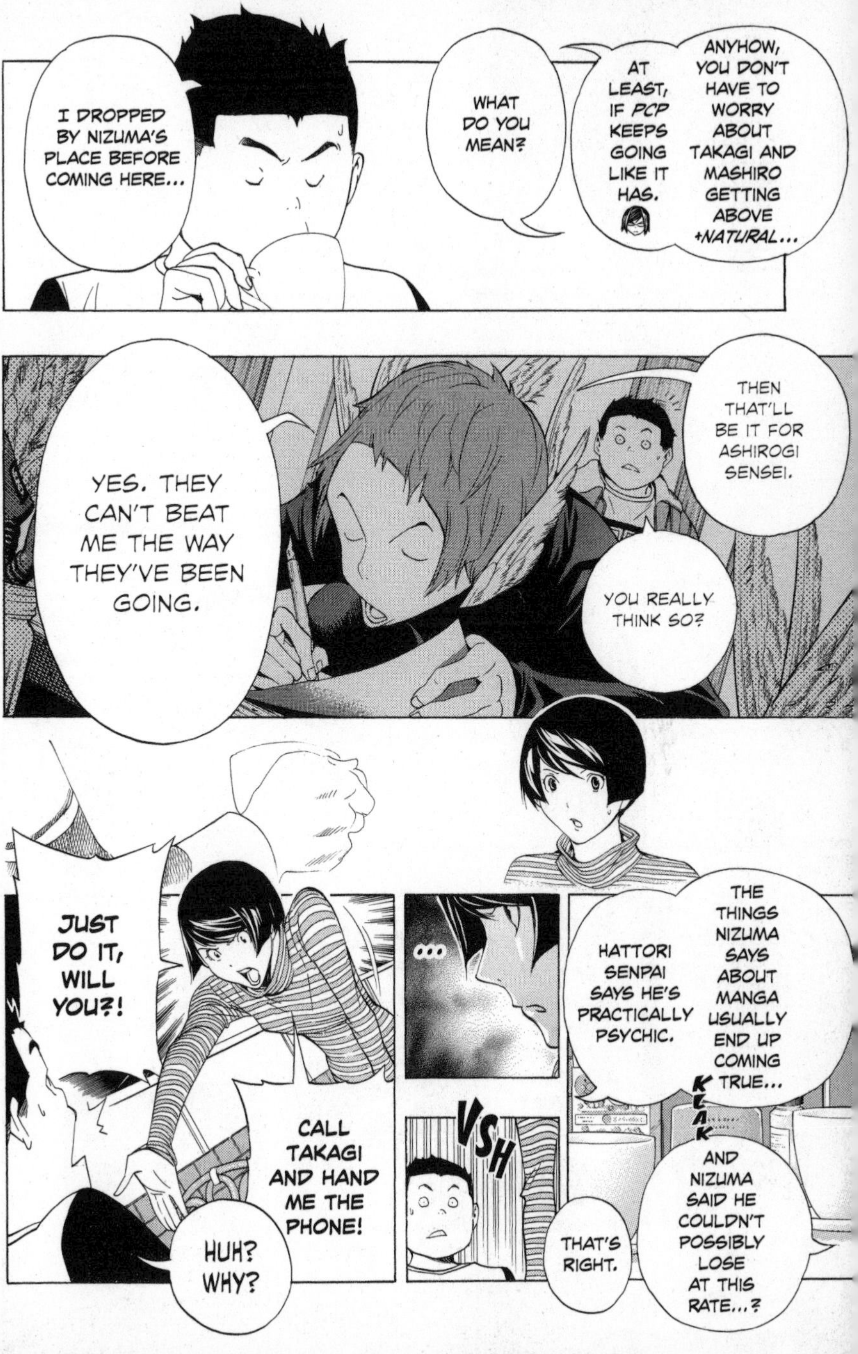
ANYHOW, YOU DON'T HAVE TO WORRY ABOUT TAKAGI AND MASHIRO GETTING ABOVE +*NATURAL*...
AT LEAST, IF *PCP* KEEPS GOING LIKE IT HAS.
WHAT DO YOU MEAN?
I DROPPED BY NIZUMA'S PLACE BEFORE COMING HERE...
THEN THAT'LL BE IT FOR ASHIROGI SENSEI.
YOU REALLY THINK SO?
YES. THEY CAN'T BEAT ME THE WAY THEY'VE BEEN GOING.
THE THINGS NIZUMA SAYS ABOUT MANGA USUALLY END UP COMING TRUE...
HATTORI SENPAI SAYS HE'S PRACTICALLY PSYCHIC.
KLAK
AND NIZUMA SAID HE COULDN'T POSSIBLY LOSE AT THIS RATE...?
THAT'S RIGHT.
...
VSH
CALL TAKAGI AND HAND ME THE PHONE!
HUH? WHY?
JUST DO IT, WILL YOU?!

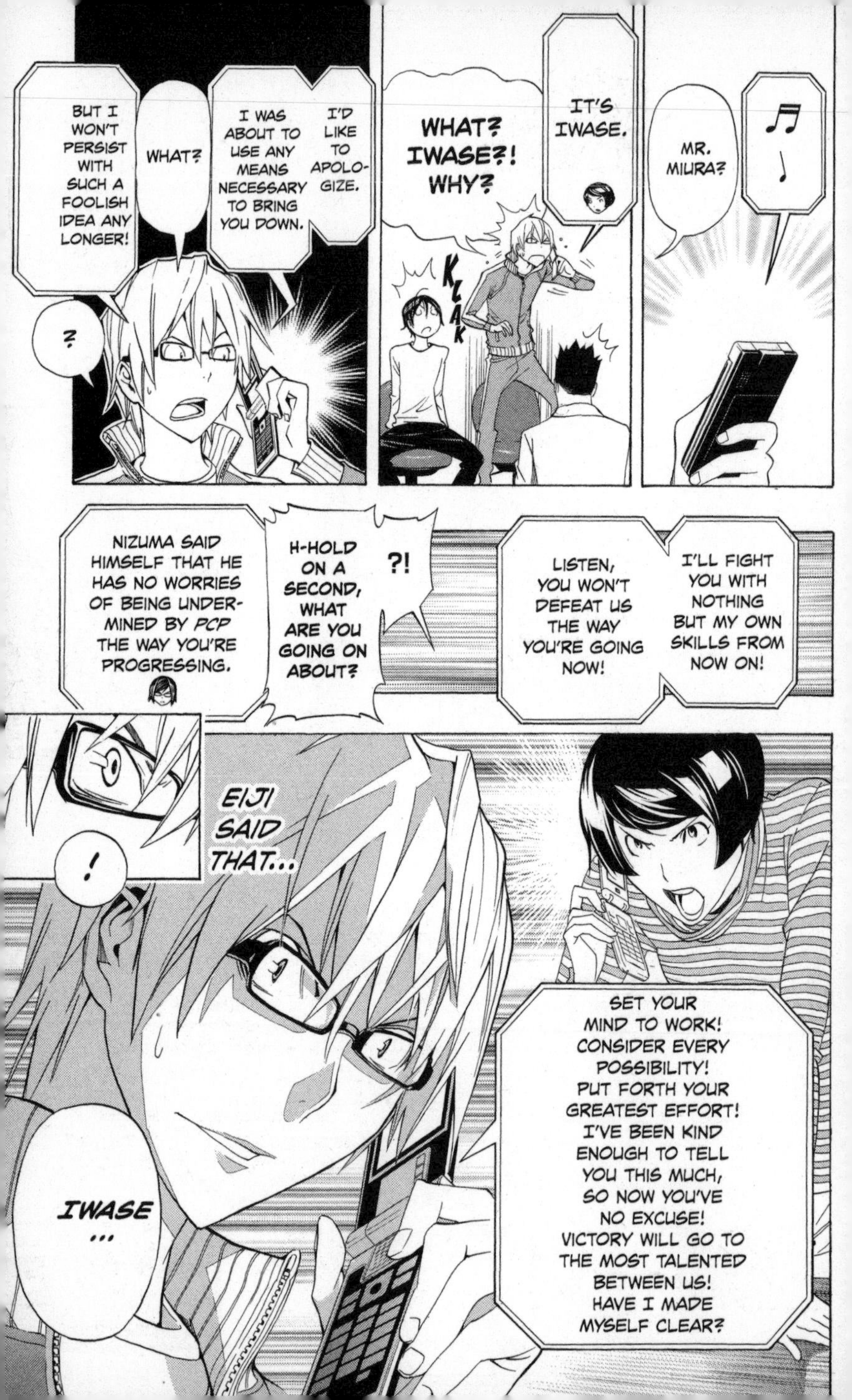
♪
MR. MIURA?
IT'S IWASE.
WHAT? IWASE?! WHY?
KLAK
I'D LIKE TO APOLOGIZE.
I WAS ABOUT TO USE ANY MEANS NECESSARY TO BRING YOU DOWN.
WHAT?
BUT I WON'T PERSIST WITH SUCH A FOOLISH IDEA ANY LONGER!
?
I'LL FIGHT YOU WITH NOTHING BUT MY OWN SKILLS FROM NOW ON!
LISTEN, YOU WON'T DEFEAT US THE WAY YOU'RE GOING NOW!
?!
H-HOLD ON A SECOND, WHAT ARE YOU GOING ON ABOUT?
NIZUMA SAID HIMSELF THAT HE HAS NO WORRIES OF BEING UNDERMINED BY *PCP* THE WAY YOU'RE PROGRESSING.
SET YOUR MIND TO WORK! CONSIDER EVERY POSSIBILITY! PUT FORTH YOUR GREATEST EFFORT! I'VE BEEN KIND ENOUGH TO TELL YOU THIS MUCH, SO NOW YOU'VE NO EXCUSE! VICTORY WILL GO TO THE MOST TALENTED BETWEEN US! HAVE I MADE MYSELF CLEAR?
EIJI SAID THAT...
!
IWASE...

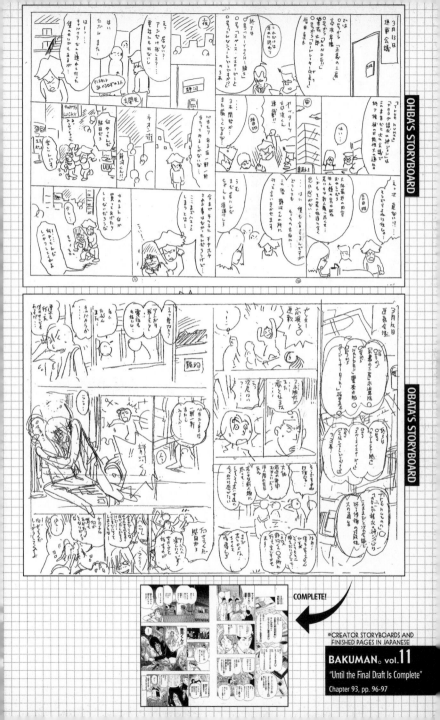

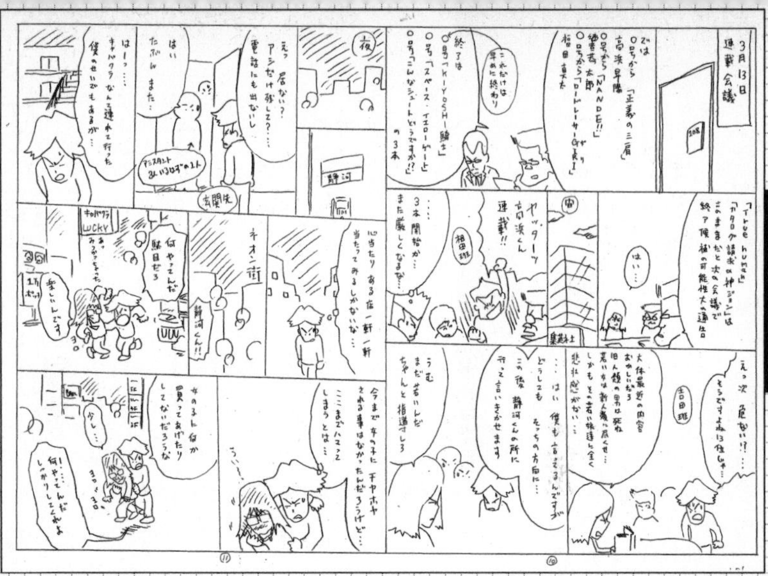
3月13日 連載会議
208
では ○号から「正義の三肩」高浜昇陽 ○号から「NANDE!!」 ○号から「ロードレーサーGIRI」 稲田
終了は ○号「KIYOSHI騎士」 ○号「スペース・イエローゲート」 ○号「こんなジュートどうですか!?」の3本
これだけは早めに終わり
「True human」「タクロウ請求の神ジーン」は このままだと次の会議で 終了候補の可能性大の通告
はい…
集英社
ヤッターッ 高浜くん 連載!!
相田班
3本開始か… また厳しくなるな…
吉田班
えっ 次 危ない!? …そうですよね 13位じゃ…
大体最近の内容 おかしいだろ 旧人類の男は死ね 若い女は新人類に尽くせ… しかもその若い女達に全く 悲壮感がない…
…はい 僕も言ってるんですが どうしても そっちの方向に… この後 静河くんの所に 行って言いますから
うむ まだ若いんだ ちゃんと指導しろ
夜
静河
えっ 居ない? アシだけ残して…? 電話にも出ないし
はい たぶん また…
アシスタント 3人いるはずの1人
玄関先
はーっ… キャバクラなんて連れて行った 僕のせいでもあるが…
心当たりある店一軒一軒 当たってみるしかないな…
ネオン街
静河くん!!
キャバクラ LUCKY
何やってんだ 駄目だろ
あっ みつかっちゃった
楽しいんです
今まで女の子にチヤホヤ される事はなかったんだろうけど… ここまでハマってしまうとは…
うい〜
女の子に何か 買ってあげたりしてないだろうな
少し…
何やってんだ しっかりしてくれよ

OHBA'S STORYBOARD

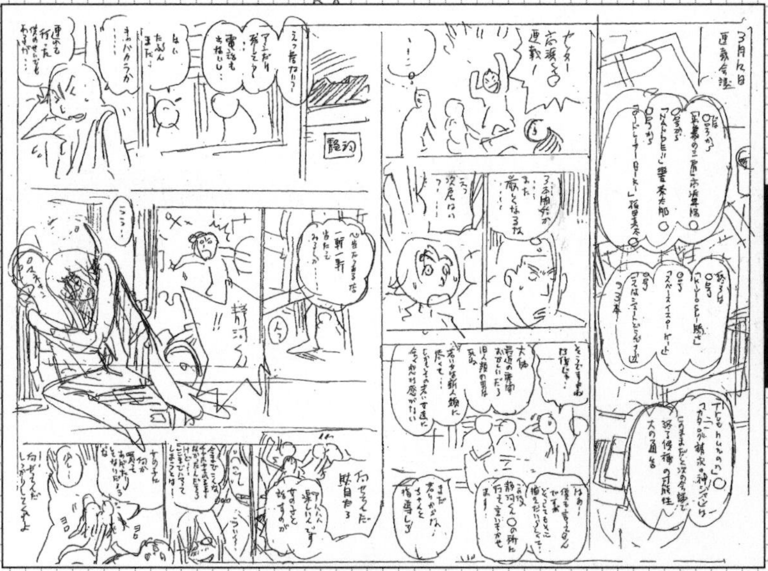
3月12日 連載会議
ヤッター 高浜くん 連載!
静河
えっ 居ない!?
電話も 出ないし…
はい たぶん また…

OBATA'S STORYBOARD

COMPLETE!

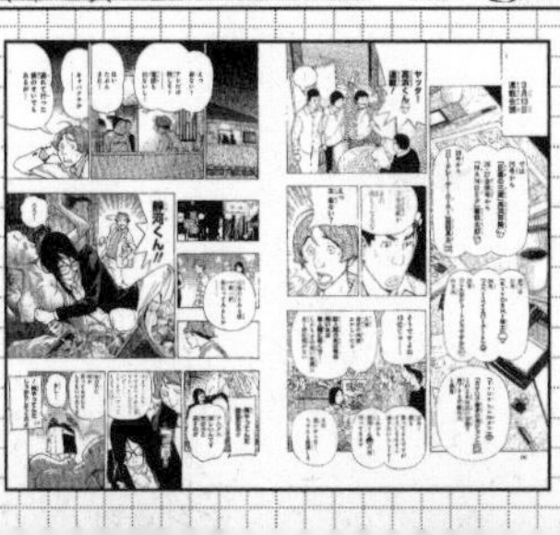

※CREATOR STORYBOARDS AND FINISHED PAGES IN JAPANESE

BAKUMAN。 vol.11

"Until the Final Draft Is Complete"

Chapter 93, pp. 96-97

CHAPTER 94 TEA AND TONE

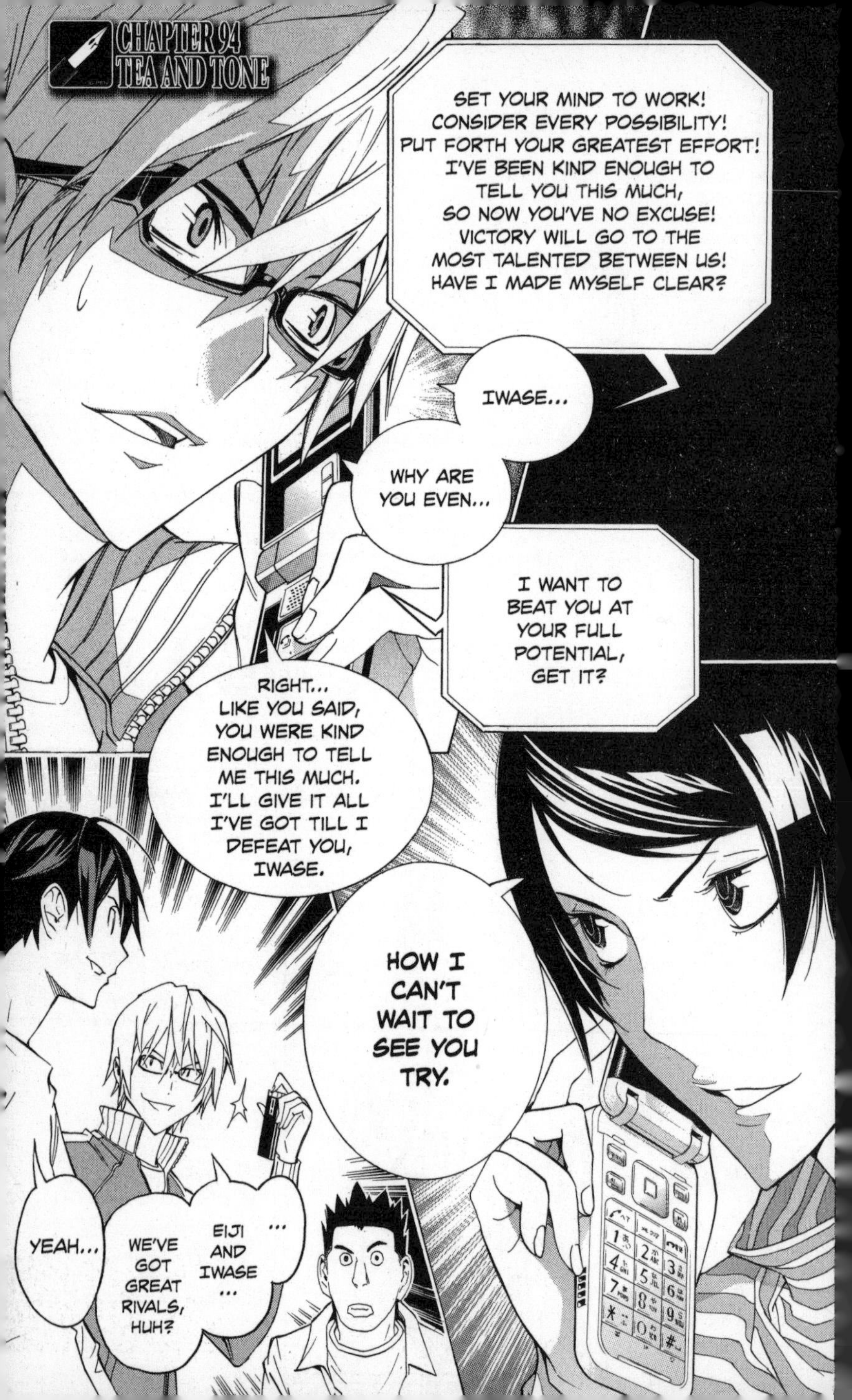
SET YOUR MIND TO WORK! CONSIDER EVERY POSSIBILITY! PUT FORTH YOUR GREATEST EFFORT! I'VE BEEN KIND ENOUGH TO TELL YOU THIS MUCH, SO NOW YOU'VE NO EXCUSE! VICTORY WILL GO TO THE MOST TALENTED BETWEEN US! HAVE I MADE MYSELF CLEAR?
IWASE...
WHY ARE YOU EVEN...
I WANT TO BEAT YOU AT YOUR FULL POTENTIAL, GET IT?
RIGHT... LIKE YOU SAID, YOU WERE KIND ENOUGH TO TELL ME THIS MUCH. I'LL GIVE IT ALL I'VE GOT TILL I DEFEAT YOU, IWASE.
HOW I CAN'T WAIT TO SEE YOU TRY.
...
EIJI AND IWASE...
WE'VE GOT GREAT RIVALS, HUH?
YEAH...

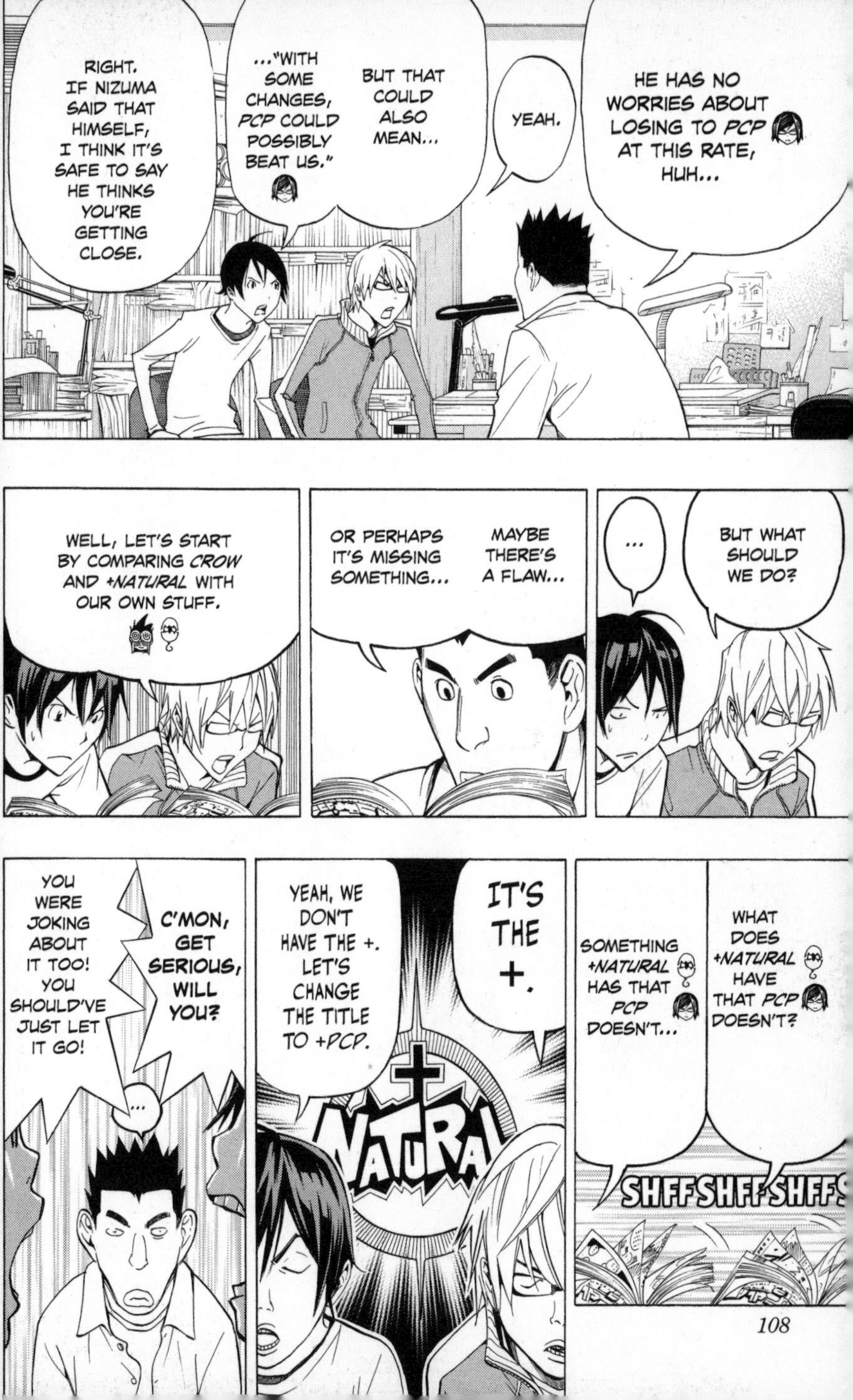
HE HAS NO WORRIES ABOUT LOSING TO *PCP* AT THIS RATE, HUH...
YEAH.
BUT THAT COULD ALSO MEAN...
..."WITH SOME CHANGES, *PCP* COULD POSSIBLY BEAT US."
RIGHT. IF NIZUMA SAID THAT HIMSELF, I THINK IT'S SAFE TO SAY HE THINKS YOU'RE GETTING CLOSE.
BUT WHAT SHOULD WE DO?
...
MAYBE THERE'S A FLAW...
OR PERHAPS IT'S MISSING SOMETHING...
WELL, LET'S START BY COMPARING *CROW* AND *+NATURAL* WITH OUR OWN STUFF.
WHAT DOES *+NATURAL* HAVE THAT *PCP* DOESN'T?
SOMETHING *+NATURAL* HAS THAT *PCP* DOESN'T...
SHFF SHFF SHFFS
IT'S THE +.
YEAH, WE DON'T HAVE THE +. LET'S CHANGE THE TITLE TO *+PCP*.
+NATURAL
C'MON, GET SERIOUS, WILL YOU?
YOU WERE JOKING ABOUT IT TOO! YOU SHOULD'VE JUST LET IT GO!
...

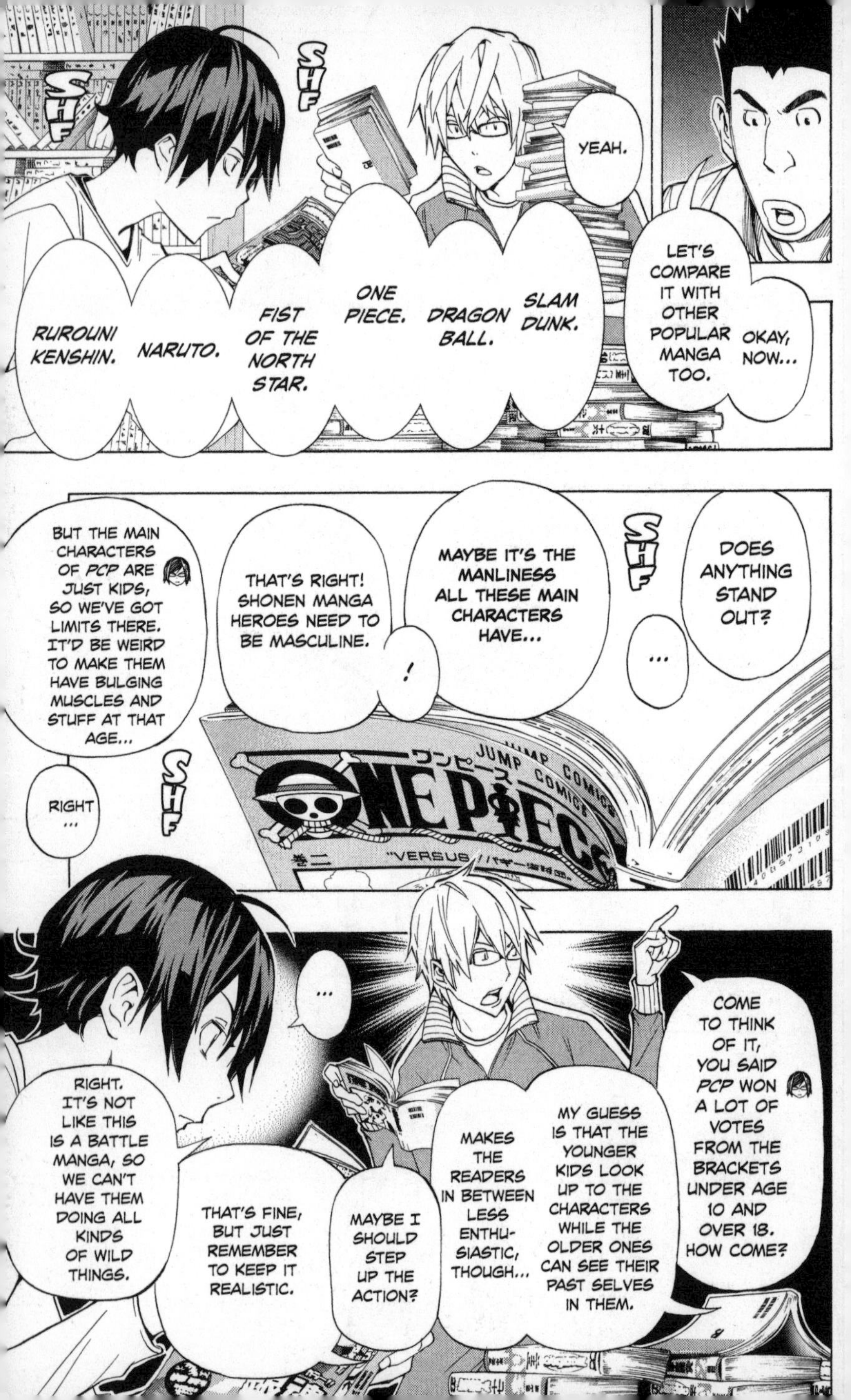
OKAY, NOW...
LET'S COMPARE IT WITH OTHER POPULAR MANGA TOO.
YEAH.
SHF
SHF
SLAM DUNK.
DRAGON BALL.
ONE PIECE.
FIST OF THE NORTH STAR.
NARUTO.
RUROUNI KENSHIN.
DOES ANYTHING STAND OUT?
...
SHF
MAYBE IT'S THE MANLINESS ALL THESE MAIN CHARACTERS HAVE...
!
THAT'S RIGHT! SHONEN MANGA HEROES NEED TO BE MASCULINE.
BUT THE MAIN CHARACTERS OF *PCP* ARE JUST KIDS, SO WE'VE GOT LIMITS THERE. IT'D BE WEIRD TO MAKE THEM HAVE BULGING MUSCLES AND STUFF AT THAT AGE...
SHF
RIGHT...
JUMP COMICS
ONE PIECE
COME TO THINK OF IT, YOU SAID *PCP* WON A LOT OF VOTES FROM THE BRACKETS UNDER AGE 10 AND OVER 18. HOW COME?
MY GUESS IS THAT THE YOUNGER KIDS LOOK UP TO THE CHARACTERS WHILE THE OLDER ONES CAN SEE THEIR PAST SELVES IN THEM.
MAKES THE READERS IN BETWEEN LESS ENTHU-SIASTIC, THOUGH...
...
MAYBE I SHOULD STEP UP THE ACTION?
THAT'S FINE, BUT JUST REMEMBER TO KEEP IT REALISTIC.
RIGHT. IT'S NOT LIKE THIS IS A BATTLE MANGA, SO WE CAN'T HAVE THEM DOING ALL KINDS OF WILD THINGS.

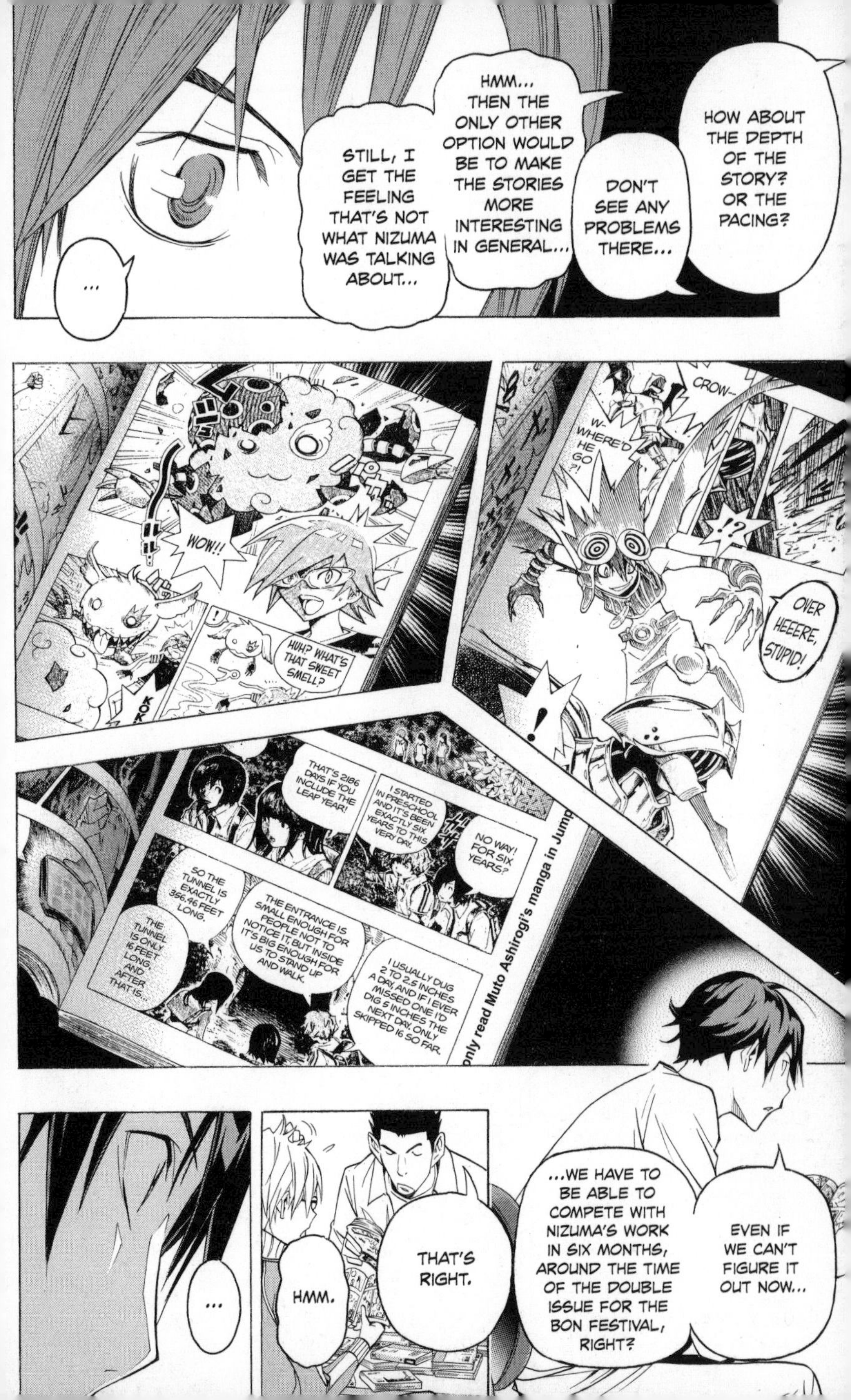
HOW ABOUT THE DEPTH OF THE STORY? OR THE PACING?
DON'T SEE ANY PROBLEMS THERE...
HMM... THEN THE ONLY OTHER OPTION WOULD BE TO MAKE THE STORIES MORE INTERESTING IN GENERAL...
STILL, I GET THE FEELING THAT'S NOT WHAT NIZUMA WAS TALKING ABOUT...
...
CROW-
W-WHERE'D HE GO?!
!?
OVER HEEERE, STUPID!
!
WOW!!
!
HUH? WHAT'S THAT SWEET SMELL?
THAT'S 2186 DAYS IF YOU INCLUDE THE LEAP YEAR!
I STARTED IN PRESCHOOL AND IT'S BEEN EXACTLY SIX YEARS TO THIS VERY DAY.
NO WAY! FOR SIX YEARS?
SO THE TUNNEL IS EXACTLY 356.46 FEET LONG.
THE ENTRANCE IS SMALL ENOUGH FOR PEOPLE NOT TO NOTICE IT, BUT INSIDE IT'S BIG ENOUGH FOR US TO STAND UP AND WALK.
I USUALLY DUG 2 TO 2.5 INCHES A DAY, AND IF I EVER MISSED ONE I'D DIG 5 INCHES THE NEXT DAY. ONLY SKIPPED 16 SO FAR.
THE TUNNEL IS ONLY 16 FEET LONG, AND AFTER THAT IS...
only read Muto Ashirogi's manga in Jump
EVEN IF WE CAN'T FIGURE IT OUT NOW...
...WE HAVE TO BE ABLE TO COMPETE WITH NIZUMA'S WORK IN SIX MONTHS, AROUND THE TIME OF THE DOUBLE ISSUE FOR THE BON FESTIVAL, RIGHT?
THAT'S RIGHT.
HMM.
...

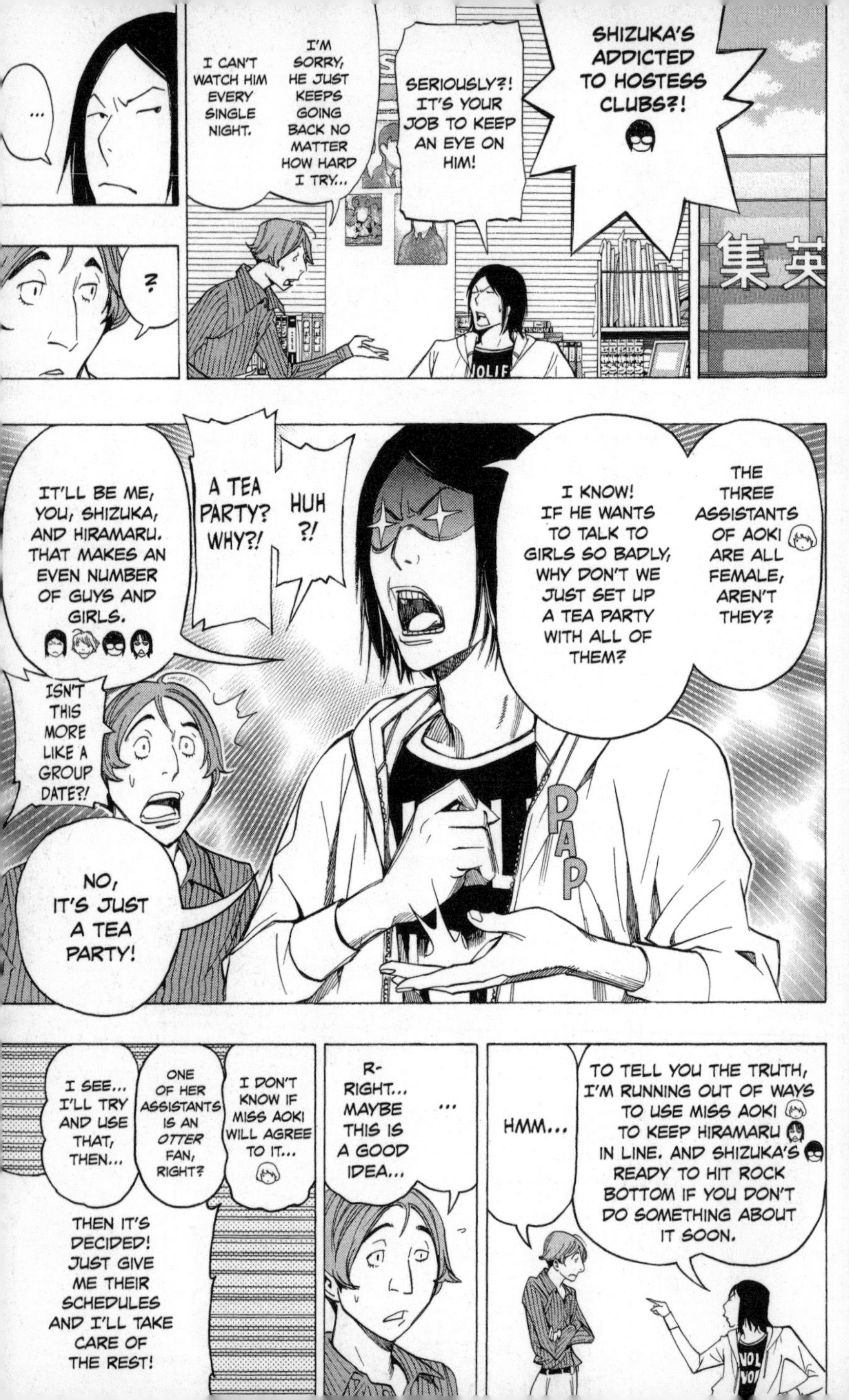
SHIZUKA'S ADDICTED TO HOSTESS CLUBS?!
SERIOUSLY?! IT'S YOUR JOB TO KEEP AN EYE ON HIM!
I'M SORRY, HE JUST KEEPS GOING BACK NO MATTER HOW HARD I TRY...
I CAN'T WATCH HIM EVERY SINGLE NIGHT.
...
?
THE THREE ASSISTANTS OF AOKI ARE ALL FEMALE, AREN'T THEY?
I KNOW! IF HE WANTS TO TALK TO GIRLS SO BADLY, WHY DON'T WE JUST SET UP A TEA PARTY WITH ALL OF THEM?
HUH ?!
A TEA PARTY? WHY?!
IT'LL BE ME, YOU, SHIZUKA, AND HIRAMARU. THAT MAKES AN EVEN NUMBER OF GUYS AND GIRLS.
PAP
ISN'T THIS MORE LIKE A GROUP DATE?!
NO, IT'S JUST A TEA PARTY!
TO TELL YOU THE TRUTH, I'M RUNNING OUT OF WAYS TO USE MISS AOKI TO KEEP HIRAMARU IN LINE. AND SHIZUKA'S READY TO HIT ROCK BOTTOM IF YOU DON'T DO SOMETHING ABOUT IT SOON.
HMM...
...
R-RIGHT... MAYBE THIS IS A GOOD IDEA...
I DON'T KNOW IF MISS AOKI WILL AGREE TO IT...
ONE OF HER ASSISTANTS IS AN *OTTER* FAN, RIGHT?
I SEE... I'LL TRY AND USE THAT, THEN...
THEN IT'S DECIDED! JUST GIVE ME THEIR SCHEDULES AND I'LL TAKE CARE OF THE REST!

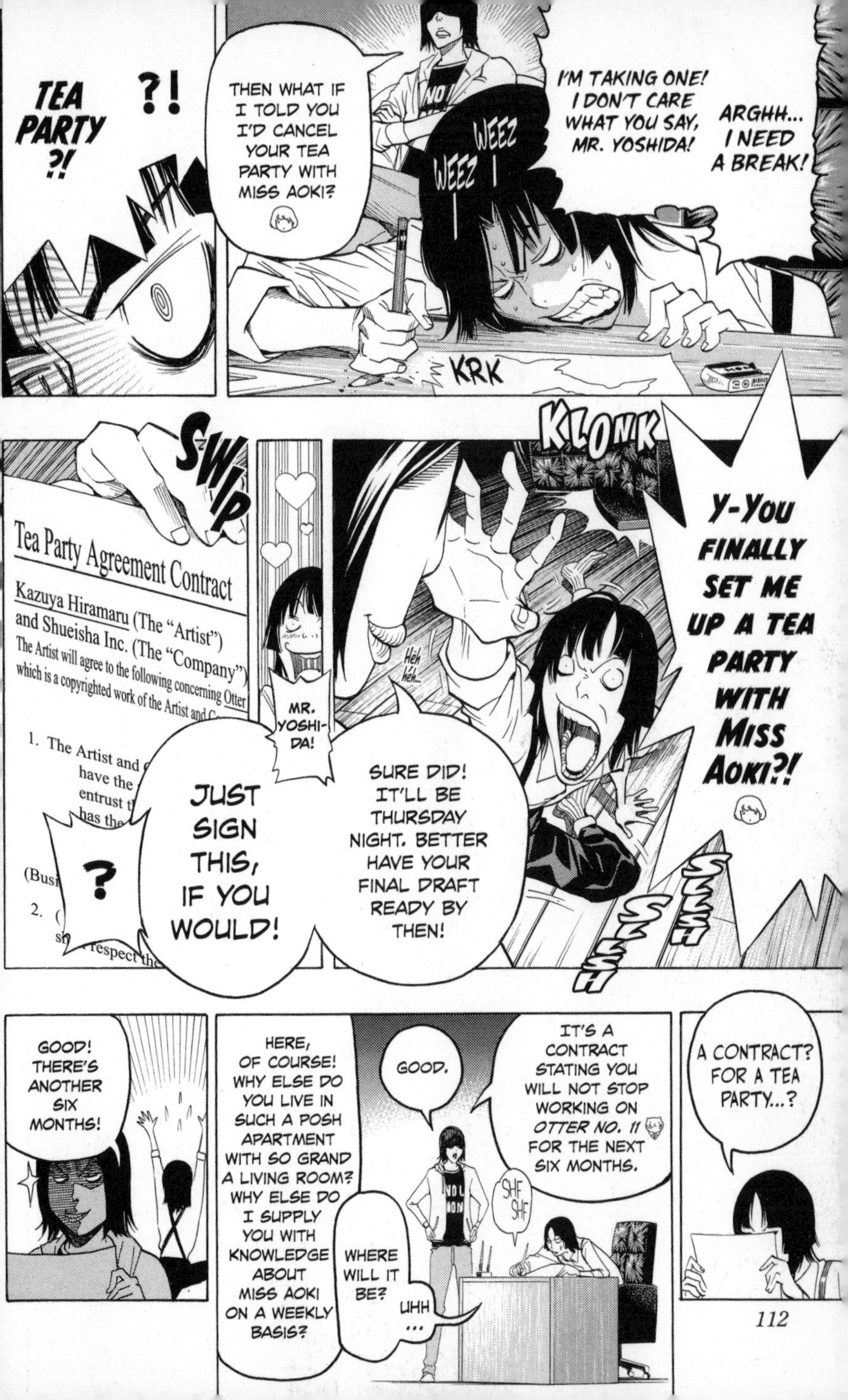
ARGHH... I NEED A BREAK!
I'M TAKING ONE! I DON'T CARE WHAT YOU SAY, MR. YOSHIDA!
WEEZ
WEEZ
THEN WHAT IF I TOLD YOU I'D CANCEL YOUR TEA PARTY WITH MISS AOKI?
KRK
?!
TEA PARTY ?!
KLONK
Y-YOU FINALLY SET ME UP A TEA PARTY WITH MISS AOKI?!
SLSH
SLSH
Heh heh...
SURE DID! IT'LL BE THURSDAY NIGHT. BETTER HAVE YOUR FINAL DRAFT READY BY THEN!
MR. YOSHIDA!
SWIP
Tea Party Agreement Contract
Kazuya Hiramaru (The "Artist")
and Shueisha Inc. (The "Company")
The Artist will agree to the following concerning Otter
which is a copyrighted work of the Artist and C
1. The Artist and
have the
entrust t
has the
(Busi
2. (
s respect the
?
JUST SIGN THIS, IF YOU WOULD!
A CONTRACT? FOR A TEA PARTY...?
IT'S A CONTRACT STATING YOU WILL NOT STOP WORKING ON OTTER NO. 11 FOR THE NEXT SIX MONTHS.
SHF SHF
GOOD.
WHERE WILL IT BE?
UHH ...
HERE, OF COURSE! WHY ELSE DO YOU LIVE IN SUCH A POSH APARTMENT WITH SO GRAND A LIVING ROOM? WHY ELSE DO I SUPPLY YOU WITH KNOWLEDGE ABOUT MISS AOKI ON A WEEKLY BASIS?
GOOD! THERE'S ANOTHER SIX MONTHS!

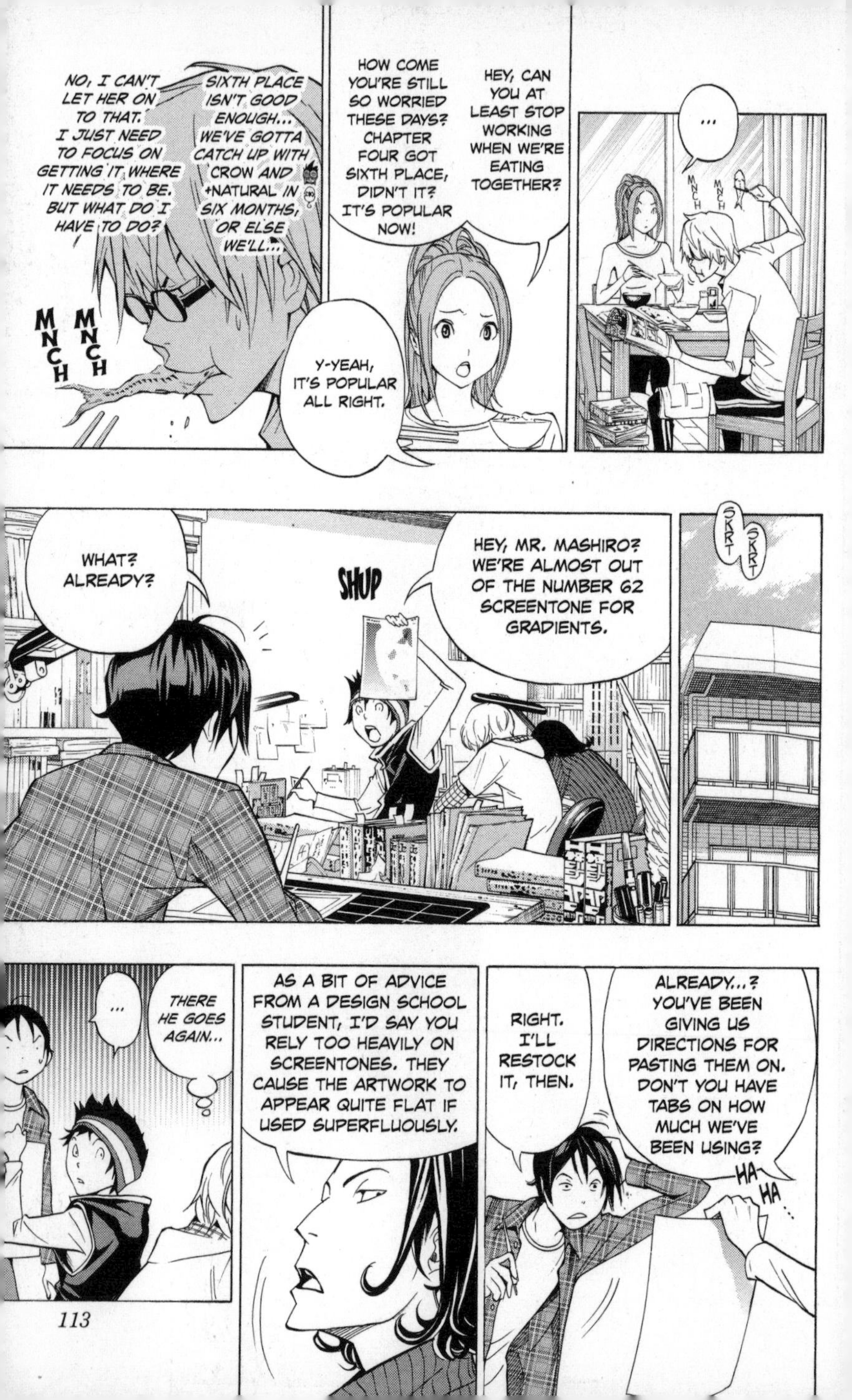
...
MNCH MNCH
HEY, CAN YOU AT LEAST STOP WORKING WHEN WE'RE EATING TOGETHER?
HOW COME YOU'RE STILL SO WORRIED THESE DAYS? CHAPTER FOUR GOT SIXTH PLACE, DIDN'T IT? IT'S POPULAR NOW!
Y-YEAH, IT'S POPULAR ALL RIGHT.
SIXTH PLACE ISN'T GOOD ENOUGH... WE'VE GOTTA CATCH UP WITH CROW AND +NATURAL IN SIX MONTHS, OR ELSE WE'LL...
NO, I CAN'T LET HER ON TO THAT. I JUST NEED TO FOCUS ON GETTING IT WHERE IT NEEDS TO BE. BUT WHAT DO I HAVE TO DO?
MNCH MNCH
SKRT SKRT
HEY, MR. MASHIRO? WE'RE ALMOST OUT OF THE NUMBER 62 SCREENTONE FOR GRADIENTS.
SHUP
WHAT? ALREADY?
ALREADY...? YOU'VE BEEN GIVING US DIRECTIONS FOR PASTING THEM ON. DON'T YOU HAVE TABS ON HOW MUCH WE'VE BEEN USING?
RIGHT. I'LL RESTOCK IT, THEN.
HA HA...
AS A BIT OF ADVICE FROM A DESIGN SCHOOL STUDENT, I'D SAY YOU RELY TOO HEAVILY ON SCREENTONES. THEY CAUSE THE ARTWORK TO APPEAR QUITE FLAT IF USED SUPERFLUOUSLY.
THERE HE GOES AGAIN...
...

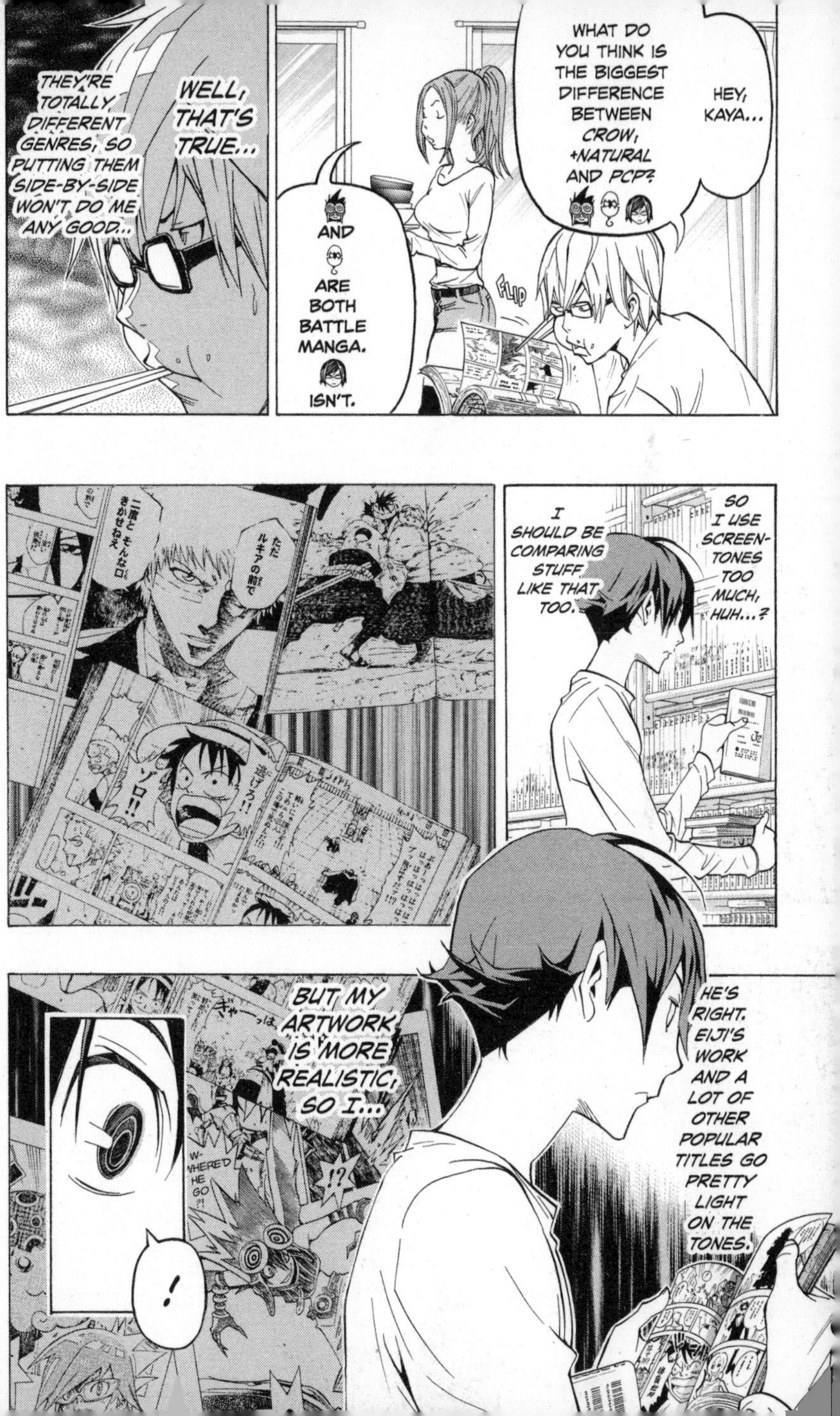
HEY, KAYA...
WHAT DO YOU THINK IS THE BIGGEST DIFFERENCE BETWEEN CROW, +NATURAL AND PCP?
AND ARE BOTH BATTLE MANGA. ISN'T.
FLIP
WELL, THAT'S TRUE...
THEY'RE TOTALLY DIFFERENT GENRES, SO PUTTING THEM SIDE-BY-SIDE WON'T DO ME ANY GOOD...
SO I USE SCREEN-TONES TOO MUCH, HUH...?
I SHOULD BE COMPARING STUFF LIKE THAT TOO.
ただ ルキアの前で
二度と もんな口 きかせねえ
ゾロ!!
逃げろ!!
HE'S RIGHT. EIJI'S WORK AND A LOT OF OTHER POPULAR TITLES GO PRETTY LIGHT ON THE TONES.
BUT MY ARTWORK IS MORE REALISTIC, SO I...
W-WHERE'D HE GO?!
!?
!

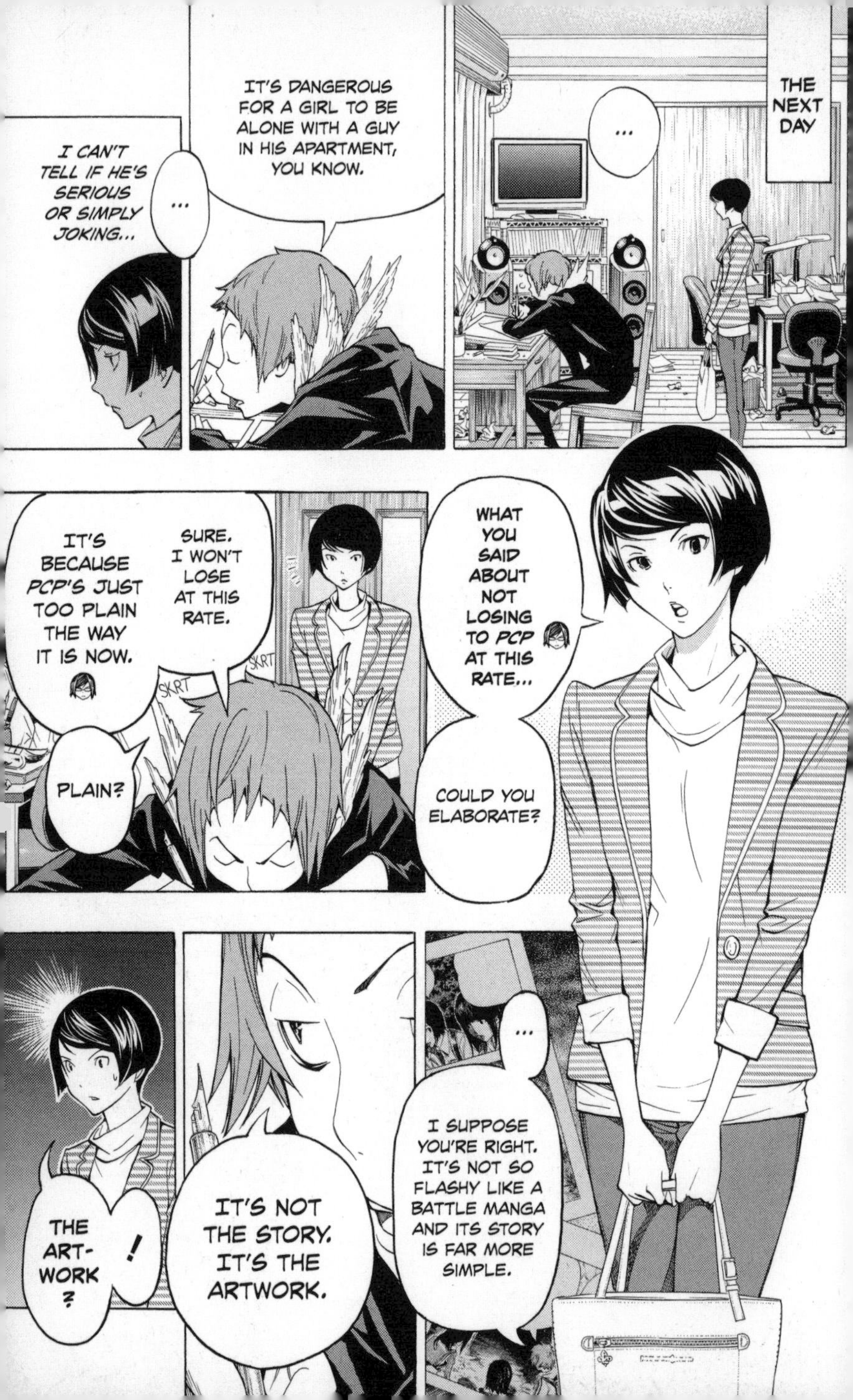
THE NEXT DAY
...
IT'S DANGEROUS FOR A GIRL TO BE ALONE WITH A GUY IN HIS APARTMENT, YOU KNOW.
...
I CAN'T TELL IF HE'S SERIOUS OR SIMPLY JOKING...
WHAT YOU SAID ABOUT NOT LOSING TO PCP AT THIS RATE...
COULD YOU ELABORATE?
SKRT
SURE. I WON'T LOSE AT THIS RATE.
SKRT
IT'S BECAUSE PCP'S JUST TOO PLAIN THE WAY IT IS NOW.
PLAIN?
...
I SUPPOSE YOU'RE RIGHT. IT'S NOT SO FLASHY LIKE A BATTLE MANGA AND ITS STORY IS FAR MORE SIMPLE.
IT'S NOT THE STORY. IT'S THE ARTWORK.
!
THE ART-WORK?

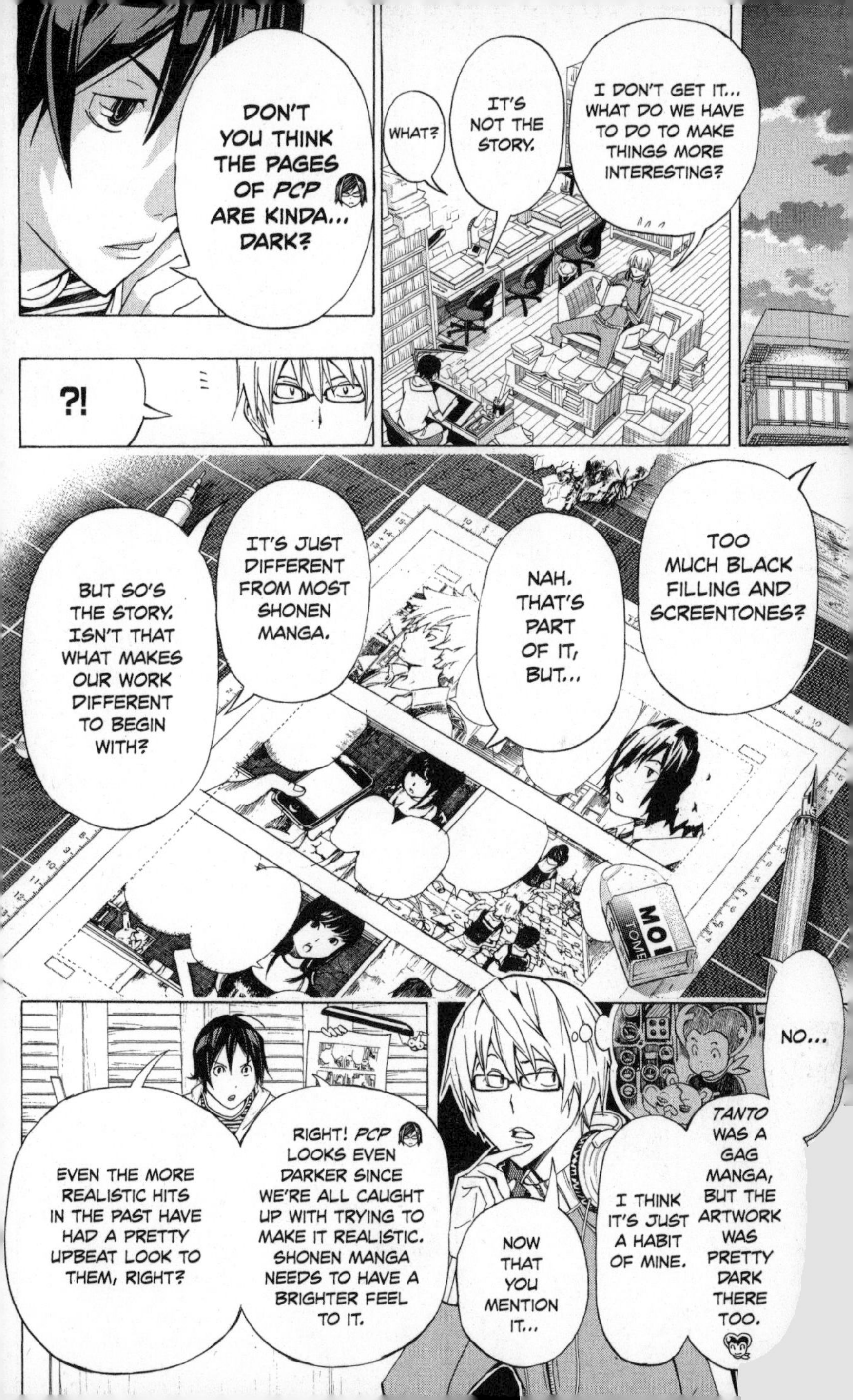
I DON'T GET IT... WHAT DO WE HAVE TO DO TO MAKE THINGS MORE INTERESTING?
IT'S NOT THE STORY.
WHAT?
DON'T YOU THINK THE PAGES OF PCP ARE KINDA... DARK?
?!
TOO MUCH BLACK FILLING AND SCREENTONES?
NAH. THAT'S PART OF IT, BUT...
IT'S JUST DIFFERENT FROM MOST SHONEN MANGA.
BUT SO'S THE STORY. ISN'T THAT WHAT MAKES OUR WORK DIFFERENT TO BEGIN WITH?
NO...
TANTO WAS A GAG MANGA, BUT THE ARTWORK WAS PRETTY DARK THERE TOO.
I THINK IT'S JUST A HABIT OF MINE.
NOW THAT YOU MENTION IT...
RIGHT! PCP LOOKS EVEN DARKER SINCE WE'RE ALL CAUGHT UP WITH TRYING TO MAKE IT REALISTIC. SHONEN MANGA NEEDS TO HAVE A BRIGHTER FEEL TO IT.
EVEN THE MORE REALISTIC HITS IN THE PAST HAVE HAD A PRETTY UPBEAT LOOK TO THEM, RIGHT?

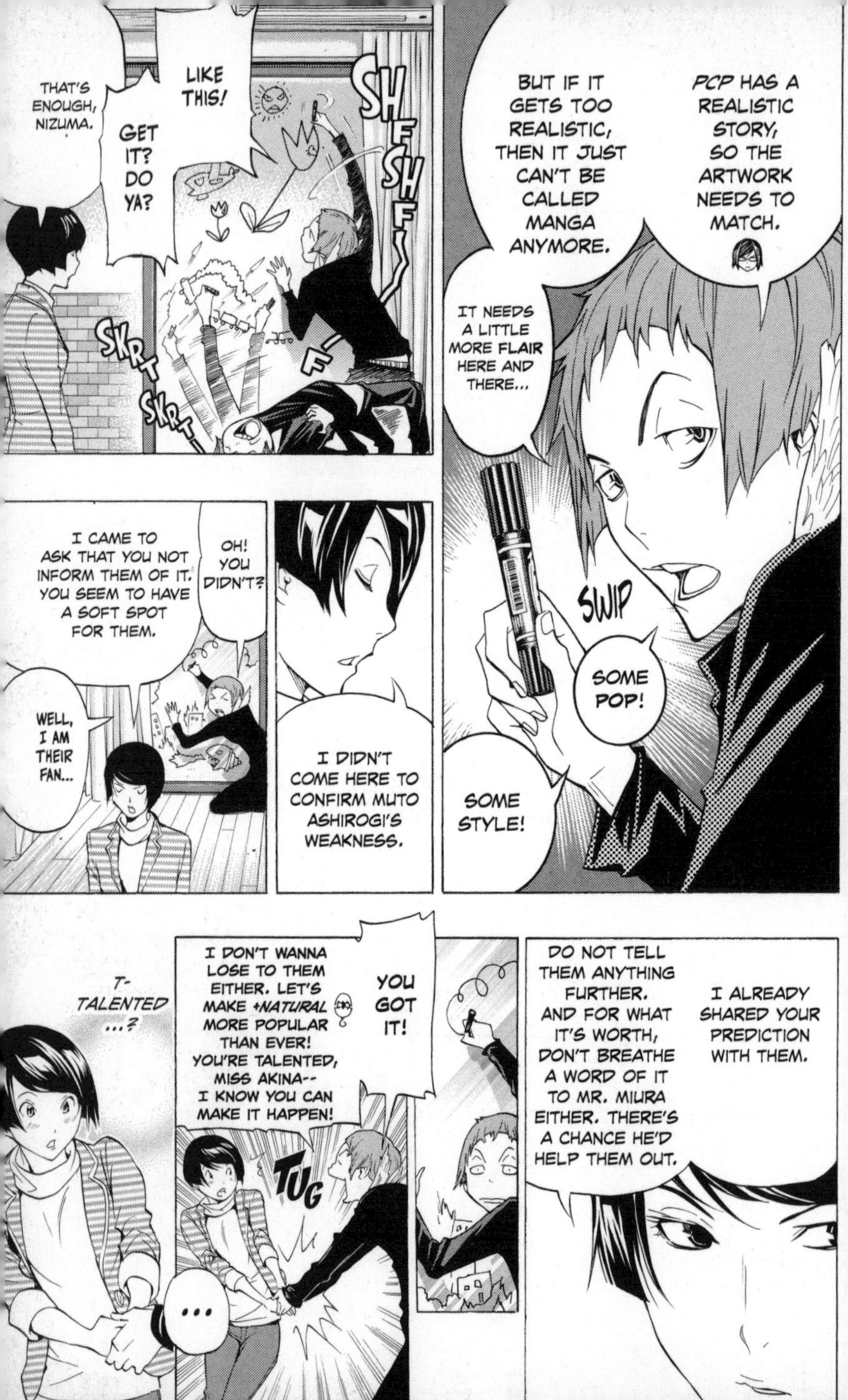

PCP HAS A REALISTIC STORY, SO THE ARTWORK NEEDS TO MATCH.
BUT IF IT GETS TOO REALISTIC, THEN IT JUST CAN'T BE CALLED MANGA ANYMORE.
IT NEEDS A LITTLE MORE FLAIR HERE AND THERE...
SWIP
SOME POP!
SOME STYLE!
SHF
SHF
LIKE THIS!
GET IT? DO YA?
THAT'S ENOUGH, NIZUMA.
F
SKRT
SKRT
I DIDN'T COME HERE TO CONFIRM MUTO ASHIROGI'S WEAKNESS.
OH! YOU DIDN'T?
I CAME TO ASK THAT YOU NOT INFORM THEM OF IT. YOU SEEM TO HAVE A SOFT SPOT FOR THEM.
WELL, I AM THEIR FAN...
I ALREADY SHARED YOUR PREDICTION WITH THEM.
DO NOT TELL THEM ANYTHING FURTHER. AND FOR WHAT IT'S WORTH, DON'T BREATHE A WORD OF IT TO MR. MIURA EITHER. THERE'S A CHANCE HE'D HELP THEM OUT.
YOU GOT IT!
I DON'T WANNA LOSE TO THEM EITHER. LET'S MAKE +NATURAL MORE POPULAR THAN EVER! YOU'RE TALENTED, MISS AKINA-- I KNOW YOU CAN MAKE IT HAPPEN!
TUG
T-TALENTED...?
...

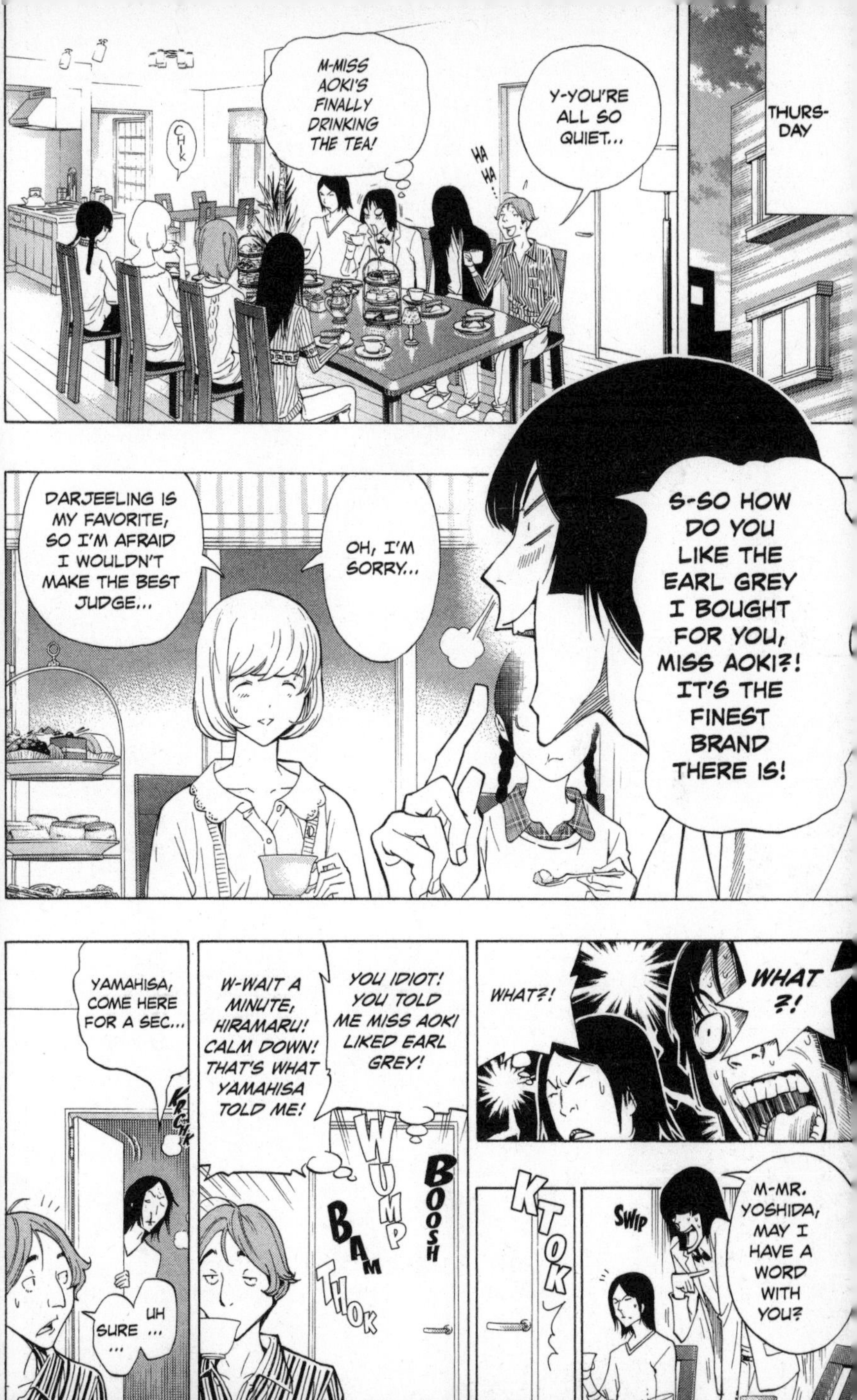
THURS-DAY
Y-YOU'RE ALL SO QUIET...
HA HA
M-MISS AOKI'S FINALLY DRINKING THE TEA!
CHIK
S-SO HOW DO YOU LIKE THE EARL GREY I BOUGHT FOR YOU, MISS AOKI?! IT'S THE FINEST BRAND THERE IS!
OH, I'M SORRY...
DARJEELING IS MY FAVORITE, SO I'M AFRAID I WOULDN'T MAKE THE BEST JUDGE...
WHAT?!
WHAT?!
M-MR. YOSHIDA, MAY I HAVE A WORD WITH YOU?
SWIP
KTOK
YOU IDIOT! YOU TOLD ME MISS AOKI LIKED EARL GREY!
W-WAIT A MINUTE, HIRAMARU! CALM DOWN! THAT'S WHAT YAMAHISA TOLD ME!
BOOSH
WUMP
BAM
THOK
YAMAHISA, COME HERE FOR A SEC...
KRCHIK
UH SURE ... ...

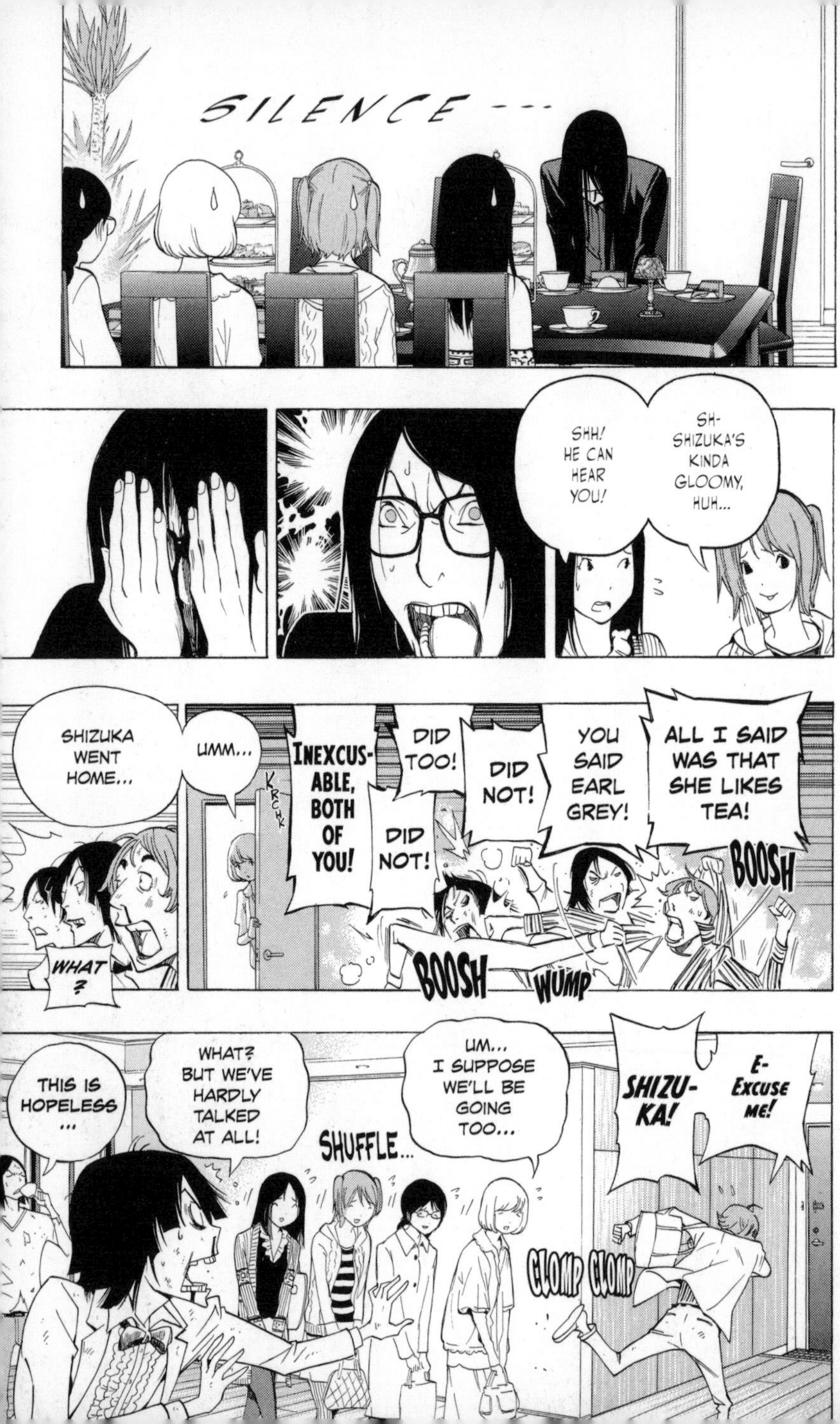
SILENCE---
SH-SHIZUKA'S KINDA GLOOMY, HUH...
SHH! HE CAN HEAR YOU!
ALL I SAID WAS THAT SHE LIKES TEA!
YOU SAID EARL GREY!
DID NOT!
DID TOO!
DID NOT!
INEXCUS-ABLE, BOTH OF YOU!
BOOSH
WUMP
BOOSH
KRCHK
UMM...
SHIZUKA WENT HOME...
WHAT?
E-EXCUSE ME!
SHIZU-KA!
CLOMP CLOMP
UM... I SUPPOSE WE'LL BE GOING TOO...
SHUFFLE...
WHAT? BUT WE'VE HARDLY TALKED AT ALL!
THIS IS HOPELESS...

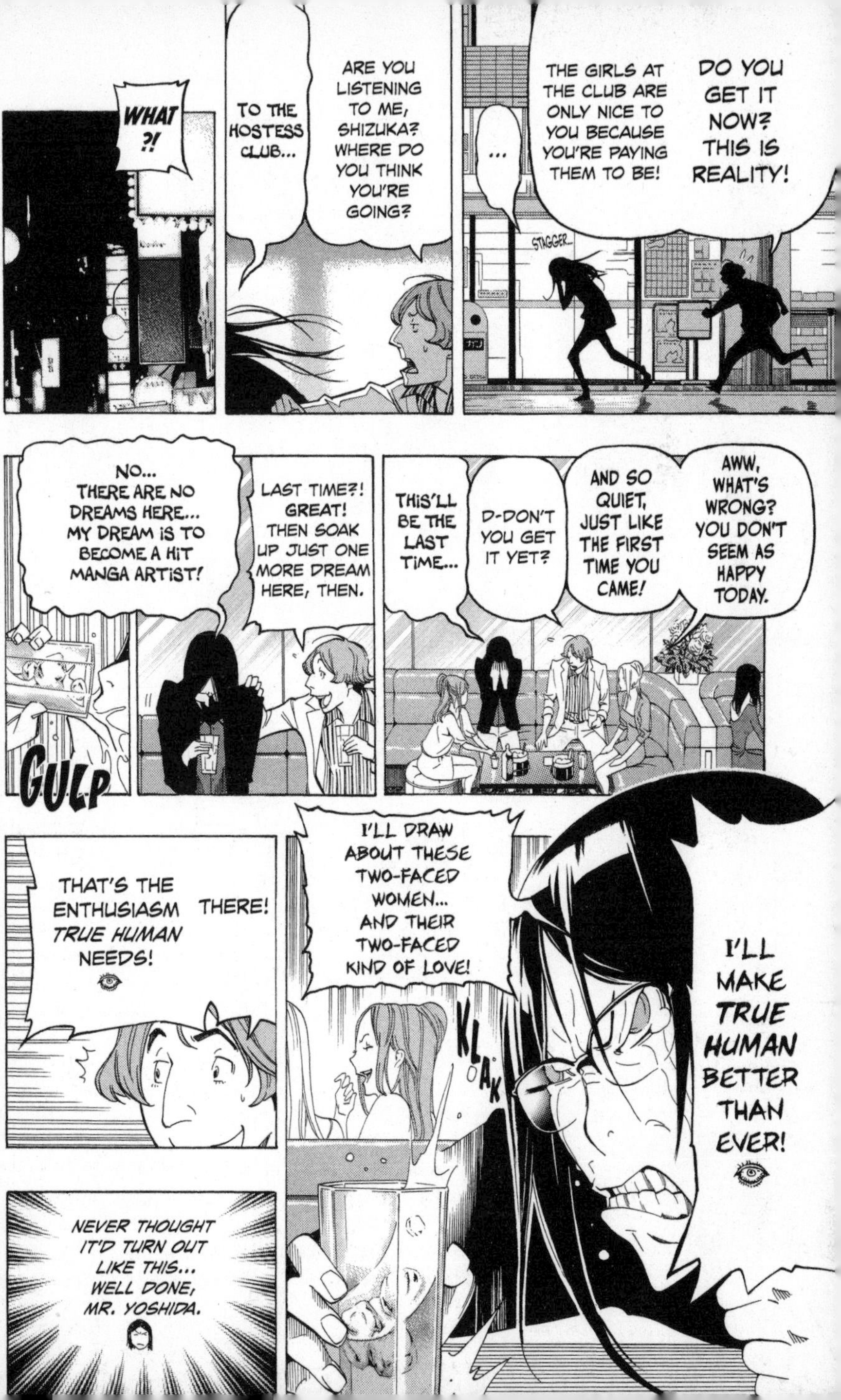
DO YOU GET IT NOW? THIS IS REALITY!
THE GIRLS AT THE CLUB ARE ONLY NICE TO YOU BECAUSE YOU'RE PAYING THEM TO BE!
...
STAGGER...
ARE YOU LISTENING TO ME, SHIZUKA? WHERE DO YOU THINK YOU'RE GOING?
TO THE HOSTESS CLUB...
WHAT ?!
AWW, WHAT'S WRONG? YOU DON'T SEEM AS HAPPY TODAY.
AND SO QUIET, JUST LIKE THE FIRST TIME YOU CAME!
D-DON'T YOU GET IT YET?
THIS'LL BE THE LAST TIME...
LAST TIME?! GREAT! THEN SOAK UP JUST ONE MORE DREAM HERE, THEN.
NO... THERE ARE NO DREAMS HERE... MY DREAM IS TO BECOME A HIT MANGA ARTIST!
GULP
I'LL MAKE *TRUE HUMAN* BETTER THAN EVER!
I'LL DRAW ABOUT THESE TWO-FACED WOMEN... AND THEIR TWO-FACED KIND OF LOVE!
KLAK
THERE!
THAT'S THE ENTHUSIASM *TRUE HUMAN* NEEDS!
NEVER THOUGHT IT'D TURN OUT LIKE THIS... WELL DONE, MR. YOSHIDA.

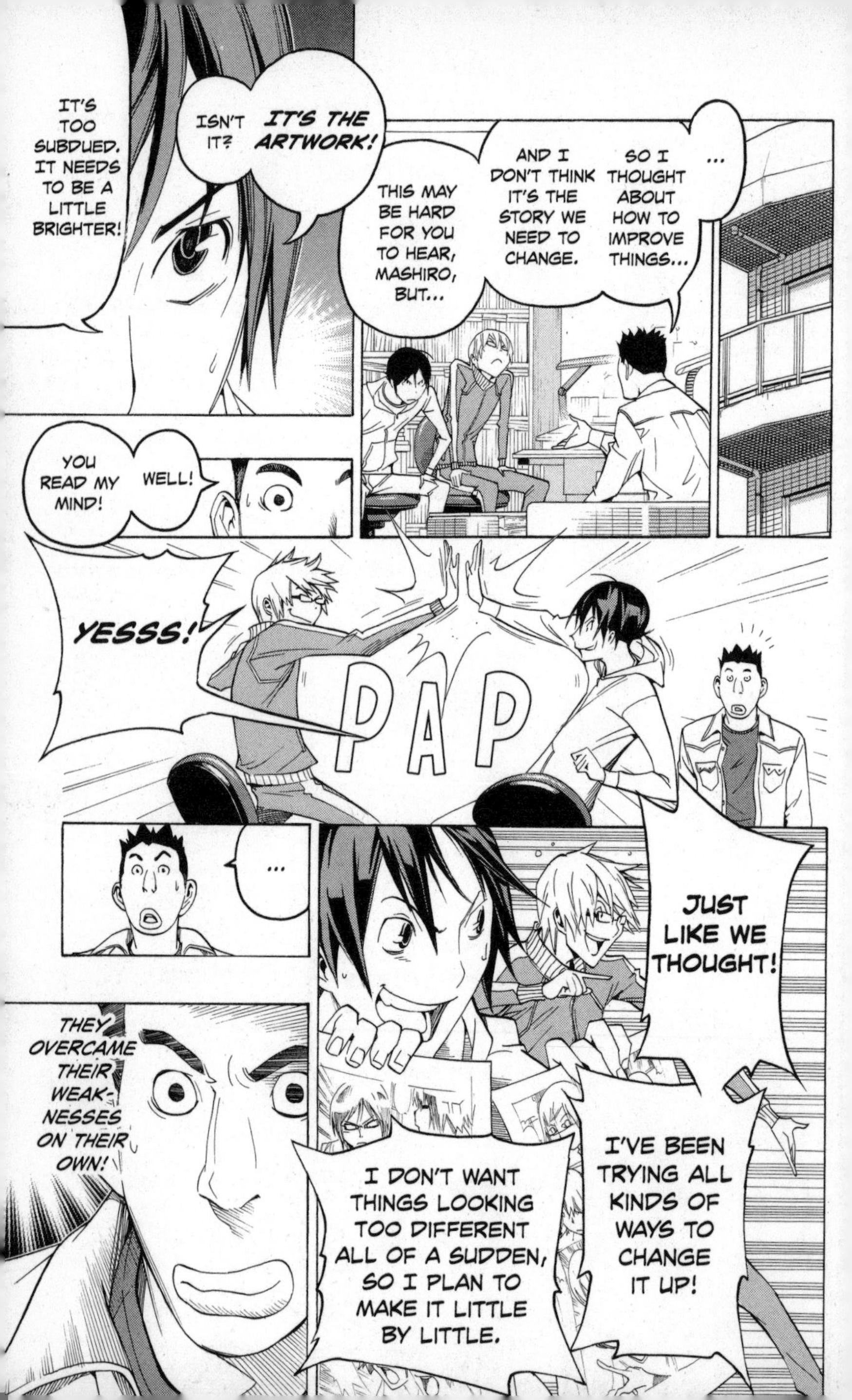
...
SO I THOUGHT ABOUT HOW TO IMPROVE THINGS...
AND I DON'T THINK IT'S THE STORY WE NEED TO CHANGE.
THIS MAY BE HARD FOR YOU TO HEAR, MASHIRO, BUT...
IT'S THE ARTWORK!
ISN'T IT?
IT'S TOO SUBDUED. IT NEEDS TO BE A LITTLE BRIGHTER!
WELL!
YOU READ MY MIND!
YESSS!
PAP
JUST LIKE WE THOUGHT!
I'VE BEEN TRYING ALL KINDS OF WAYS TO CHANGE IT UP!
I DON'T WANT THINGS LOOKING TOO DIFFERENT ALL OF A SUDDEN, SO I PLAN TO MAKE IT LITTLE BY LITTLE.
...
THEY OVERCAME THEIR WEAKNESSES ON THEIR OWN!

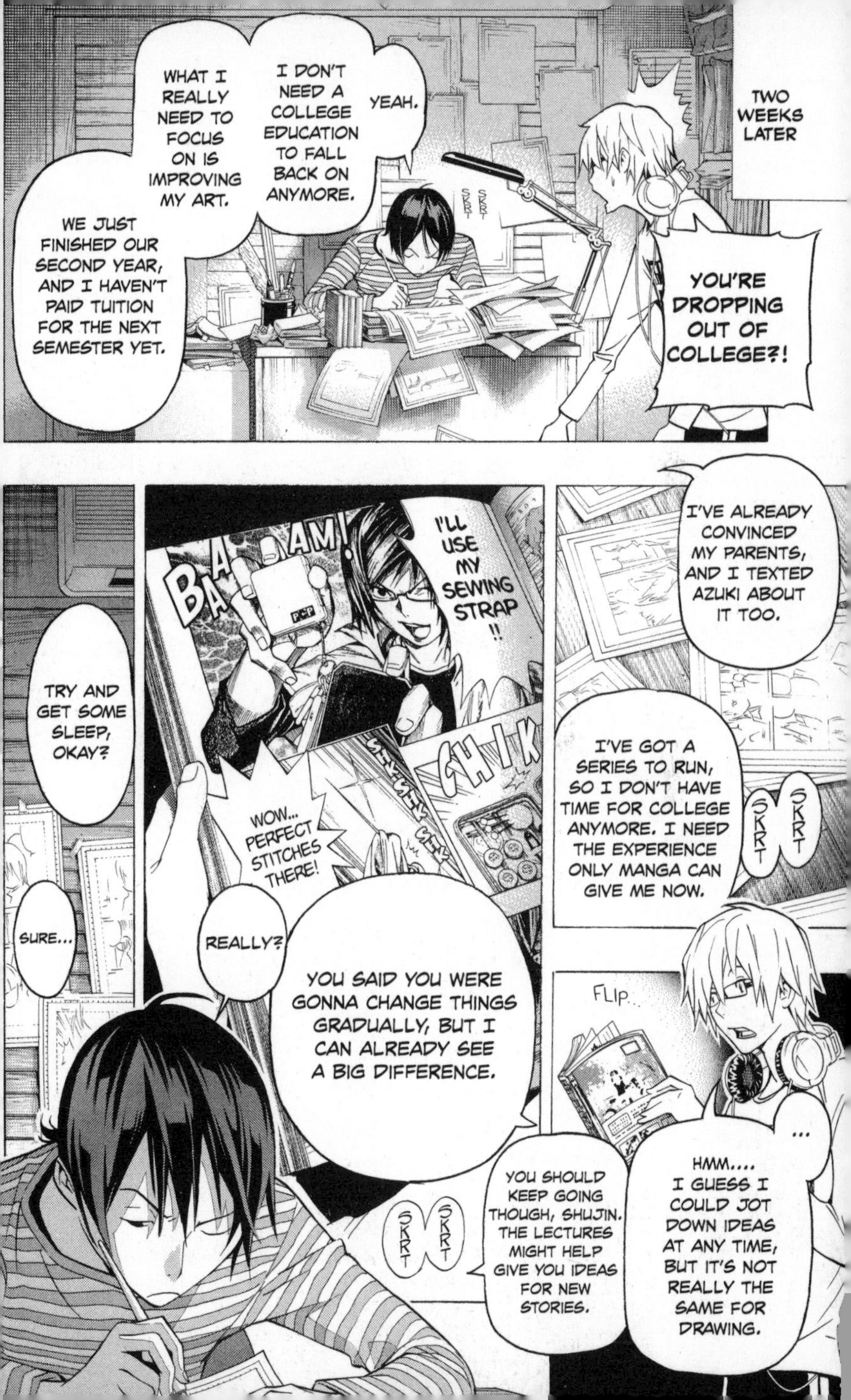

TWO WEEKS LATER
YOU'RE DROPPING OUT OF COLLEGE?!
YEAH.
I DON'T NEED A COLLEGE EDUCATION TO FALL BACK ON ANYMORE.
WHAT I REALLY NEED TO FOCUS ON IS IMPROVING MY ART.
WE JUST FINISHED OUR SECOND YEAR, AND I HAVEN'T PAID TUITION FOR THE NEXT SEMESTER YET.
SKRT SKRT
I'VE ALREADY CONVINCED MY PARENTS, AND I TEXTED AZUKI ABOUT IT TOO.
I'VE GOT A SERIES TO RUN, SO I DON'T HAVE TIME FOR COLLEGE ANYMORE. I NEED THE EXPERIENCE ONLY MANGA CAN GIVE ME NOW.
SKRT SKRT
BAAAM!
I'LL USE MY SEWING STRAP!!
CHIK
WOW... PERFECT STITCHES THERE!
YOU SAID YOU WERE GONNA CHANGE THINGS GRADUALLY, BUT I CAN ALREADY SEE A BIG DIFFERENCE.
REALLY?
FLIP...
YOU SHOULD KEEP GOING THOUGH, SHUJIN. THE LECTURES MIGHT HELP GIVE YOU IDEAS FOR NEW STORIES.
SKRT SKRT
...
HMM.... I GUESS I COULD JOT DOWN IDEAS AT ANY TIME, BUT IT'S NOT REALLY THE SAME FOR DRAWING.
TRY AND GET SOME SLEEP, OKAY?
SURE...

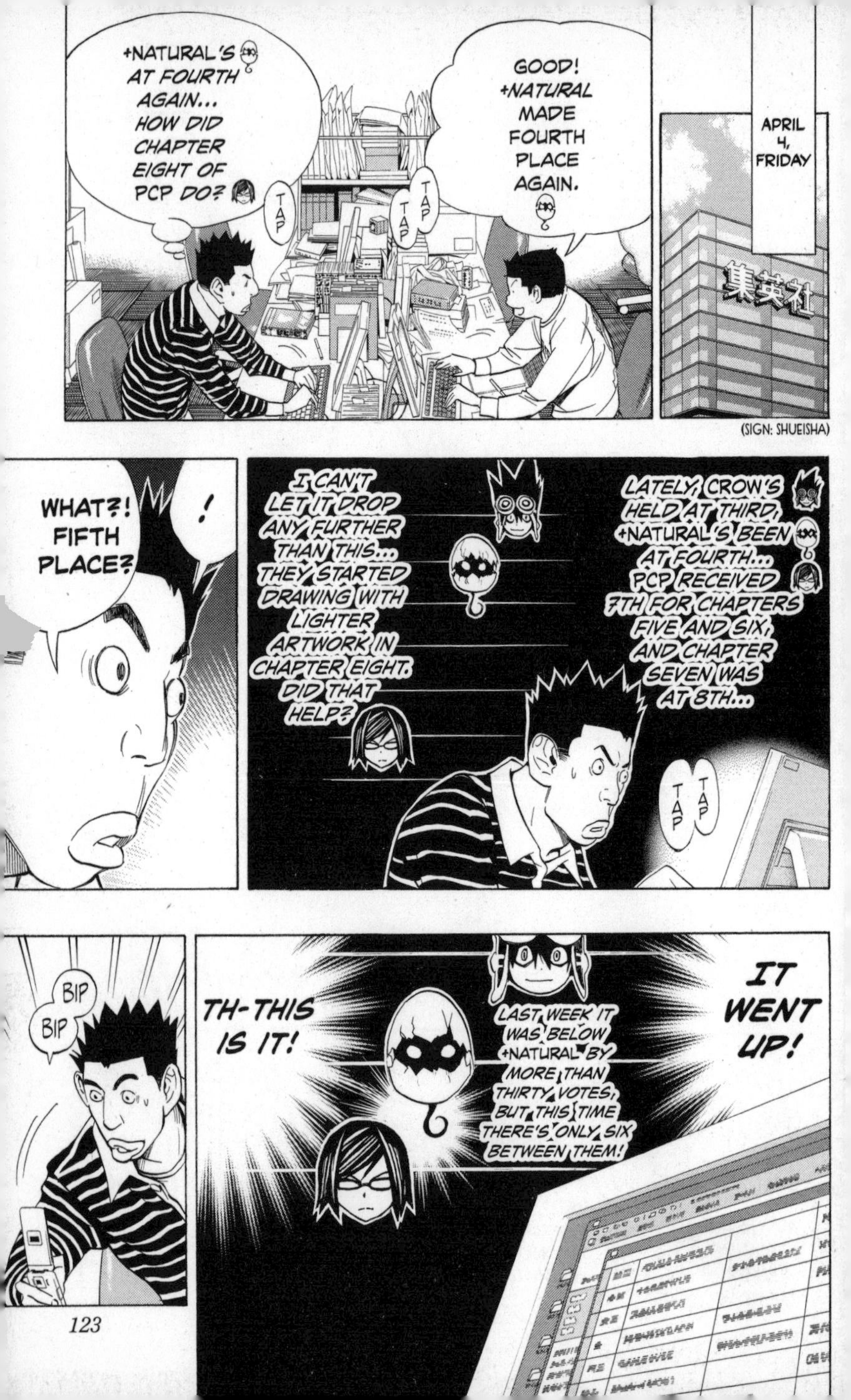
APRIL 4, FRIDAY
(SIGN: SHUEISHA)
GOOD! +NATURAL MADE FOURTH PLACE AGAIN.
TAP TAP
+NATURAL'S AT FOURTH AGAIN... HOW DID CHAPTER EIGHT OF PCP DO?
TAP
LATELY, CROW'S HELD AT THIRD, +NATURAL'S BEEN AT FOURTH... PCP RECEIVED 7TH FOR CHAPTERS FIVE AND SIX, AND CHAPTER SEVEN WAS AT 8TH...
I CAN'T LET IT DROP ANY FURTHER THAN THIS... THEY STARTED DRAWING WITH LIGHTER ARTWORK IN CHAPTER EIGHT. DID THAT HELP?
TAP TAP
!
WHAT?! FIFTH PLACE?
IT WENT UP!
LAST WEEK IT WAS BELOW +NATURAL BY MORE THAN THIRTY VOTES, BUT THIS TIME THERE'S ONLY SIX BETWEEN THEM!
TH-THIS IS IT!
BIP BIP

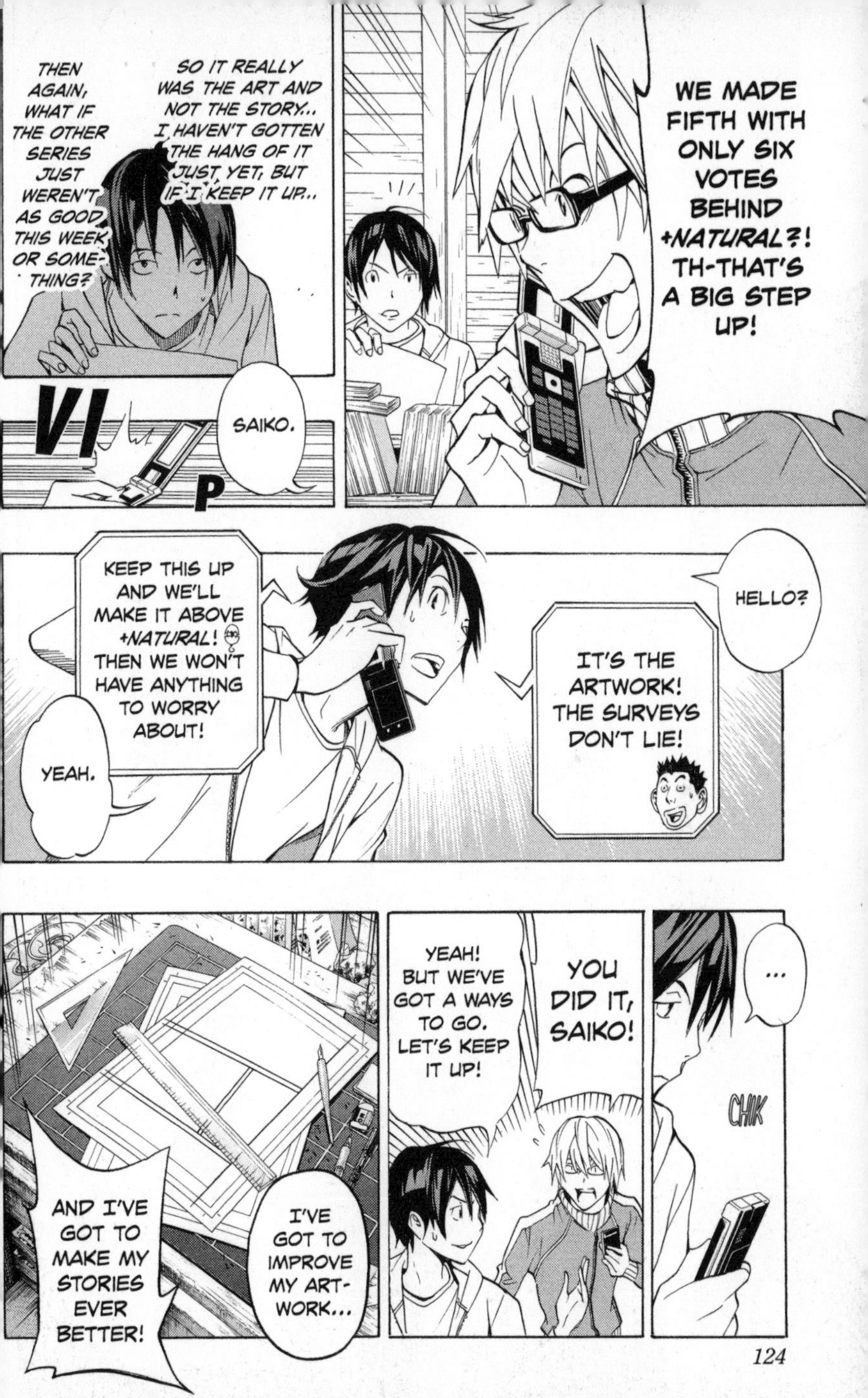
WE MADE FIFTH WITH ONLY SIX VOTES BEHIND +NATURAL?! TH-THAT'S A BIG STEP UP!
SO IT REALLY WAS THE ART AND NOT THE STORY... I HAVEN'T GOTTEN THE HANG OF IT JUST YET, BUT IF I KEEP IT UP...
THEN AGAIN, WHAT IF THE OTHER SERIES JUST WEREN'T AS GOOD THIS WEEK OR SOME-THING?
SAIKO.
VIP
HELLO?
IT'S THE ARTWORK! THE SURVEYS DON'T LIE!
KEEP THIS UP AND WE'LL MAKE IT ABOVE +NATURAL! THEN WE WON'T HAVE ANYTHING TO WORRY ABOUT!
YEAH.
...
CHIK
YOU DID IT, SAIKO!
YEAH! BUT WE'VE GOT A WAYS TO GO. LET'S KEEP IT UP!
I'VE GOT TO IMPROVE MY ART-WORK...
AND I'VE GOT TO MAKE MY STORIES EVER BETTER!

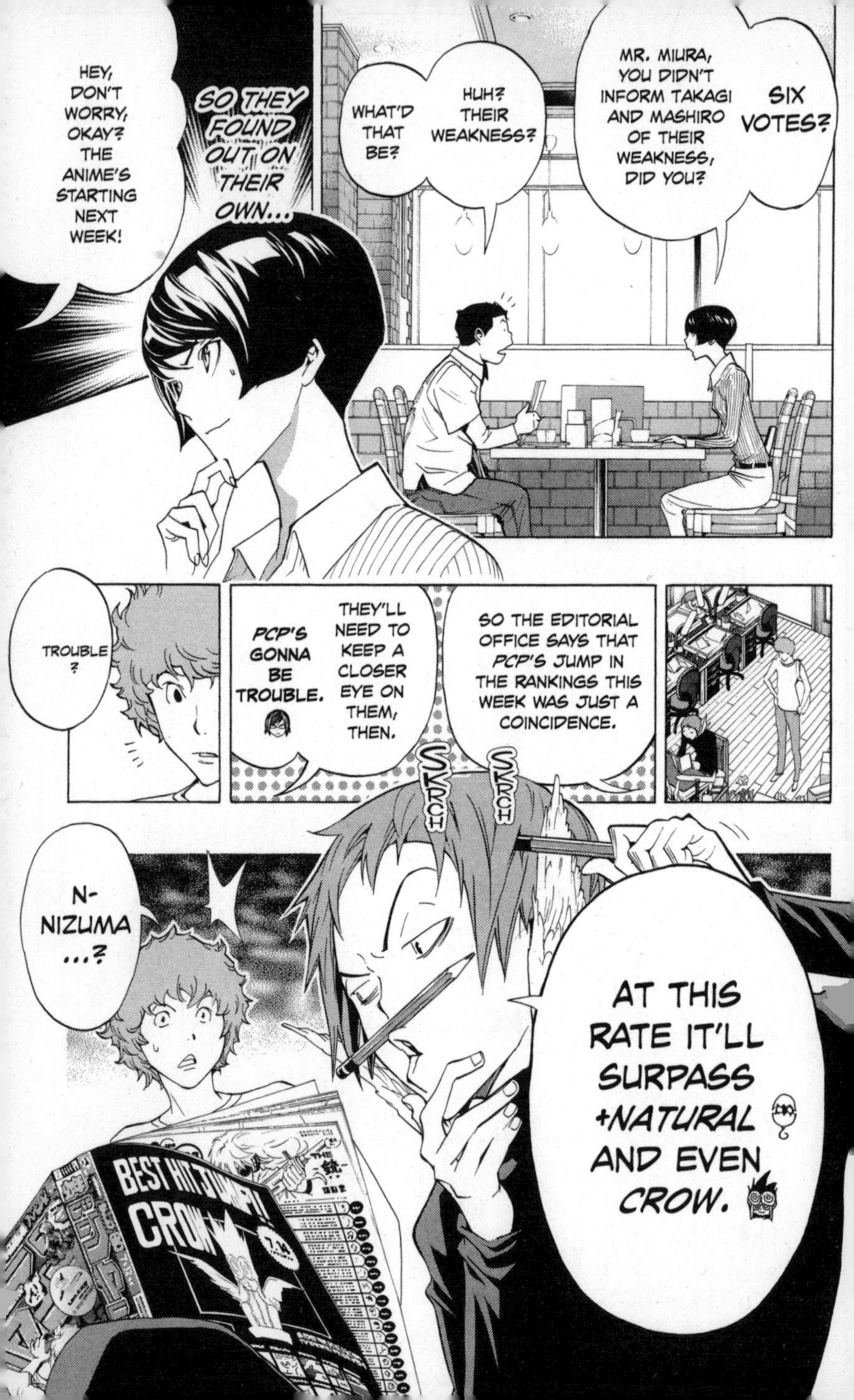
SIX VOTES?
MR. MIURA, YOU DIDN'T INFORM TAKAGI AND MASHIRO OF THEIR WEAKNESS, DID YOU?
HUH? THEIR WEAKNESS?
WHAT'D THAT BE?
SO THEY FOUND OUT ON THEIR OWN...
HEY, DON'T WORRY, OKAY? THE ANIME'S STARTING NEXT WEEK!
SO THE EDITORIAL OFFICE SAYS THAT *PCP'S* JUMP IN THE RANKINGS THIS WEEK WAS JUST A COINCIDENCE.
THEY'LL NEED TO KEEP A CLOSER EYE ON THEM, THEN.
PCP'S GONNA BE TROUBLE.
TROUBLE?
SKRCH
SKRCH
AT THIS RATE IT'LL SURPASS *+NATURAL* AND EVEN *CROW*.
N-NIZUMA...?

OHBA'S STORYBOARD

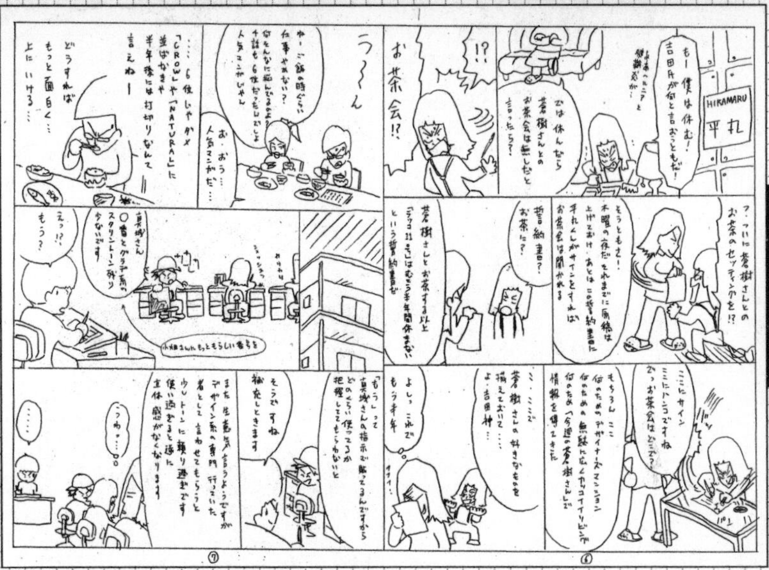
HIRAMARU
平丸
もー僕は休む！吉田氏が何と言おうともだ！
ふぁ～ヘルニアと腱鞘炎が…
では休んなら蒼樹さんとのお茶会は無しだと言ったら？
!?
お茶会!?
フ・ついに蒼樹さんとのお茶のセッティングを!?
そうともさ！木曜の夜だそれまでに原稿は上げておけ。あとはこの誓約書に平丸くんがサインをすればお茶会は開かれる
誓約書？お茶に？
蒼樹さんとお茶する以上「ラッコ11号」はむこう半年間休まない という誓約書だ
ここにサイン
ここにトンコですね
で…お茶会はどこで？
もちろんここ 何のためのデザイナーズマンション 何のための無駄に広くカッコイイリビング 何のため「今週の蒼樹さん」で情報を得てきた
こ…ここで蒼樹さんの好きなものを揃えておいて…
よ…吉田神…
よしっこれでもう半年
オフィ…
う～ん
やーご飯の時ぐらい仕事やめない？何をそんなに悩んでるのよ？十話も6位だったしでしょ人気マンガじゃん
お…おう…人気マンガだ…
…6位じゃダメ「CROW」や「NATURAL」に並ばなきゃ半年後には打切りなんて言えねー
どうすればもっと面白く…上にいける…
カリカリ
シュッシュッ
真城さん○番とグラデ系のスクリントーン残り少ないです
小畑さんもっともらしい番号を
えっ!?もう？
「もう」って真城さんの指示で貼ってるんですからどのくらい使ってるか把握してもらわないと
そうですね補充しときます
また生意気言うようですがデザイン系の専門行っていた者として言わせてもらうとスクリーントーンに頼り過ぎです使い過ぎると逆に立体感がなくなります
うわ…
……
⑥
⑦

OBATA'S STORYBOARD

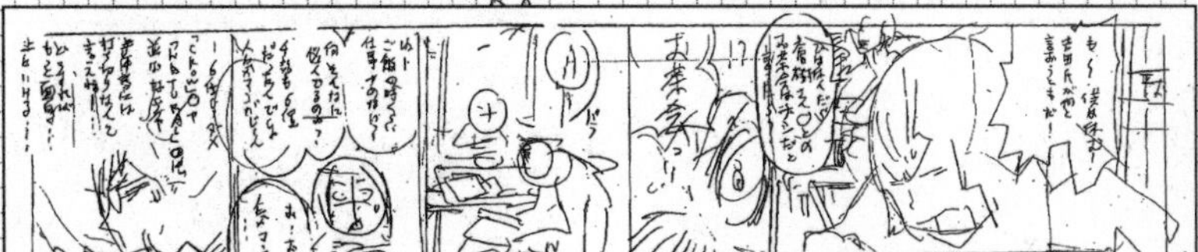

COMPLETE!

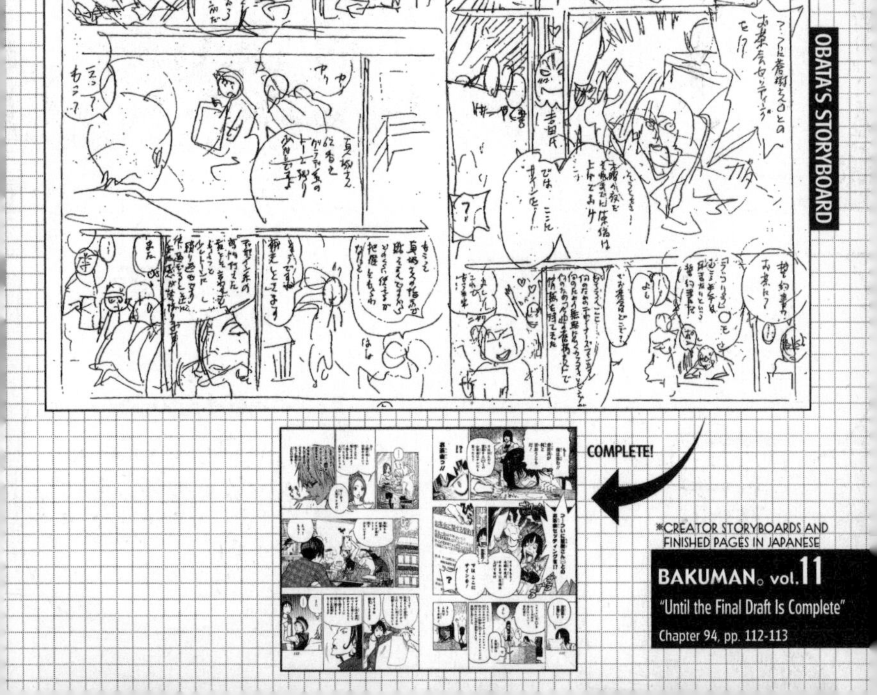

※CREATOR STORYBOARDS AND FINISHED PAGES IN JAPANESE

BAKUMAN。 vol.11

"Until the Final Draft Is Complete"

Chapter 94, pp. 112-113

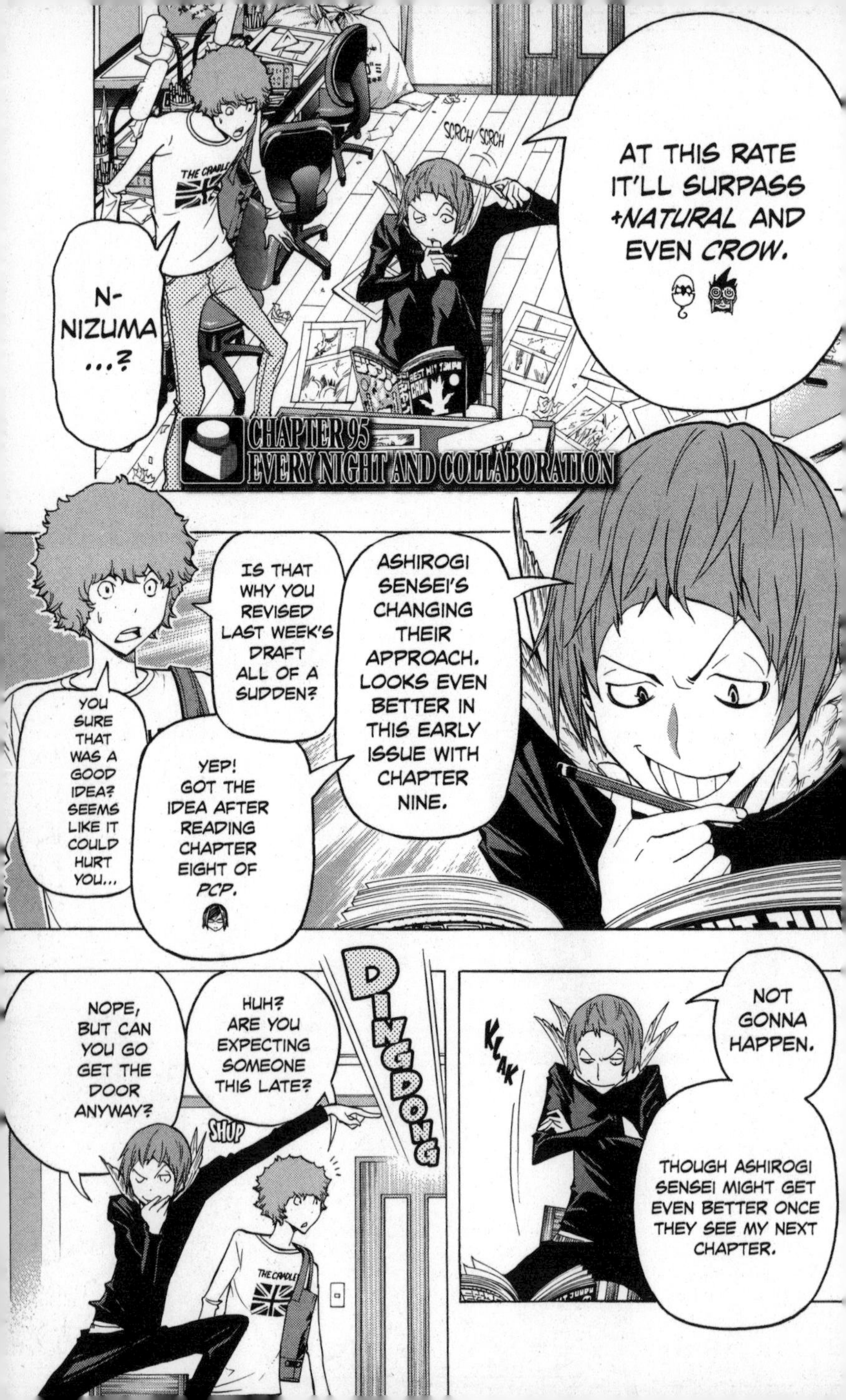
AT THIS RATE IT'LL SURPASS +NATURAL AND EVEN CROW.
SCRCH SCRCH
N-NIZUMA...?
CHAPTER 95 EVERY NIGHT AND COLLABORATION
ASHIROGI SENSEI'S CHANGING THEIR APPROACH. LOOKS EVEN BETTER IN THIS EARLY ISSUE WITH CHAPTER NINE.
IS THAT WHY YOU REVISED LAST WEEK'S DRAFT ALL OF A SUDDEN?
YEP! GOT THE IDEA AFTER READING CHAPTER EIGHT OF PCP.
YOU SURE THAT WAS A GOOD IDEA? SEEMS LIKE IT COULD HURT YOU...
NOT GONNA HAPPEN.
KLAK
THOUGH ASHIROGI SENSEI MIGHT GET EVEN BETTER ONCE THEY SEE MY NEXT CHAPTER.
DINGDONG
HUH? ARE YOU EXPECTING SOMEONE THIS LATE?
NOPE, BUT CAN YOU GO GET THE DOOR ANYWAY?
SHUP

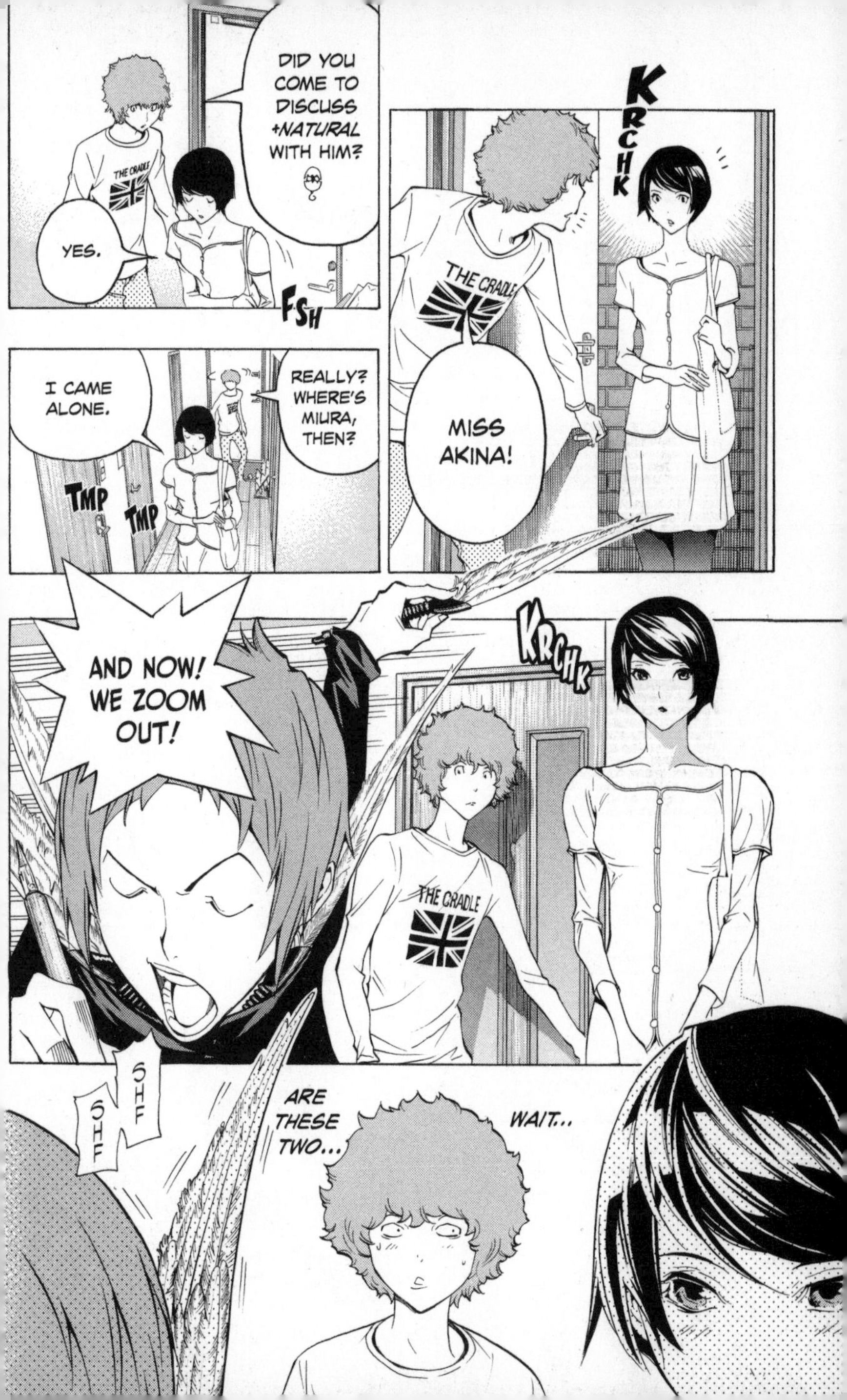
KRCHK
MISS AKINA!
DID YOU COME TO DISCUSS +NATURAL WITH HIM?
YES.
FSH
REALLY? WHERE'S MIURA, THEN?
I CAME ALONE.
TMP
TMP
KRCHK
AND NOW! WE ZOOM OUT!
WAIT...
ARE THESE TWO...
SHF
SHF

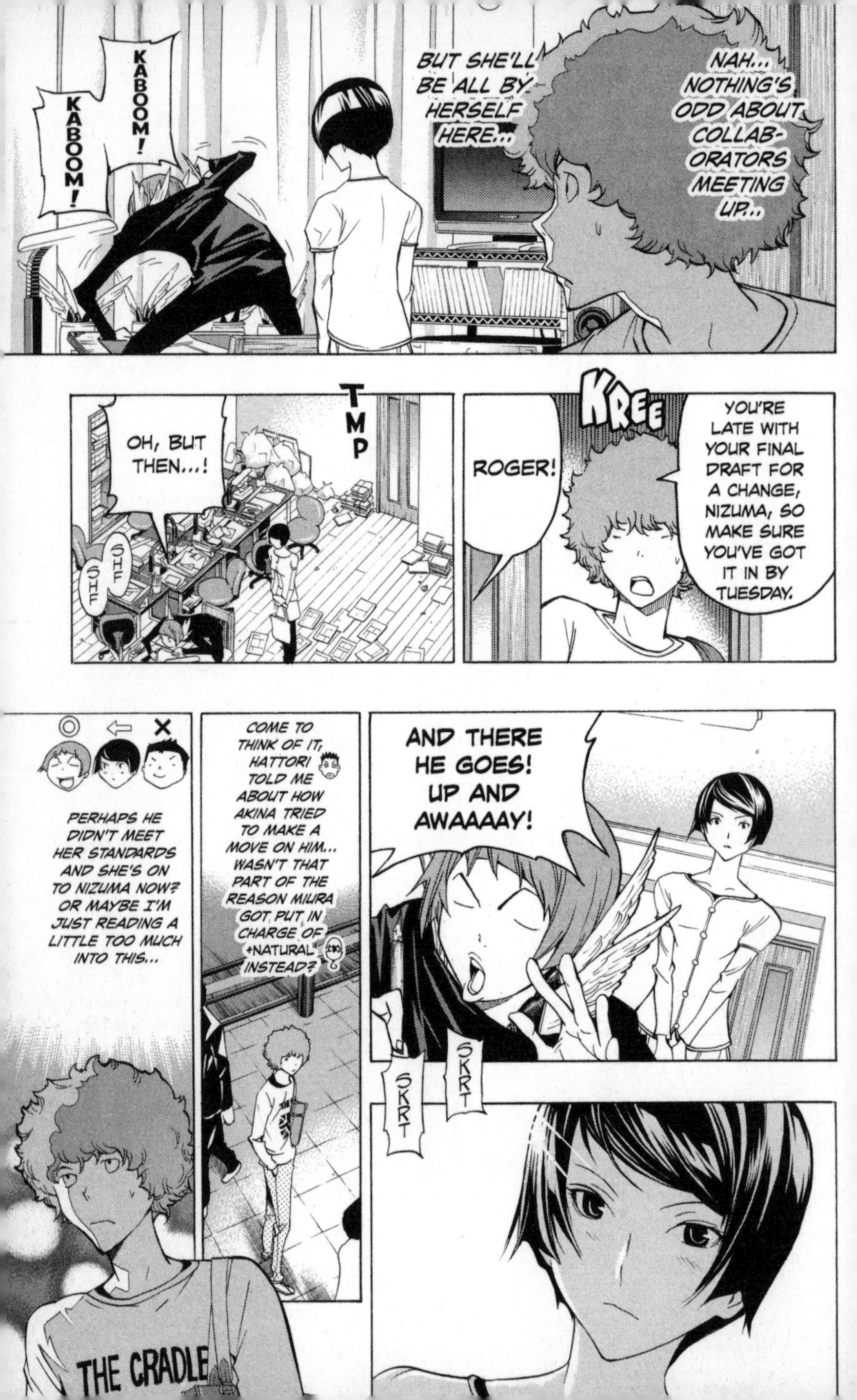
NAH... NOTHING'S ODD ABOUT COLLABORATORS MEETING UP...
BUT SHE'LL BE ALL BY HERSELF HERE...
KABOOM!
KABOOM!
KREE
YOU'RE LATE WITH YOUR FINAL DRAFT FOR A CHANGE, NIZUMA, SO MAKE SURE YOU'VE GOT IT IN BY TUESDAY.
ROGER!
TMP
OH, BUT THEN...!
SHF
SHF
AND THERE HE GOES! UP AND AWAAAAY!
SKRT
SKRT
COME TO THINK OF IT, HATTORI TOLD ME ABOUT HOW AKINA TRIED TO MAKE A MOVE ON HIM... WASN'T THAT PART OF THE REASON MIURA GOT PUT IN CHARGE OF +NATURAL INSTEAD?
◎ ← ×
PERHAPS HE DIDN'T MEET HER STANDARDS AND SHE'S ON TO NIZUMA NOW? OR MAYBE I'M JUST READING A LITTLE TOO MUCH INTO THIS...
THE CRADLE

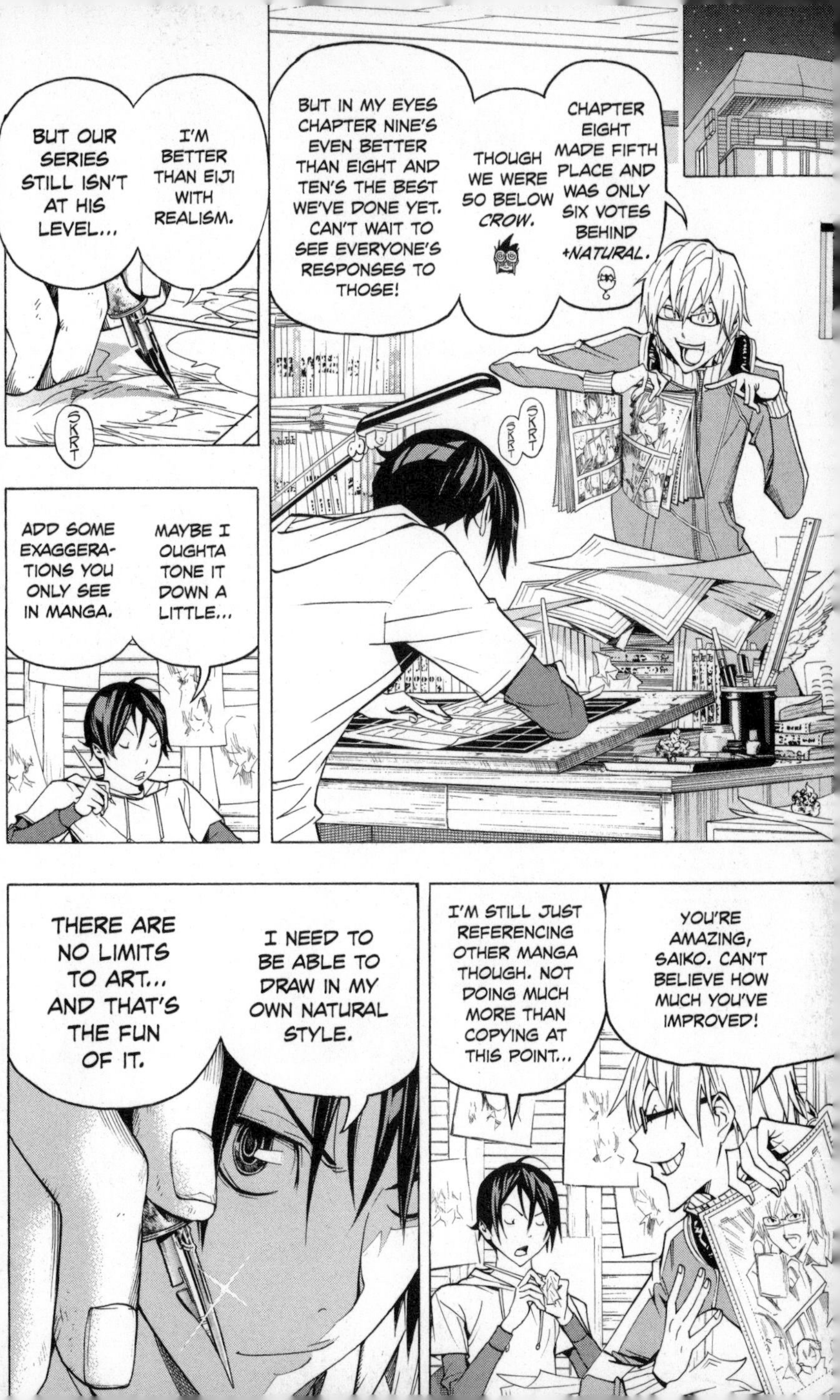
CHAPTER EIGHT MADE FIFTH PLACE AND WAS ONLY SIX VOTES BEHIND +NATURAL.
THOUGH WE WERE 50 BELOW CROW.
BUT IN MY EYES CHAPTER NINE'S EVEN BETTER THAN EIGHT AND TEN'S THE BEST WE'VE DONE YET. CAN'T WAIT TO SEE EVERYONE'S RESPONSES TO THOSE!
SKRT
SKRT
I'M BETTER THAN EIJI WITH REALISM.
BUT OUR SERIES STILL ISN'T AT HIS LEVEL...
SKRT
MAYBE I OUGHTA TONE IT DOWN A LITTLE...
ADD SOME EXAGGERATIONS YOU ONLY SEE IN MANGA.
YOU'RE AMAZING, SAIKO. CAN'T BELIEVE HOW MUCH YOU'VE IMPROVED!
I'M STILL JUST REFERENCING OTHER MANGA THOUGH. NOT DOING MUCH MORE THAN COPYING AT THIS POINT...
I NEED TO BE ABLE TO DRAW IN MY OWN NATURAL STYLE.
THERE ARE NO LIMITS TO ART... AND THAT'S THE FUN OF IT.

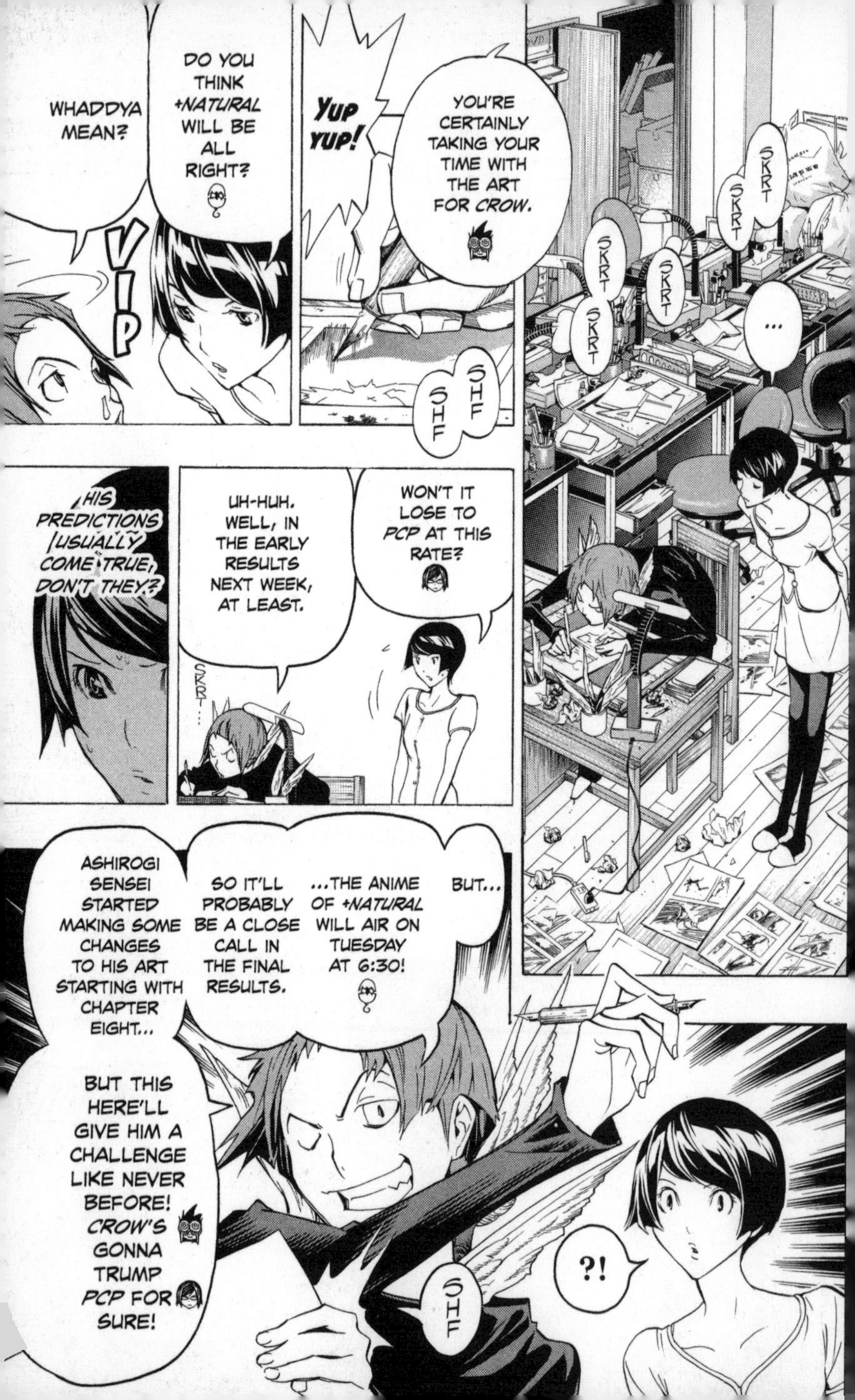
SKRT
SKRT
SKRT
SKRT
SKRT
...
SHF SHF
YOU'RE CERTAINLY TAKING YOUR TIME WITH THE ART FOR CROW.
YUP YUP!
DO YOU THINK +NATURAL WILL BE ALL RIGHT?
WHADDYA MEAN?
VIP
WON'T IT LOSE TO PCP AT THIS RATE?
UH-HUH. WELL, IN THE EARLY RESULTS NEXT WEEK, AT LEAST.
SKRT...
HIS PREDICTIONS USUALLY COME TRUE, DON'T THEY?
BUT...
...THE ANIME OF +NATURAL WILL AIR ON TUESDAY AT 6:30!
SO IT'LL PROBABLY BE A CLOSE CALL IN THE FINAL RESULTS.
ASHIROGI SENSEI STARTED MAKING SOME CHANGES TO HIS ART STARTING WITH CHAPTER EIGHT...
BUT THIS HERE'LL GIVE HIM A CHALLENGE LIKE NEVER BEFORE! CROW'S GONNA TRUMP PCP FOR SURE!
SHF
?!

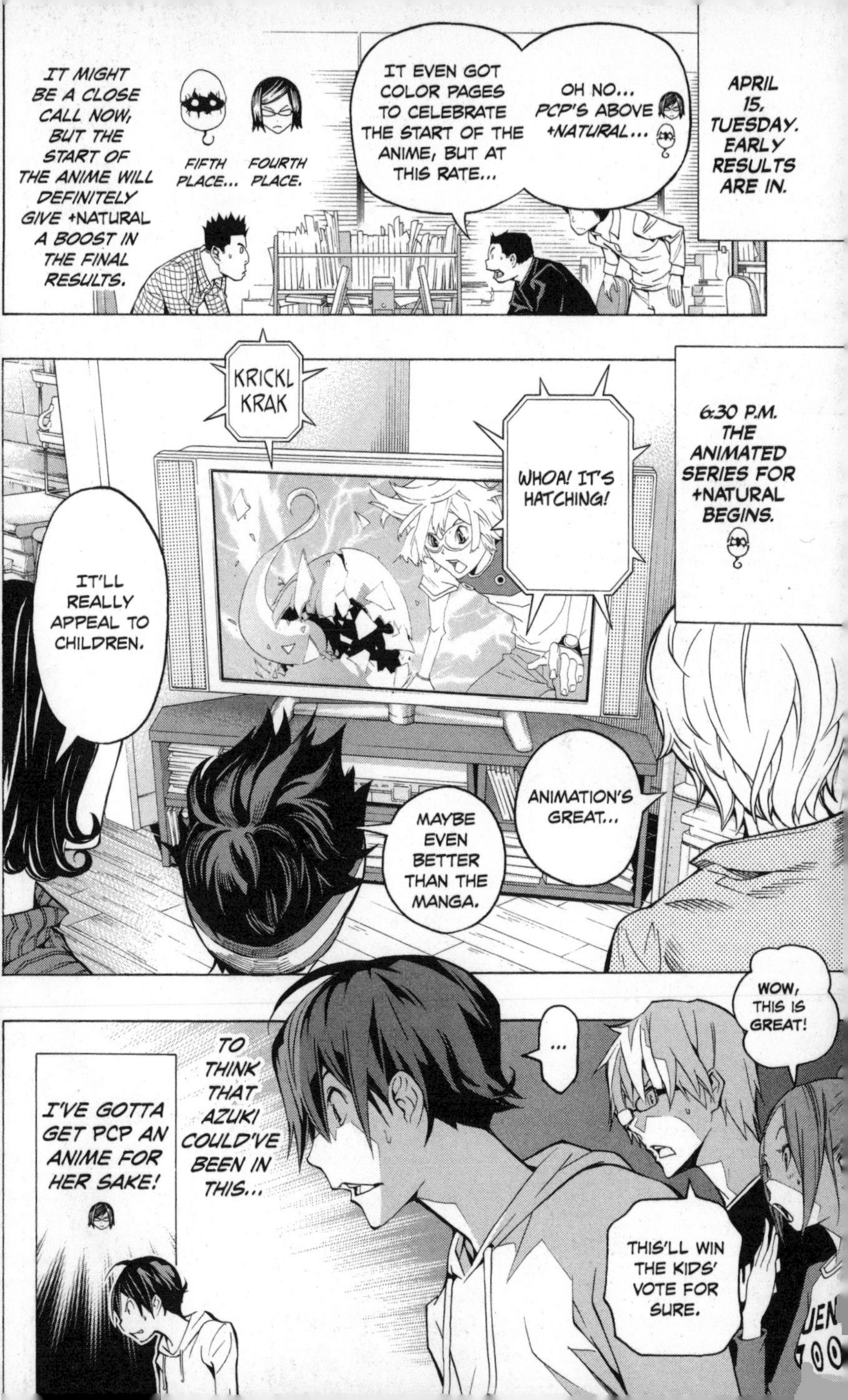
APRIL 15, TUESDAY. EARLY RESULTS ARE IN.
OH NO... PCP'S ABOVE +NATURAL...
IT EVEN GOT COLOR PAGES TO CELEBRATE THE START OF THE ANIME, BUT AT THIS RATE...
FOURTH PLACE.
FIFTH PLACE...
IT MIGHT BE A CLOSE CALL NOW, BUT THE START OF THE ANIME WILL DEFINITELY GIVE +NATURAL A BOOST IN THE FINAL RESULTS.
6:30 P.M. THE ANIMATED SERIES FOR +NATURAL BEGINS.
WHOA! IT'S HATCHING!
KRICKL KRAK
ANIMATION'S GREAT...
MAYBE EVEN BETTER THAN THE MANGA.
IT'LL REALLY APPEAL TO CHILDREN.
WOW, THIS IS GREAT!
...
THIS'LL WIN THE KIDS' VOTE FOR SURE.
TO THINK THAT AZUKI COULD'VE BEEN IN THIS...
I'VE GOTTA GET PCP AN ANIME FOR HER SAKE!

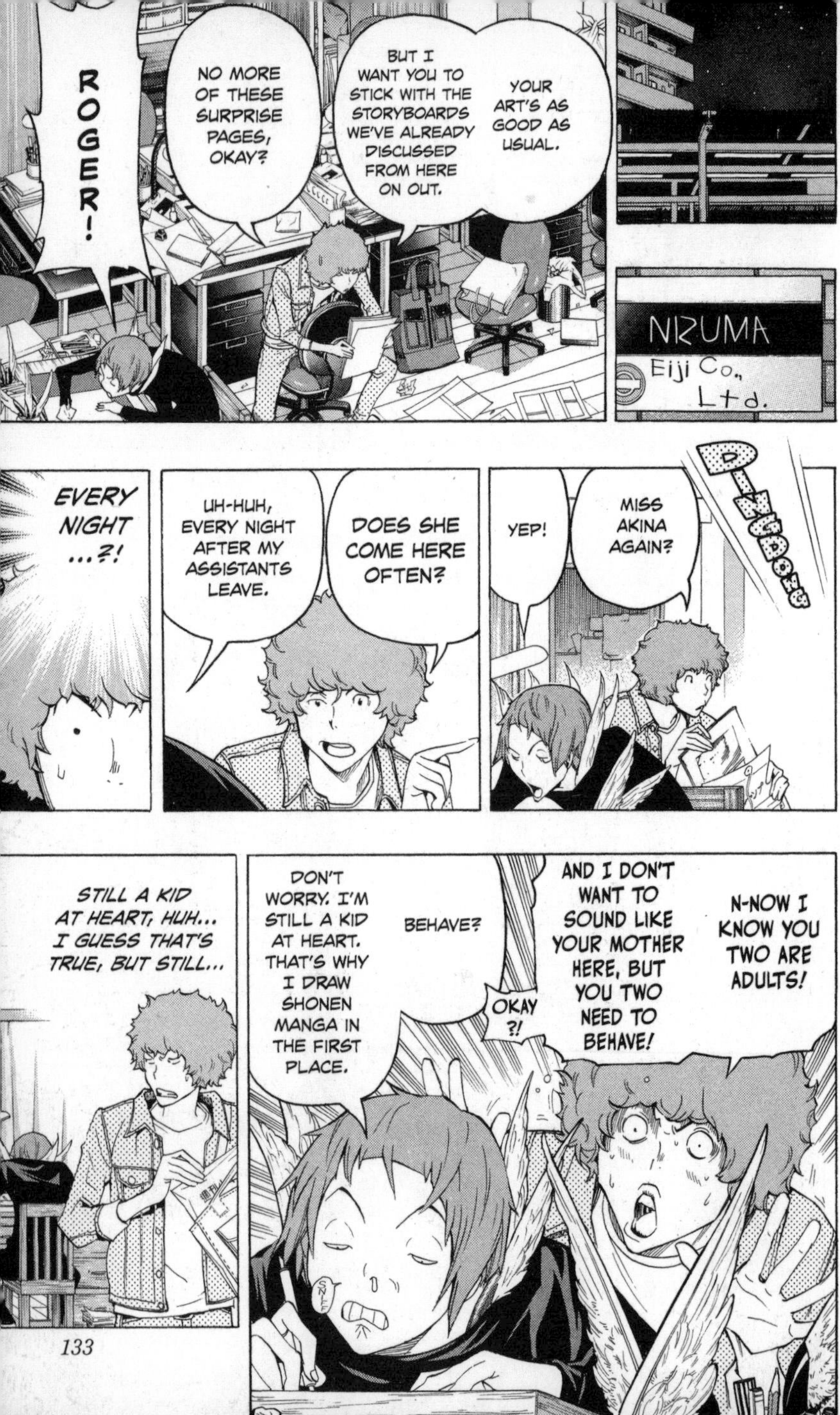
NIZUMA
Eiji Co., Ltd.
YOUR ART'S AS GOOD AS USUAL.
BUT I WANT YOU TO STICK WITH THE STORYBOARDS WE'VE ALREADY DISCUSSED FROM HERE ON OUT.
NO MORE OF THESE SURPRISE PAGES, OKAY?
ROGER!
DINGDONG
MISS AKINA AGAIN?
YEP!
DOES SHE COME HERE OFTEN?
UH-HUH, EVERY NIGHT AFTER MY ASSISTANTS LEAVE.
EVERY NIGHT ...?!
N-NOW I KNOW YOU TWO ARE ADULTS!
AND I DON'T WANT TO SOUND LIKE YOUR MOTHER HERE, BUT YOU TWO NEED TO BEHAVE!
OKAY ?!
BEHAVE?
DON'T WORRY. I'M STILL A KID AT HEART. THAT'S WHY I DRAW SHONEN MANGA IN THE FIRST PLACE.
SNIFF
STILL A KID AT HEART, HUH... I GUESS THAT'S TRUE, BUT STILL...

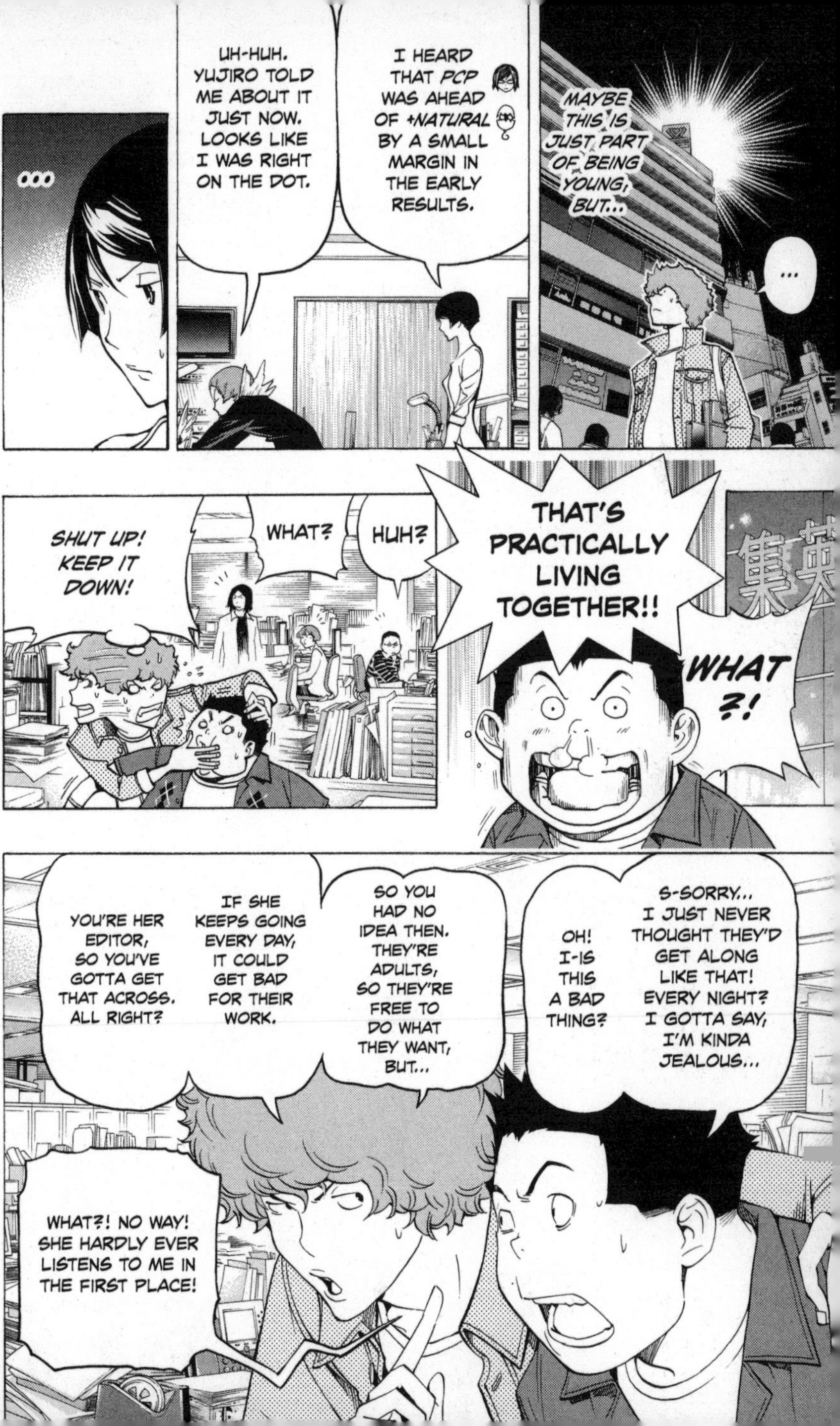
MAYBE THIS IS JUST PART OF BEING YOUNG, BUT...
...
I HEARD THAT PCP WAS AHEAD OF +NATURAL BY A SMALL MARGIN IN THE EARLY RESULTS.
UH-HUH. YUJIRO TOLD ME ABOUT IT JUST NOW. LOOKS LIKE I WAS RIGHT ON THE DOT.
...
THAT'S PRACTICALLY LIVING TOGETHER!!
WHAT?!
HUH?
WHAT?
SHUT UP! KEEP IT DOWN!
S-SORRY... I JUST NEVER THOUGHT THEY'D GET ALONG LIKE THAT! EVERY NIGHT? I GOTTA SAY, I'M KINDA JEALOUS...
OH! I-IS THIS A BAD THING?
SO YOU HAD NO IDEA THEN. THEY'RE ADULTS, SO THEY'RE FREE TO DO WHAT THEY WANT, BUT...
IF SHE KEEPS GOING EVERY DAY, IT COULD GET BAD FOR THEIR WORK.
YOU'RE HER EDITOR, SO YOU'VE GOTTA GET THAT ACROSS. ALL RIGHT?
WHAT?! NO WAY! SHE HARDLY EVER LISTENS TO ME IN THE FIRST PLACE!

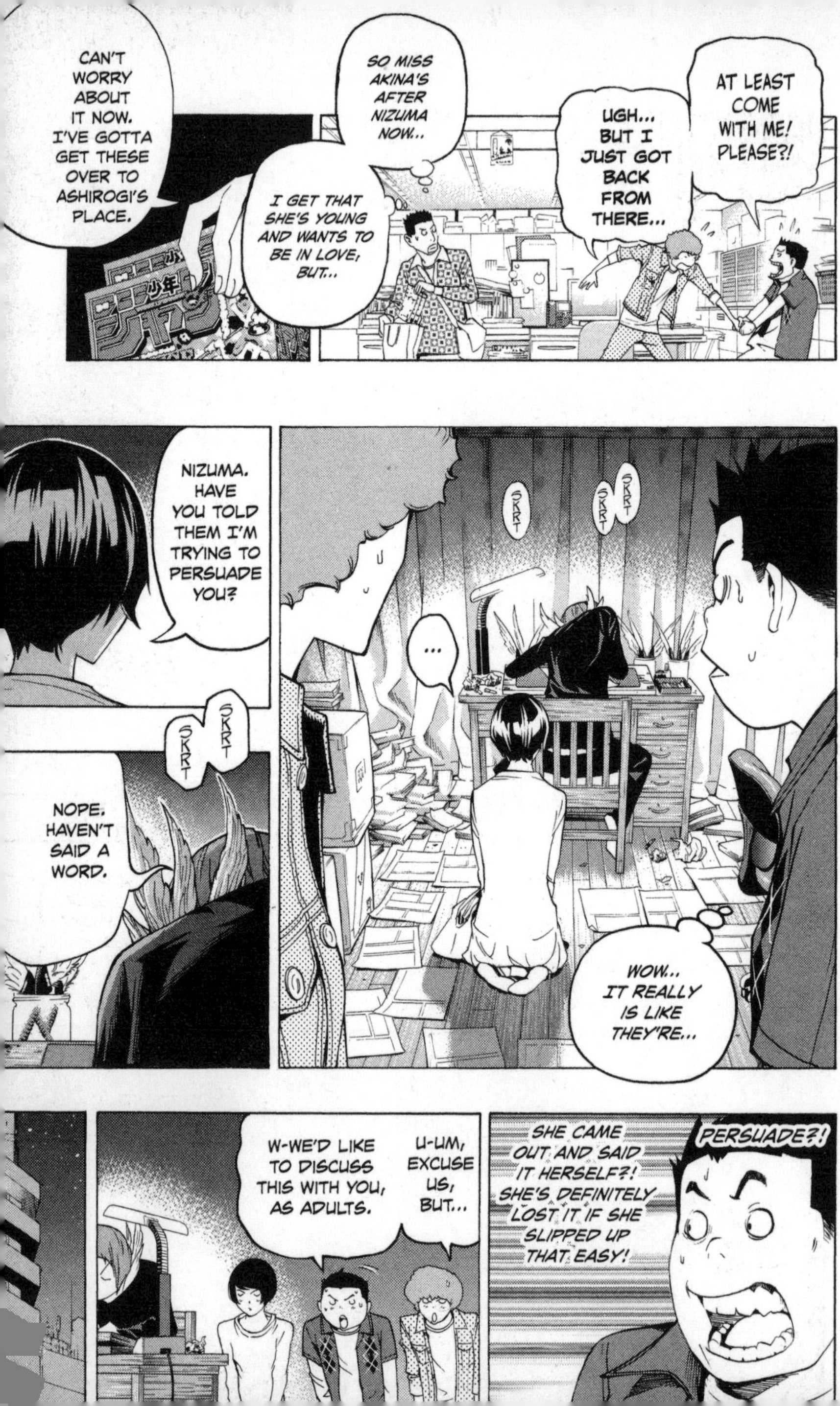
AT LEAST COME WITH ME! PLEASE?!
UGH... BUT I JUST GOT BACK FROM THERE...
SO MISS AKINA'S AFTER NIZUMA NOW...
I GET THAT SHE'S YOUNG AND WANTS TO BE IN LOVE, BUT...
CAN'T WORRY ABOUT IT NOW. I'VE GOTTA GET THESE OVER TO ASHIROGI'S PLACE.
SKRT
SKRT
SKRT
...
WOW... IT REALLY IS LIKE THEY'RE...
NIZUMA. HAVE YOU TOLD THEM I'M TRYING TO PERSUADE YOU?
SKRT
SKRT
NOPE. HAVEN'T SAID A WORD.
PERSUADE?!
SHE CAME OUT AND SAID IT HERSELF?! SHE'S DEFINITELY LOST IT IF SHE SLIPPED UP THAT EASY!
U-UM, EXCUSE US, BUT...
W-WE'D LIKE TO DISCUSS THIS WITH YOU, AS ADULTS.

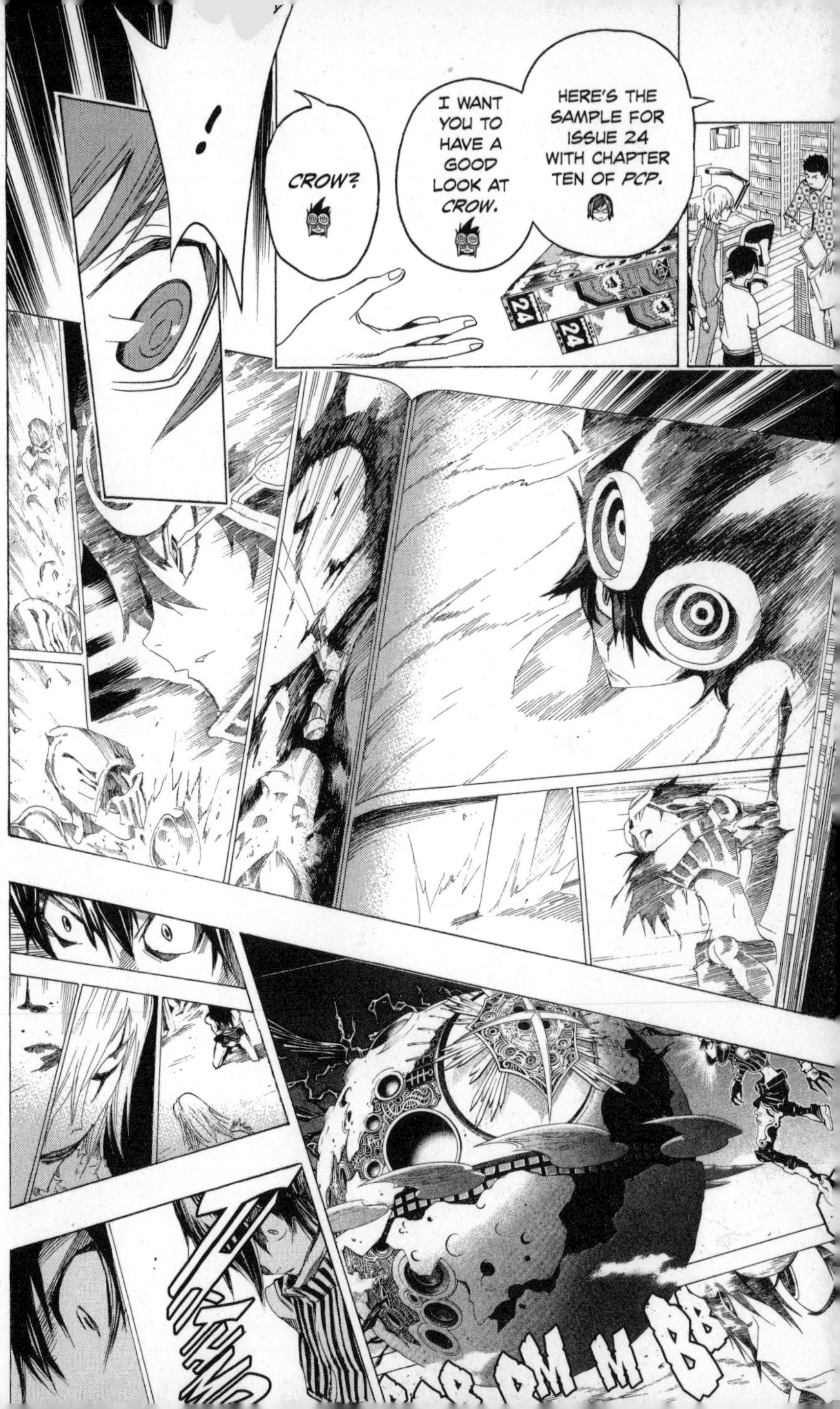
HERE'S THE SAMPLE FOR ISSUE 24 WITH CHAPTER TEN OF *PCP*.
I WANT YOU TO HAVE A GOOD LOOK AT *CROW*.
CROW?
!

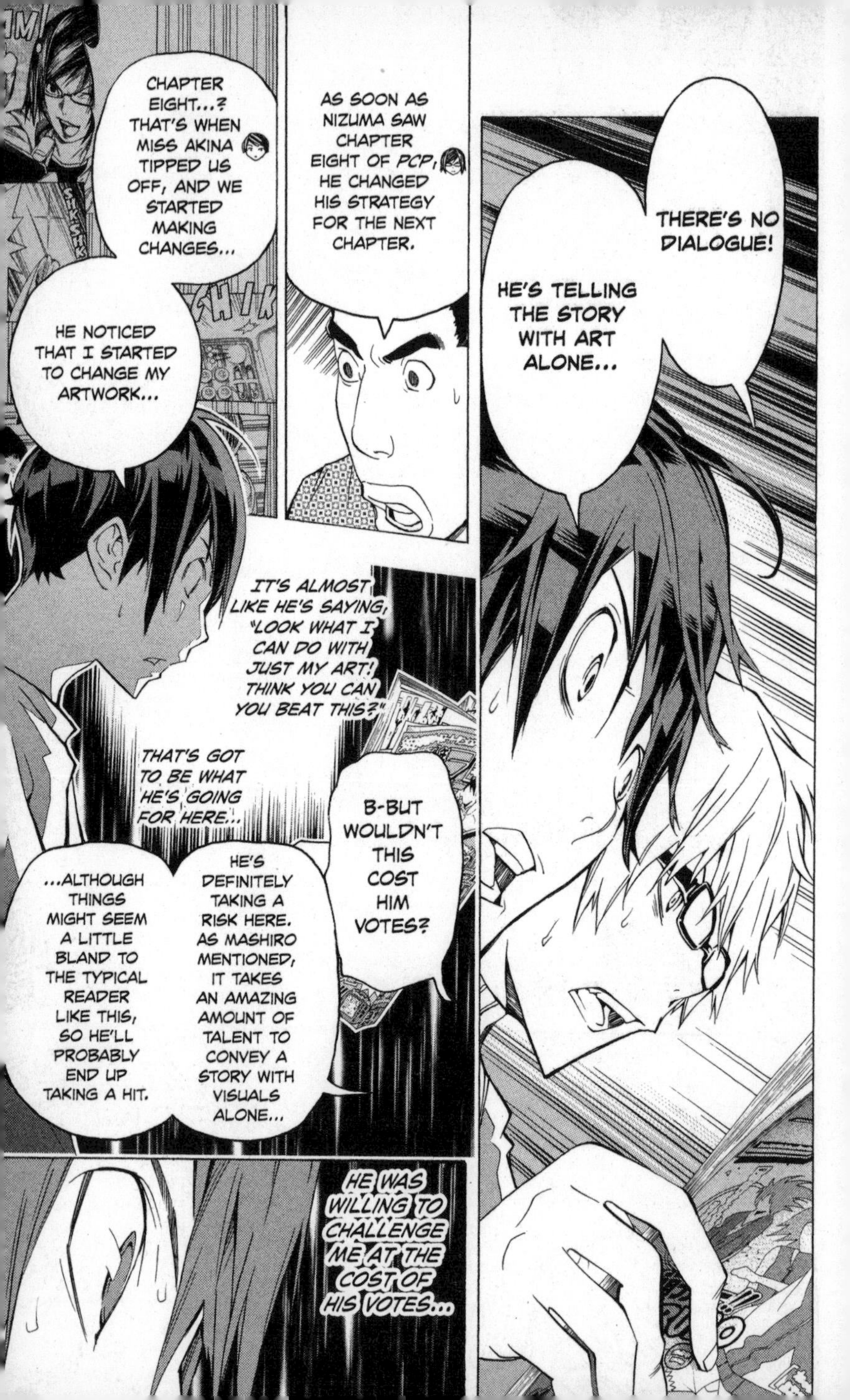

THERE'S NO DIALOGUE!
HE'S TELLING THE STORY WITH ART ALONE...
AS SOON AS NIZUMA SAW CHAPTER EIGHT OF PCP, HE CHANGED HIS STRATEGY FOR THE NEXT CHAPTER.
CHAPTER EIGHT...? THAT'S WHEN MISS AKINA TIPPED US OFF, AND WE STARTED MAKING CHANGES...
HE NOTICED THAT I STARTED TO CHANGE MY ARTWORK...
SHIK
IT'S ALMOST LIKE HE'S SAYING, "LOOK WHAT I CAN DO WITH JUST MY ART! THINK YOU CAN YOU BEAT THIS?"
THAT'S GOT TO BE WHAT HE'S GOING FOR HERE...
B-BUT WOULDN'T THIS COST HIM VOTES?
HE'S DEFINITELY TAKING A RISK HERE. AS MASHIRO MENTIONED, IT TAKES AN AMAZING AMOUNT OF TALENT TO CONVEY A STORY WITH VISUALS ALONE...
...ALTHOUGH THINGS MIGHT SEEM A LITTLE BLAND TO THE TYPICAL READER LIKE THIS, SO HE'LL PROBABLY END UP TAKING A HIT.
HE WAS WILLING TO CHALLENGE ME AT THE COST OF HIS VOTES...

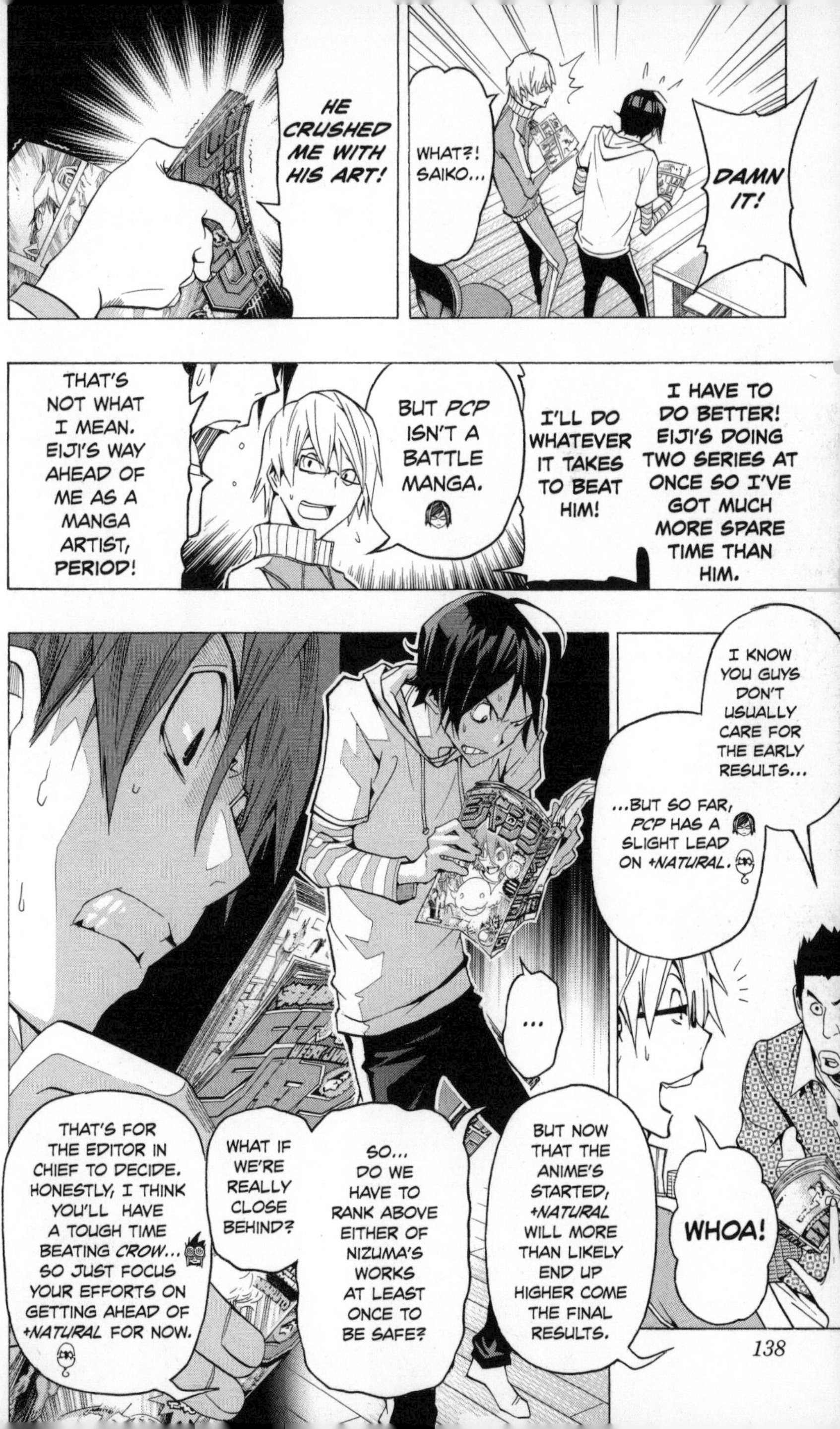
DAMN IT!
WHAT?! SAIKO...
HE CRUSHED ME WITH HIS ART!
I HAVE TO DO BETTER! EIJI'S DOING TWO SERIES AT ONCE SO I'VE GOT MUCH MORE SPARE TIME THAN HIM.
I'LL DO WHATEVER IT TAKES TO BEAT HIM!
BUT *PCP* ISN'T A BATTLE MANGA.
THAT'S NOT WHAT I MEAN. EIJI'S WAY AHEAD OF ME AS A MANGA ARTIST, PERIOD!
I KNOW YOU GUYS DON'T USUALLY CARE FOR THE EARLY RESULTS...
...BUT SO FAR, *PCP* HAS A SLIGHT LEAD ON *+NATURAL*.
WHOA!
...
BUT NOW THAT THE ANIME'S STARTED, *+NATURAL* WILL MORE THAN LIKELY END UP HIGHER COME THE FINAL RESULTS.
SO... DO WE HAVE TO RANK ABOVE EITHER OF NIZUMA'S WORKS AT LEAST ONCE TO BE SAFE?
WHAT IF WE'RE REALLY CLOSE BEHIND?
THAT'S FOR THE EDITOR IN CHIEF TO DECIDE. HONESTLY, I THINK YOU'LL HAVE A TOUGH TIME BEATING *CROW*... SO JUST FOCUS YOUR EFFORTS ON GETTING AHEAD OF *+NATURAL* FOR NOW.

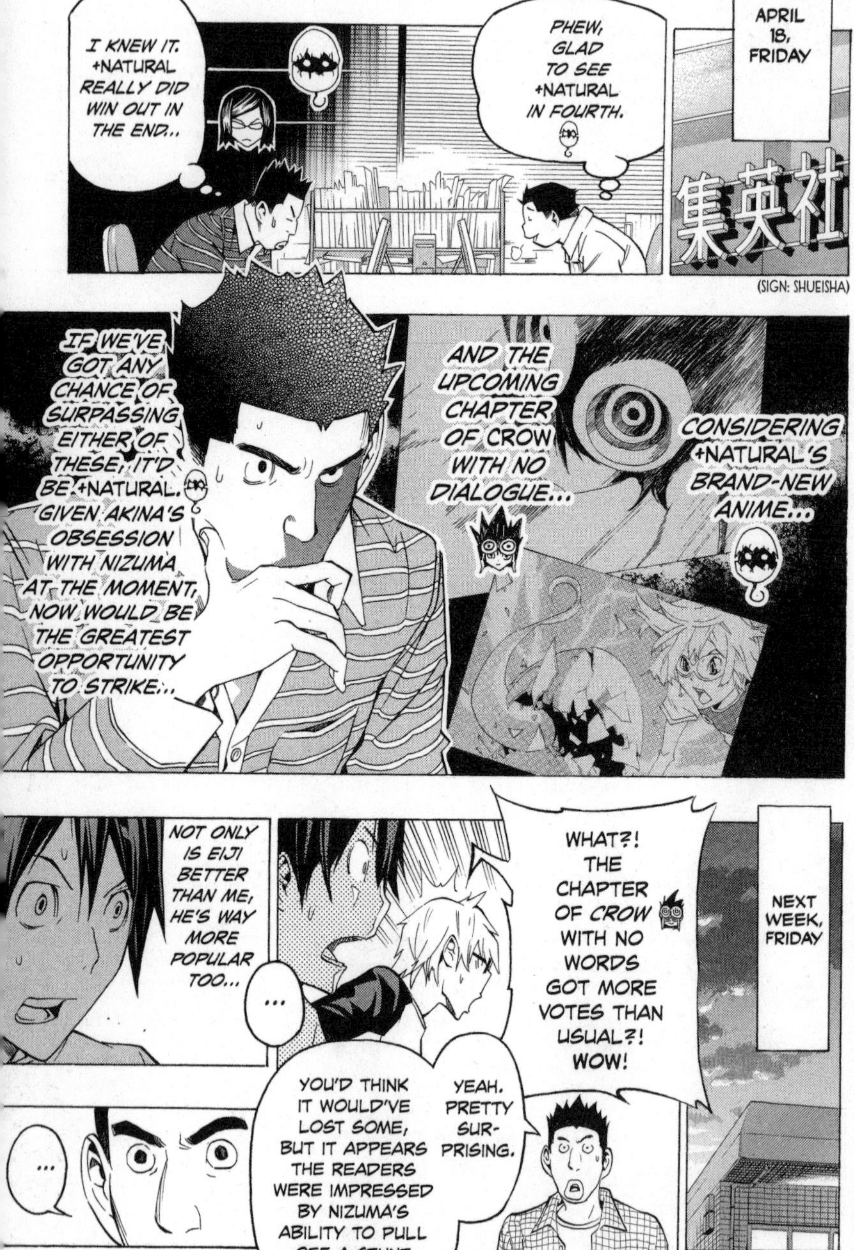
APRIL 18, FRIDAY
集英社
(SIGN: SHUEISHA)
PHEW, GLAD TO SEE +NATURAL IN FOURTH.
I KNEW IT. +NATURAL REALLY DID WIN OUT IN THE END...
CONSIDERING +NATURAL'S BRAND-NEW ANIME...
AND THE UPCOMING CHAPTER OF CROW WITH NO DIALOGUE...
IF WE'VE GOT ANY CHANCE OF SURPASSING EITHER OF THESE, IT'D BE +NATURAL. GIVEN AKINA'S OBSESSION WITH NIZUMA AT THE MOMENT, NOW WOULD BE THE GREATEST OPPORTUNITY TO STRIKE...
NEXT WEEK, FRIDAY
WHAT?! THE CHAPTER OF *CROW* WITH NO WORDS GOT MORE VOTES THAN USUAL?! WOW!
...
YEAH. PRETTY SURPRISING.
YOU'D THINK IT WOULD'VE LOST SOME, BUT IT APPEARS THE READERS WERE IMPRESSED BY NIZUMA'S ABILITY TO PULL OFF A STUNT LIKE THAT.
NOT ONLY IS EIJI BETTER THAN ME, HE'S WAY MORE POPULAR TOO...
...

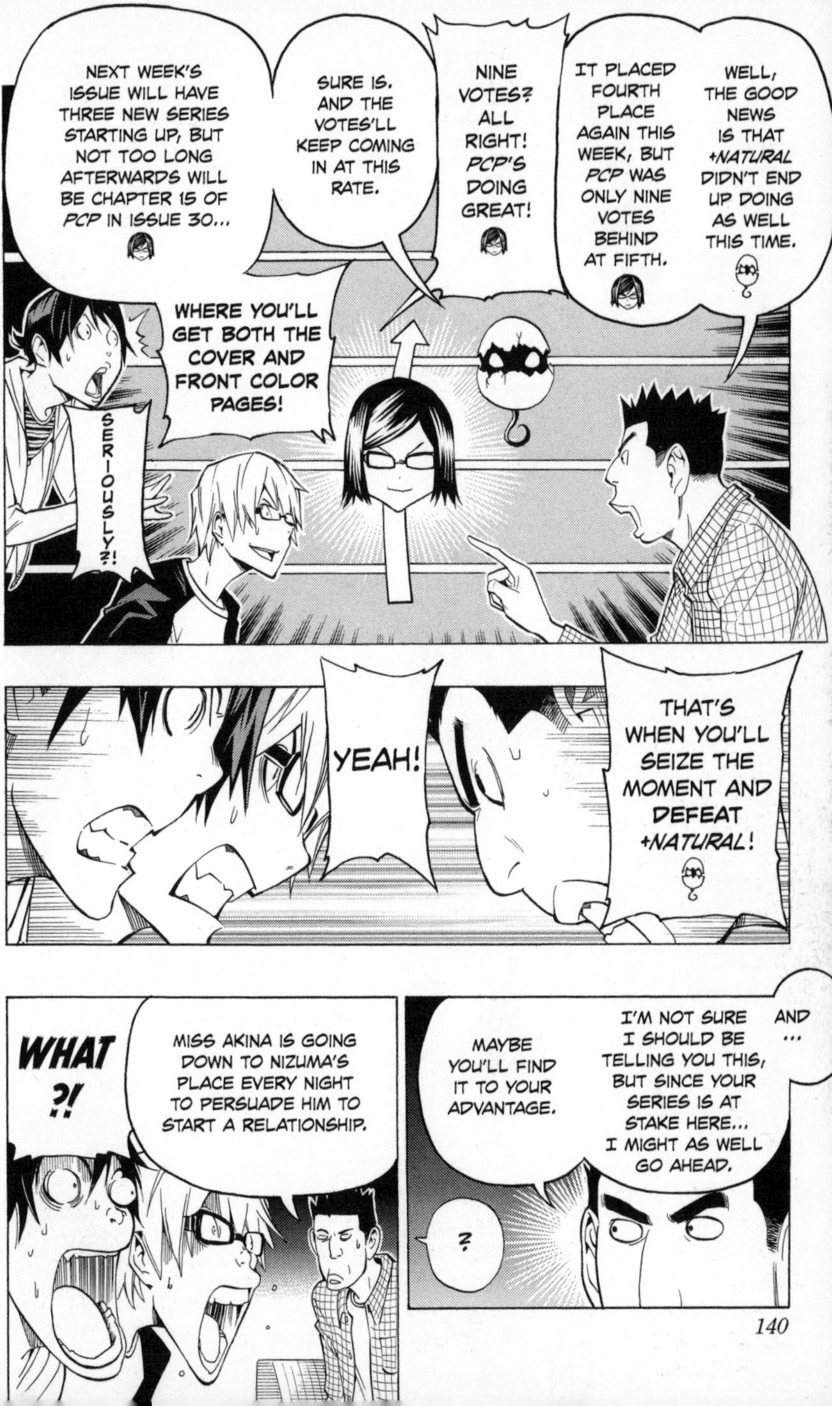
WELL, THE GOOD NEWS IS THAT +NATURAL DIDN'T END UP DOING AS WELL THIS TIME.
IT PLACED FOURTH PLACE AGAIN THIS WEEK, BUT PCP WAS ONLY NINE VOTES BEHIND AT FIFTH.
NINE VOTES? ALL RIGHT! PCP'S DOING GREAT!
SURE IS. AND THE VOTES'LL KEEP COMING IN AT THIS RATE.
NEXT WEEK'S ISSUE WILL HAVE THREE NEW SERIES STARTING UP, BUT NOT TOO LONG AFTERWARDS WILL BE CHAPTER 15 OF PCP IN ISSUE 30...
WHERE YOU'LL GET BOTH THE COVER AND FRONT COLOR PAGES!
SERIOUSLY?!
THAT'S WHEN YOU'LL SEIZE THE MOMENT AND DEFEAT +NATURAL!
YEAH!
AND...
I'M NOT SURE I SHOULD BE TELLING YOU THIS, BUT SINCE YOUR SERIES IS AT STAKE HERE... I MIGHT AS WELL GO AHEAD.
MAYBE YOU'LL FIND IT TO YOUR ADVANTAGE.
?
MISS AKINA IS GOING DOWN TO NIZUMA'S PLACE EVERY NIGHT TO PERSUADE HIM TO START A RELATIONSHIP.
WHAT?!

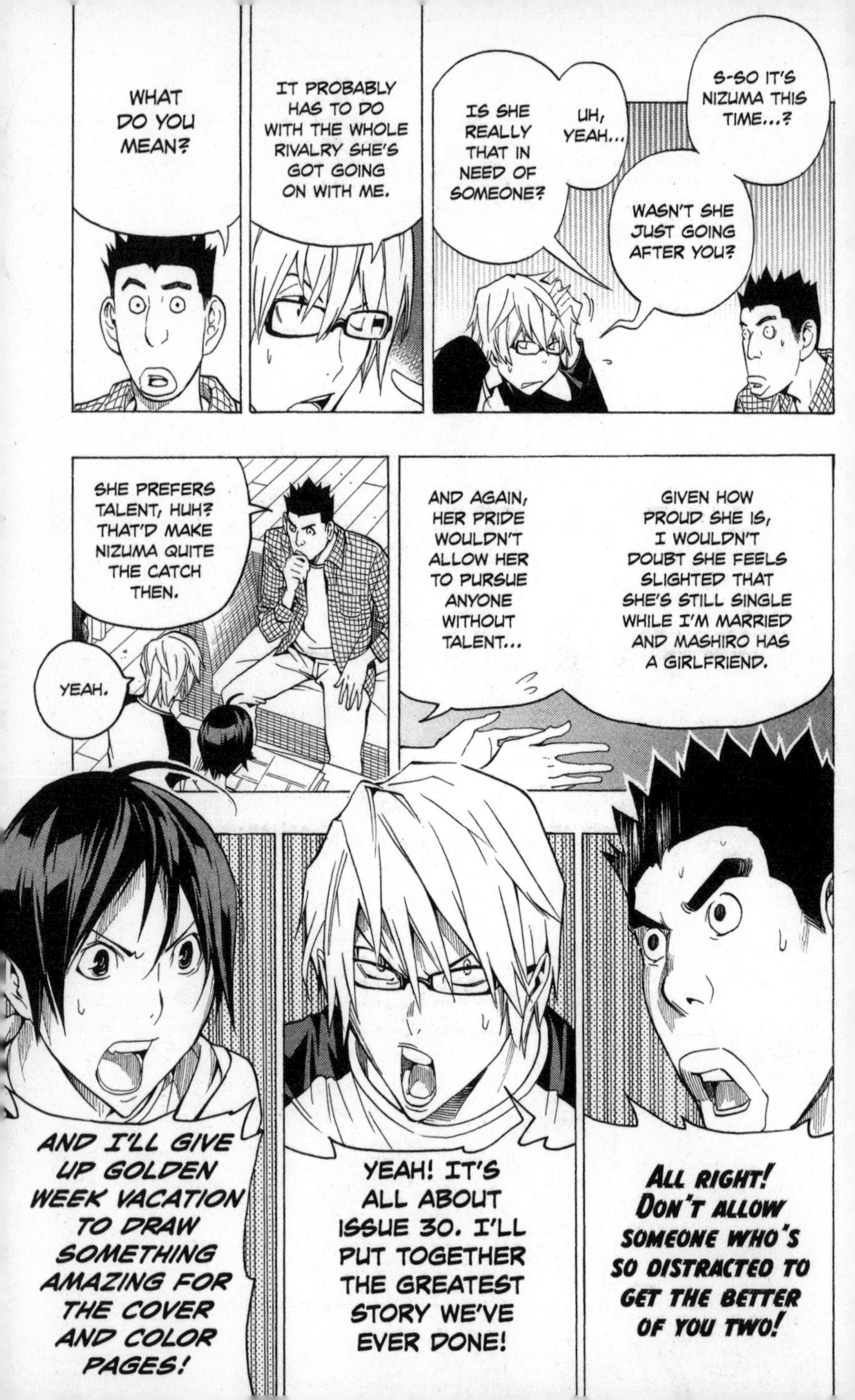

S-SO IT'S NIZUMA THIS TIME...?
WASN'T SHE JUST GOING AFTER YOU?
UH, YEAH...
IS SHE REALLY THAT IN NEED OF SOMEONE?
IT PROBABLY HAS TO DO WITH THE WHOLE RIVALRY SHE'S GOT GOING ON WITH ME.
WHAT DO YOU MEAN?
GIVEN HOW PROUD SHE IS, I WOULDN'T DOUBT SHE FEELS SLIGHTED THAT SHE'S STILL SINGLE WHILE I'M MARRIED AND MASHIRO HAS A GIRLFRIEND.
AND AGAIN, HER PRIDE WOULDN'T ALLOW HER TO PURSUE ANYONE WITHOUT TALENT...
SHE PREFERS TALENT, HUH? THAT'D MAKE NIZUMA QUITE THE CATCH THEN.
YEAH.
ALL RIGHT! DON'T ALLOW SOMEONE WHO'S SO DISTRACTED TO GET THE BETTER OF YOU TWO!
YEAH! IT'S ALL ABOUT ISSUE 30. I'LL PUT TOGETHER THE GREATEST STORY WE'VE EVER DONE!
AND I'LL GIVE UP GOLDEN WEEK VACATION TO DRAW SOMETHING AMAZING FOR THE COVER AND COLOR PAGES!

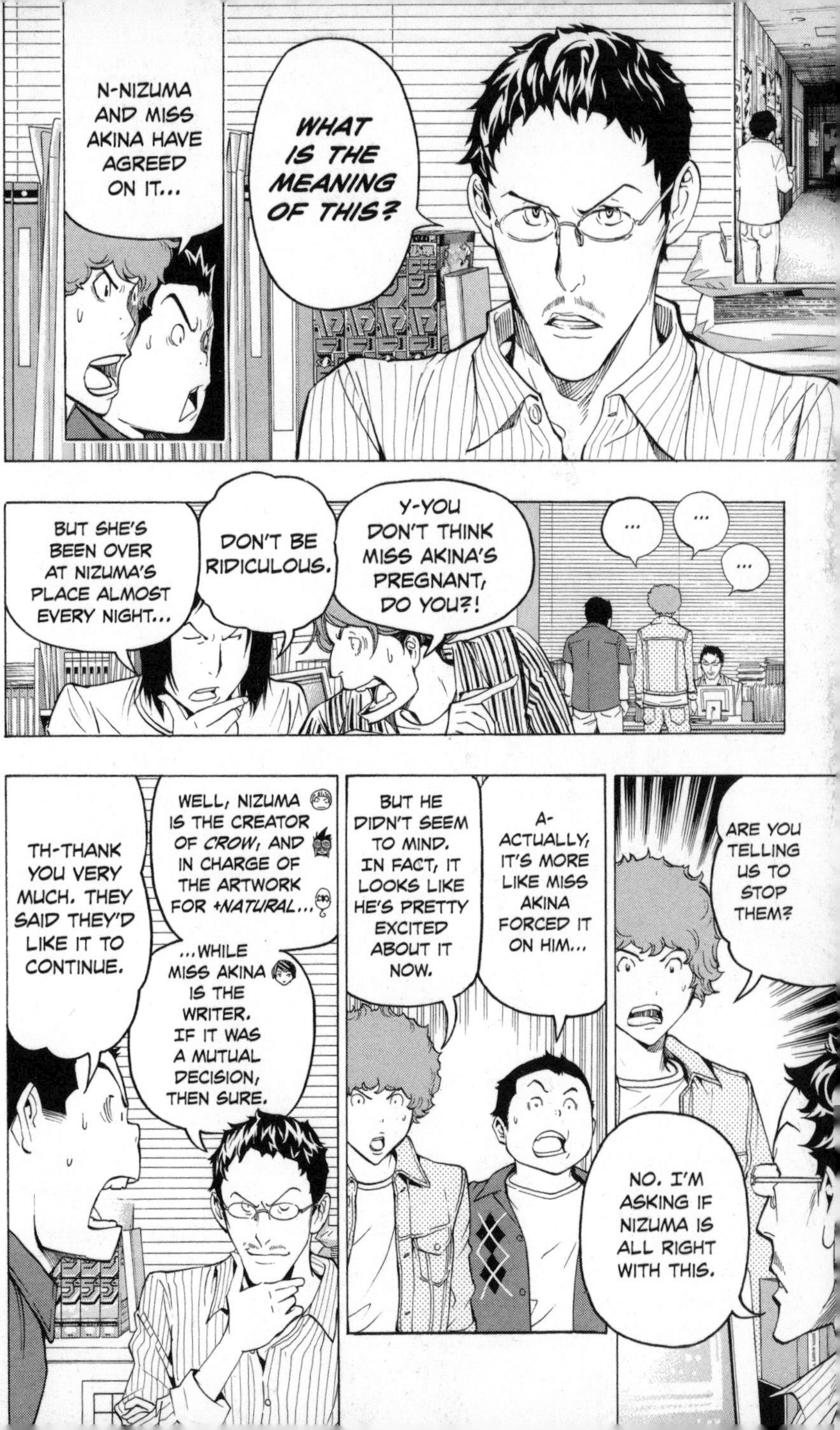
WHAT IS THE MEANING OF THIS?
N-NIZUMA AND MISS AKINA HAVE AGREED ON IT...
...
...
...
Y-YOU DON'T THINK MISS AKINA'S PREGNANT, DO YOU?!
DON'T BE RIDICULOUS.
BUT SHE'S BEEN OVER AT NIZUMA'S PLACE ALMOST EVERY NIGHT...
ARE YOU TELLING US TO STOP THEM?
NO. I'M ASKING IF NIZUMA IS ALL RIGHT WITH THIS.
A-ACTUALLY, IT'S MORE LIKE MISS AKINA FORCED IT ON HIM...
BUT HE DIDN'T SEEM TO MIND. IN FACT, IT LOOKS LIKE HE'S PRETTY EXCITED ABOUT IT NOW.
WELL, NIZUMA IS THE CREATOR OF *CROW*, AND IN CHARGE OF THE ARTWORK FOR *+NATURAL*...
...WHILE MISS AKINA IS THE WRITER. IF IT WAS A MUTUAL DECISION, THEN SURE.
TH-THANK YOU VERY MUCH. THEY SAID THEY'D LIKE IT TO CONTINUE.

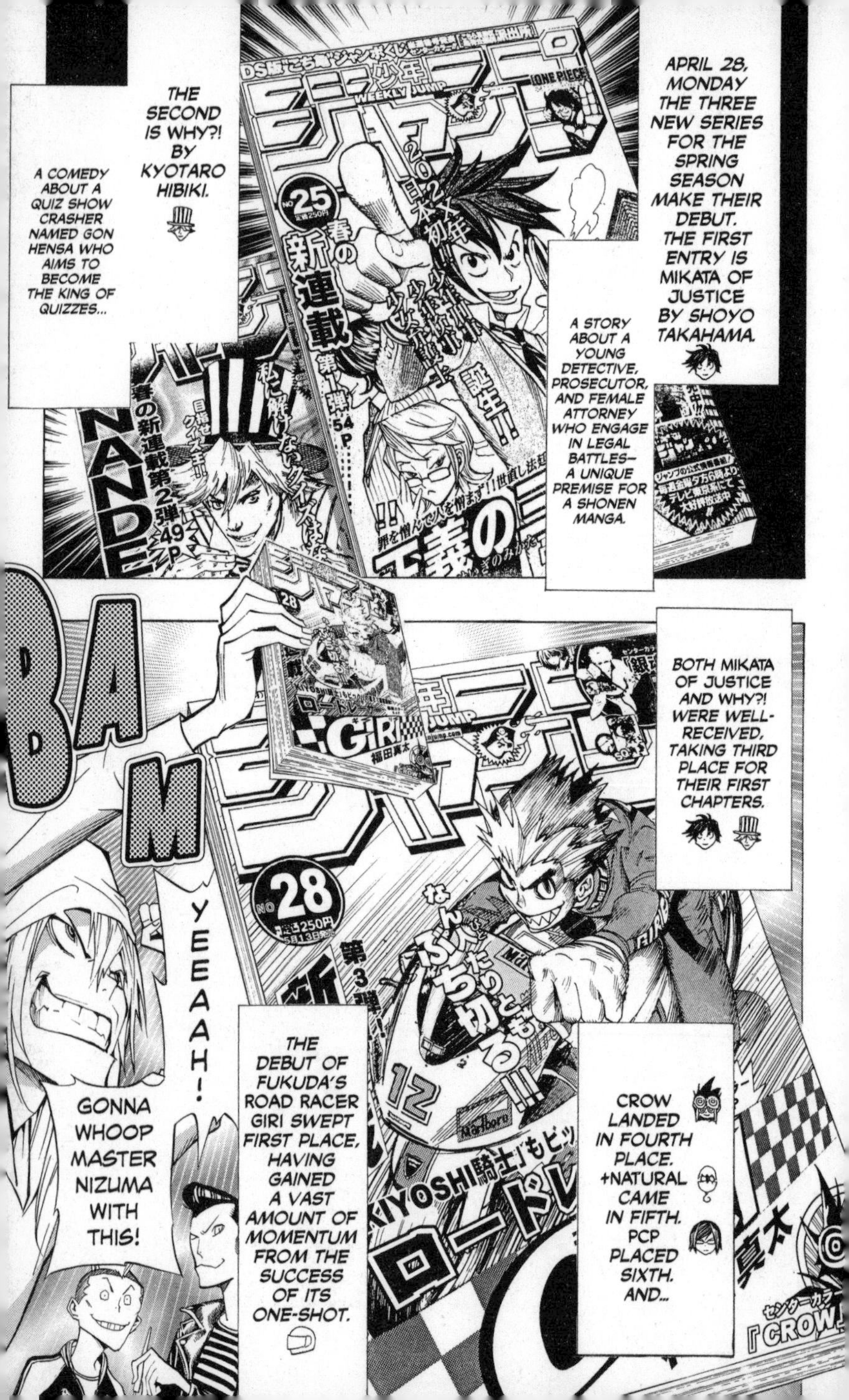
APRIL 28, MONDAY THE THREE NEW SERIES FOR THE SPRING SEASON MAKE THEIR DEBUT. THE FIRST ENTRY IS MIKATA OF JUSTICE BY SHOYO TAKAHAMA.
A STORY ABOUT A YOUNG DETECTIVE, PROSECUTOR, AND FEMALE ATTORNEY WHO ENGAGE IN LEGAL BATTLES— A UNIQUE PREMISE FOR A SHONEN MANGA.
THE SECOND IS WHY?! BY KYOTARO HIBIKI.
A COMEDY ABOUT A QUIZ SHOW CRASHER NAMED GON HENSA WHO AIMS TO BECOME THE KING OF QUIZZES...
BOTH MIKATA OF JUSTICE AND WHY?! WERE WELL-RECEIVED, TAKING THIRD PLACE FOR THEIR FIRST CHAPTERS.
BAM
CROW LANDED IN FOURTH PLACE. +NATURAL CAME IN FIFTH. PCP PLACED SIXTH. AND...
THE DEBUT OF FUKUDA'S ROAD RACER GIRI SWEPT FIRST PLACE, HAVING GAINED A VAST AMOUNT OF MOMENTUM FROM THE SUCCESS OF ITS ONE-SHOT.
YEEAAAH!
GONNA WHOOP MASTER NIZUMA WITH THIS!

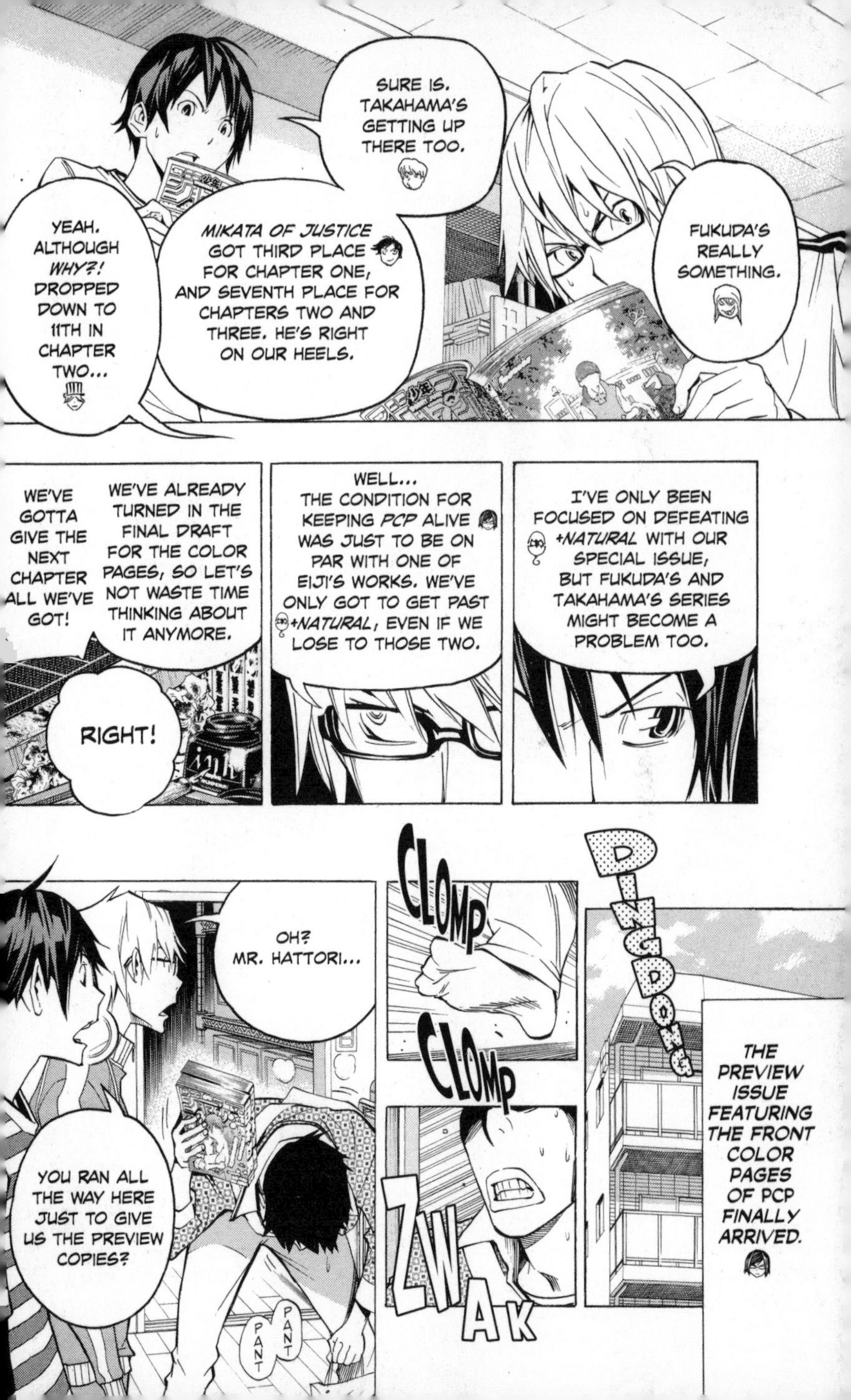
FUKUDA'S REALLY SOMETHING.
SURE IS. TAKAHAMA'S GETTING UP THERE TOO.
MIKATA OF JUSTICE GOT THIRD PLACE FOR CHAPTER ONE, AND SEVENTH PLACE FOR CHAPTERS TWO AND THREE. HE'S RIGHT ON OUR HEELS.
YEAH. ALTHOUGH *WHY?!* DROPPED DOWN TO 11TH IN CHAPTER TWO...
I'VE ONLY BEEN FOCUSED ON DEFEATING *+NATURAL* WITH OUR SPECIAL ISSUE, BUT FUKUDA'S AND TAKAHAMA'S SERIES MIGHT BECOME A PROBLEM TOO.
WELL... THE CONDITION FOR KEEPING *PCP* ALIVE WAS JUST TO BE ON PAR WITH ONE OF EIJI'S WORKS. WE'VE ONLY GOT TO GET PAST *+NATURAL*, EVEN IF WE LOSE TO THOSE TWO.
WE'VE ALREADY TURNED IN THE FINAL DRAFT FOR THE COLOR PAGES, SO LET'S NOT WASTE TIME THINKING ABOUT IT ANYMORE.
WE'VE GOTTA GIVE THE NEXT CHAPTER ALL WE'VE GOT!
RIGHT!
DINGDONG
THE PREVIEW ISSUE FEATURING THE FRONT COLOR PAGES OF PCP FINALLY ARRIVED.
CLOMP
CLOMP
ZWAK
OH? MR. HATTORI...
YOU RAN ALL THE WAY HERE JUST TO GIVE US THE PREVIEW COPIES?
PANT
PANT
PANT

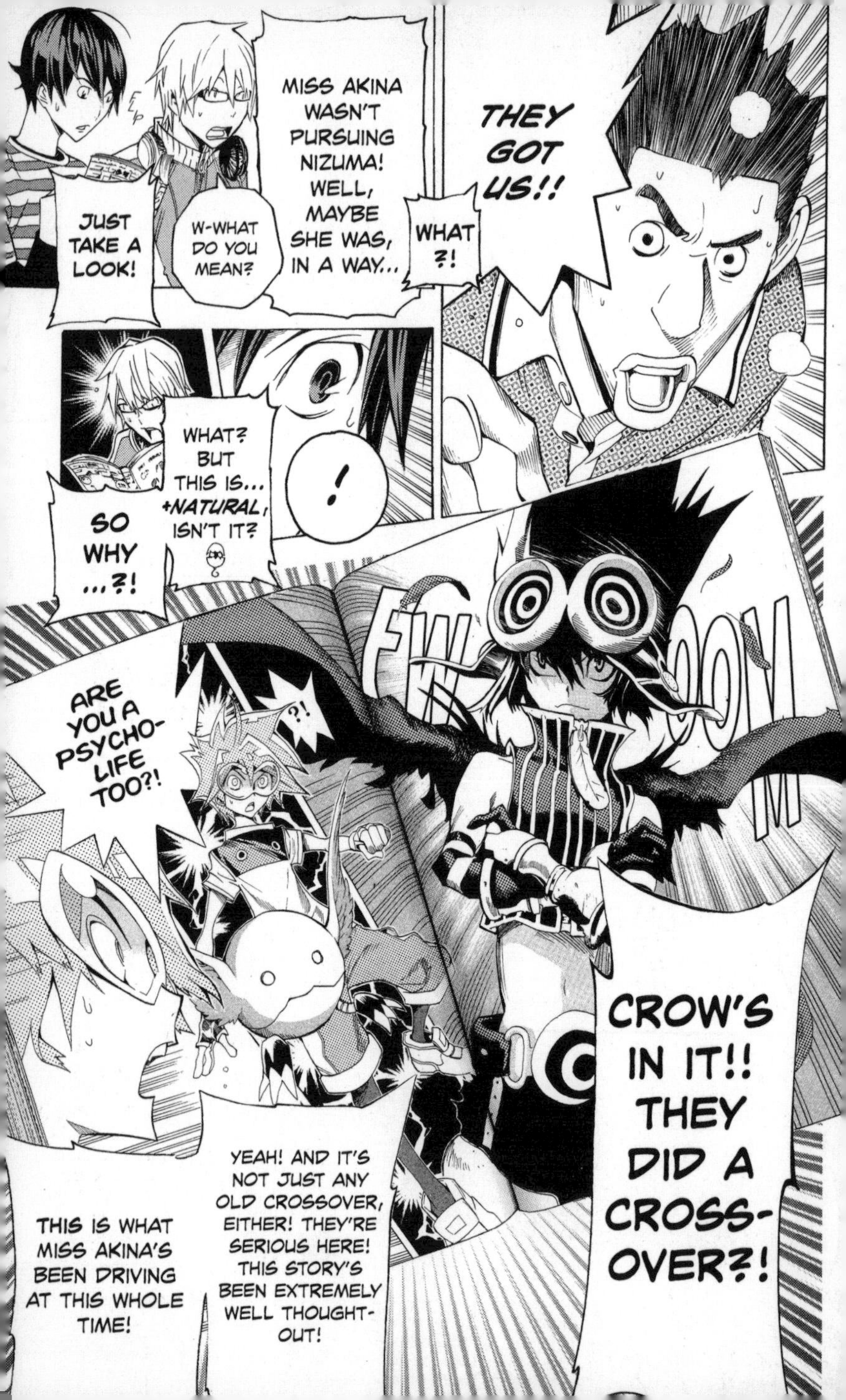
THEY GOT US!!
WHAT ?!
MISS AKINA WASN'T PURSUING NIZUMA! WELL, MAYBE SHE WAS, IN A WAY...
W-WHAT DO YOU MEAN?
JUST TAKE A LOOK!
!
WHAT? BUT THIS IS... +NATURAL, ISN'T IT?
SO WHY ...?!
CROW'S IN IT!! THEY DID A CROSS-OVER?!
ARE YOU A PSYCHO-LIFE TOO?!
?!
YEAH! AND IT'S NOT JUST ANY OLD CROSSOVER, EITHER! THEY'RE SERIOUS HERE! THIS STORY'S BEEN EXTREMELY WELL THOUGHT-OUT!
THIS IS WHAT MISS AKINA'S BEEN DRIVING AT THIS WHOLE TIME!

OHBA'S STORYBOARD

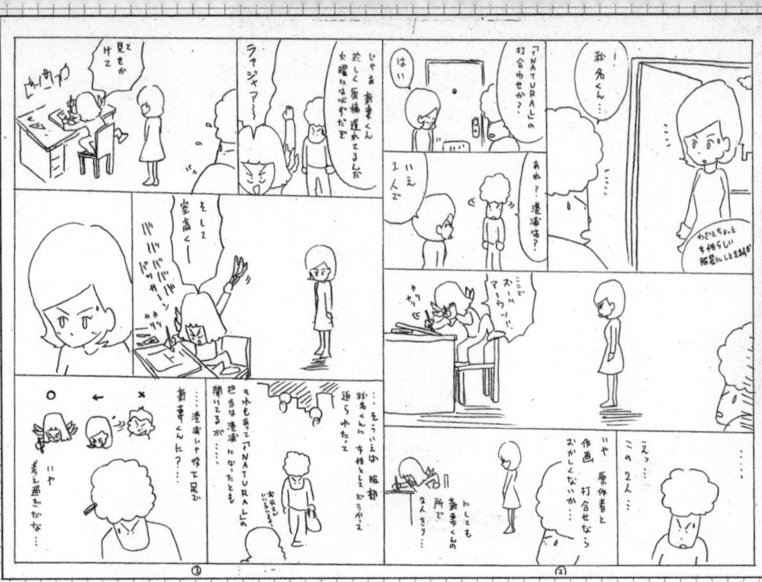

！秋名くん…
「NATURAL」の打合わせか？
はい
あれ？港浦は？
いえ1人で
ここでズームアウトー!!
えっ……この2人……
いや原作者と作画打合せならおかしくないか…
にしても新妻くんの所で2人きり…
じゃあ新妻くん珍しく原稿遅れてるんだ火曜には必ずだぞ
ラジャアー〜〜
…そういえば服部秋名くんに女性としてどうかって迫られたって
そんなもあって「NATURAL」の担当は港浦になったとも聞いてるが…
…港浦じゃ役不足で新妻くんに？…
いや考え過ぎだな…

OBATA'S STORYBOARD

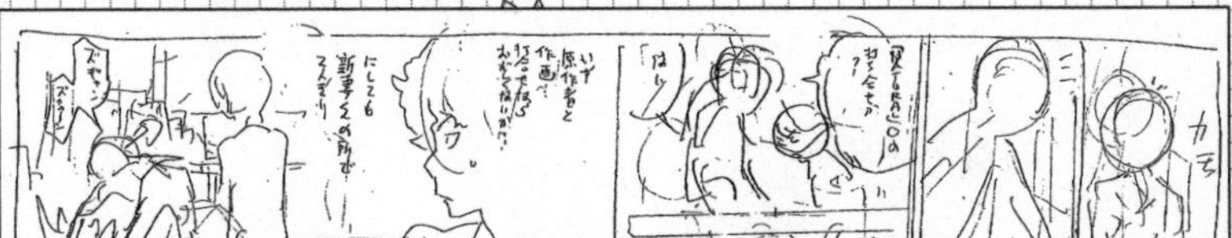

COMPLETE!

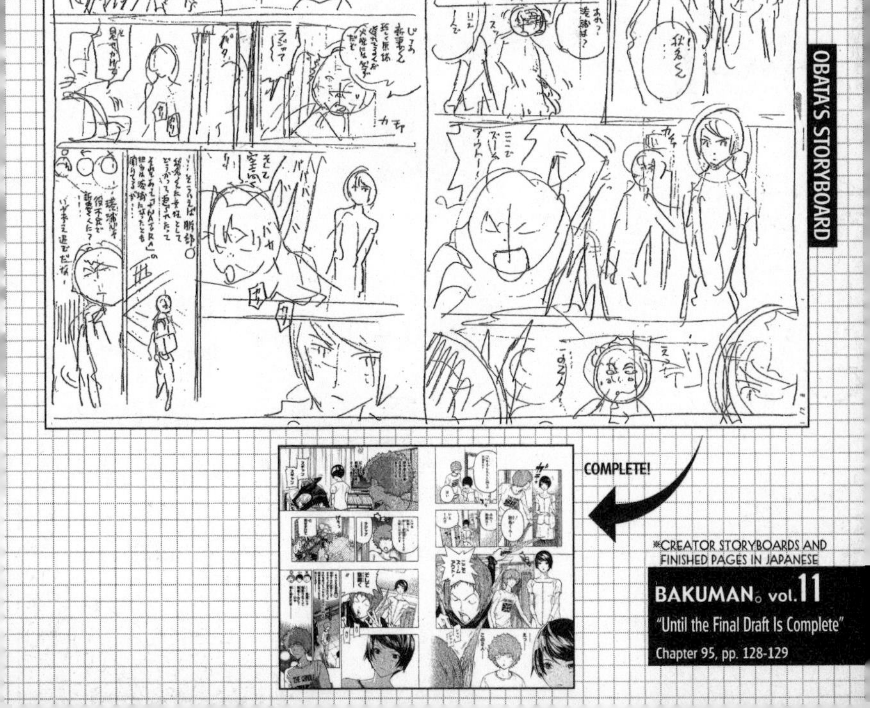

※CREATOR STORYBOARDS AND FINISHED PAGES IN JAPANESE

BAKUMAN。 vol.11

"Until the Final Draft Is Complete"

Chapter 95, pp. 128-129

CHAPTER 96
4TH PLACE VOTES AND SERIES

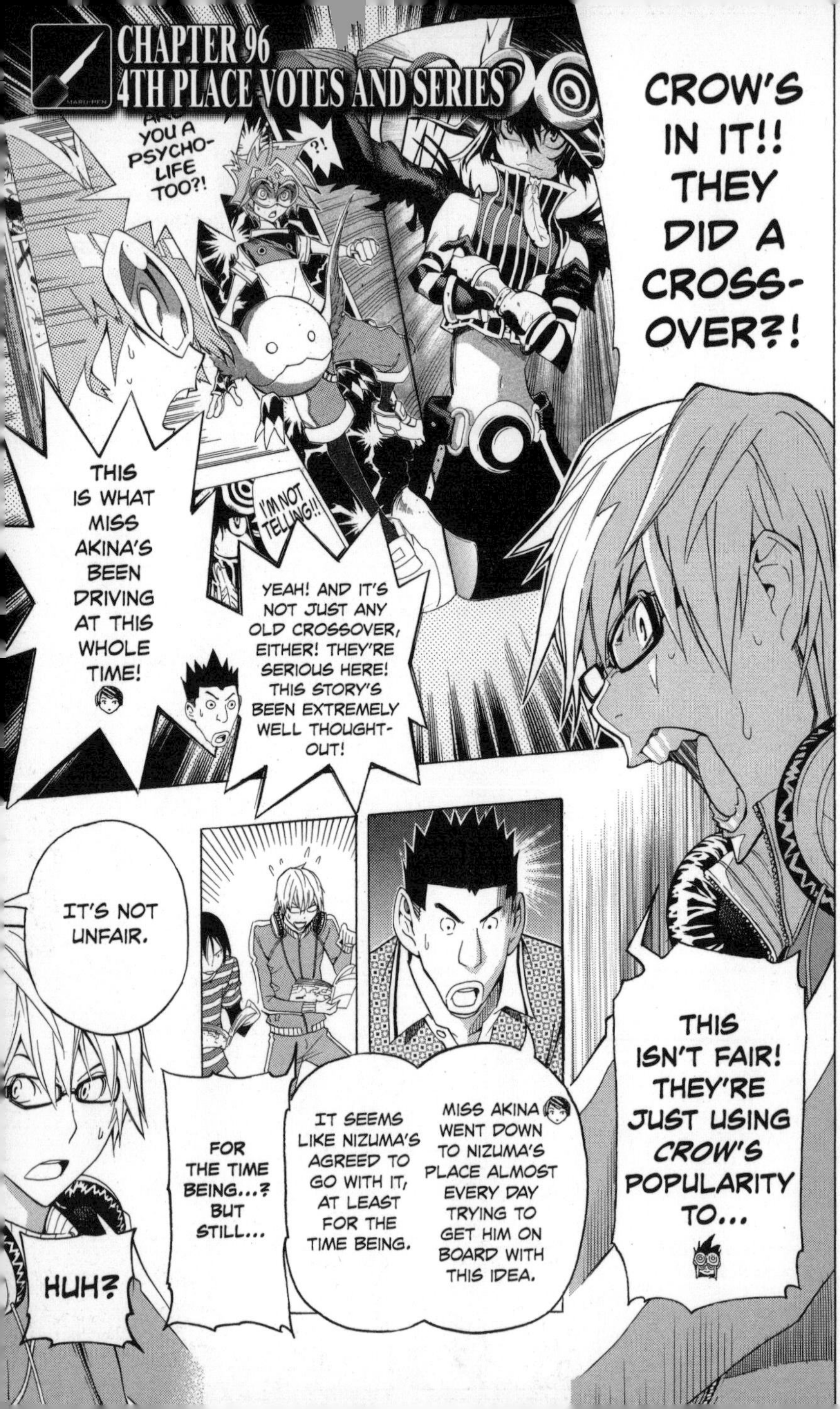
CROW'S IN IT!! THEY DID A CROSSOVER?!
YOU A PSYCHO-LIFE TOO?!
?!
I'M NOT TELLING!!!
YEAH! AND IT'S NOT JUST ANY OLD CROSSOVER, EITHER! THEY'RE SERIOUS HERE! THIS STORY'S BEEN EXTREMELY WELL THOUGHT-OUT!
THIS IS WHAT MISS AKINA'S BEEN DRIVING AT THIS WHOLE TIME!
THIS ISN'T FAIR! THEY'RE JUST USING CROW'S POPULARITY TO...
MISS AKINA WENT DOWN TO NIZUMA'S PLACE ALMOST EVERY DAY TRYING TO GET HIM ON BOARD WITH THIS IDEA.
IT SEEMS LIKE NIZUMA'S AGREED TO GO WITH IT, AT LEAST FOR THE TIME BEING.
FOR THE TIME BEING...? BUT STILL...
IT'S NOT UNFAIR.
HUH?

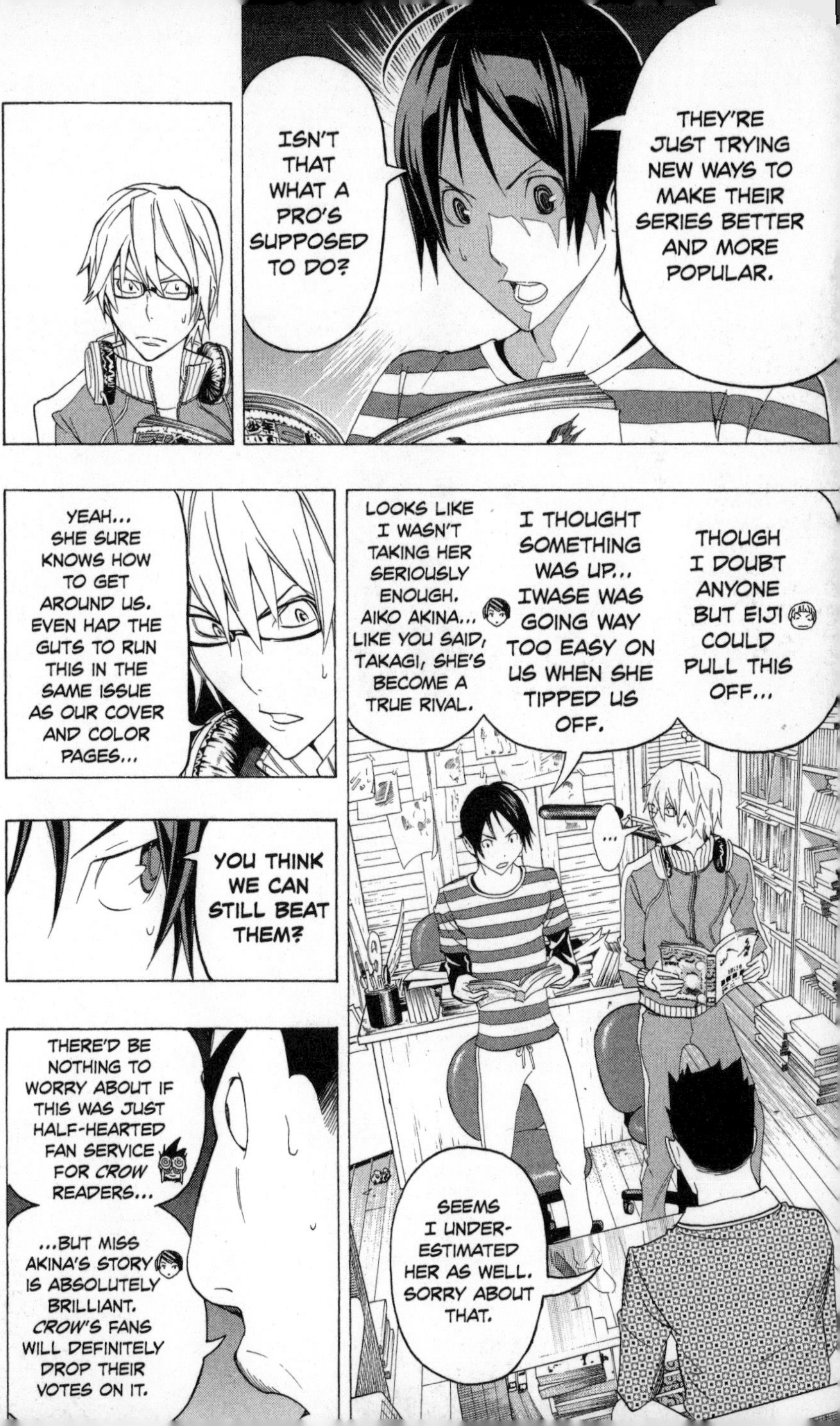
THEY'RE JUST TRYING NEW WAYS TO MAKE THEIR SERIES BETTER AND MORE POPULAR.
ISN'T THAT WHAT A PRO'S SUPPOSED TO DO?
THOUGH I DOUBT ANYONE BUT EIJI COULD PULL THIS OFF...
I THOUGHT SOMETHING WAS UP... IWASE WAS GOING WAY TOO EASY ON US WHEN SHE TIPPED US OFF.
LOOKS LIKE I WASN'T TAKING HER SERIOUSLY ENOUGH. AIKO AKINA... LIKE YOU SAID, TAKAGI, SHE'S BECOME A TRUE RIVAL.
...
SEEMS I UNDER-ESTIMATED HER AS WELL. SORRY ABOUT THAT.
YEAH... SHE SURE KNOWS HOW TO GET AROUND US. EVEN HAD THE GUTS TO RUN THIS IN THE SAME ISSUE AS OUR COVER AND COLOR PAGES...
YOU THINK WE CAN STILL BEAT THEM?
THERE'D BE NOTHING TO WORRY ABOUT IF THIS WAS JUST HALF-HEARTED FAN SERVICE FOR *CROW* READERS...
...BUT MISS AKINA'S STORY IS ABSOLUTELY BRILLIANT. *CROW'S* FANS WILL DEFINITELY DROP THEIR VOTES ON IT.

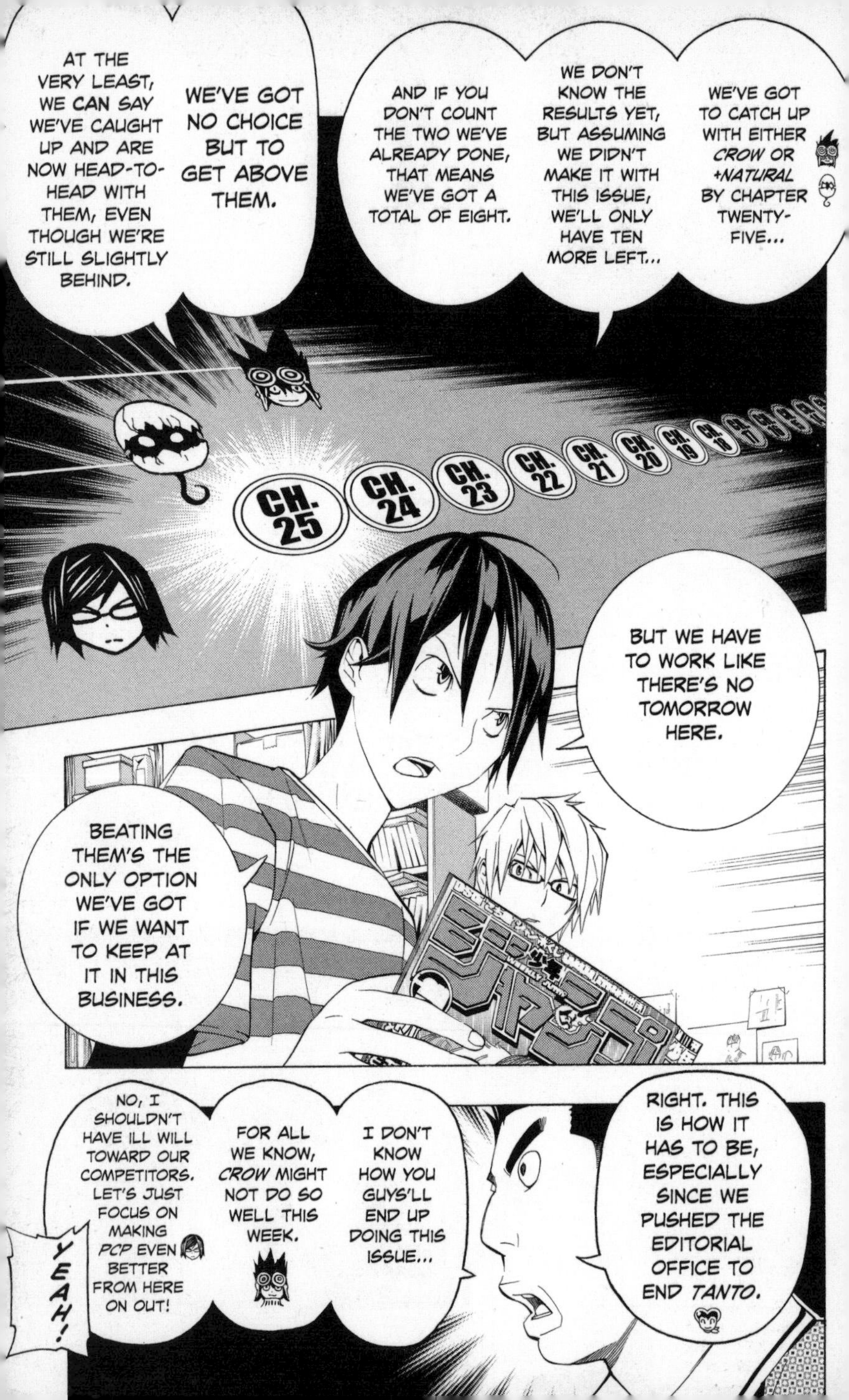
WE'VE GOT TO CATCH UP WITH EITHER *CROW* OR *+NATURAL* BY CHAPTER TWENTY-FIVE...
WE DON'T KNOW THE RESULTS YET, BUT ASSUMING WE DIDN'T MAKE IT WITH THIS ISSUE, WE'LL ONLY HAVE TEN MORE LEFT...
AND IF YOU DON'T COUNT THE TWO WE'VE ALREADY DONE, THAT MEANS WE'VE GOT A TOTAL OF EIGHT.
WE'VE GOT NO CHOICE BUT TO GET ABOVE THEM.
AT THE VERY LEAST, WE CAN SAY WE'VE CAUGHT UP AND ARE NOW HEAD-TO-HEAD WITH THEM, EVEN THOUGH WE'RE STILL SLIGHTLY BEHIND.
CH. 25
CH. 24
CH. 23
CH. 22
CH. 21
CH. 20
CH. 19
CH. 18
BUT WE HAVE TO WORK LIKE THERE'S NO TOMORROW HERE.
BEATING THEM'S THE ONLY OPTION WE'VE GOT IF WE WANT TO KEEP AT IT IN THIS BUSINESS.
RIGHT. THIS IS HOW IT HAS TO BE, ESPECIALLY SINCE WE PUSHED THE EDITORIAL OFFICE TO END *TANTO*.
I DON'T KNOW HOW YOU GUYS'LL END UP DOING THIS ISSUE...
FOR ALL WE KNOW, *CROW* MIGHT NOT DO SO WELL THIS WEEK.
NO, I SHOULDN'T HAVE ILL WILL TOWARD OUR COMPETITORS. LET'S JUST FOCUS ON MAKING *PCP* EVEN BETTER FROM HERE ON OUT!
YEAH!

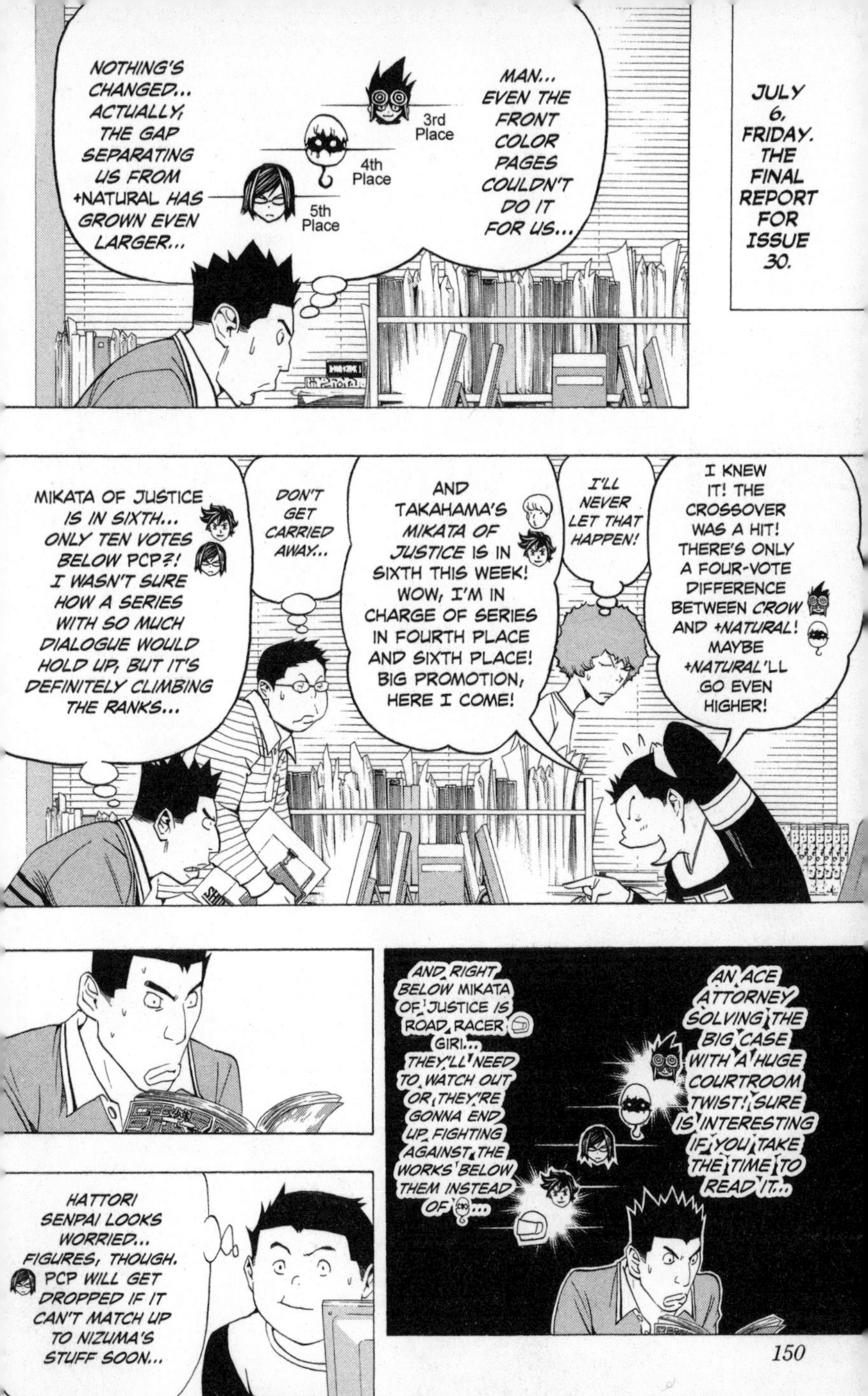
JULY 6, FRIDAY. THE FINAL REPORT FOR ISSUE 30.
MAN... EVEN THE FRONT COLOR PAGES COULDN'T DO IT FOR US...
3rd Place
4th Place
5th Place
NOTHING'S CHANGED... ACTUALLY, THE GAP SEPARATING US FROM +NATURAL HAS GROWN EVEN LARGER...
I KNEW IT! THE CROSSOVER WAS A HIT! THERE'S ONLY A FOUR-VOTE DIFFERENCE BETWEEN CROW AND +NATURAL! MAYBE +NATURAL'LL GO EVEN HIGHER!
I'LL NEVER LET THAT HAPPEN!
AND TAKAHAMA'S MIKATA OF JUSTICE IS IN SIXTH THIS WEEK! WOW, I'M IN CHARGE OF SERIES IN FOURTH PLACE AND SIXTH PLACE! BIG PROMOTION, HERE I COME!
DON'T GET CARRIED AWAY...
MIKATA OF JUSTICE IS IN SIXTH... ONLY TEN VOTES BELOW PCP?! I WASN'T SURE HOW A SERIES WITH SO MUCH DIALOGUE WOULD HOLD UP, BUT IT'S DEFINITELY CLIMBING THE RANKS...
AN ACE ATTORNEY SOLVING THE BIG CASE WITH A HUGE COURTROOM TWIST! SURE IS INTERESTING IF YOU TAKE THE TIME TO READ IT...
AND RIGHT BELOW MIKATA OF JUSTICE IS ROAD RACER GIRI... THEY'LL NEED TO WATCH OUT OR THEY'RE GONNA END UP FIGHTING AGAINST THE WORKS BELOW THEM INSTEAD OF ...
HATTORI SENPAI LOOKS WORRIED... FIGURES, THOUGH. PCP WILL GET DROPPED IF IT CAN'T MATCH UP TO NIZUMA'S STUFF SOON...

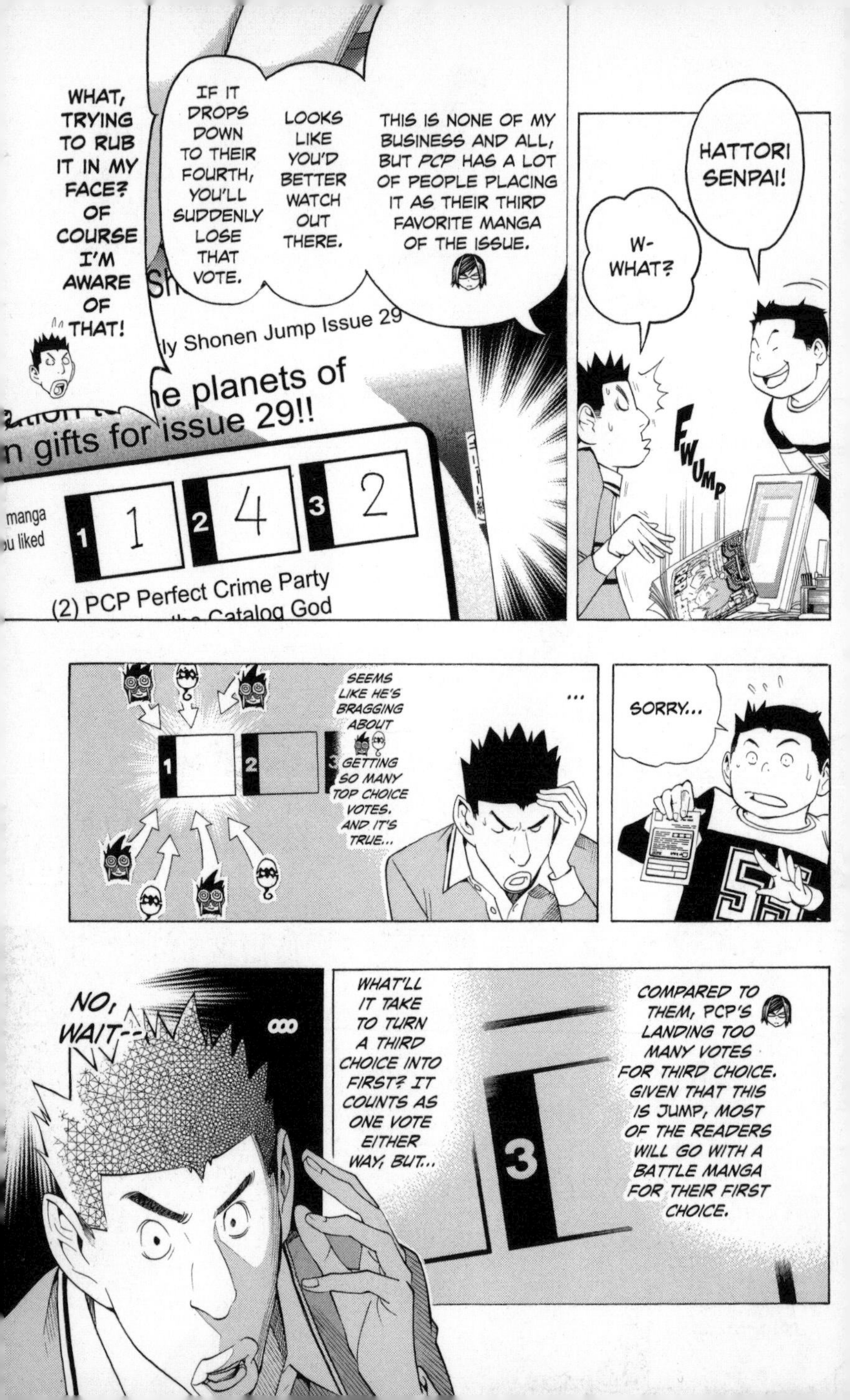
HATTORI SENPAI!
W-WHAT?
FWUMP
THIS IS NONE OF MY BUSINESS AND ALL, BUT PCP HAS A LOT OF PEOPLE PLACING IT AS THEIR THIRD FAVORITE MANGA OF THE ISSUE.
LOOKS LIKE YOU'D BETTER WATCH OUT THERE.
IF IT DROPS DOWN TO THEIR FOURTH, YOU'LL SUDDENLY LOSE THAT VOTE.
WHAT, TRYING TO RUB IT IN MY FACE? OF COURSE I'M AWARE OF THAT!
ly Shonen Jump Issue 29
e planets of
n gifts for issue 29!!
manga
u liked
1 1 2 4 3 2
(2) PCP Perfect Crime Party
SORRY...
...
SEEMS LIKE HE'S BRAGGING ABOUT GETTING SO MANY TOP CHOICE VOTES. AND IT'S TRUE...
1 2
COMPARED TO THEM, PCP'S LANDING TOO MANY VOTES FOR THIRD CHOICE. GIVEN THAT THIS IS JUMP, MOST OF THE READERS WILL GO WITH A BATTLE MANGA FOR THEIR FIRST CHOICE.
3
WHAT'LL IT TAKE TO TURN A THIRD CHOICE INTO FIRST? IT COUNTS AS ONE VOTE EITHER WAY, BUT...
NO, WAIT--
...

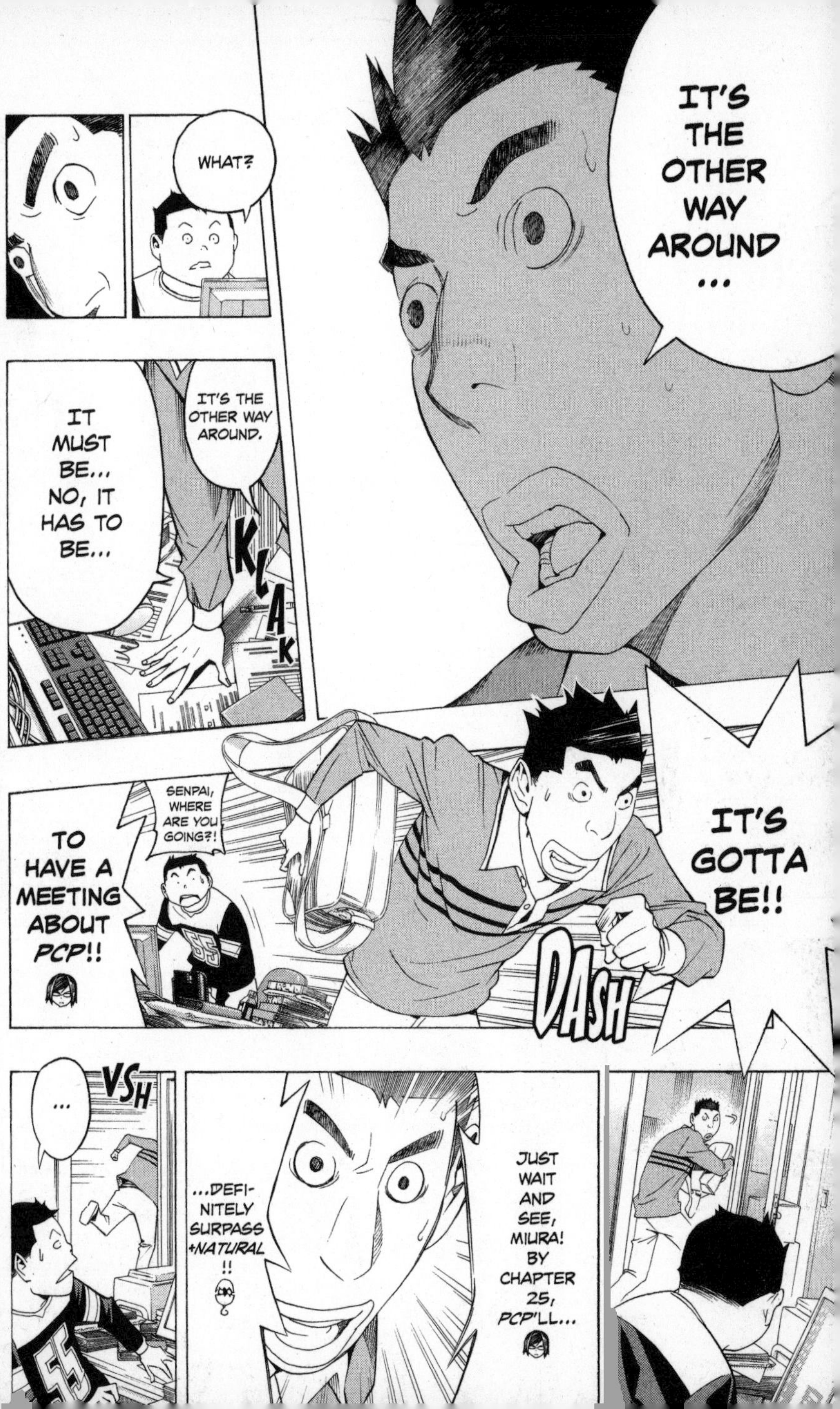
IT'S THE OTHER WAY AROUND...
WHAT?
IT'S THE OTHER WAY AROUND.
IT MUST BE... NO, IT HAS TO BE...
KLAK
IT'S GOTTA BE!!
DASH
SENPAI, WHERE ARE YOU GOING?!
TO HAVE A MEETING ABOUT *PCP*!!
JUST WAIT AND SEE, MIURA! BY CHAPTER 25, *PCP*'LL...
...DEFINITELY SURPASS *+NATURAL*!!
VSH
...

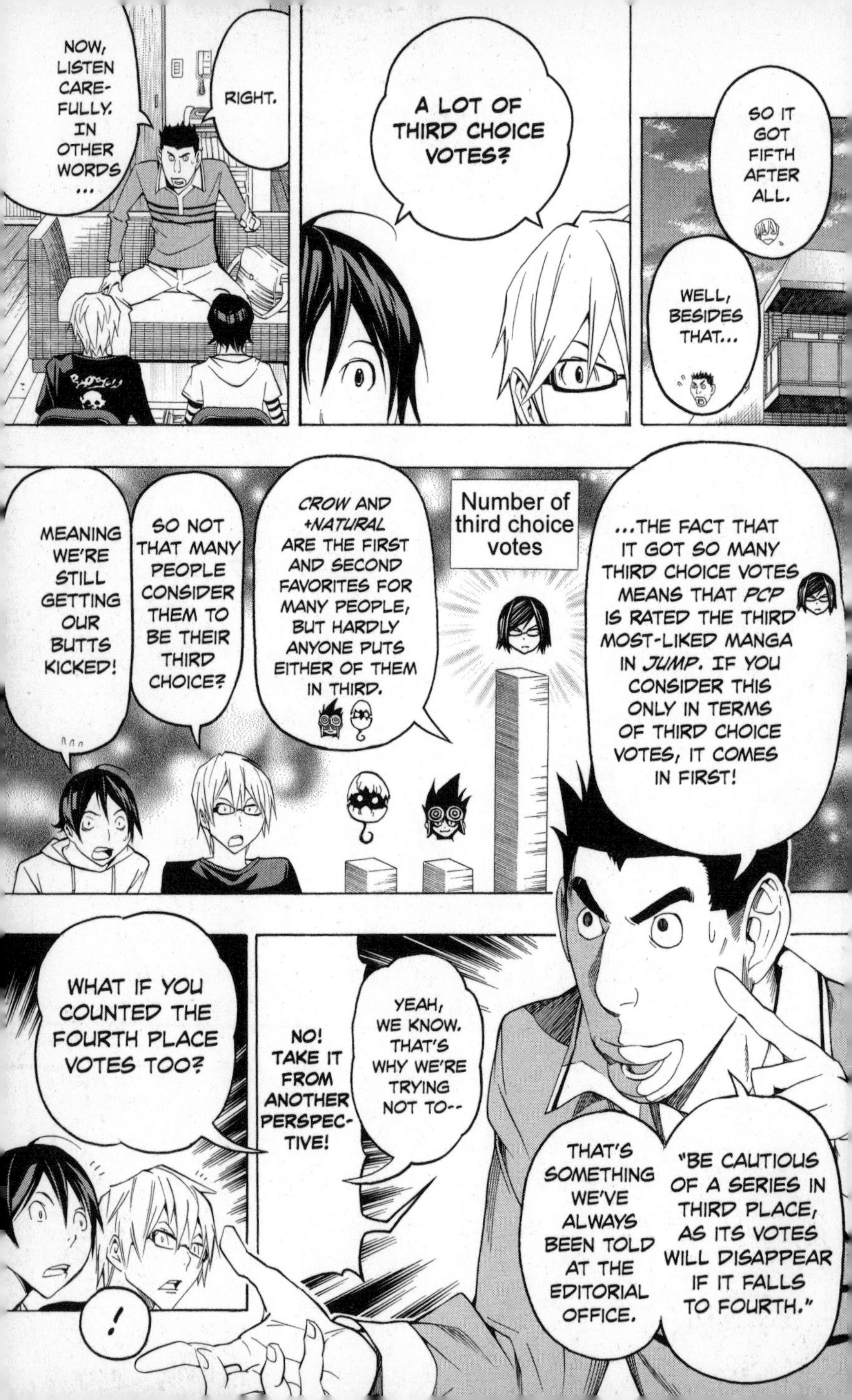
SO IT GOT FIFTH AFTER ALL.
WELL, BESIDES THAT...
A LOT OF THIRD CHOICE VOTES?
NOW, LISTEN CARE-FULLY. IN OTHER WORDS...
RIGHT.
...THE FACT THAT IT GOT SO MANY THIRD CHOICE VOTES MEANS THAT *PCP* IS RATED THE THIRD MOST-LIKED MANGA IN *JUMP*. IF YOU CONSIDER THIS ONLY IN TERMS OF THIRD CHOICE VOTES, IT COMES IN FIRST!
Number of third choice votes
CROW AND *+NATURAL* ARE THE FIRST AND SECOND FAVORITES FOR MANY PEOPLE, BUT HARDLY ANYONE PUTS EITHER OF THEM IN THIRD.
SO NOT THAT MANY PEOPLE CONSIDER THEM TO BE THEIR THIRD CHOICE?
MEANING WE'RE STILL GETTING OUR BUTTS KICKED!
"BE CAUTIOUS OF A SERIES IN THIRD PLACE, AS ITS VOTES WILL DISAPPEAR IF IT FALLS TO FOURTH."
THAT'S SOMETHING WE'VE ALWAYS BEEN TOLD AT THE EDITORIAL OFFICE.
YEAH, WE KNOW. THAT'S WHY WE'RE TRYING NOT TO--
NO! TAKE IT FROM ANOTHER PERSPEC-TIVE!
WHAT IF YOU COUNTED THE FOURTH PLACE VOTES TOO?
!

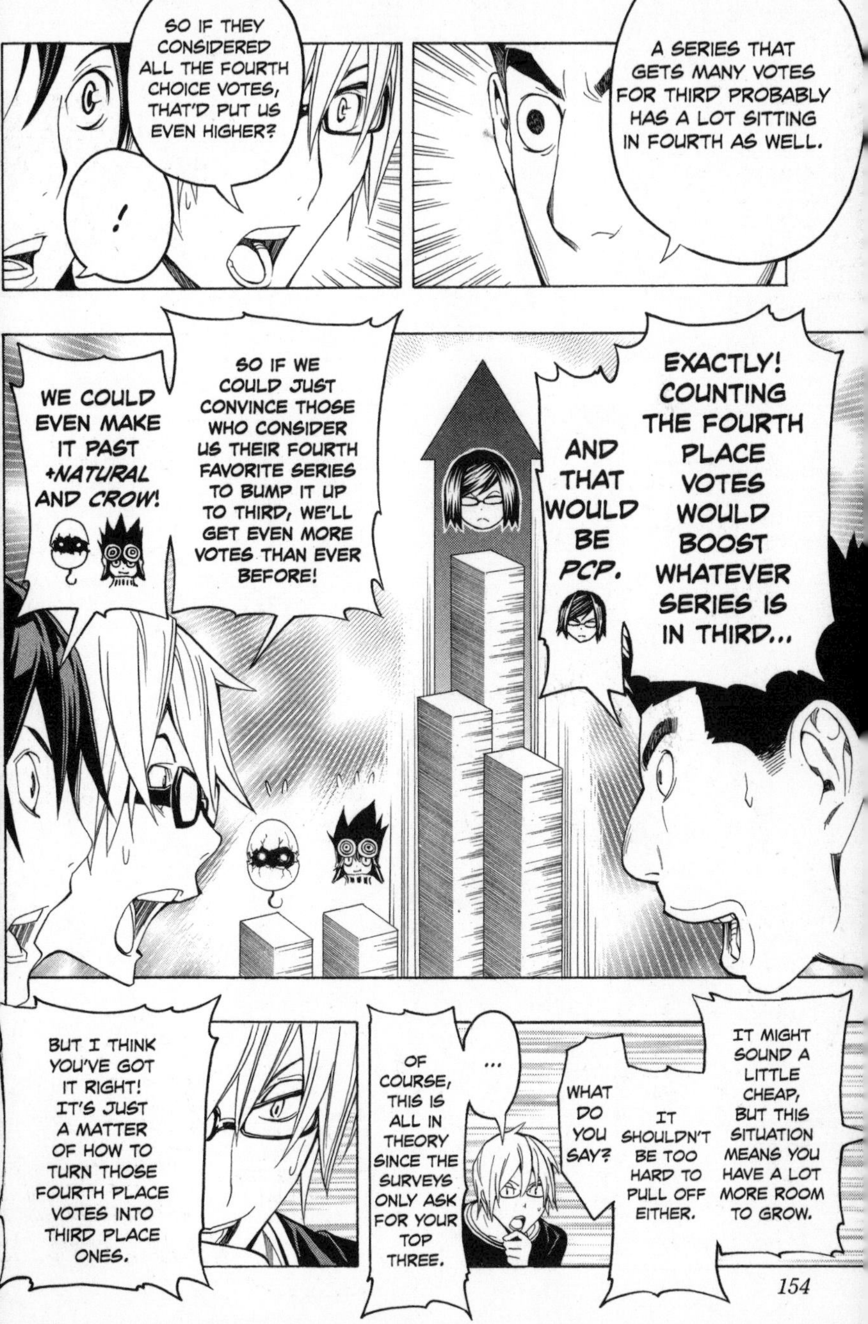
A SERIES THAT GETS MANY VOTES FOR THIRD PROBABLY HAS A LOT SITTING IN FOURTH AS WELL.
SO IF THEY CONSIDERED ALL THE FOURTH CHOICE VOTES, THAT'D PUT US EVEN HIGHER?
!
EXACTLY! COUNTING THE FOURTH PLACE VOTES WOULD BOOST WHATEVER SERIES IS IN THIRD...
AND THAT WOULD BE *PCP*.
SO IF WE COULD JUST CONVINCE THOSE WHO CONSIDER US THEIR FOURTH FAVORITE SERIES TO BUMP IT UP TO THIRD, WE'LL GET EVEN MORE VOTES THAN EVER BEFORE!
WE COULD EVEN MAKE IT PAST *+NATURAL* AND *CROW*!
IT MIGHT SOUND A LITTLE CHEAP, BUT THIS SITUATION MEANS YOU HAVE A LOT MORE ROOM TO GROW.
IT SHOULDN'T BE TOO HARD TO PULL OFF EITHER.
WHAT DO YOU SAY?
...
OF COURSE, THIS IS ALL IN THEORY SINCE THE SURVEYS ONLY ASK FOR YOUR TOP THREE.
BUT I THINK YOU'VE GOT IT RIGHT! IT'S JUST A MATTER OF HOW TO TURN THOSE FOURTH PLACE VOTES INTO THIRD PLACE ONES.

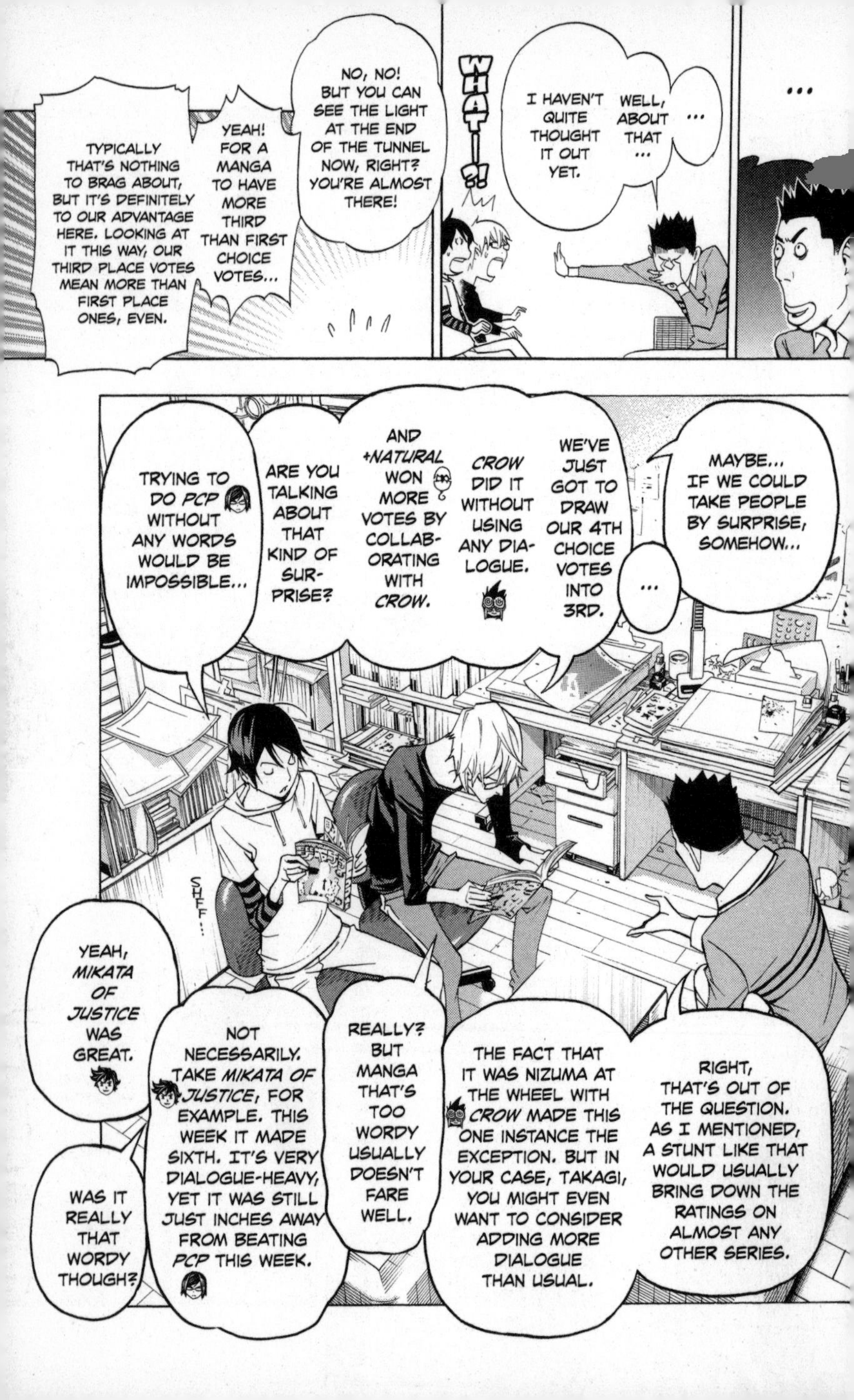
...
WELL, ABOUT THAT...
...
I HAVEN'T QUITE THOUGHT IT OUT YET.
WHAT!?
NO, NO! BUT YOU CAN SEE THE LIGHT AT THE END OF THE TUNNEL NOW, RIGHT? YOU'RE ALMOST THERE!
YEAH! FOR A MANGA TO HAVE MORE THIRD THAN FIRST CHOICE VOTES...
TYPICALLY THAT'S NOTHING TO BRAG ABOUT, BUT IT'S DEFINITELY TO OUR ADVANTAGE HERE. LOOKING AT IT THIS WAY, OUR THIRD PLACE VOTES MEAN MORE THAN FIRST PLACE ONES, EVEN.
MAYBE... IF WE COULD TAKE PEOPLE BY SURPRISE, SOMEHOW...
...
WE'VE JUST GOT TO DRAW OUR 4TH CHOICE VOTES INTO 3RD.
CROW DID IT WITHOUT USING ANY DIALOGUE.
AND +NATURAL WON MORE VOTES BY COLLABORATING WITH CROW.
ARE YOU TALKING ABOUT THAT KIND OF SURPRISE?
TRYING TO DO PCP WITHOUT ANY WORDS WOULD BE IMPOSSIBLE...
SHFF...
RIGHT, THAT'S OUT OF THE QUESTION. AS I MENTIONED, A STUNT LIKE THAT WOULD USUALLY BRING DOWN THE RATINGS ON ALMOST ANY OTHER SERIES.
THE FACT THAT IT WAS NIZUMA AT THE WHEEL WITH CROW MADE THIS ONE INSTANCE THE EXCEPTION. BUT IN YOUR CASE, TAKAGI, YOU MIGHT EVEN WANT TO CONSIDER ADDING MORE DIALOGUE THAN USUAL.
REALLY? BUT MANGA THAT'S TOO WORDY USUALLY DOESN'T FARE WELL.
NOT NECESSARILY. TAKE MIKATA OF JUSTICE, FOR EXAMPLE. THIS WEEK IT MADE SIXTH. IT'S VERY DIALOGUE-HEAVY, YET IT WAS STILL JUST INCHES AWAY FROM BEATING PCP THIS WEEK.
YEAH, MIKATA OF JUSTICE WAS GREAT.
WAS IT REALLY THAT WORDY THOUGH?

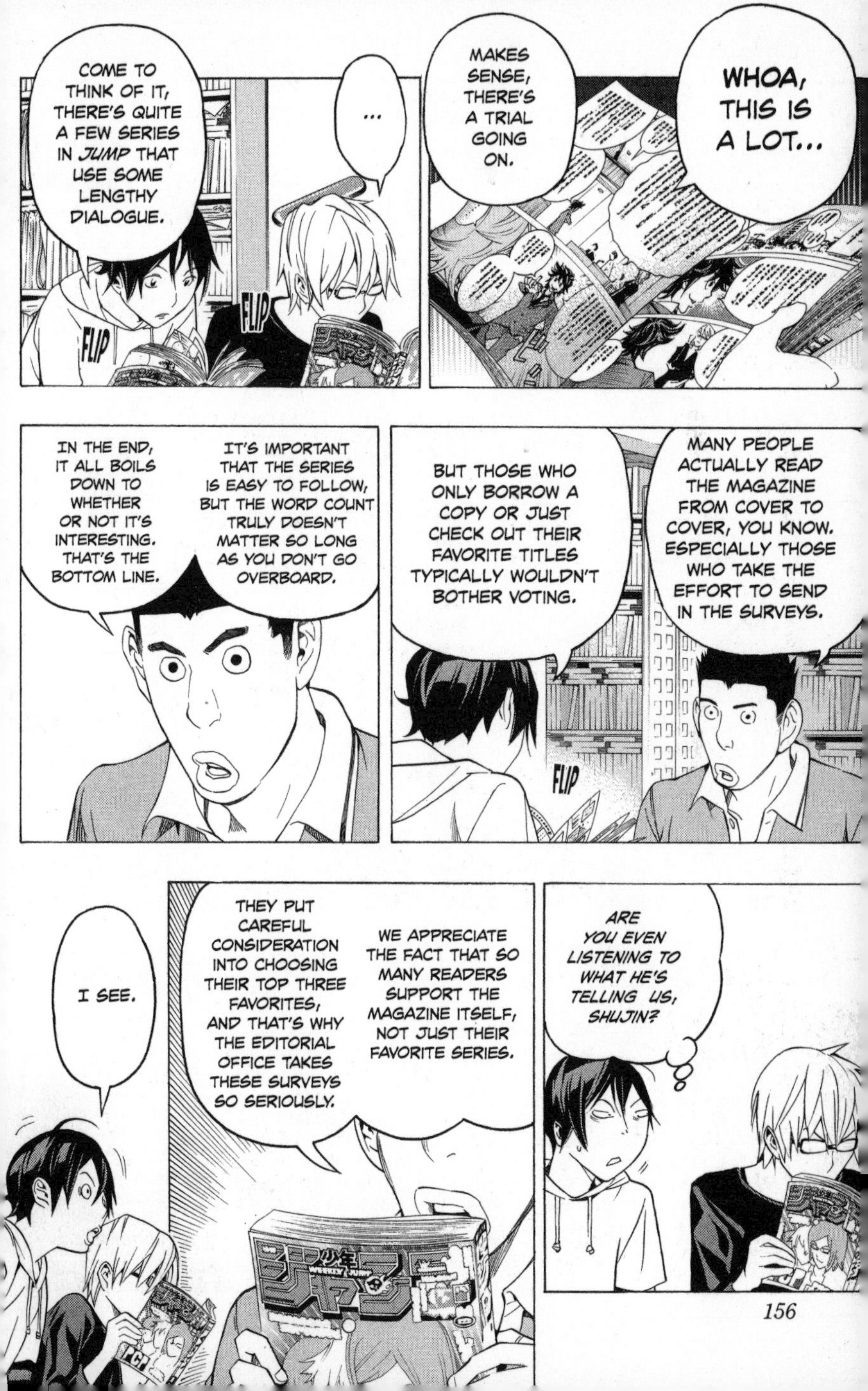
WHOA, THIS IS A LOT...
MAKES SENSE, THERE'S A TRIAL GOING ON.
...
COME TO THINK OF IT, THERE'S QUITE A FEW SERIES IN *JUMP* THAT USE SOME LENGTHY DIALOGUE.
FLIP
FLIP
MANY PEOPLE ACTUALLY READ THE MAGAZINE FROM COVER TO COVER, YOU KNOW. ESPECIALLY THOSE WHO TAKE THE EFFORT TO SEND IN THE SURVEYS.
BUT THOSE WHO ONLY BORROW A COPY OR JUST CHECK OUT THEIR FAVORITE TITLES TYPICALLY WOULDN'T BOTHER VOTING.
FLIP
IT'S IMPORTANT THAT THE SERIES IS EASY TO FOLLOW, BUT THE WORD COUNT TRULY DOESN'T MATTER SO LONG AS YOU DON'T GO OVERBOARD.
IN THE END, IT ALL BOILS DOWN TO WHETHER OR NOT IT'S INTERESTING. THAT'S THE BOTTOM LINE.
ARE YOU EVEN LISTENING TO WHAT HE'S TELLING US, SHUJIN?
WE APPRECIATE THE FACT THAT SO MANY READERS SUPPORT THE MAGAZINE ITSELF, NOT JUST THEIR FAVORITE SERIES.
THEY PUT CAREFUL CONSIDERATION INTO CHOOSING THEIR TOP THREE FAVORITES, AND THAT'S WHY THE EDITORIAL OFFICE TAKES THESE SURVEYS SO SERIOUSLY.
I SEE.

READ THIS WAY

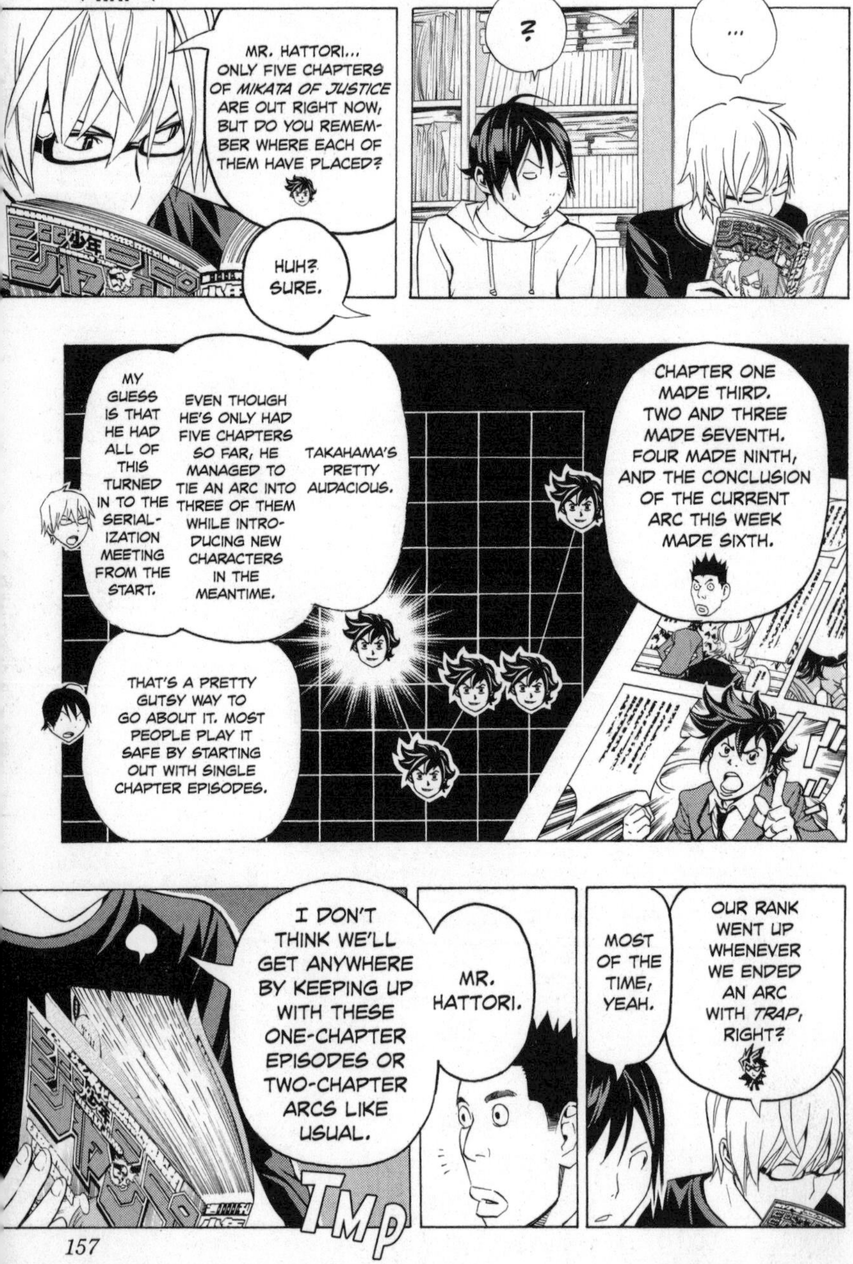

...
?
MR. HATTORI... ONLY FIVE CHAPTERS OF *MIKATA OF JUSTICE* ARE OUT RIGHT NOW, BUT DO YOU REMEMBER WHERE EACH OF THEM HAVE PLACED?
HUH? SURE.
CHAPTER ONE MADE THIRD. TWO AND THREE MADE SEVENTH. FOUR MADE NINTH, AND THE CONCLUSION OF THE CURRENT ARC THIS WEEK MADE SIXTH.
TAKAHAMA'S PRETTY AUDACIOUS.
EVEN THOUGH HE'S ONLY HAD FIVE CHAPTERS SO FAR, HE MANAGED TO TIE AN ARC INTO THREE OF THEM WHILE INTRODUCING NEW CHARACTERS IN THE MEANTIME.
MY GUESS IS THAT HE HAD ALL OF THIS TURNED IN TO THE SERIALIZATION MEETING FROM THE START.
THAT'S A PRETTY GUTSY WAY TO GO ABOUT IT. MOST PEOPLE PLAY IT SAFE BY STARTING OUT WITH SINGLE CHAPTER EPISODES.
OUR RANK WENT UP WHENEVER WE ENDED AN ARC WITH *TRAP*, RIGHT?
MOST OF THE TIME, YEAH.
MR. HATTORI.
I DON'T THINK WE'LL GET ANYWHERE BY KEEPING UP WITH THESE ONE-CHAPTER EPISODES OR TWO-CHAPTER ARCS LIKE USUAL.
TMP

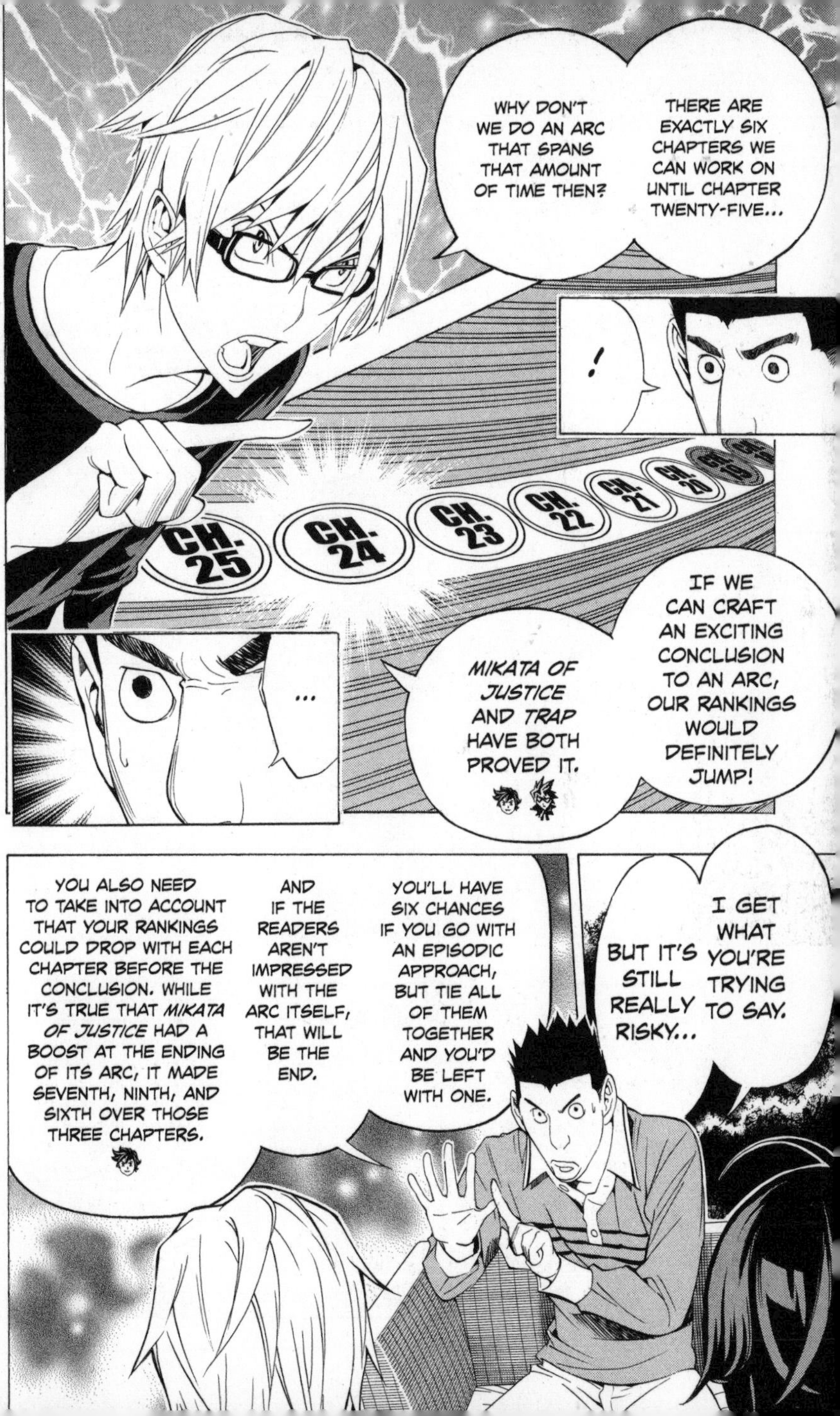
THERE ARE EXACTLY SIX CHAPTERS WE CAN WORK ON UNTIL CHAPTER TWENTY-FIVE...
WHY DON'T WE DO AN ARC THAT SPANS THAT AMOUNT OF TIME THEN?
!
CH. 21
CH. 22
CH. 23
CH. 24
CH. 25
IF WE CAN CRAFT AN EXCITING CONCLUSION TO AN ARC, OUR RANKINGS WOULD DEFINITELY JUMP!
MIKATA OF JUSTICE AND *TRAP* HAVE BOTH PROVED IT.
...
I GET WHAT YOU'RE TRYING TO SAY.
BUT IT'S STILL REALLY RISKY...
YOU'LL HAVE SIX CHANCES IF YOU GO WITH AN EPISODIC APPROACH, BUT TIE ALL OF THEM TOGETHER AND YOU'D BE LEFT WITH ONE.
AND IF THE READERS AREN'T IMPRESSED WITH THE ARC ITSELF, THAT WILL BE THE END.
YOU ALSO NEED TO TAKE INTO ACCOUNT THAT YOUR RANKINGS COULD DROP WITH EACH CHAPTER BEFORE THE CONCLUSION. WHILE IT'S TRUE THAT *MIKATA OF JUSTICE* HAD A BOOST AT THE ENDING OF ITS ARC, IT MADE SEVENTH, NINTH, AND SIXTH OVER THOSE THREE CHAPTERS.

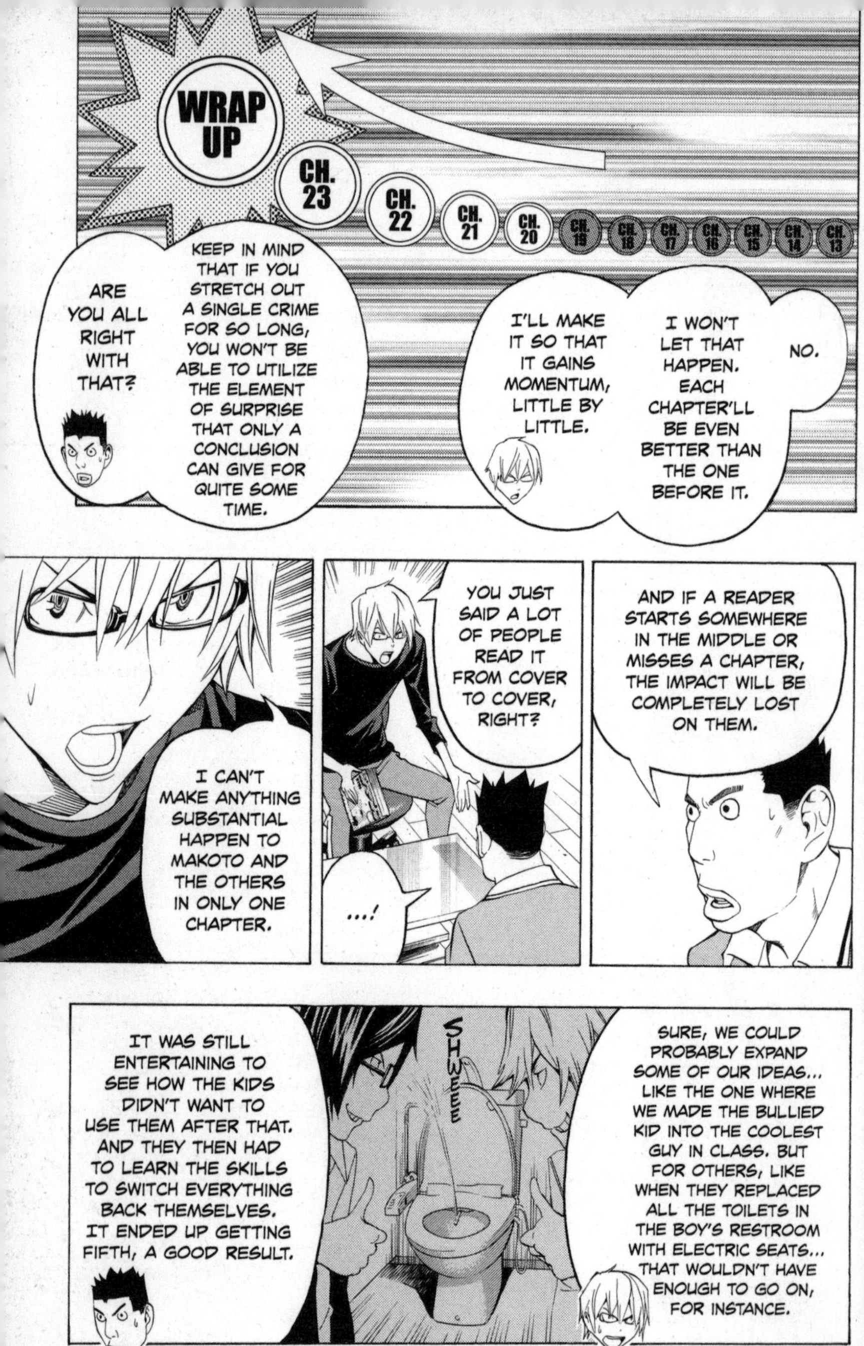
WRAP UP
CH. 23
CH. 22
CH. 21
CH. 20
CH. 19
CH. 18
CH. 17
CH. 16
CH. 15
CH. 14
CH. 13
NO.
I WON'T LET THAT HAPPEN. EACH CHAPTER'LL BE EVEN BETTER THAN THE ONE BEFORE IT.
I'LL MAKE IT SO THAT IT GAINS MOMENTUM, LITTLE BY LITTLE.
KEEP IN MIND THAT IF YOU STRETCH OUT A SINGLE CRIME FOR SO LONG, YOU WON'T BE ABLE TO UTILIZE THE ELEMENT OF SURPRISE THAT ONLY A CONCLUSION CAN GIVE FOR QUITE SOME TIME.
ARE YOU ALL RIGHT WITH THAT?
AND IF A READER STARTS SOMEWHERE IN THE MIDDLE OR MISSES A CHAPTER, THE IMPACT WILL BE COMPLETELY LOST ON THEM.
YOU JUST SAID A LOT OF PEOPLE READ IT FROM COVER TO COVER, RIGHT?
...!
I CAN'T MAKE ANYTHING SUBSTANTIAL HAPPEN TO MAKOTO AND THE OTHERS IN ONLY ONE CHAPTER.
SURE, WE COULD PROBABLY EXPAND SOME OF OUR IDEAS... LIKE THE ONE WHERE WE MADE THE BULLIED KID INTO THE COOLEST GUY IN CLASS. BUT FOR OTHERS, LIKE WHEN THEY REPLACED ALL THE TOILETS IN THE BOY'S RESTROOM WITH ELECTRIC SEATS... THAT WOULDN'T HAVE ENOUGH TO GO ON, FOR INSTANCE.
SHWEEE
IT WAS STILL ENTERTAINING TO SEE HOW THE KIDS DIDN'T WANT TO USE THEM AFTER THAT. AND THEY THEN HAD TO LEARN THE SKILLS TO SWITCH EVERYTHING BACK THEMSELVES. IT ENDED UP GETTING FIFTH, A GOOD RESULT.

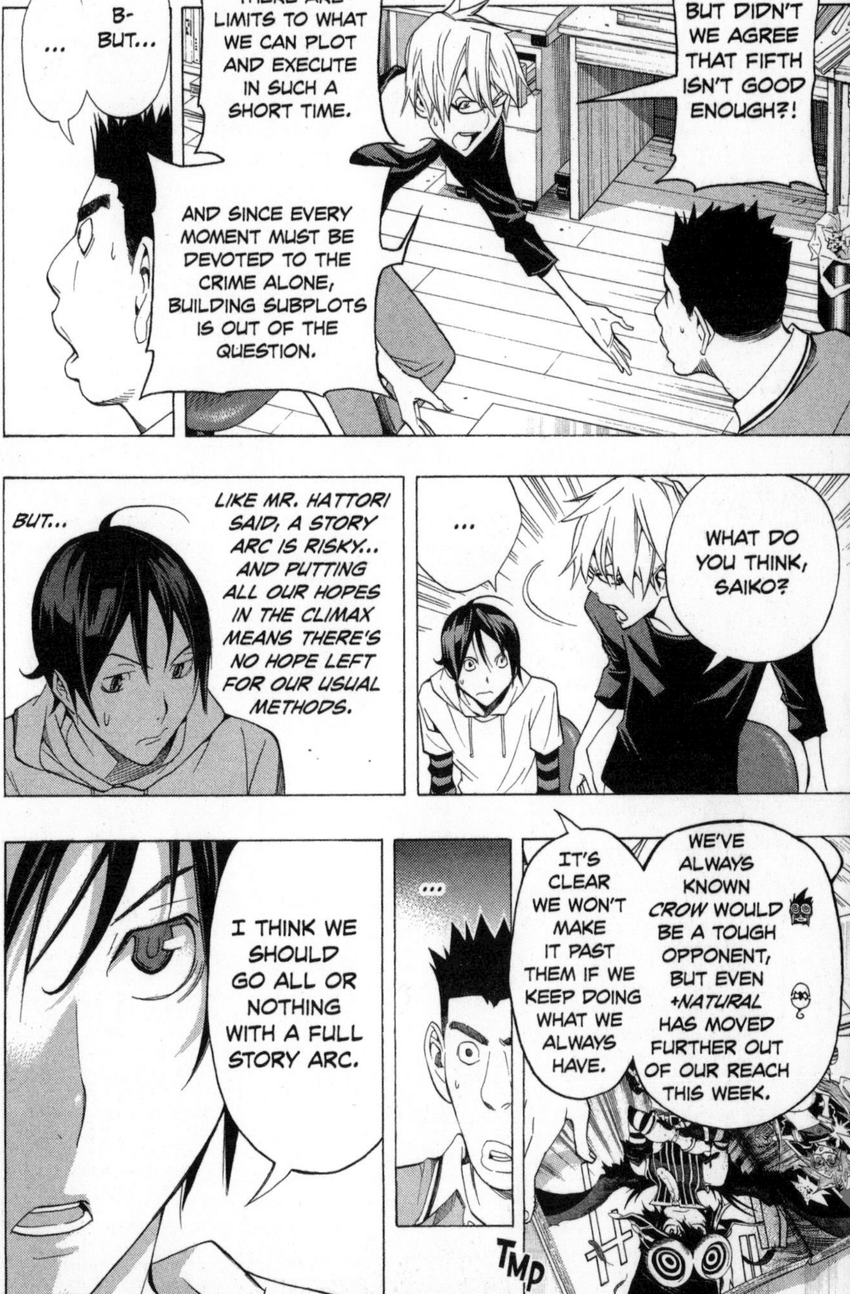
BUT DIDN'T WE AGREE THAT FIFTH ISN'T GOOD ENOUGH?!
THERE ARE LIMITS TO WHAT WE CAN PLOT AND EXECUTE IN SUCH A SHORT TIME.
B-BUT...
...
AND SINCE EVERY MOMENT MUST BE DEVOTED TO THE CRIME ALONE, BUILDING SUBPLOTS IS OUT OF THE QUESTION.
WHAT DO YOU THINK, SAIKO?
...
LIKE MR. HATTORI SAID, A STORY ARC IS RISKY... AND PUTTING ALL OUR HOPES IN THE CLIMAX MEANS THERE'S NO HOPE LEFT FOR OUR USUAL METHODS.
BUT...
WE'VE ALWAYS KNOWN *CROW* WOULD BE A TOUGH OPPONENT, BUT EVEN *+NATURAL* HAS MOVED FURTHER OUT OF OUR REACH THIS WEEK.
IT'S CLEAR WE WON'T MAKE IT PAST THEM IF WE KEEP DOING WHAT WE ALWAYS HAVE.
TMP
...
I THINK WE SHOULD GO ALL OR NOTHING WITH A FULL STORY ARC.

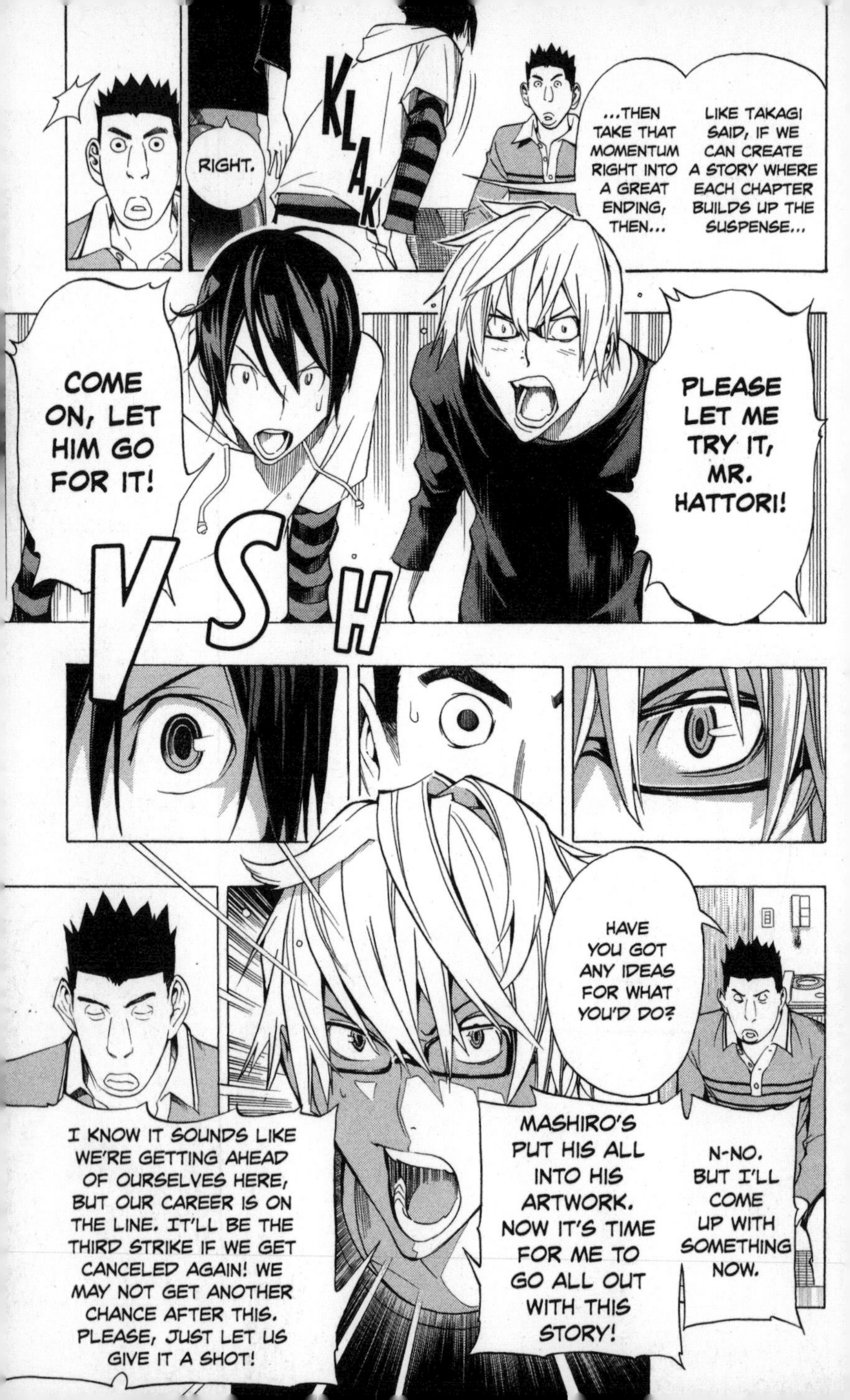
LIKE TAKAGI SAID, IF WE CAN CREATE A STORY WHERE EACH CHAPTER BUILDS UP THE SUSPENSE...
...THEN TAKE THAT MOMENTUM RIGHT INTO A GREAT ENDING, THEN...
KLAK
RIGHT.
PLEASE LET ME TRY IT, MR. HATTORI!
COME ON, LET HIM GO FOR IT!
VSH
HAVE YOU GOT ANY IDEAS FOR WHAT YOU'D DO?
N-NO. BUT I'LL COME UP WITH SOMETHING NOW.
MASHIRO'S PUT HIS ALL INTO HIS ARTWORK. NOW IT'S TIME FOR ME TO GO ALL OUT WITH THIS STORY!
I KNOW IT SOUNDS LIKE WE'RE GETTING AHEAD OF OURSELVES HERE, BUT OUR CAREER IS ON THE LINE. IT'LL BE THE THIRD STRIKE IF WE GET CANCELED AGAIN! WE MAY NOT GET ANOTHER CHANCE AFTER THIS. PLEASE, JUST LET US GIVE IT A SHOT!

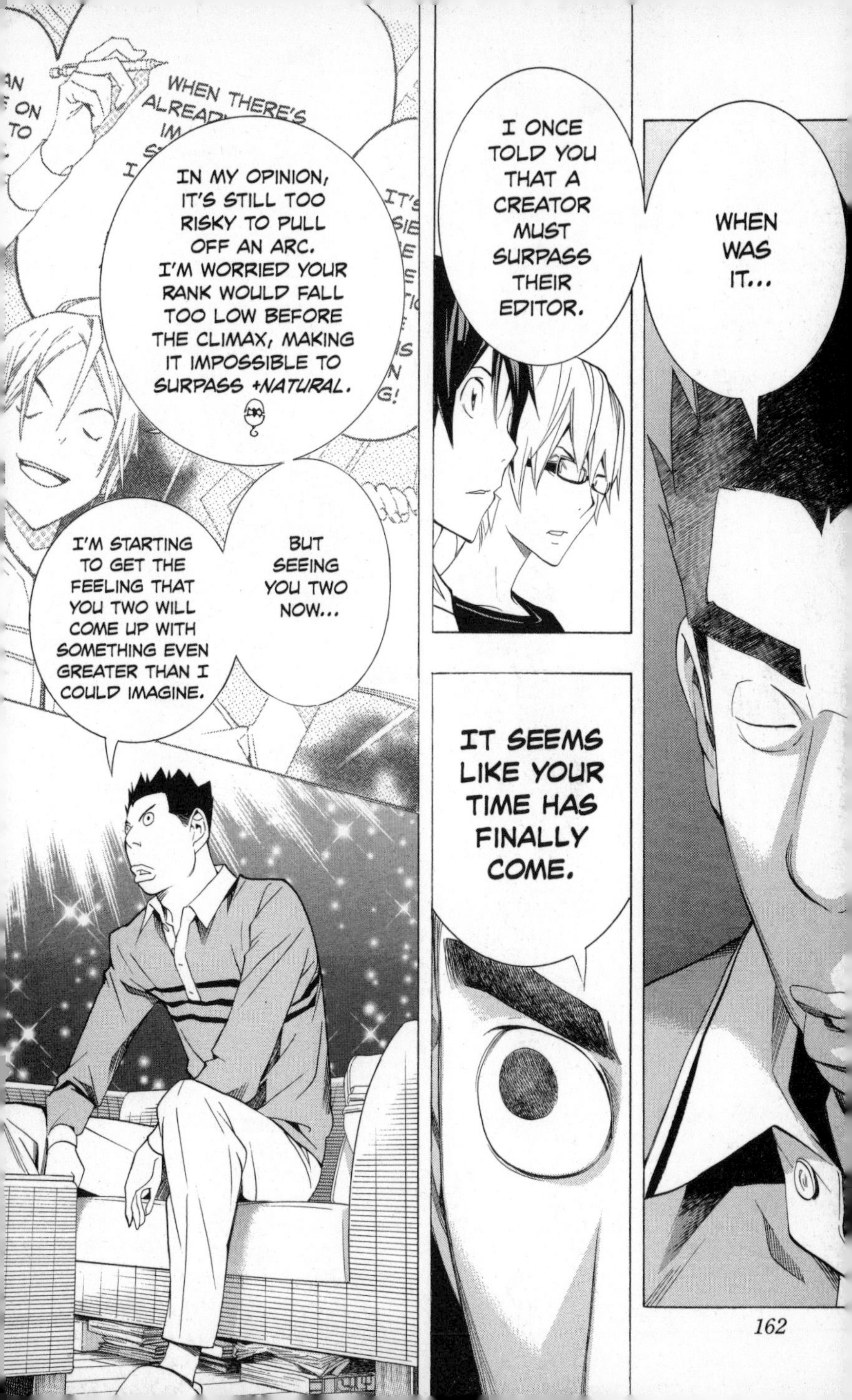
WHEN WAS IT...
I ONCE TOLD YOU THAT A CREATOR MUST SURPASS THEIR EDITOR.
IT SEEMS LIKE YOUR TIME HAS FINALLY COME.
IN MY OPINION, IT'S STILL TOO RISKY TO PULL OFF AN ARC. I'M WORRIED YOUR RANK WOULD FALL TOO LOW BEFORE THE CLIMAX, MAKING IT IMPOSSIBLE TO SURPASS +NATURAL.
BUT SEEING YOU TWO NOW...
I'M STARTING TO GET THE FEELING THAT YOU TWO WILL COME UP WITH SOMETHING EVEN GREATER THAN I COULD IMAGINE.

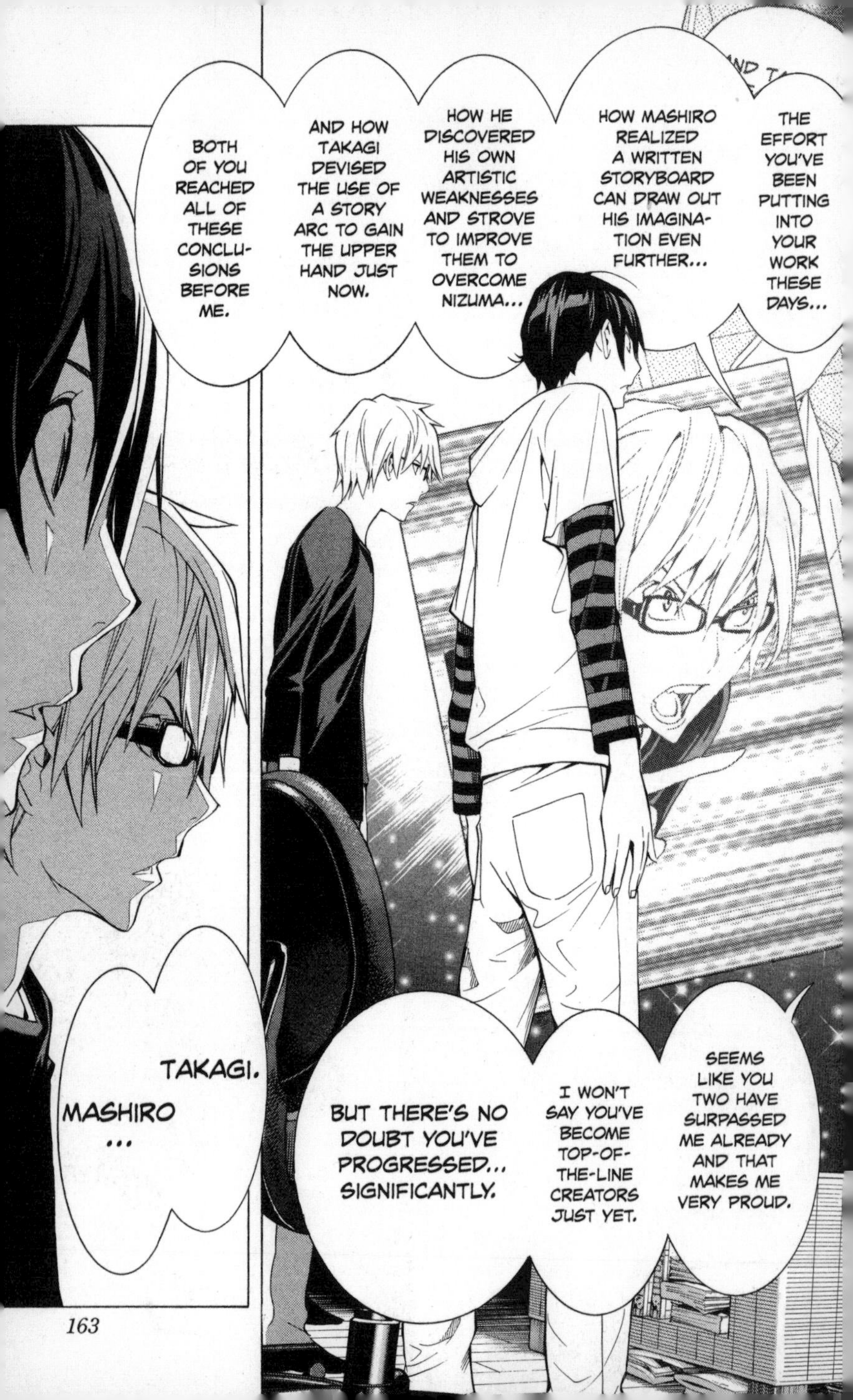

THE EFFORT YOU'VE BEEN PUTTING INTO YOUR WORK THESE DAYS...
HOW MASHIRO REALIZED A WRITTEN STORYBOARD CAN DRAW OUT HIS IMAGINATION EVEN FURTHER...
HOW HE DISCOVERED HIS OWN ARTISTIC WEAKNESSES AND STROVE TO IMPROVE THEM TO OVERCOME NIZUMA...
AND HOW TAKAGI DEVISED THE USE OF A STORY ARC TO GAIN THE UPPER HAND JUST NOW.
BOTH OF YOU REACHED ALL OF THESE CONCLUSIONS BEFORE ME.
SEEMS LIKE YOU TWO HAVE SURPASSED ME ALREADY AND THAT MAKES ME VERY PROUD.
I WON'T SAY YOU'VE BECOME TOP-OF-THE-LINE CREATORS JUST YET.
BUT THERE'S NO DOUBT YOU'VE PROGRESSED... SIGNIFICANTLY.
TAKAGI.
MASHIRO...

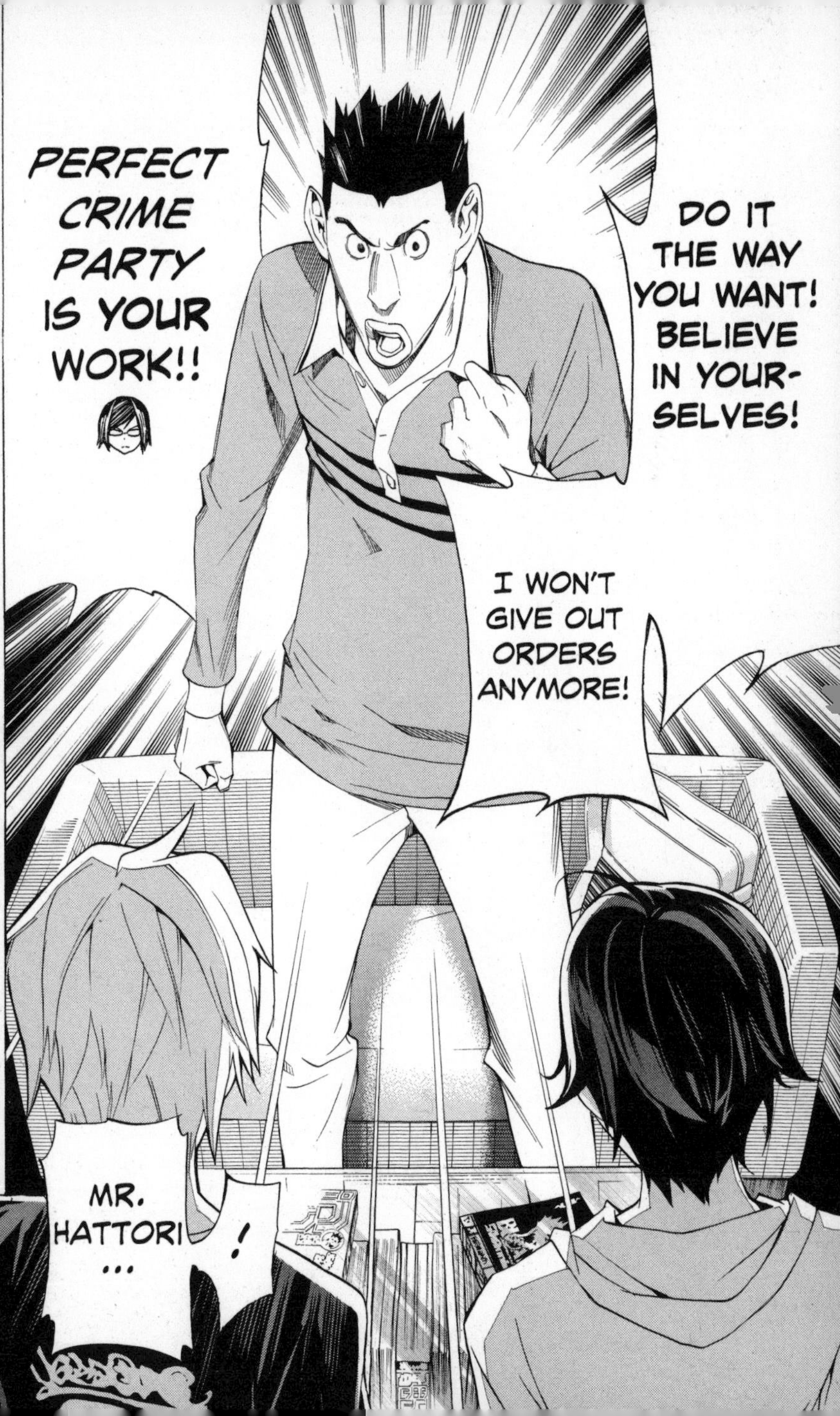
DO IT THE WAY YOU WANT! BELIEVE IN YOUR-SELVES!
I WON'T GIVE OUT ORDERS ANYMORE!
PERFECT CRIME PARTY IS YOUR WORK!!
!
MR. HATTORI ...

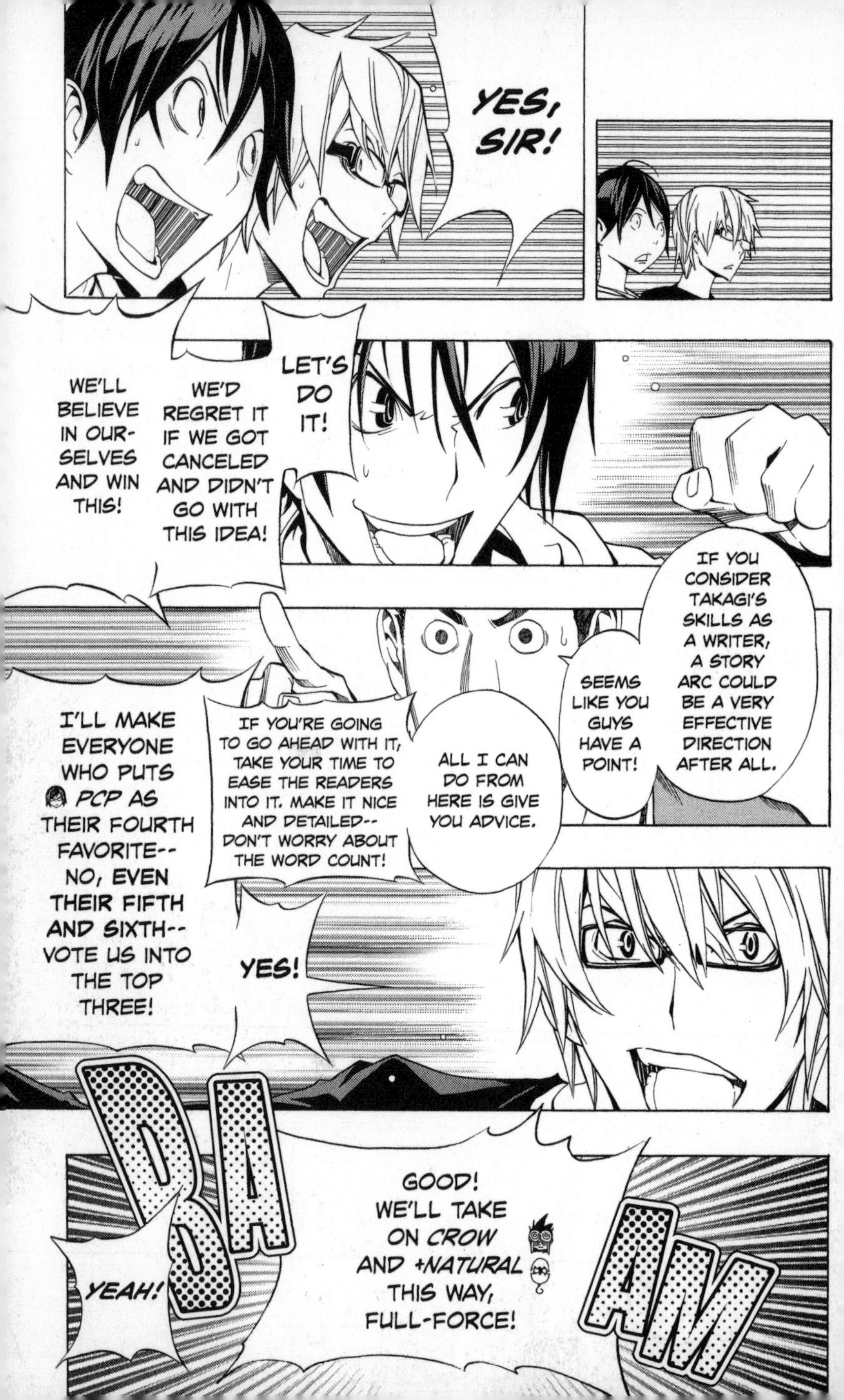
YES, SIR!
LET'S DO IT!
WE'D REGRET IT IF WE GOT CANCELED AND DIDN'T GO WITH THIS IDEA!
WE'LL BELIEVE IN OUR-SELVES AND WIN THIS!
IF YOU CONSIDER TAKAGI'S SKILLS AS A WRITER, A STORY ARC COULD BE A VERY EFFECTIVE DIRECTION AFTER ALL.
SEEMS LIKE YOU GUYS HAVE A POINT!
ALL I CAN DO FROM HERE IS GIVE YOU ADVICE.
IF YOU'RE GOING TO GO AHEAD WITH IT, TAKE YOUR TIME TO EASE THE READERS INTO IT. MAKE IT NICE AND DETAILED-- DON'T WORRY ABOUT THE WORD COUNT!
I'LL MAKE EVERYONE WHO PUTS *PCP* AS THEIR FOURTH FAVORITE-- NO, EVEN THEIR FIFTH AND SIXTH-- VOTE US INTO THE TOP THREE!
YES!
BAAM
GOOD! WE'LL TAKE ON *CROW* AND *+NATURAL* THIS WAY, FULL-FORCE!
YEAH!

OHBA'S STORYBOARD

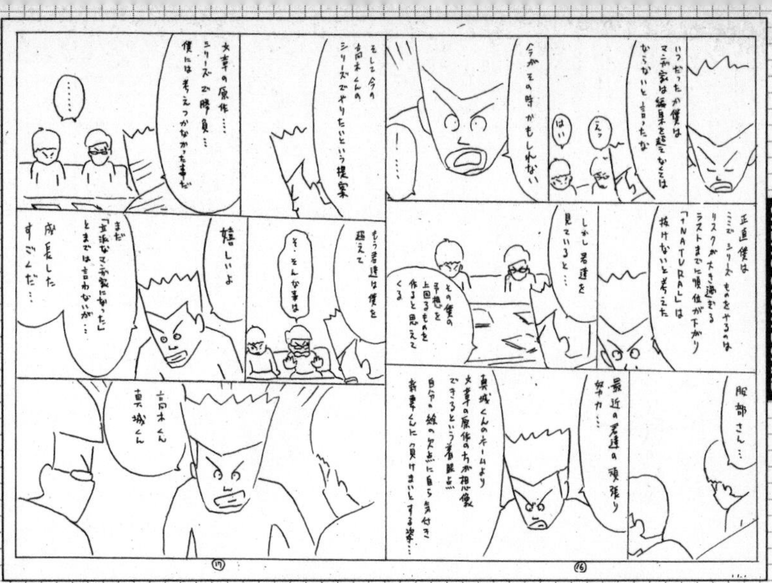

いつだったか僕は マンガ家は編集を超えなくてはならないと言ったな
えっ
はい
今がその時かもしれない
!…
正直 僕は ここでシリーズものをやるのは リスクが大き過ぎる ラストまでに順位が下がり 「ＮＡＴＵＲＡＬ」は抜けないと考えた
しかし君達を見ていると…
その僕の予想を上回るものを作ると思えてくる
服部さん…
最近の君達の頑張り 努力…
真城くんのネームより文章の原作の方が想像できるという着眼点 自分の絵の欠点に自ら気付き新妻くんに負けまいとする姿…
もし今の高木くんのシリーズでやりたいという提案
文章の原作… シリーズで勝負… 僕には考えつかなかった事だ
……
もう君達は僕を超えて
そ、そんな事は
嬉しいよ
まだ「立派なマンガ家になった」とまでは言わないが…
成長した すごくんだ…
高木くん 真城くん

OBATA'S STORYBOARD

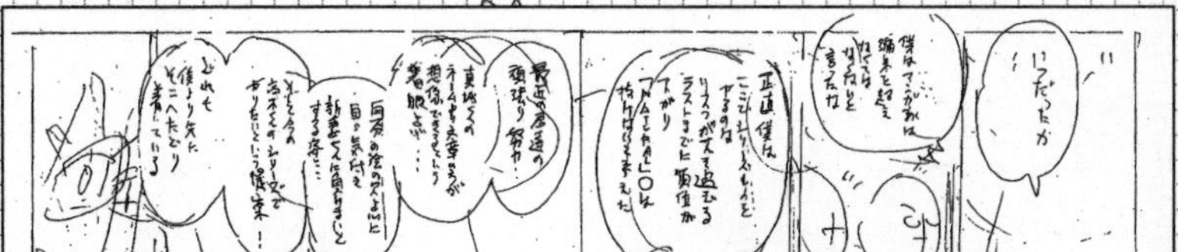

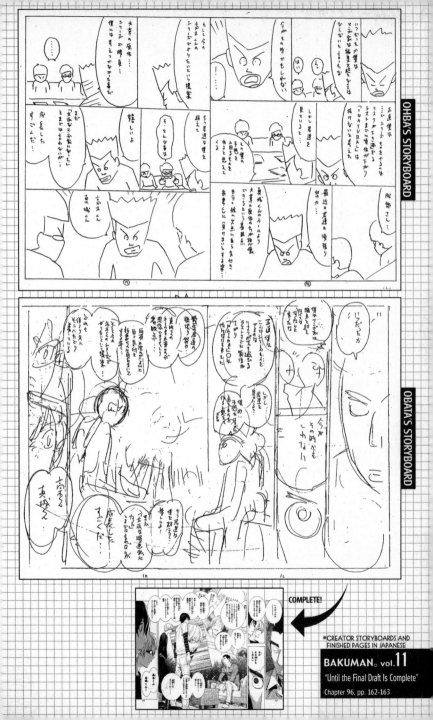

COMPLETE!

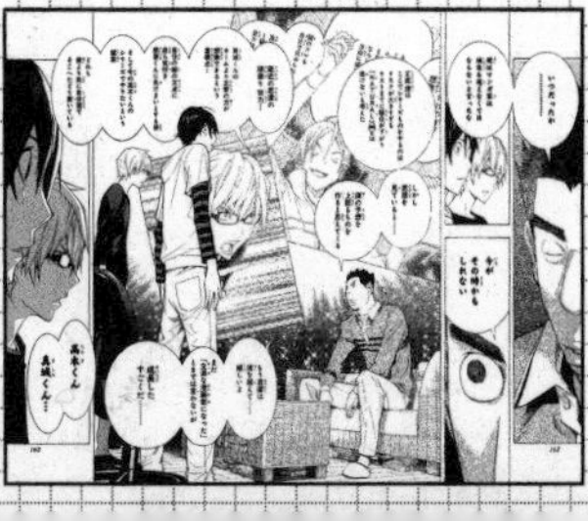

※CREATOR STORYBOARDS AND FINISHED PAGES IN JAPANESE

BAKUMAN。 vol.11

"Until the Final Draft Is Complete"

Chapter 96, pp. 162-163

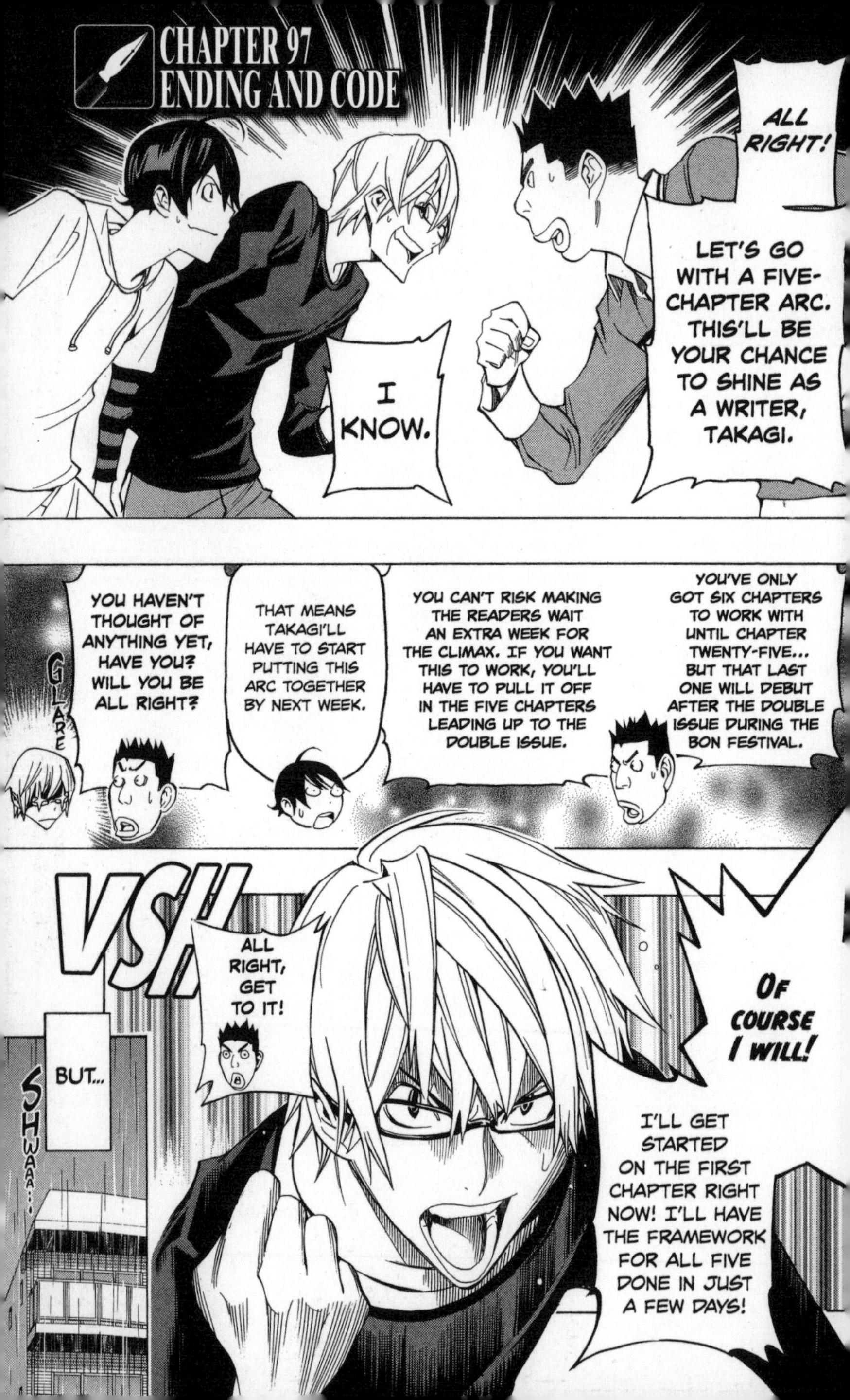
CHAPTER 97
ENDING AND CODE
ALL RIGHT!
LET'S GO WITH A FIVE-CHAPTER ARC. THIS'LL BE YOUR CHANCE TO SHINE AS A WRITER, TAKAGI.
I KNOW.
YOU'VE ONLY GOT SIX CHAPTERS TO WORK WITH UNTIL CHAPTER TWENTY-FIVE... BUT THAT LAST ONE WILL DEBUT AFTER THE DOUBLE ISSUE DURING THE BON FESTIVAL.
YOU CAN'T RISK MAKING THE READERS WAIT AN EXTRA WEEK FOR THE CLIMAX. IF YOU WANT THIS TO WORK, YOU'LL HAVE TO PULL IT OFF IN THE FIVE CHAPTERS LEADING UP TO THE DOUBLE ISSUE.
THAT MEANS TAKAGI'LL HAVE TO START PUTTING THIS ARC TOGETHER BY NEXT WEEK.
YOU HAVEN'T THOUGHT OF ANYTHING YET, HAVE YOU? WILL YOU BE ALL RIGHT?
GLARE
OF COURSE I WILL!
I'LL GET STARTED ON THE FIRST CHAPTER RIGHT NOW! I'LL HAVE THE FRAMEWORK FOR ALL FIVE DONE IN JUST A FEW DAYS!
ALL RIGHT, GET TO IT!
VSH
BUT...
SHWAAA...

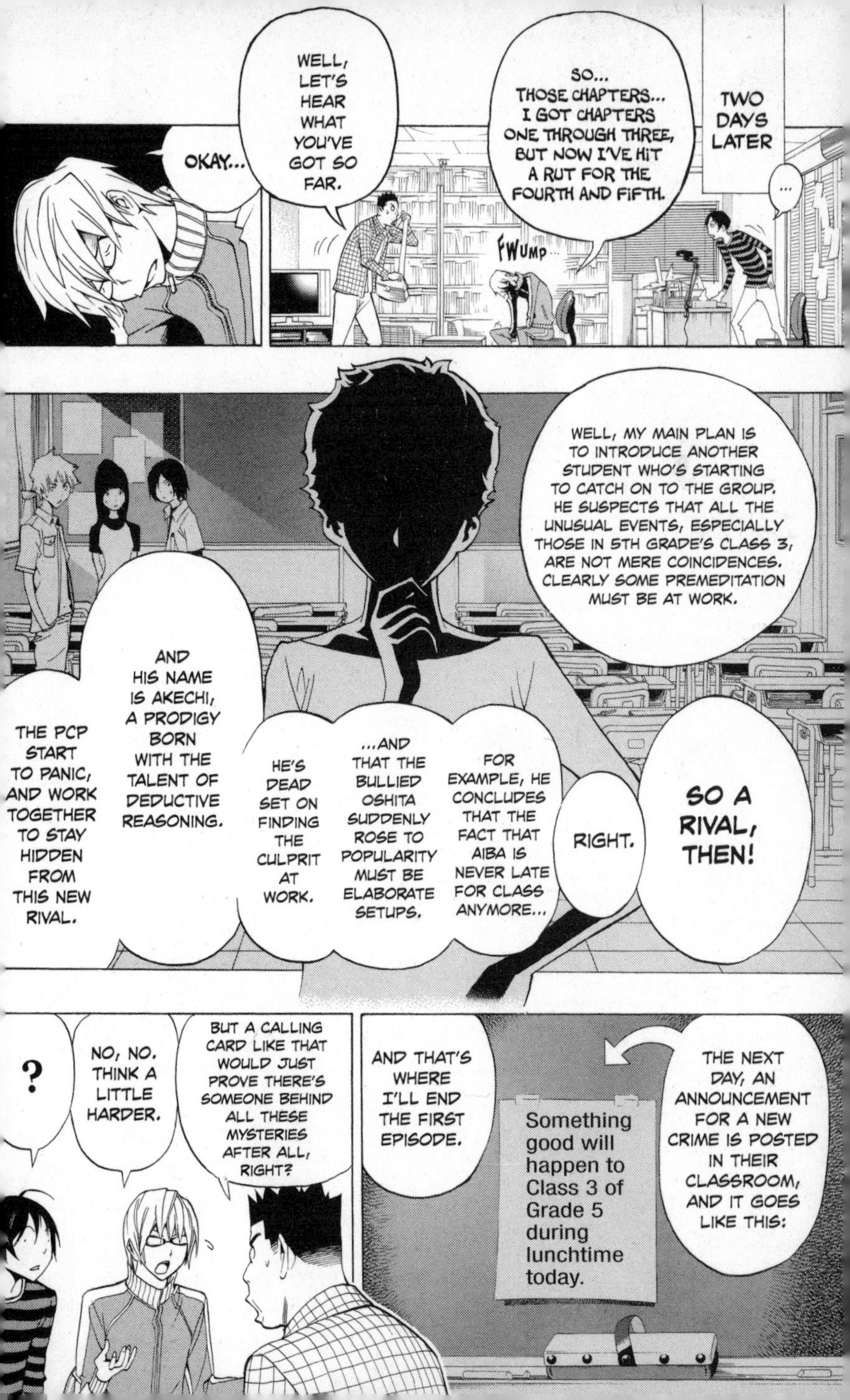
TWO DAYS LATER
...
FWUMP...
SO... THOSE CHAPTERS... I GOT CHAPTERS ONE THROUGH THREE, BUT NOW I'VE HIT A RUT FOR THE FOURTH AND FIFTH.
WELL, LET'S HEAR WHAT YOU'VE GOT SO FAR.
OKAY...
WELL, MY MAIN PLAN IS TO INTRODUCE ANOTHER STUDENT WHO'S STARTING TO CATCH ON TO THE GROUP. HE SUSPECTS THAT ALL THE UNUSUAL EVENTS, ESPECIALLY THOSE IN 5TH GRADE'S CLASS 3, ARE NOT MERE COINCIDENCES. CLEARLY SOME PREMEDITATION MUST BE AT WORK.
SO A RIVAL, THEN!
RIGHT.
FOR EXAMPLE, HE CONCLUDES THAT THE FACT THAT AIBA IS NEVER LATE FOR CLASS ANYMORE...
...AND THAT THE BULLIED OSHITA SUDDENLY ROSE TO POPULARITY MUST BE ELABORATE SETUPS.
HE'S DEAD SET ON FINDING THE CULPRIT AT WORK.
AND HIS NAME IS AKECHI, A PRODIGY BORN WITH THE TALENT OF DEDUCTIVE REASONING.
THE PCP START TO PANIC, AND WORK TOGETHER TO STAY HIDDEN FROM THIS NEW RIVAL.
THE NEXT DAY, AN ANNOUNCEMENT FOR A NEW CRIME IS POSTED IN THEIR CLASSROOM, AND IT GOES LIKE THIS:
Something good will happen to Class 3 of Grade 5 during lunchtime today.
AND THAT'S WHERE I'LL END THE FIRST EPISODE.
BUT A CALLING CARD LIKE THAT WOULD JUST PROVE THERE'S SOMEONE BEHIND ALL THESE MYSTERIES AFTER ALL, RIGHT?
NO, NO. THINK A LITTLE HARDER.
?

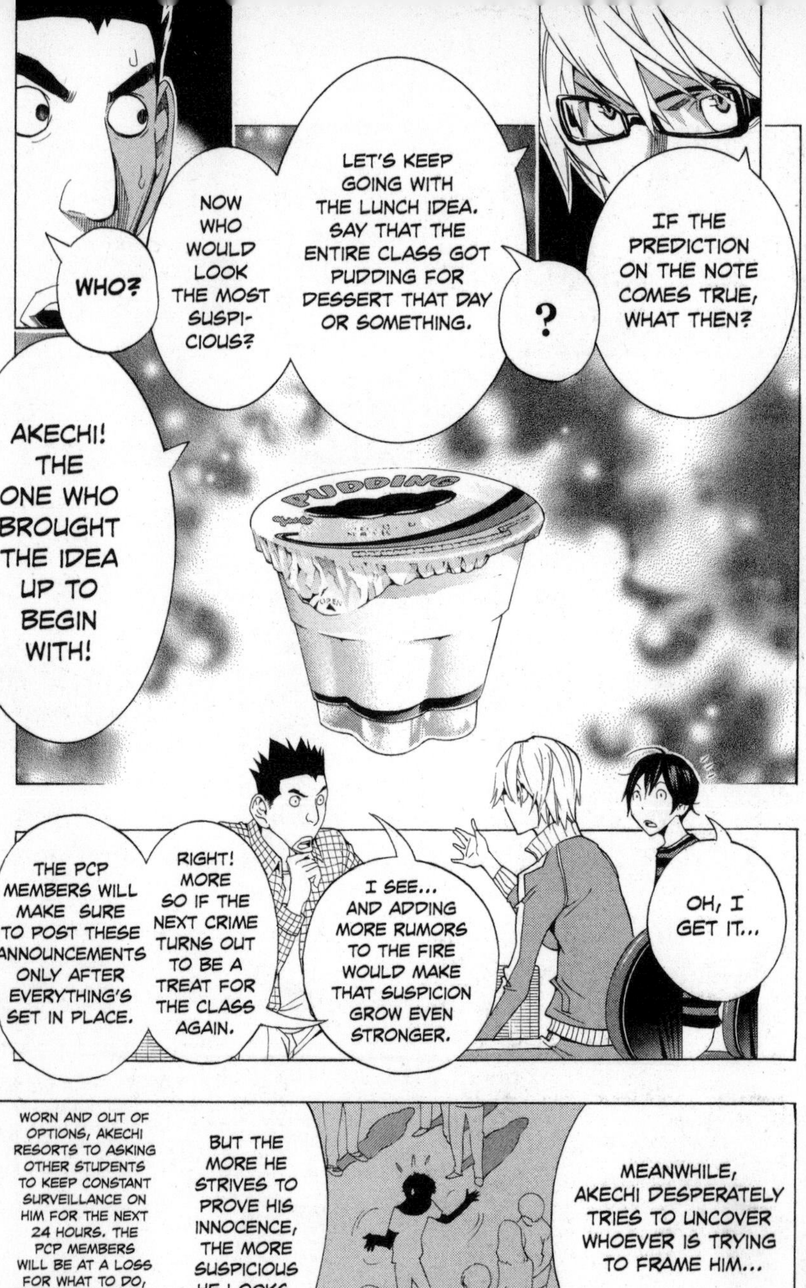
IF THE PREDICTION ON THE NOTE COMES TRUE, WHAT THEN?
?
LET'S KEEP GOING WITH THE LUNCH IDEA. SAY THAT THE ENTIRE CLASS GOT PUDDING FOR DESSERT THAT DAY OR SOMETHING.
NOW WHO WOULD LOOK THE MOST SUSPI-CIOUS?
WHO?
AKECHI! THE ONE WHO BROUGHT THE IDEA UP TO BEGIN WITH!
PUDDING
OH, I GET IT...
I SEE... AND ADDING MORE RUMORS TO THE FIRE WOULD MAKE THAT SUSPICION GROW EVEN STRONGER.
RIGHT! MORE SO IF THE NEXT CRIME TURNS OUT TO BE A TREAT FOR THE CLASS AGAIN.
THE PCP MEMBERS WILL MAKE SURE TO POST THESE ANNOUNCEMENTS ONLY AFTER EVERYTHING'S SET IN PLACE.
MEANWHILE, AKECHI DESPERATELY TRIES TO UNCOVER WHOEVER IS TRYING TO FRAME HIM...
BUT THE MORE HE STRIVES TO PROVE HIS INNOCENCE, THE MORE SUSPICIOUS HE LOOKS.
WORN AND OUT OF OPTIONS, AKECHI RESORTS TO ASKING OTHER STUDENTS TO KEEP CONSTANT SURVEILLANCE ON HIM FOR THE NEXT 24 HOURS. THE PCP MEMBERS WILL BE AT A LOSS FOR WHAT TO DO, AND THAT'S WHERE THE SECOND CHAPTER WILL END.

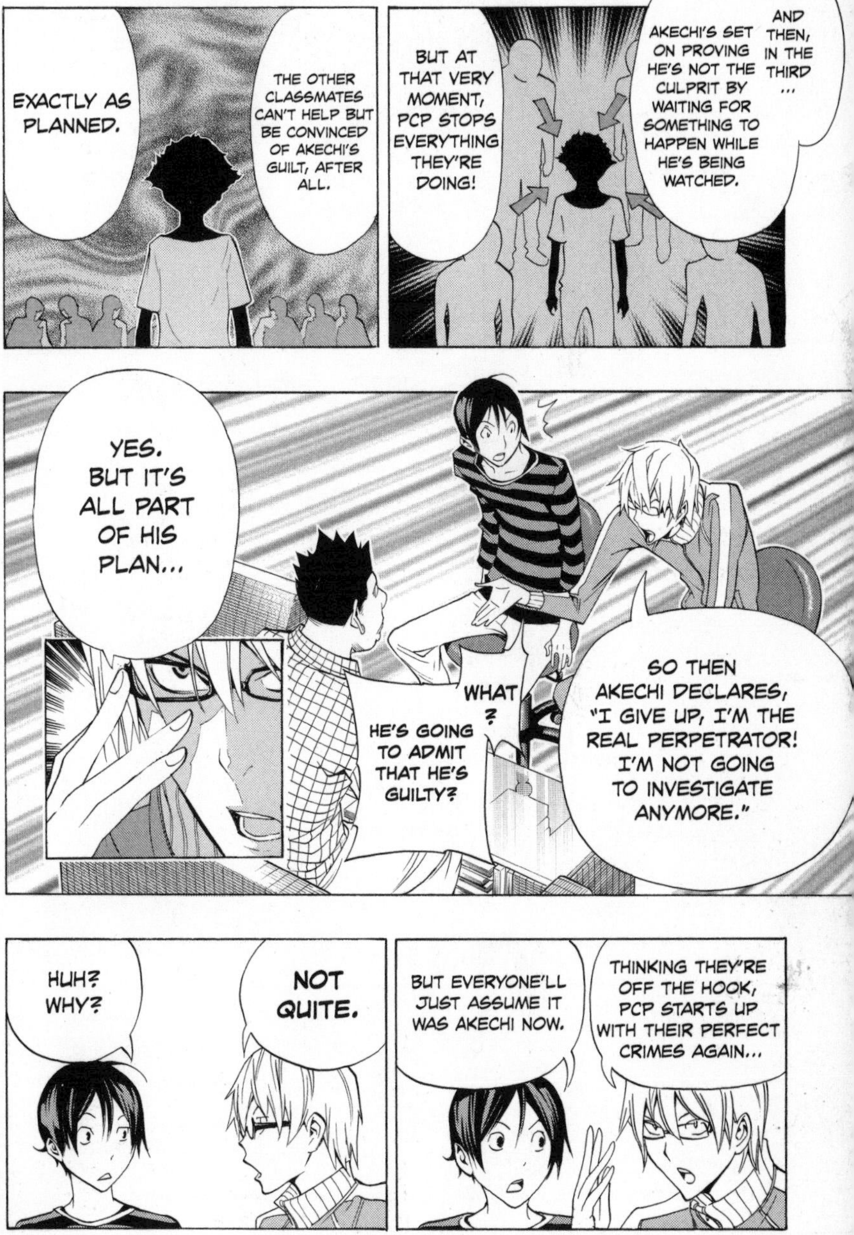
AND THEN, IN THE THIRD ...
AKECHI'S SET ON PROVING HE'S NOT THE CULPRIT BY WAITING FOR SOMETHING TO HAPPEN WHILE HE'S BEING WATCHED.
BUT AT THAT VERY MOMENT, PCP STOPS EVERYTHING THEY'RE DOING!
THE OTHER CLASSMATES CAN'T HELP BUT BE CONVINCED OF AKECHI'S GUILT, AFTER ALL.
EXACTLY AS PLANNED.
SO THEN AKECHI DECLARES, "I GIVE UP, I'M THE REAL PERPETRATOR! I'M NOT GOING TO INVESTIGATE ANYMORE."
WHAT?
HE'S GOING TO ADMIT THAT HE'S GUILTY?
YES. BUT IT'S ALL PART OF HIS PLAN...
THINKING THEY'RE OFF THE HOOK, PCP STARTS UP WITH THEIR PERFECT CRIMES AGAIN...
BUT EVERYONE'LL JUST ASSUME IT WAS AKECHI NOW.
NOT QUITE.
HUH? WHY?

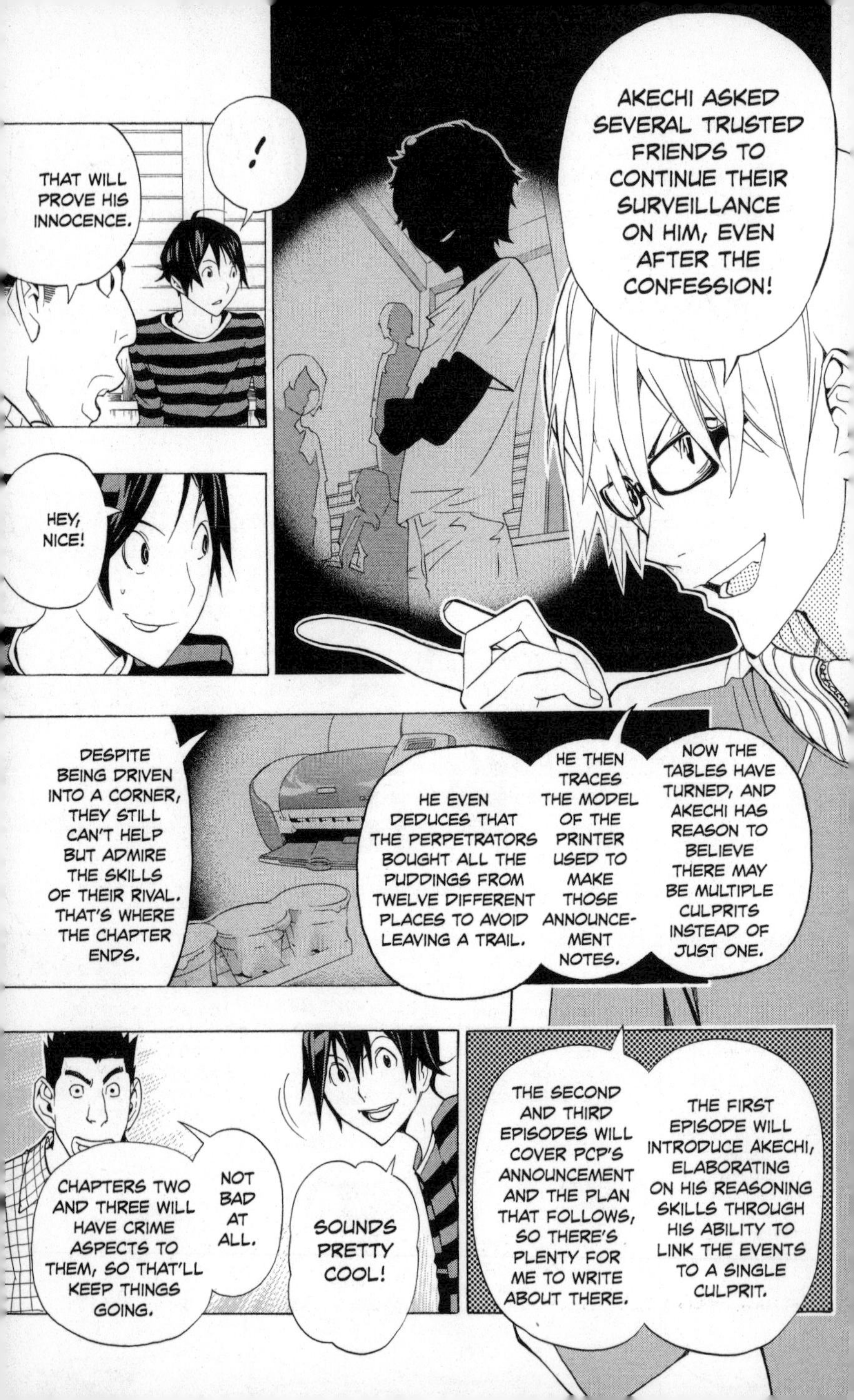
AKECHI ASKED SEVERAL TRUSTED FRIENDS TO CONTINUE THEIR SURVEILLANCE ON HIM, EVEN AFTER THE CONFESSION!
!
THAT WILL PROVE HIS INNOCENCE.
HEY, NICE!
NOW THE TABLES HAVE TURNED, AND AKECHI HAS REASON TO BELIEVE THERE MAY BE MULTIPLE CULPRITS INSTEAD OF JUST ONE.
HE THEN TRACES THE MODEL OF THE PRINTER USED TO MAKE THOSE ANNOUNCE-MENT NOTES.
HE EVEN DEDUCES THAT THE PERPETRATORS BOUGHT ALL THE PUDDINGS FROM TWELVE DIFFERENT PLACES TO AVOID LEAVING A TRAIL.
DESPITE BEING DRIVEN INTO A CORNER, THEY STILL CAN'T HELP BUT ADMIRE THE SKILLS OF THEIR RIVAL. THAT'S WHERE THE CHAPTER ENDS.
THE FIRST EPISODE WILL INTRODUCE AKECHI, ELABORATING ON HIS REASONING SKILLS THROUGH HIS ABILITY TO LINK THE EVENTS TO A SINGLE CULPRIT.
THE SECOND AND THIRD EPISODES WILL COVER PCP'S ANNOUNCEMENT AND THE PLAN THAT FOLLOWS, SO THERE'S PLENTY FOR ME TO WRITE ABOUT THERE.
SOUNDS PRETTY COOL!
NOT BAD AT ALL.
CHAPTERS TWO AND THREE WILL HAVE CRIME ASPECTS TO THEM, SO THAT'LL KEEP THINGS GOING.

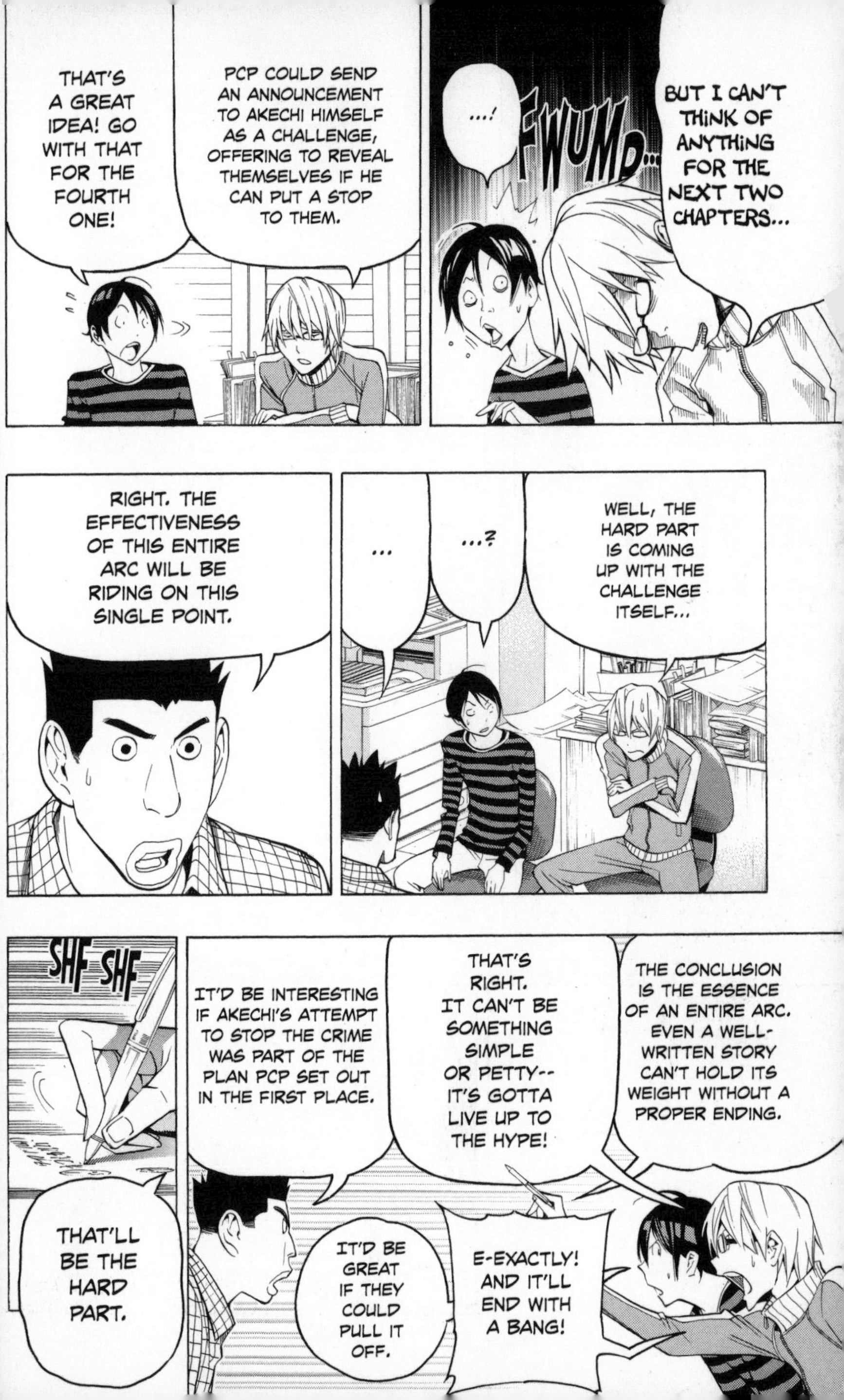
BUT I CAN'T THINK OF ANYTHING FOR THE NEXT TWO CHAPTERS...
FWUMP...
...!
PCP COULD SEND AN ANNOUNCEMENT TO AKECHI HIMSELF AS A CHALLENGE, OFFERING TO REVEAL THEMSELVES IF HE CAN PUT A STOP TO THEM.
THAT'S A GREAT IDEA! GO WITH THAT FOR THE FOURTH ONE!
WELL, THE HARD PART IS COMING UP WITH THE CHALLENGE ITSELF...
...?
...
RIGHT. THE EFFECTIVENESS OF THIS ENTIRE ARC WILL BE RIDING ON THIS SINGLE POINT.
THE CONCLUSION IS THE ESSENCE OF AN ENTIRE ARC. EVEN A WELL-WRITTEN STORY CAN'T HOLD ITS WEIGHT WITHOUT A PROPER ENDING.
THAT'S RIGHT. IT CAN'T BE SOMETHING SIMPLE OR PETTY--IT'S GOTTA LIVE UP TO THE HYPE!
IT'D BE INTERESTING IF AKECHI'S ATTEMPT TO STOP THE CRIME WAS PART OF THE PLAN PCP SET OUT IN THE FIRST PLACE.
E-EXACTLY! AND IT'LL END WITH A BANG!
IT'D BE GREAT IF THEY COULD PULL IT OFF.
SHF SHF
THAT'LL BE THE HARD PART.

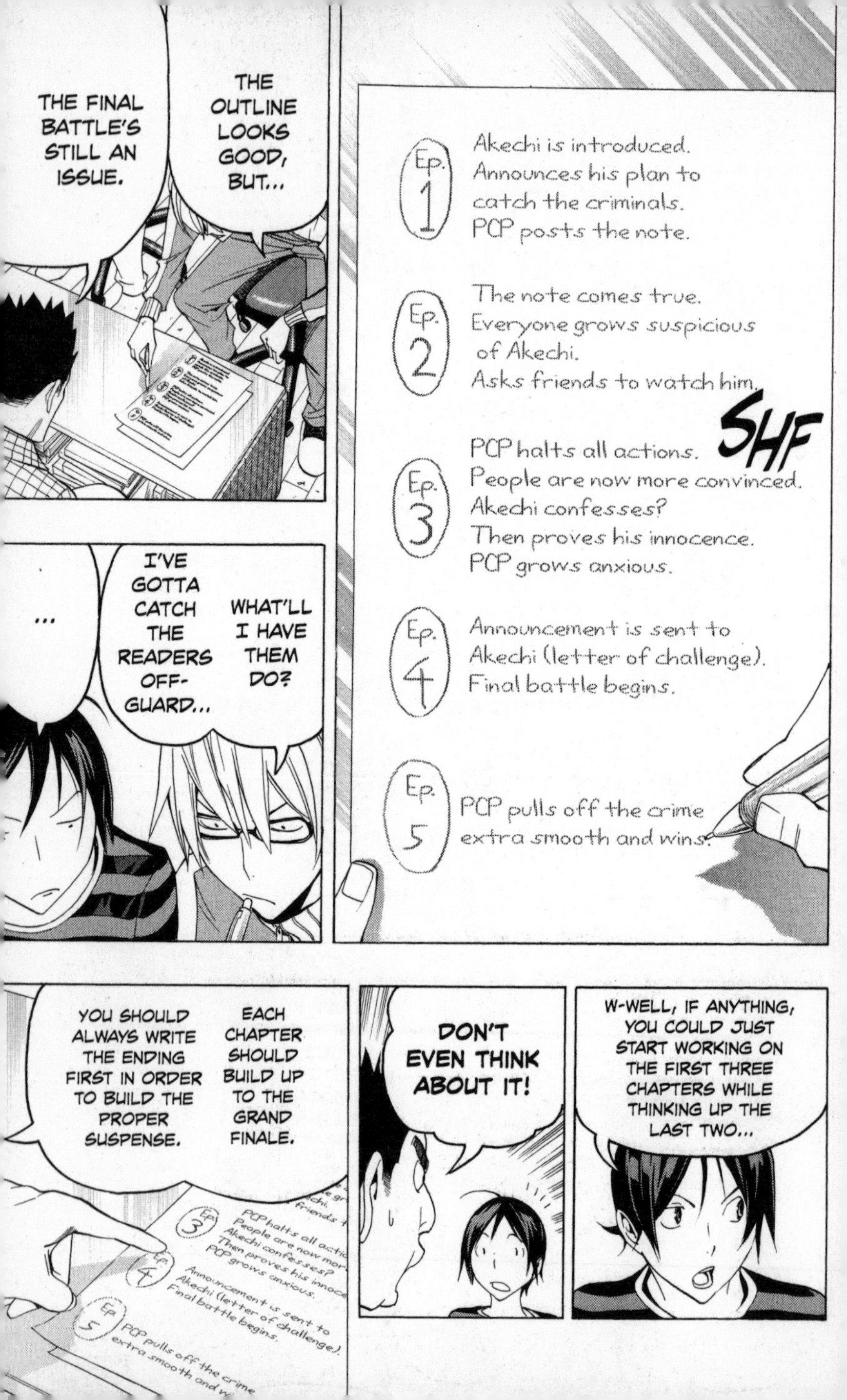
Ep. 1 Akechi is introduced. Announces his plan to catch the criminals. PCP posts the note.
Ep. 2 The note comes true. Everyone grows suspicious of Akechi. Asks friends to watch him.
Ep. 3 PCP halts all actions. People are now more convinced. Akechi confesses? Then proves his innocence. PCP grows anxious.
Ep. 4 Announcement is sent to Akechi (letter of challenge). Final battle begins.
Ep. 5 PCP pulls off the crime extra smooth and wins.
SHF
THE OUTLINE LOOKS GOOD, BUT...
THE FINAL BATTLE'S STILL AN ISSUE.
WHAT'LL I HAVE THEM DO?
I'VE GOTTA CATCH THE READERS OFF-GUARD...
...
W-WELL, IF ANYTHING, YOU COULD JUST START WORKING ON THE FIRST THREE CHAPTERS WHILE THINKING UP THE LAST TWO...
DON'T EVEN THINK ABOUT IT!
EACH CHAPTER SHOULD BUILD UP TO THE GRAND FINALE.
YOU SHOULD ALWAYS WRITE THE ENDING FIRST IN ORDER TO BUILD THE PROPER SUSPENSE.

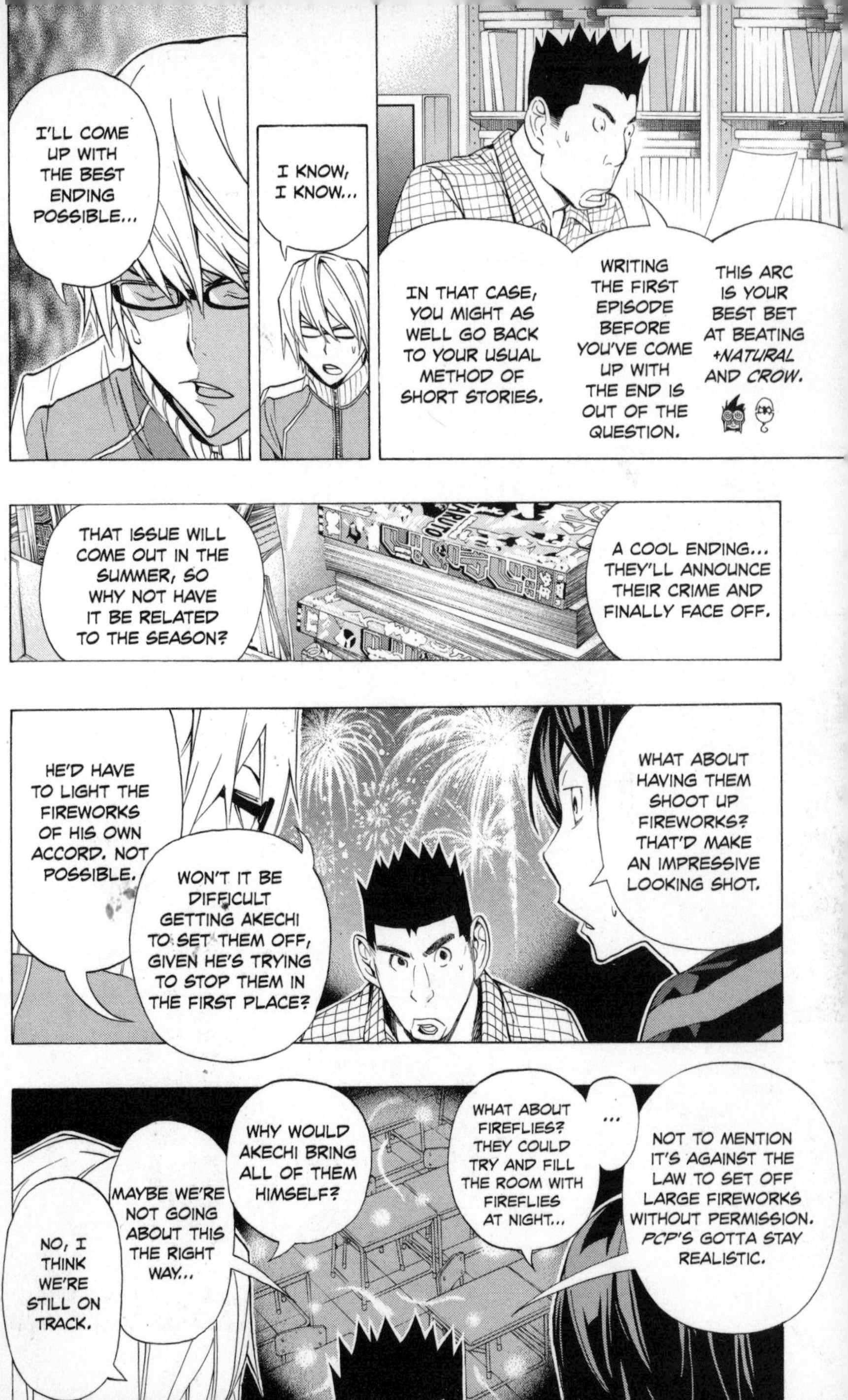
THIS ARC IS YOUR BEST BET AT BEATING +NATURAL AND CROW.
WRITING THE FIRST EPISODE BEFORE YOU'VE COME UP WITH THE END IS OUT OF THE QUESTION.
IN THAT CASE, YOU MIGHT AS WELL GO BACK TO YOUR USUAL METHOD OF SHORT STORIES.
I KNOW, I KNOW...
I'LL COME UP WITH THE BEST ENDING POSSIBLE...
A COOL ENDING... THEY'LL ANNOUNCE THEIR CRIME AND FINALLY FACE OFF.
THAT ISSUE WILL COME OUT IN THE SUMMER, SO WHY NOT HAVE IT BE RELATED TO THE SEASON?
WHAT ABOUT HAVING THEM SHOOT UP FIREWORKS? THAT'D MAKE AN IMPRESSIVE LOOKING SHOT.
WON'T IT BE DIFFICULT GETTING AKECHI TO SET THEM OFF, GIVEN HE'S TRYING TO STOP THEM IN THE FIRST PLACE?
HE'D HAVE TO LIGHT THE FIREWORKS OF HIS OWN ACCORD. NOT POSSIBLE.
NOT TO MENTION IT'S AGAINST THE LAW TO SET OFF LARGE FIREWORKS WITHOUT PERMISSION. *PCP*'S GOTTA STAY REALISTIC.
...
WHAT ABOUT FIREFLIES? THEY COULD TRY AND FILL THE ROOM WITH FIREFLIES AT NIGHT...
WHY WOULD AKECHI BRING ALL OF THEM HIMSELF?
MAYBE WE'RE NOT GOING ABOUT THIS THE RIGHT WAY...
NO, I THINK WE'RE STILL ON TRACK.

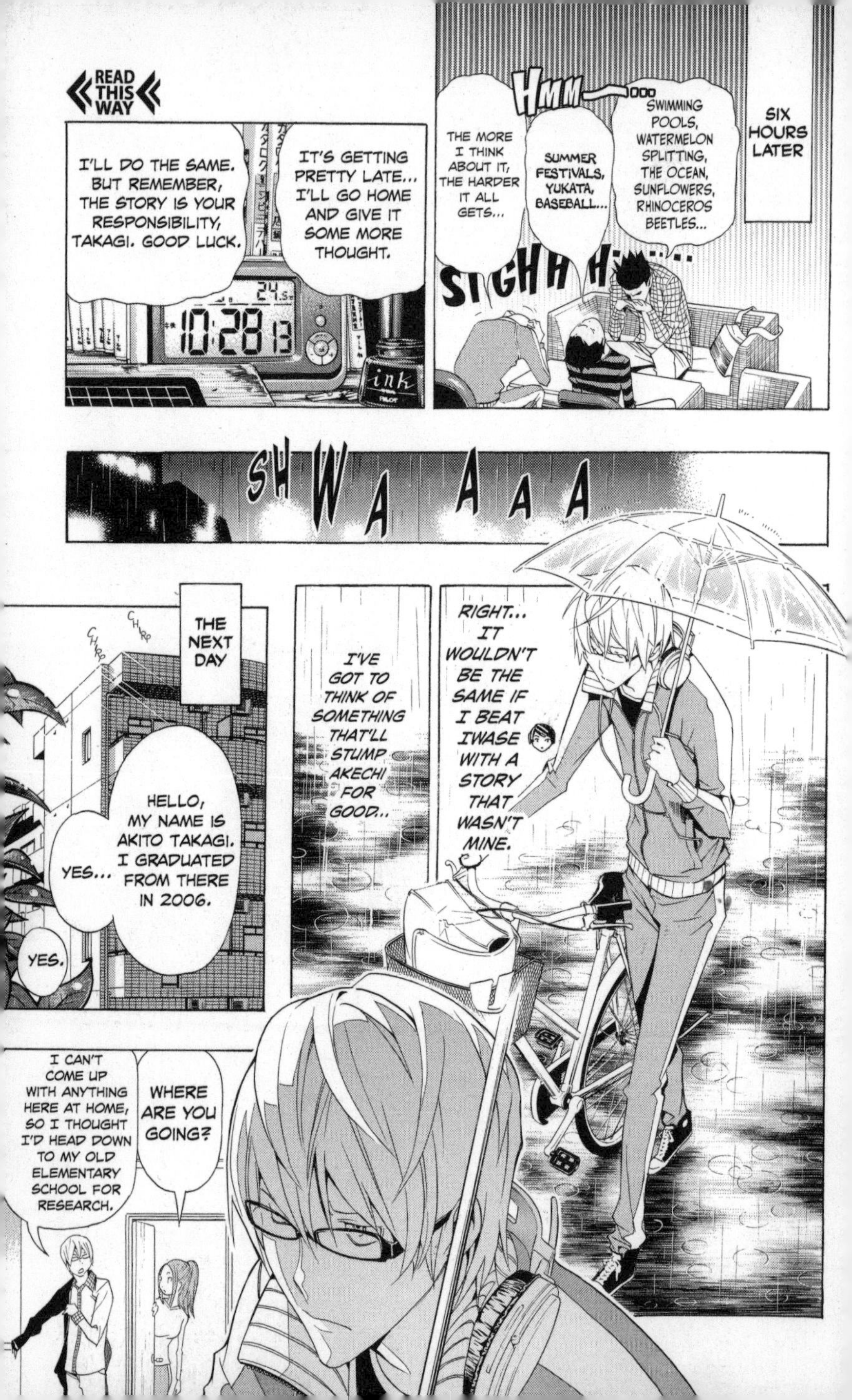
READ THIS WAY
SIX HOURS LATER
HMM—...
SWIMMING POOLS, WATERMELON SPLITTING, THE OCEAN, SUNFLOWERS, RHINOCEROS BEETLES...
SUMMER FESTIVALS, YUKATA, BASEBALL...
THE MORE I THINK ABOUT IT, THE HARDER IT ALL GETS...
SIGHHH...
IT'S GETTING PRETTY LATE... I'LL GO HOME AND GIVE IT SOME MORE THOUGHT.
I'LL DO THE SAME. BUT REMEMBER, THE STORY IS YOUR RESPONSIBILITY, TAKAGI. GOOD LUCK.
SHWAAAA
RIGHT... IT WOULDN'T BE THE SAME IF I BEAT IWASE WITH A STORY THAT WASN'T MINE.
I'VE GOT TO THINK OF SOMETHING THAT'LL STUMP AKECHI FOR GOOD...
THE NEXT DAY
CHIRP CHIRP
HELLO, MY NAME IS AKITO TAKAGI. I GRADUATED FROM THERE IN 2006.
YES...
YES.
WHERE ARE YOU GOING?
I CAN'T COME UP WITH ANYTHING HERE AT HOME, SO I THOUGHT I'D HEAD DOWN TO MY OLD ELEMENTARY SCHOOL FOR RESEARCH.

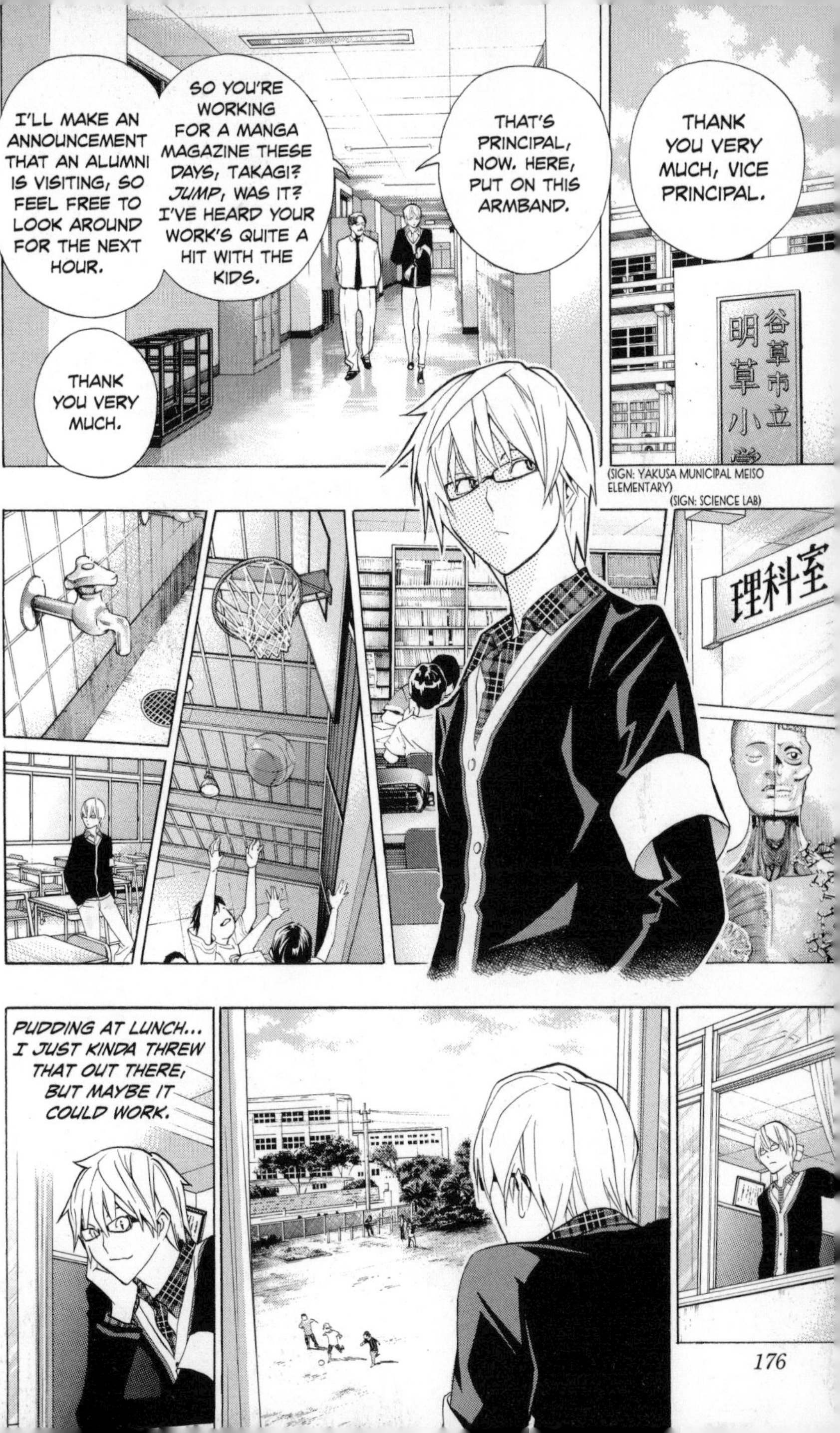
THANK YOU VERY MUCH, VICE PRINCIPAL.
THAT'S PRINCIPAL, NOW. HERE, PUT ON THIS ARMBAND.
SO YOU'RE WORKING FOR A MANGA MAGAZINE THESE DAYS, TAKAGI? *JUMP*, WAS IT? I'VE HEARD YOUR WORK'S QUITE A HIT WITH THE KIDS.
I'LL MAKE AN ANNOUNCEMENT THAT AN ALUMNI IS VISITING, SO FEEL FREE TO LOOK AROUND FOR THE NEXT HOUR.
THANK YOU VERY MUCH.
谷草市立
明草小
(SIGN: YAKUSA MUNICIPAL MEISO ELEMENTARY)
理科室
(SIGN: SCIENCE LAB)
PUDDING AT LUNCH... I JUST KINDA THREW THAT OUT THERE, BUT MAYBE IT COULD WORK.

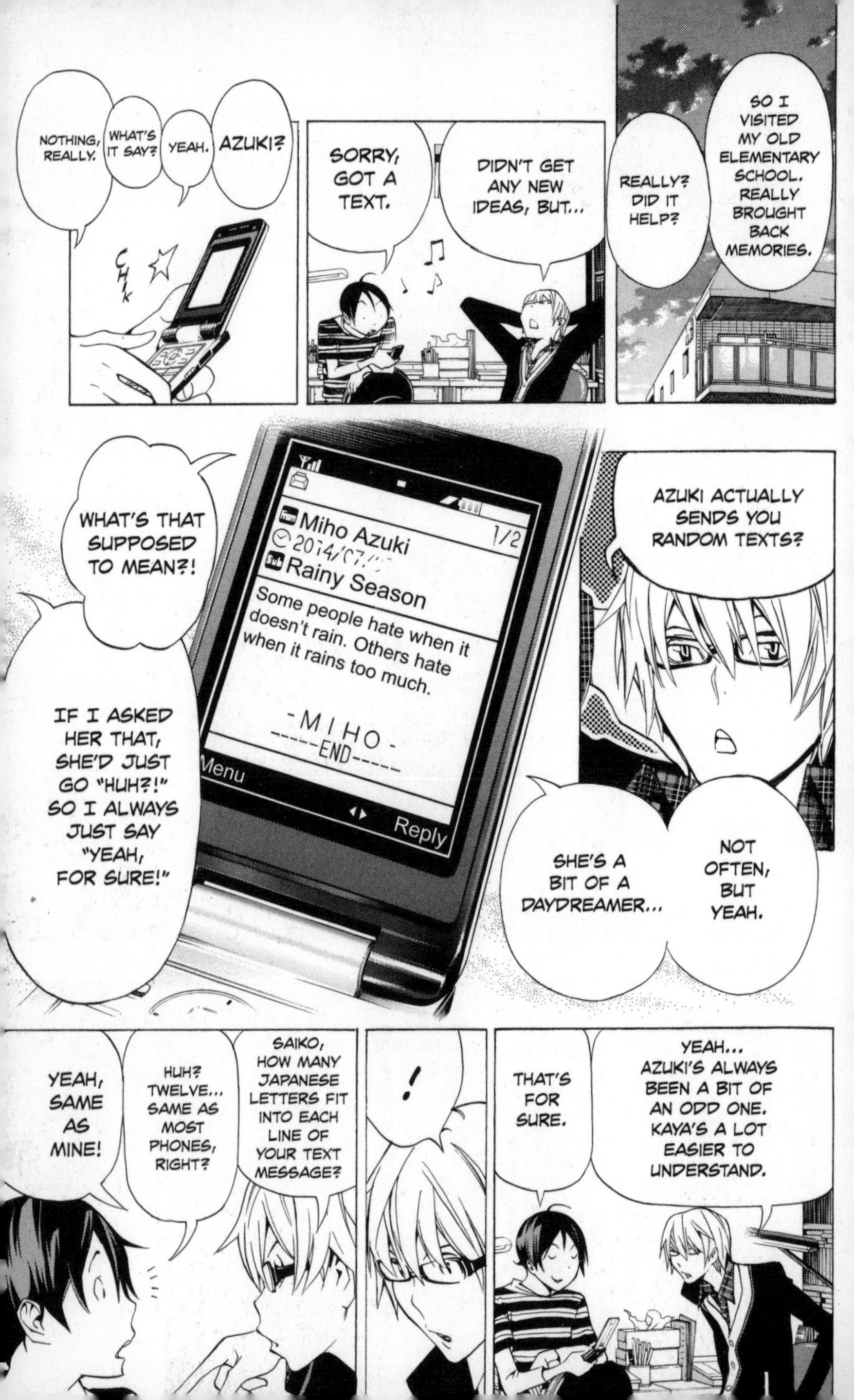
SO I VISITED MY OLD ELEMENTARY SCHOOL. REALLY BROUGHT BACK MEMORIES.
REALLY? DID IT HELP?
DIDN'T GET ANY NEW IDEAS, BUT...
SORRY, GOT A TEXT.
AZUKI?
YEAH.
WHAT'S IT SAY?
NOTHING, REALLY.
CHIK
AZUKI ACTUALLY SENDS YOU RANDOM TEXTS?
NOT OFTEN, BUT YEAH.
SHE'S A BIT OF A DAYDREAMER...
Miho Azuki
1/2
Rainy Season
Some people hate when it doesn't rain. Others hate when it rains too much.
-MIHO-
-----END-----
Menu
Reply
WHAT'S THAT SUPPOSED TO MEAN?!
IF I ASKED HER THAT, SHE'D JUST GO "HUH?!" SO I ALWAYS JUST SAY "YEAH, FOR SURE!"
YEAH... AZUKI'S ALWAYS BEEN A BIT OF AN ODD ONE. KAYA'S A LOT EASIER TO UNDERSTAND.
THAT'S FOR SURE.
!
SAIKO, HOW MANY JAPANESE LETTERS FIT INTO EACH LINE OF YOUR TEXT MESSAGE?
HUH? TWELVE... SAME AS MOST PHONES, RIGHT?
YEAH, SAME AS MINE!

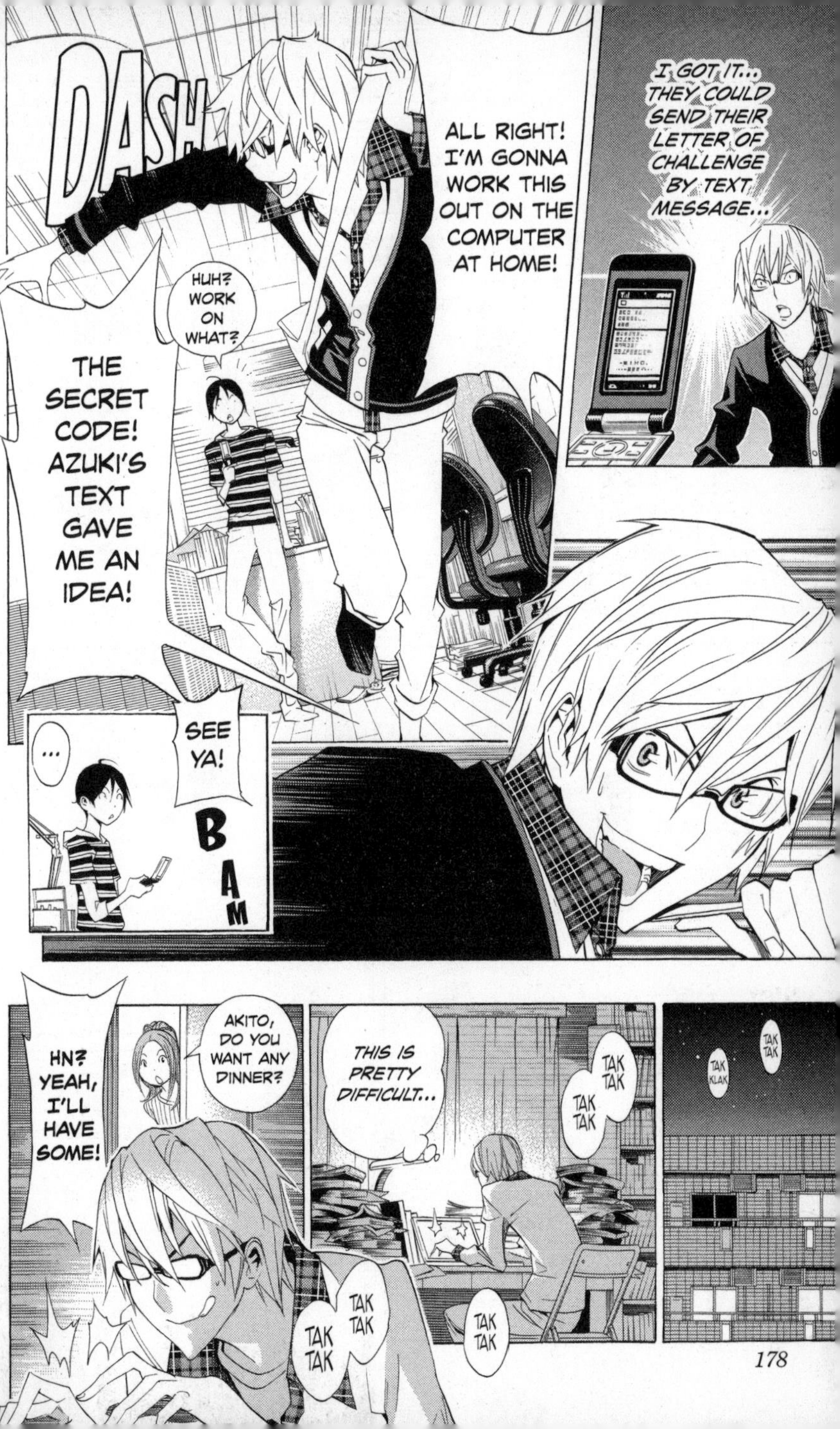

I GOT IT... THEY COULD SEND THEIR LETTER OF CHALLENGE BY TEXT MESSAGE...
ALL RIGHT! I'M GONNA WORK THIS OUT ON THE COMPUTER AT HOME!
DASH
HUH? WORK ON WHAT?
THE SECRET CODE! AZUKI'S TEXT GAVE ME AN IDEA!
SEE YA!
...
BAM
TAK TAK
TAK KLAK
TAK TAK
TAK TAK
THIS IS PRETTY DIFFICULT...
TAK TAK
AKITO, DO YOU WANT ANY DINNER?
HN? YEAH, I'LL HAVE SOME!
TAK TAK
TAK TAK

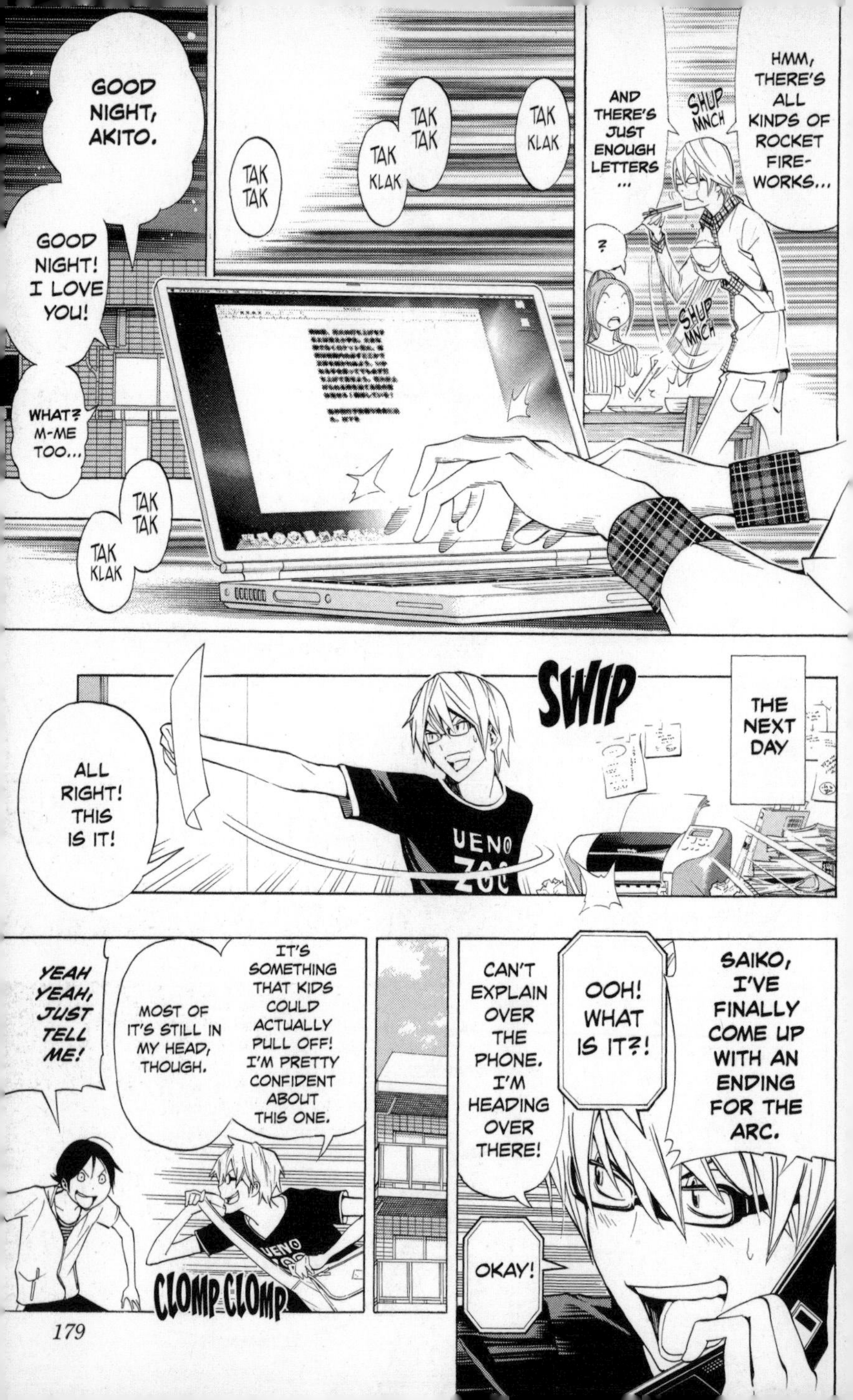
HMM, THERE'S ALL KINDS OF ROCKET FIRE-WORKS...
SHUP MNCH
AND THERE'S JUST ENOUGH LETTERS ...
?
SHUP MNCH
TAK KLAK
TAK TAK
TAK KLAK
TAK TAK
GOOD NIGHT, AKITO.
GOOD NIGHT! I LOVE YOU!
WHAT? M-ME TOO...
TAK TAK
TAK KLAK
THE NEXT DAY
SWIP
ALL RIGHT! THIS IS IT!
SAIKO, I'VE FINALLY COME UP WITH AN ENDING FOR THE ARC.
OOH! WHAT IS IT?!
CAN'T EXPLAIN OVER THE PHONE. I'M HEADING OVER THERE!
OKAY!
IT'S SOMETHING THAT KIDS COULD ACTUALLY PULL OFF! I'M PRETTY CONFIDENT ABOUT THIS ONE.
MOST OF IT'S STILL IN MY HEAD, THOUGH.
YEAH YEAH, JUST TELL ME!
CLOMP CLOMP

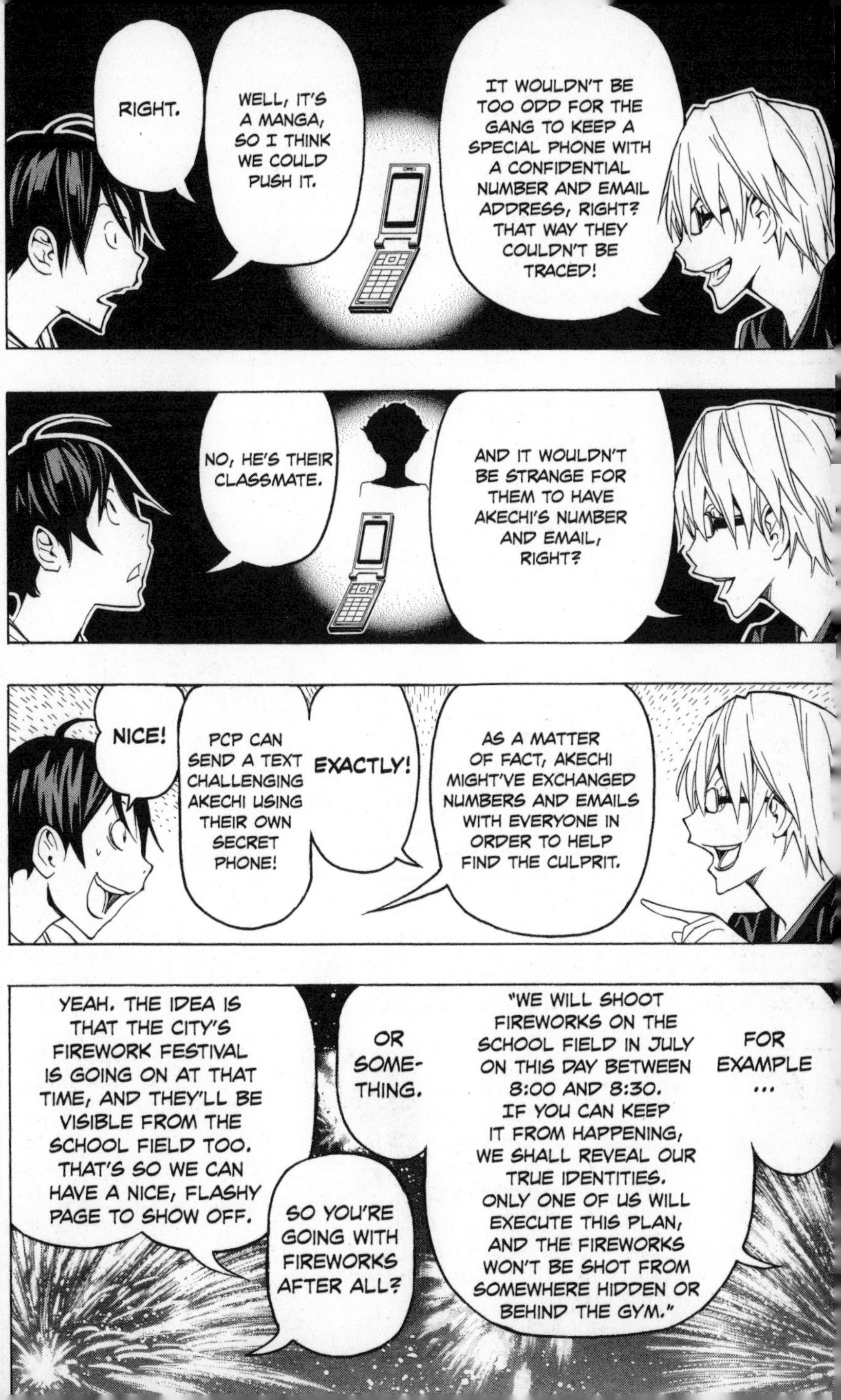
IT WOULDN'T BE TOO ODD FOR THE GANG TO KEEP A SPECIAL PHONE WITH A CONFIDENTIAL NUMBER AND EMAIL ADDRESS, RIGHT? THAT WAY THEY COULDN'T BE TRACED!
WELL, IT'S A MANGA, SO I THINK WE COULD PUSH IT.
RIGHT.
AND IT WOULDN'T BE STRANGE FOR THEM TO HAVE AKECHI'S NUMBER AND EMAIL, RIGHT?
NO, HE'S THEIR CLASSMATE.
AS A MATTER OF FACT, AKECHI MIGHT'VE EXCHANGED NUMBERS AND EMAILS WITH EVERYONE IN ORDER TO HELP FIND THE CULPRIT.
EXACTLY!
PCP CAN SEND A TEXT CHALLENGING AKECHI USING THEIR OWN SECRET PHONE!
NICE!
FOR EXAMPLE...
"WE WILL SHOOT FIREWORKS ON THE SCHOOL FIELD IN JULY ON THIS DAY BETWEEN 8:00 AND 8:30. IF YOU CAN KEEP IT FROM HAPPENING, WE SHALL REVEAL OUR TRUE IDENTITIES. ONLY ONE OF US WILL EXECUTE THIS PLAN, AND THE FIREWORKS WON'T BE SHOT FROM SOMEWHERE HIDDEN OR BEHIND THE GYM."
OR SOME-THING.
SO YOU'RE GOING WITH FIREWORKS AFTER ALL?
YEAH. THE IDEA IS THAT THE CITY'S FIREWORK FESTIVAL IS GOING ON AT THAT TIME, AND THEY'LL BE VISIBLE FROM THE SCHOOL FIELD TOO. THAT'S SO WE CAN HAVE A NICE, FLASHY PAGE TO SHOW OFF.

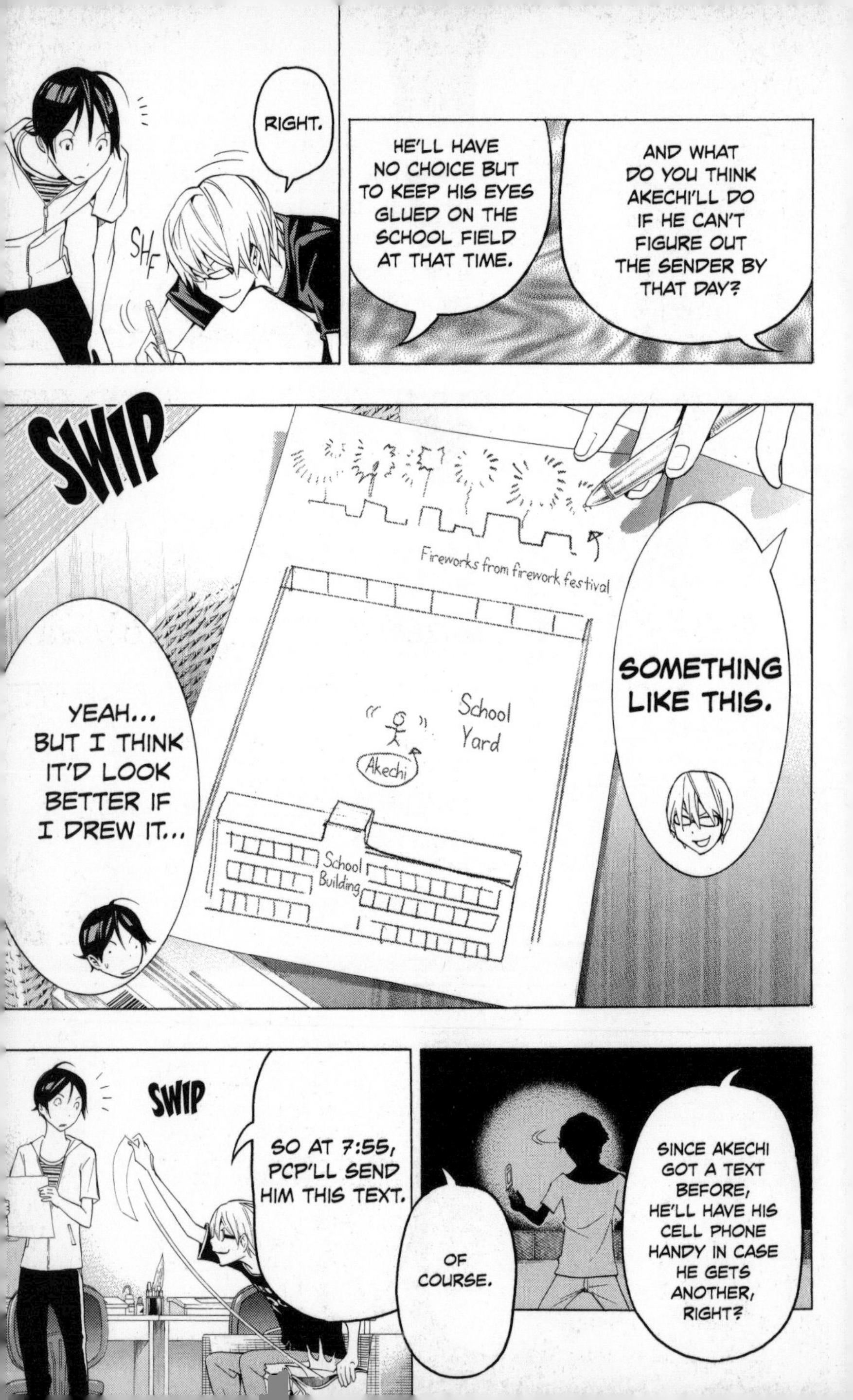
AND WHAT DO YOU THINK AKECHI'LL DO IF HE CAN'T FIGURE OUT THE SENDER BY THAT DAY?
HE'LL HAVE NO CHOICE BUT TO KEEP HIS EYES GLUED ON THE SCHOOL FIELD AT THAT TIME.
RIGHT.
SHF
SOMETHING LIKE THIS.
Fireworks from firework festival
School Yard
Akechi
School Building
YEAH... BUT I THINK IT'D LOOK BETTER IF I DREW IT...
SWIP
SINCE AKECHI GOT A TEXT BEFORE, HE'LL HAVE HIS CELL PHONE HANDY IN CASE HE GETS ANOTHER, RIGHT?
OF COURSE.
SO AT 7:55, PCP'LL SEND HIM THIS TEXT.
SWIP

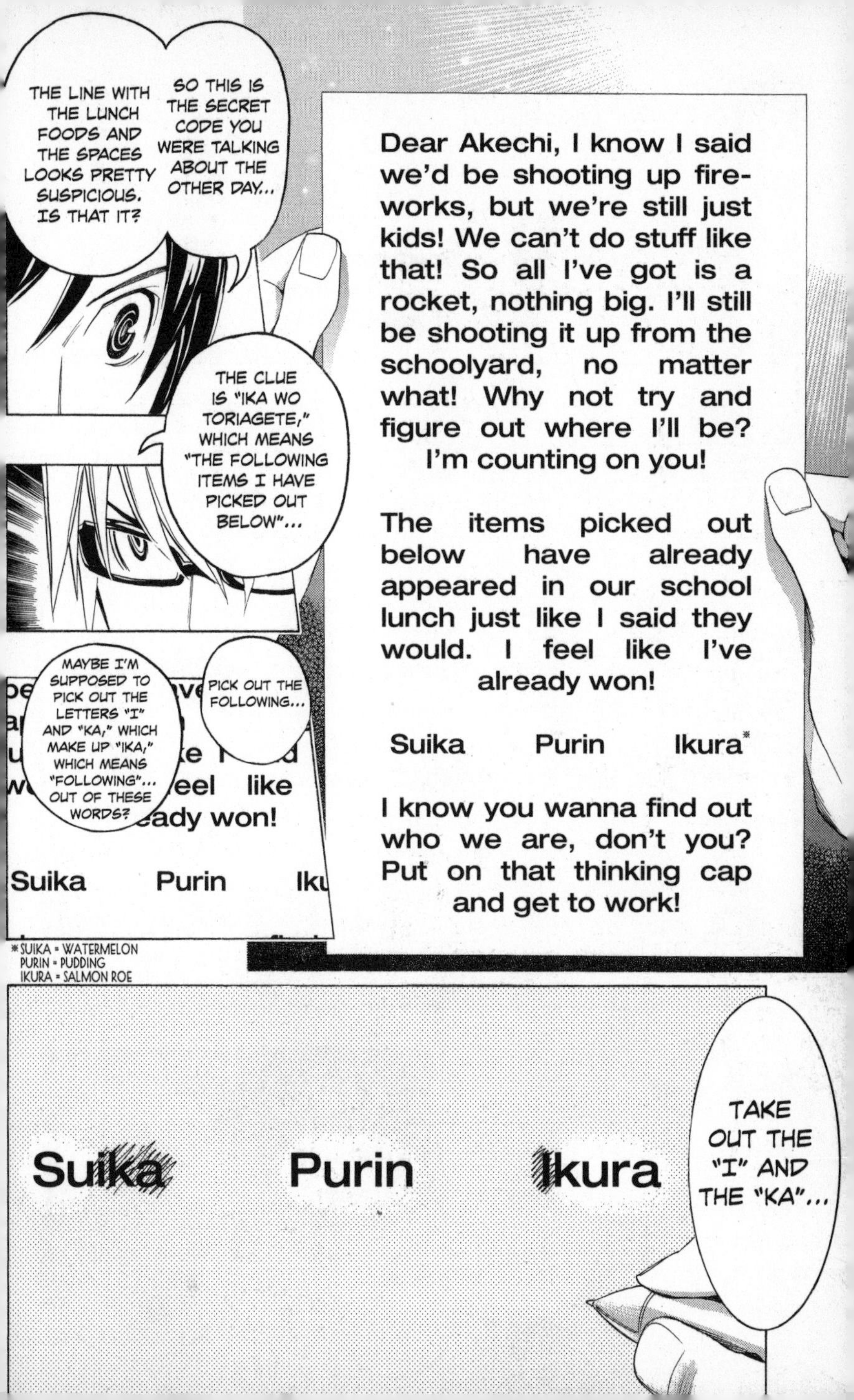
Dear Akechi, I know I said we'd be shooting up fire-works, but we're still just kids! We can't do stuff like that! So all I've got is a rocket, nothing big. I'll still be shooting it up from the schoolyard, no matter what! Why not try and figure out where I'll be? I'm counting on you!
The items picked out below have already appeared in our school lunch just like I said they would. I feel like I've already won!
Suika Purin Ikura*
I know you wanna find out who we are, don't you? Put on that thinking cap and get to work!
SO THIS IS THE SECRET CODE YOU WERE TALKING ABOUT THE OTHER DAY...
THE LINE WITH THE LUNCH FOODS AND THE SPACES LOOKS PRETTY SUSPICIOUS. IS THAT IT?
THE CLUE IS "IKA WO TORIAGETE," WHICH MEANS "THE FOLLOWING ITEMS I HAVE PICKED OUT BELOW"...
PICK OUT THE FOLLOWING...
MAYBE I'M SUPPOSED TO PICK OUT THE LETTERS "I" AND "KA," WHICH MAKE UP "IKA," WHICH MEANS "FOLLOWING"... OUT OF THESE WORDS?
*SUIKA = WATERMELON
PURIN = PUDDING
IKURA = SALMON ROE
Suika Purin Ikura
TAKE OUT THE "I" AND THE "KA"...

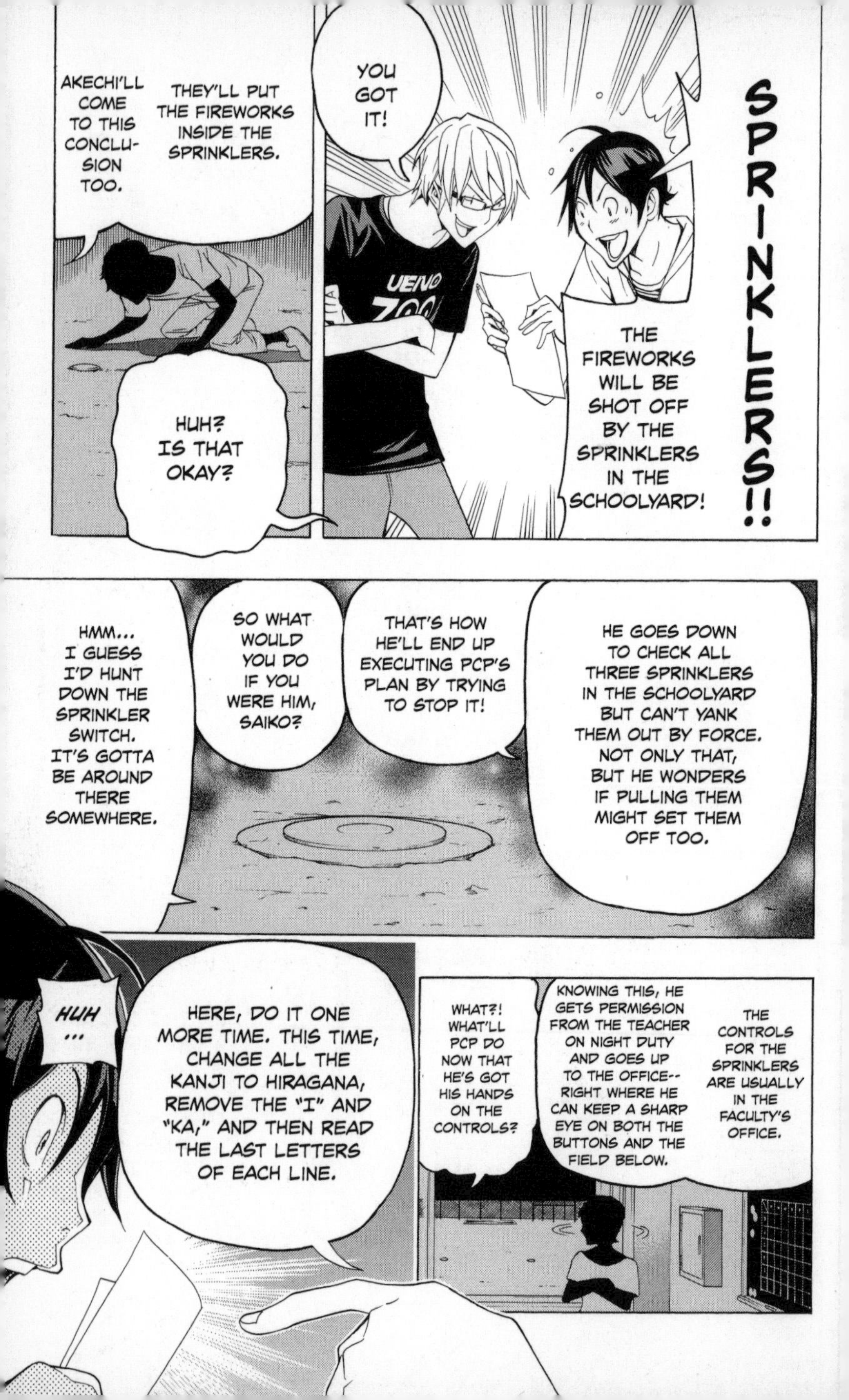
SPRINKLERS!!
THE FIREWORKS WILL BE SHOT OFF BY THE SPRINKLERS IN THE SCHOOLYARD!
YOU GOT IT!
THEY'LL PUT THE FIREWORKS INSIDE THE SPRINKLERS.
AKECHI'LL COME TO THIS CONCLUSION TOO.
HUH? IS THAT OKAY?
HE GOES DOWN TO CHECK ALL THREE SPRINKLERS IN THE SCHOOLYARD BUT CAN'T YANK THEM OUT BY FORCE. NOT ONLY THAT, BUT HE WONDERS IF PULLING THEM MIGHT SET THEM OFF TOO.
THAT'S HOW HE'LL END UP EXECUTING PCP'S PLAN BY TRYING TO STOP IT!
SO WHAT WOULD YOU DO IF YOU WERE HIM, SAIKO?
HMM... I GUESS I'D HUNT DOWN THE SPRINKLER SWITCH. IT'S GOTTA BE AROUND THERE SOMEWHERE.
THE CONTROLS FOR THE SPRINKLERS ARE USUALLY IN THE FACULTY'S OFFICE.
KNOWING THIS, HE GETS PERMISSION FROM THE TEACHER ON NIGHT DUTY AND GOES UP TO THE OFFICE-- RIGHT WHERE HE CAN KEEP A SHARP EYE ON BOTH THE BUTTONS AND THE FIELD BELOW.
WHAT?! WHAT'LL PCP DO NOW THAT HE'S GOT HIS HANDS ON THE CONTROLS?
HERE, DO IT ONE MORE TIME. THIS TIME, CHANGE ALL THE KANJI TO HIRAGANA, REMOVE THE "I" AND "KA," AND THEN READ THE LAST LETTERS OF EACH LINE.
HUH...
UENO ZOO

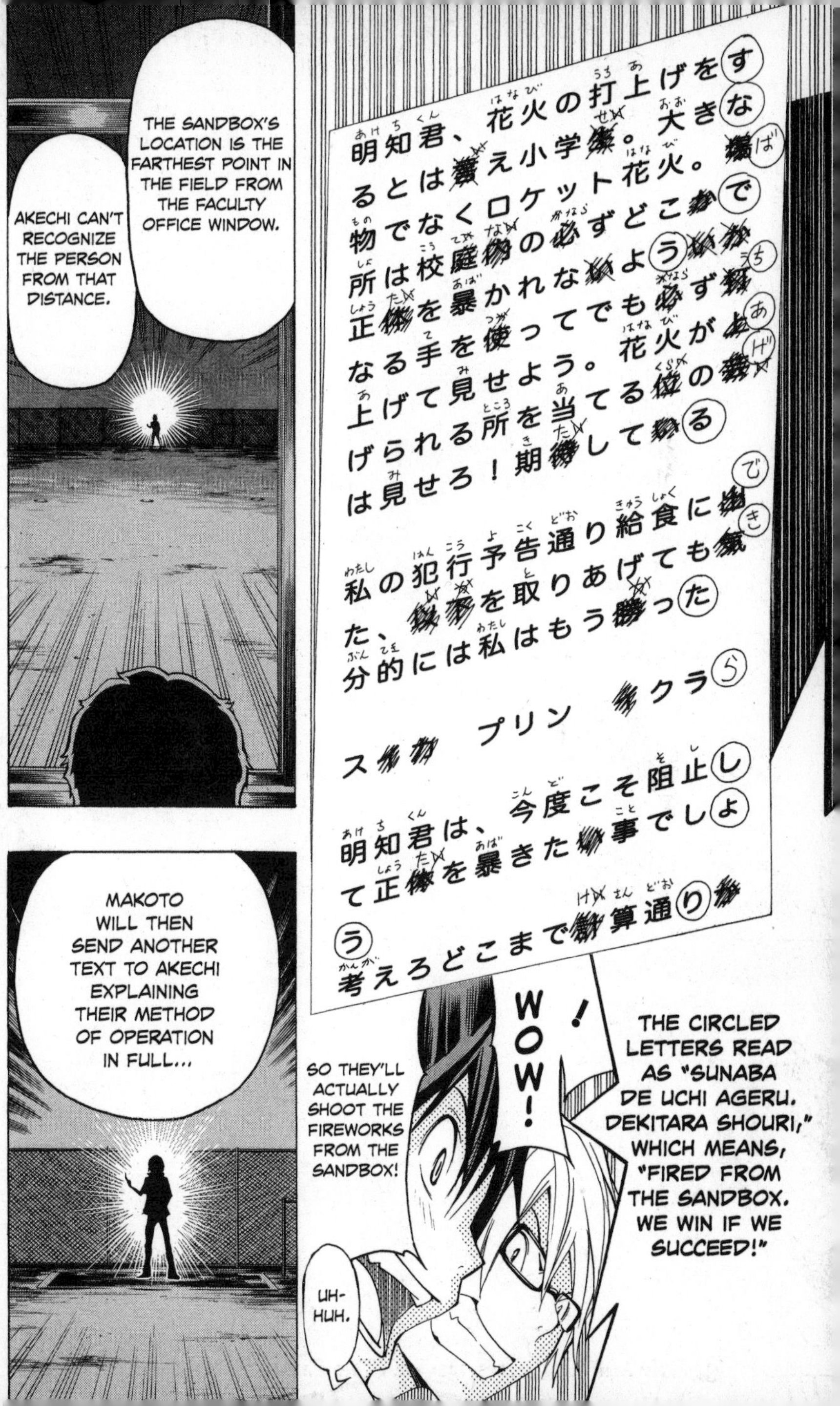

明知君、花火の打上げをす
るとは え小学 。大きな
物でなくロケット花火。 ば
所は校庭 の ずどこ で
正 を暴かれな よう ち
なる手を ってでも ず
上げて見せよう。花火が あ
げられる所を当てる の ゲ
は見せろ！期 して る
私の犯行予告通り給食に で
た、 を取りあげても き
分的には私はもう った
ス プリン クラら
明知君は、今度こそ阻止し
て正 を暴きた 事でしょ
う考えろどこまで 算通り
WOW!
THE CIRCLED LETTERS READ AS "SUNABA DE UCHI AGERU. DEKITARA SHOURI," WHICH MEANS, "FIRED FROM THE SANDBOX. WE WIN IF WE SUCCEED!"
SO THEY'LL ACTUALLY SHOOT THE FIREWORKS FROM THE SANDBOX!
UH-HUH.
THE SANDBOX'S LOCATION IS THE FARTHEST POINT IN THE FIELD FROM THE FACULTY OFFICE WINDOW.
AKECHI CAN'T RECOGNIZE THE PERSON FROM THAT DISTANCE.
MAKOTO WILL THEN SEND ANOTHER TEXT TO AKECHI EXPLAINING THEIR METHOD OF OPERATION IN FULL...

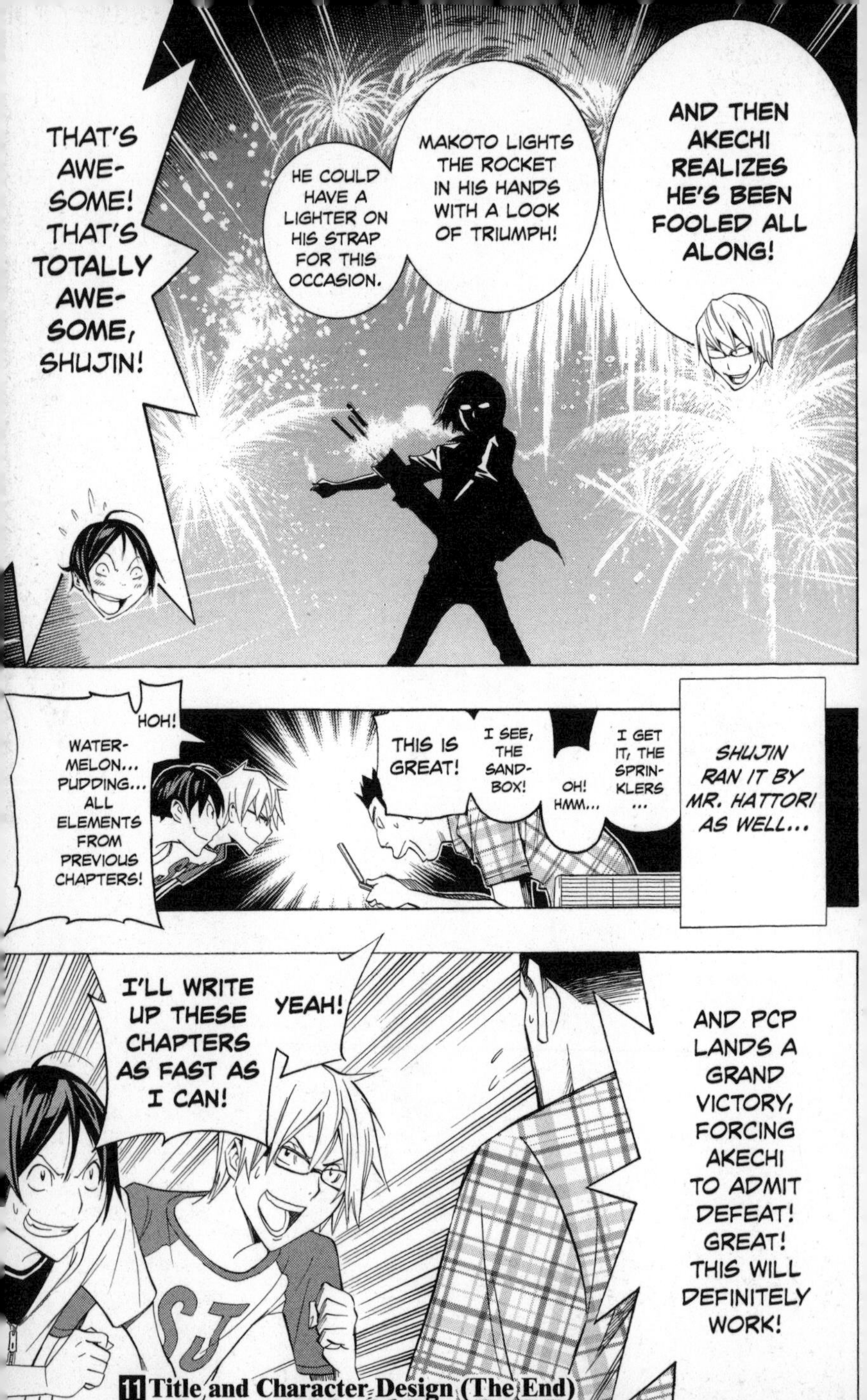
AND THEN AKECHI REALIZES HE'S BEEN FOOLED ALL ALONG!
MAKOTO LIGHTS THE ROCKET IN HIS HANDS WITH A LOOK OF TRIUMPH!
HE COULD HAVE A LIGHTER ON HIS STRAP FOR THIS OCCASION.
THAT'S AWE-SOME! THAT'S TOTALLY AWE-SOME, SHUJIN!
SHUJIN RAN IT BY MR. HATTORI AS WELL...
I GET IT, THE SPRIN-KLERS ...
OH! HMM...
I SEE, THE SAND-BOX!
THIS IS GREAT!
HOH! WATER-MELON... PUDDING... ALL ELEMENTS FROM PREVIOUS CHAPTERS!
AND PCP LANDS A GRAND VICTORY, FORCING AKECHI TO ADMIT DEFEAT! GREAT! THIS WILL DEFINITELY WORK!
YEAH!
I'LL WRITE UP THESE CHAPTERS AS FAST AS I CAN!

11 Title and Character Design (The End)

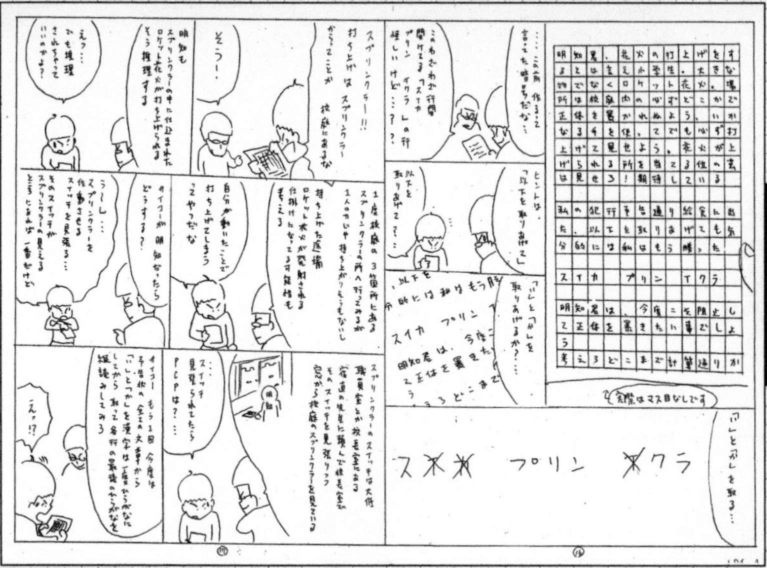
明知君、花火の打上げをするとは言え小学生。大きな物でなくロケット花火。場所は校舎内のどこかで
スイカ　プリン　イクラ
スプリンクラー!!

OHBA'S STORYBOARD

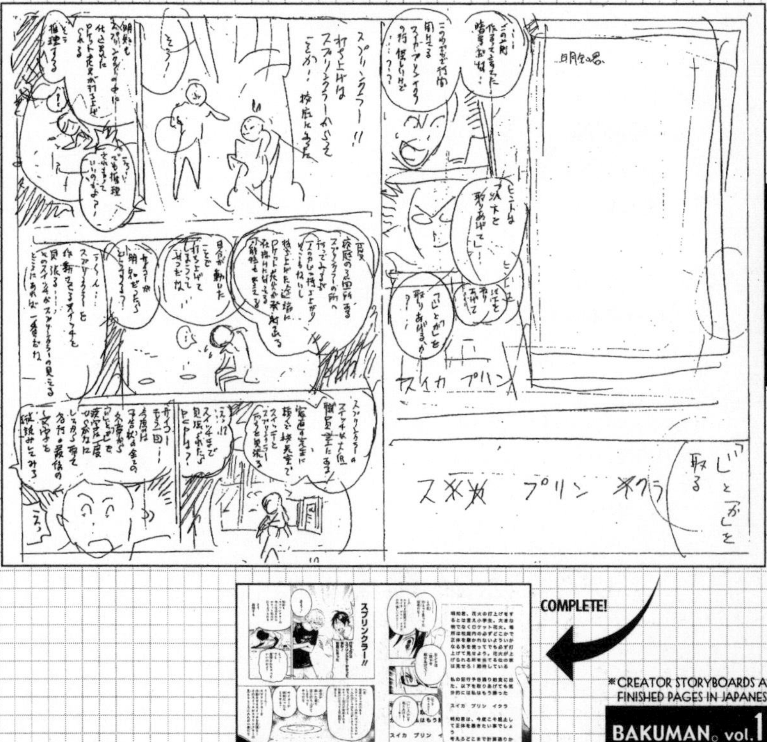
スプリンクラー!!
スイカ　プリン　イクラ

OBATA'S STORYBOARD

COMPLETE!

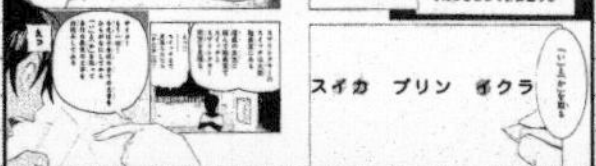
スプリンクラー!!
スイカ　プリン　イクラ

※CREATOR STORYBOARDS AND FINISHED PAGES IN JAPANESE

BAKUMAN。vol.11

"Until the Final Draft Is Complete"

Chapter 97, pp. 182-183

BAKUMAN

In the NEXT VOLUME

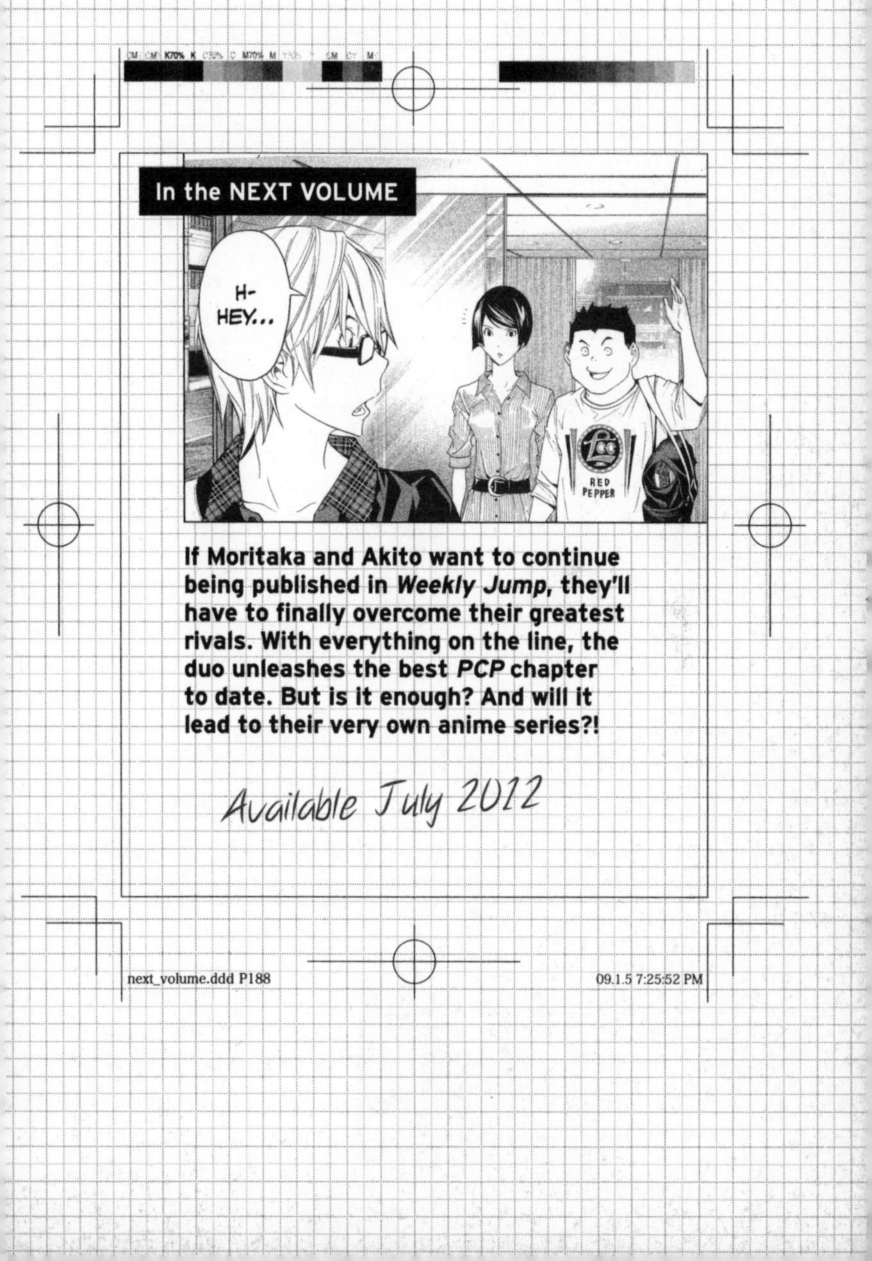
H-
HEY...
RED
PEPPER

If Moritaka and Akito want to continue being published in *Weekly Jump*, they'll have to finally overcome their greatest rivals. With everything on the line, the duo unleashes the best *PCP* chapter to date. But is it enough? And will it lead to their very own anime series?!

Available July 2012

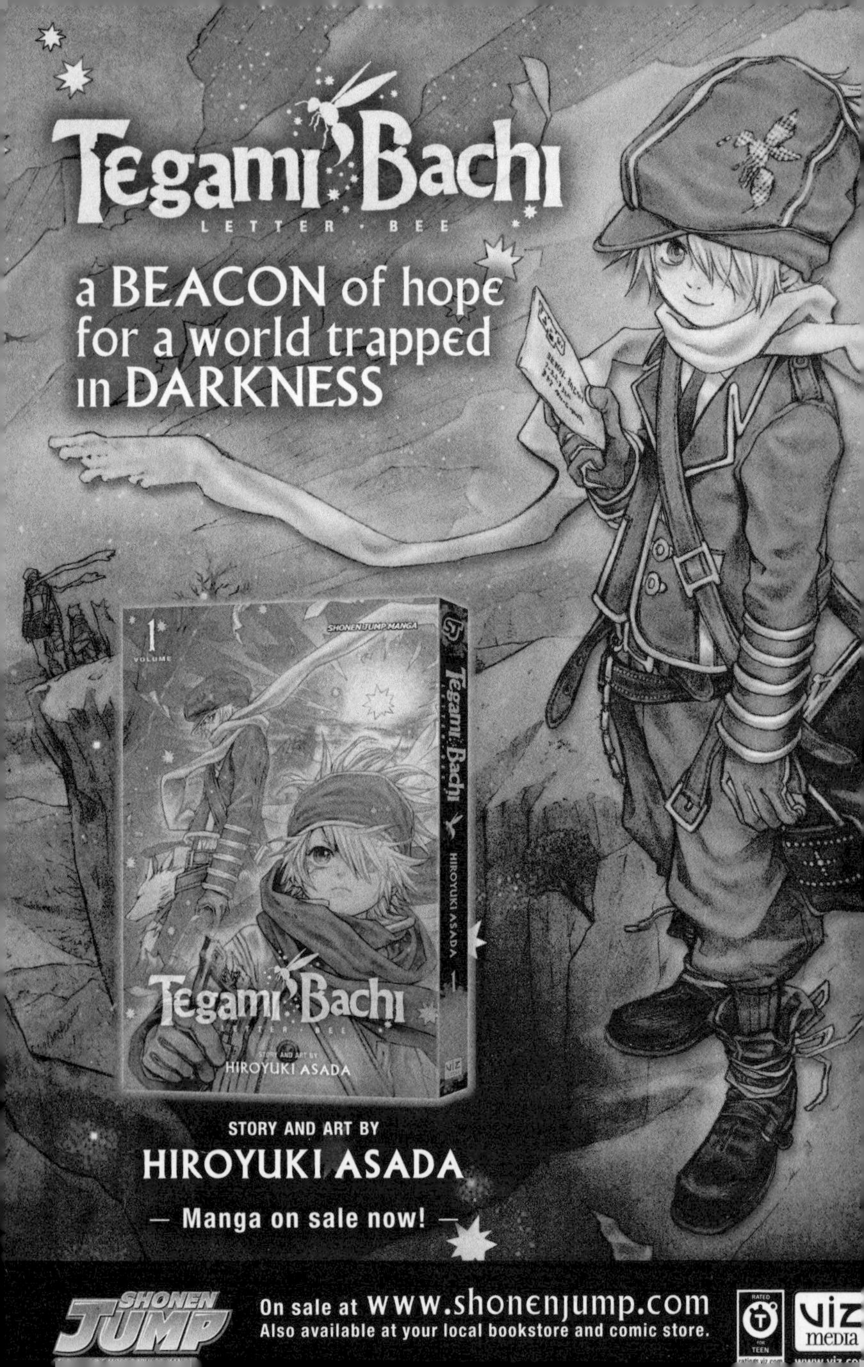
Tegami Bachi
LETTER BEE
a BEACON of hope
for a world trapped
in DARKNESS
1
VOLUME
SHONEN JUMP MANGA
Tegami Bachi
HIROYUKI ASADA
1
Tegami Bachi
LETTER BEE
STORY AND ART BY
HIROYUKI ASADA
STORY AND ART BY
HIROYUKI ASADA
— Manga on sale now! —
SHONEN JUMP
On sale at www.shonenjump.com
Also available at your local bookstore and comic store.
RATED
T
TEEN
VIZ media

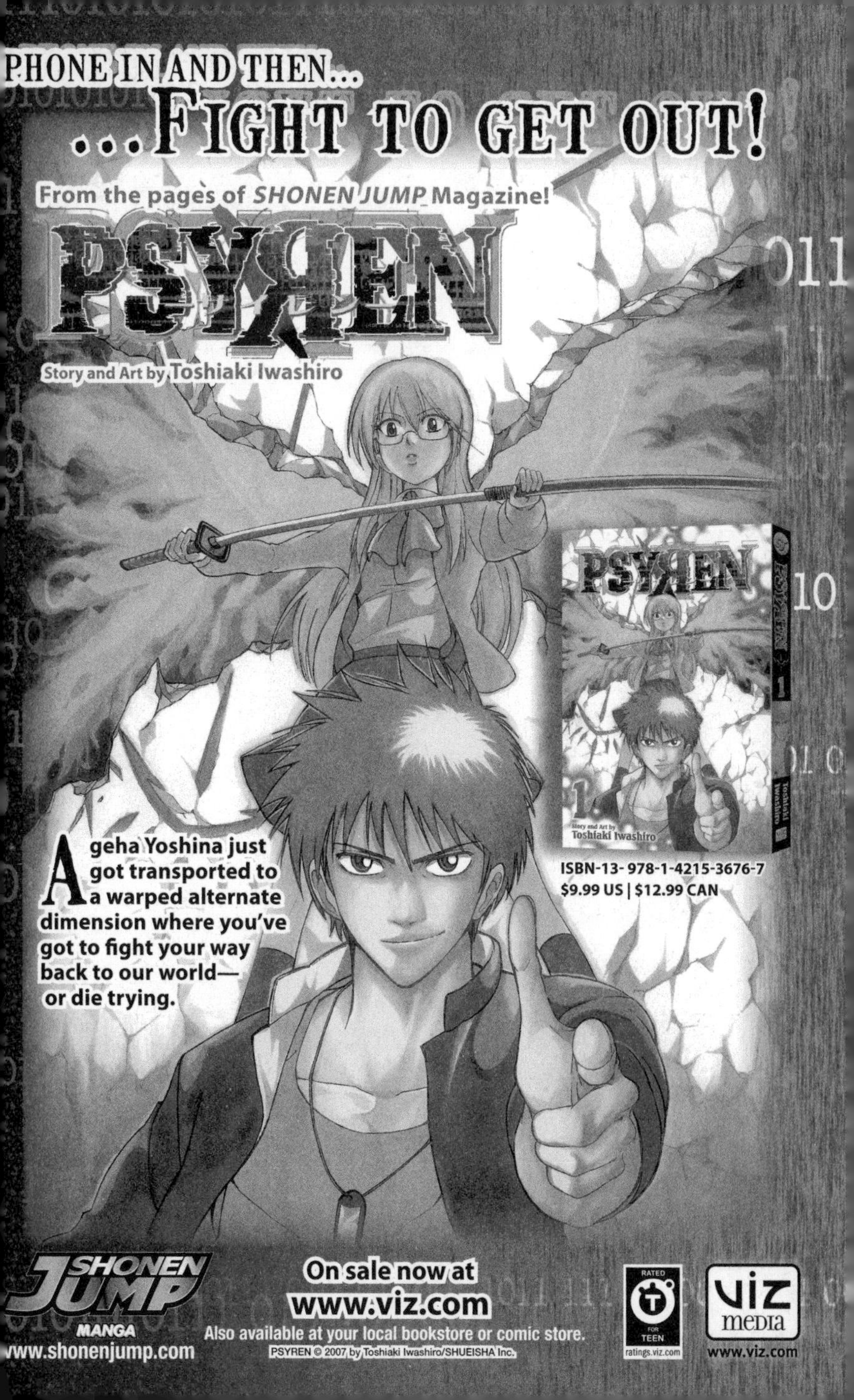
PHONE IN AND THEN...
...FIGHT TO GET OUT!
From the pages of SHONEN JUMP Magazine!
PSYREN
Story and Art by Toshiaki Iwashiro
Ageha Yoshina just got transported to a warped alternate dimension where you've got to fight your way back to our world—or die trying.
PSYREN
1
Story and Art by Toshiaki Iwashiro
ISBN-13- 978-1-4215-3676-7
$9.99 US | $12.99 CAN
SHONEN JUMP MANGA
www.shonenjump.com
On sale now at
www.viz.com
Also available at your local bookstore or comic store.
PSYREN © 2007 by Toshiaki Iwashiro/SHUEISHA Inc.
RATED T FOR TEEN
ratings.viz.com
viz media
www.viz.com

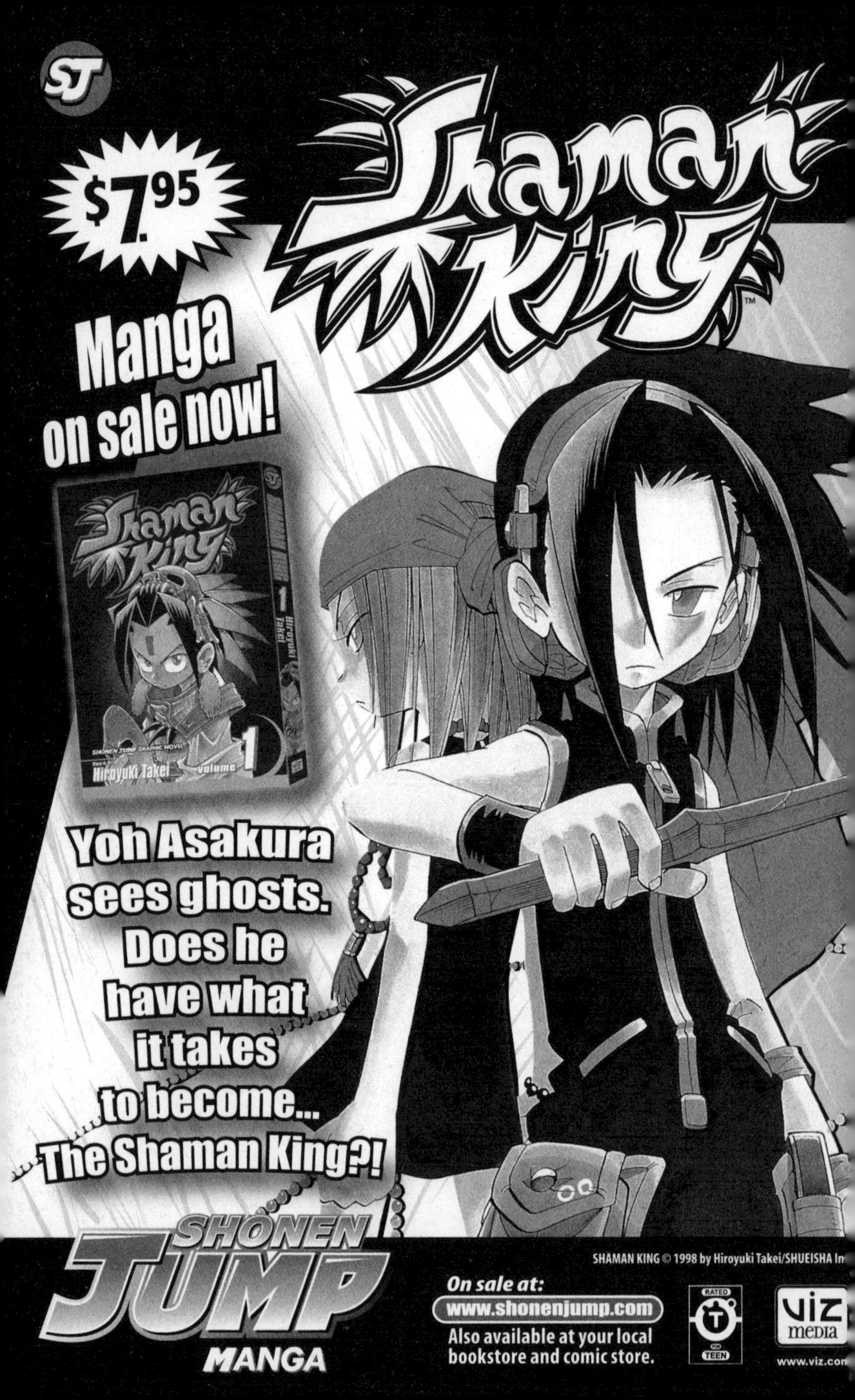

SJ
$7.95
Shaman King™
Manga on sale now!
Shaman King
SHONEN JUMP GRAPHIC NOVEL
Hiroyuki Takei volume 1
Yoh Asakura sees ghosts. Does he have what it takes to become... The Shaman King?!
SHONEN JUMP MANGA
SHAMAN KING © 1998 by Hiroyuki Takei/SHUEISHA In
On sale at:
www.shonenjump.com
Also available at your local bookstore and comic store.
RATED T TEEN
viz media
www.viz.co

This is the LAST PAGE.

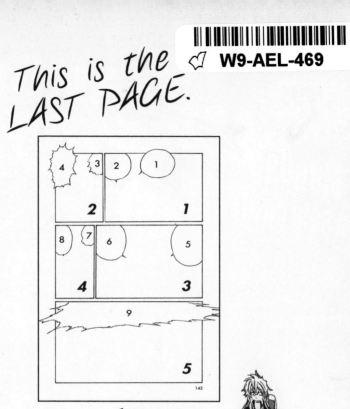

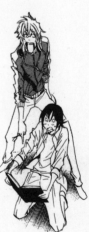

← Follow the action this way.

BAKUMAN。 has been printed in the original Japanese format in order to preserve the orientation of the original artwork.

Please turn it around and begin reading from right to left. Unlike English, Japanese is read right to left, so Japanese comics are read in reverse order from the way English comics are typically read. Have fun with it!